Twentieth-Century Short Story Explication New Series

Volume II   1991–1992

With Checklists of Books and Journals Used

Wendell M. Aycock
Professor of English
Texas Tech University

The Shoe String Press, 1995

© 1995 The Shoe String Press, Inc.
All rights reserved.
First published by The Shoe String Press, Inc.,
North Haven, Connecticut 06473.

Library of Congress Cataloging-in-Publication Data

(Revised for vol. 2)

Walker, Warren S.
    Twentieth century short story explication.
    Vol. 2 compiled by Wendell M. Aycock.
    Includes bibliographical references and
indexes.
        Contents: v. 1. 1989–1990 — v. 2. 1991–1992.
        1. Short stories—Indexes. [1. Short
stories—Indexes]. I. Aycock, Wendell M.
Z5917.S5W35   1993   [PN3373]   92-22790
ISBN 0-208-02340-2 (v. 1)
ISBN 0-208-02370-4 (v. 2)

The paper in this publication meets the minimum
requirements of American National Standard for
Information Science—Permanence of Paper for
Printed Library Materials, ANSI Z39.48-1984. ∞

For
Warren Walker
in recognition of
his contributions to
the study of short stories

Contents

Preface   vii

Short Story Explications   1

A Checklist of Books Used   261

A Checklist of Journals Used   275

Index of Short Story Writers   289

Preface

From 1961 until 1992, Warren Walker provided students and scholars of the short story with volume after volume of excellent research that uncovered explications of almost two centuries of short stories written throughout the world. The original series of *Twentieth-Century Short Story Explication* was concluded in 1992 with the publication of *An Index to the Third Edition and Its Five Supplements*. In 1992, Warren Walker continued his work by creating Volume I of the New Series, covering 1989–1990. While Volume I was in preparation in 1992, Professor Walker decided he would give up the work of searching out short story explications in order to devote his energies full-time to the Archive of Turkish Oral Narrative at Texas Tech University. Because he knew of my interest in the short story, he pressed me into service as a bibliographer. Although the present volume, Volume II of the New Series, was prepared with the help and advice of Warren Walker (I could not have done it otherwise), I am responsible for whatever shortcomings it has. The two years' work that I have done make me appreciate anew Warren Walker's intelligence, tenacity, and sheer hard work. Legions of scholars and students have benefited from the enormous contributions that he has made.

This current volume carries the coverage of the *Third Edition* forward through December 31, 1992, and includes more than 4,940 entries. Of the 662 authors cited, 175 appear here for the first time, bringing to 2,822 the total number of authors represented in both the original and New Series of *Twentieth-Century Short Story Explication*. Many of the authors explicated for the first time come from the burgeoning interest in Latin American and Spanish literature. In fact, 115 of the authors cited in the following pages have Hispanic surnames, and 38 of these are new authors. Explications of new authors, however, appear from almost all parts of the globe, including the Middle East, Australia, Africa, the Philippines, and many parts of Europe and the Orient.

I follow Professor Walker's parameters insofar as the languages of explication are concerned; i.e., no matter what the original language of the short stories themselves, the explications within are limited to those published in the major languages of Western Europe. As he pointed out, these languages encompass the vast majority of critical studies of the genre.

As in the past, *Twentieth-Century Short Story Explication* is a bibliography of interpretations that have appeared since 1900 of short stories published since 1800. The term *short story* here has the same meaning it carries in the Wilson Company's *Short Story Index*: "A brief narrative of not more than 150 average-sized pages." *Explication* is meant to suggest simply interpretation or explanation of the meaning of the story, including observations on theme, symbol, and sometimes structure. This excludes from the bibliography what are essentially studies of source, biographical data, and background materials. Occasionally there are explicatory passages cited in works otherwise devoted to these external considerations. All page numbers refer strictly to interpretative passages, not to the longer works in which they occur.

Over the years, Professor Walker developed a very convenient, useful system for handling great numbers of explications. We will continue to follow his system in this volume. Each book is cited by author or editor and a short title; the full title and publication data are provided in "A Checklist of Books Used"—and 336 were used in the compilation of this Supplement. For an article in a journal or an essay in a critical collection, the full publication information is provided in the text the first time the study is cited. In subsequent entries, only the critic's or scholar's name and a short title are used as long as these entries appear under the name of the same short story author. If an article or essay explicates stories of two or more authors, a complete initial entry is made for each author. As in previous volumes, we have again included a "Checklist of Journals Used"—and this time 332 were used. This information should be especially helpful to students who may not be familiar with titles of professional journals, much less the abbreviations for such titles.

Although most of the entries in Volume II were published during 1991 and 1992, there are some entries with earlier dates. A few of these are earlier interpretations that were either unavailable or overlooked previously. A few are reprintings of earlier studies and these are preceded by a plus sign (+). Any such entry can be located in the original series by consulting the *Index to the Third Edition and Its Five Supplements, 1961–1991*.

In preparing this book, I have been indebted to a number of people. Already apparent is the great debt that I owe to Warren Walker, who was a constant source of information, help, and encouragement. In addition, I must acknowledge the contributions from such journals as *PMLA*, *Studies in Short Fiction*, *Modern Fiction Studies*, and *Journal of Modern Literature*. I depended constantly upon the considerable support and help from the Texas Tech University Library and the Interlibrary Loan Department of Texas Tech University Library, especially from its Director, Amy Chang, and her extremely capable assistants, Carol Roberts, Delia Arteaga, and Dale Poulter. I also extend my appreciation to three very capable graduate students: Liliana Anglada, Marlene Selker and Chandrashekhar Veera. And I wish to thank Adriel Alvarado for his valuable help with computer-related problems. Finally, for her patience, assistance, and encouragement, I thank my wife, Diane.

WENDELL M. AYCOCK
TEXAS TECH UNIVERSITY

MERCEDES ABAD

"Ligeros libertinajes sabáticos"
Pérez, Janet. "Characteristics of Erotic Brief Fiction by Women in Spain," *Monographic R*, 7 (1991), 175–178.

"Pascualino y los globos"
Pérez, Janet. "Characteristics . . . ," 178–179.

MENA ABDULLAH [WITH RAY MATHEW]

"The Babu from Bengal"
MacDermott, Doireann. "*The Time of the Peacock*: Indian Rural Life in Australia," in Bardolph, Jacquelin, Ed. *Short Fiction* . . . , 207–208.

"Because of the Rusilla"
MacDermott, Doireann. "*The Time* . . . ," 205–206.

"Grandfather Tiger"
MacDermott, Doireann. "*The Time* . . . ," 208.

"High Maharaja"
MacDermott, Doireann. "*The Time* . . . ," 206–207.

"The Time of the Peacock"
MacDermott, Doireann. "*The Time* . . . ," 204–205.

RICHARD ABERNATHY

"Axolotl"
Vonarburg, Elisabeth. "The Reproduction of the Body in Space," in Ruddick, Nicholas, Ed. *State* . . . , 61, 62.

CHINUA ACHEBE

"Akueke"
Balogun, F. Odun. *Tradition and Modernity* . . . , 78–79.

"Dead Man's Path"
Balogun, F. Odun. *Tradition and Modernity* . . . , 70–71.
Charters, Ann, and William E. Sheidley. *Resources for Teaching* . . . , 3rd ed., 1.

"Girls at War"
Balogun, F. Odun. *Tradition and Modernity* . . . , 77.
Niven, Alastair. "Achebe and Okri: Contrasts in the Response to Civil War," in Bardolph, Jacquelin, Ed. *Short Fiction* . . . , 279–282.

"The Madman"
Balogun, F. Odun. *Tradition and Modernity* . . . , 66–68, 91.

"Marriage Is a Private Thing"
Balogun, F. Odun. *Tradition and Modernity* . . . , 68–69.

"Polar Undergraduate"
Balogun, F. Odun. *Tradition and Modernity* . . . , 73–74.
"The Sacrificial Egg"
Balogun, F. Odun. *Tradition and Modernity* . . . , 84.
"Sugar Baby"
Balogun, F. Odun. *Tradition and Modernity* . . . , 76.
"Uncle Ben's Choice"
Balogun, F. Odun. *Tradition and Modernity* . . . , 92.
"Vengeful Creditor"
Balogun, F. Odun. *Tradition and Modernity* . . . , 72–75.
"The Voter"
Balogun, F. Odun. *Tradition and Modernity* . . . , 75–76, 92–93.

ALICE ADAMS

"The Oasis"
Charters, Ann, and William E. Sheidley. *Resources for Teaching* . . . ,
3rd ed., 2–3.
"Roses, Rhododendron"
+ Bohner, Charles H. *Instructor's Manual* . . . , 1–2.

JAMES AGEE

"Dream Sequence"
Kramer, Victor A. *Agee and Actuality* . . . , 114–117.

SHMUEL [SHAY] YOSEF AGNON [SHMUEL YOSEF CZACZKES]

"Agunot"
Hoffman, Anne G. *Between Exile and Return* . . . , 66–69.
"The Book of Deeds"
Hoffman, Anne G. *Between Exile and Return* . . . , 59–60.
"The Document"
Hoffman, Anne G. *Between Exile and Return* . . . , 112–114.
"Edo and Enam" [same as "Iddo and Aynam"]
Knapp, Bettina L. *Exile and the Writer* . . . , 111–129.
"Forevermore"
Hoffman, Anne G. *Between Exile and Return* . . . , 161.
"In the Heart of the Seas"
Hoffman, Anne G. *Between Exile and Return* . . . , 177.
"Knots upon Knots"
Hoffman, Anne G. *Between Exile and Return* . . . , 163.
"A Little Hero"
Hoffman, Anne G. *Between Exile and Return* . . . , 63.

"The Secret of Writing Stories"
   Hoffman, Anne G. *Between Exile and Return* . . . , 32.
"The Sense of Smell"
   Hoffman, Anne G. *Between Exile and Return* . . . , 115–122.
"Tale of the Scribe"
   Hoffman, Anne G. *Between Exile and Return* . . . , 30–39.
"Upon a Stone"
   Hoffman, Anne G. *Between Exile and Return* . . . , 106–112.
"A Whole Loaf"
   Hoffman, Anne G. *Between Exile and Return* . . . , 44–52.

TOMAS F. AGULTO

"The Beautiful Woman at St. Elena"
   Lucero, Rosario Cruz. "The Philippine Short Story, 1981–1990: The
   Voice of the Self-Authenticating Other," *Tenggara*, 26 (1990),
   83–84.

ILSE AICHINGER

"Eliza Eliza"
   Knauer, Bettina. "Der Text als Entfaltung des Namens: Ilse
   Aichingers Erzählung 'Eliza Eliza,' " *Sprachkunst*, 23, ii (1992),
   246–250, 253–265.
"Der Gefesselte"
   Nicolai, Ralf R. "Ilse Aichingers 'Der Gefesselte.' Kommentare zum
   Text," *Archiv*, 228, i (1991), 2–10.

AMA ATA AIDOO

"The Message"
   Rooney, Caroline. "Are We in the Company of Feminists? A Preface
   for Bessie Head and Ama Ata Aidoo," in Jump, Harriet D., Ed.
   Diverse Voices . . . , 217–223.

LOUISA MAY ALCOTT

"The Brothers"
   Diffley, Kathleen. *Where My Heart* . . . , 34–38.
"Marion Earle; or, Only an Actress!"
   Stern, Madeleine B. "An Early Alcott Sensation Story: 'Marion
   Earle; or, Only an Actress!' " *Nineteenth-Century Lit*, 47 (1992),
   91–98.
"My Contraband" [same as "My Brothers"]
   Elberg, Sarah. "Introduction," *Moods* [by Louisa May Alcott],
   xxiv–xxv.

"Whisper"
Elberg, Sarah. "Introduction," xxiv.

SHOLEM ALEICHEM [SHOLOM RABINOWITZ]

"On Account of a Hat"
Saposnik, Irving. "The Yiddish Are Coming! The Yiddish Are
Coming! Some Thoughts on Yiddish Comedy," in Grimm,
Reinhold, and Jost Hermand, Eds. *Laughter Unlimited* . . . ,
103–105.

ESTRELLA ALFON

"Magnificence"
Arambulo, Thelma E. "The Filipina as Writer: Against All Odds," in
Kintanar, Thelma B., Ed. *Women Reading* . . . , 171, 173–174.
"Servant Girl"
Evasco, Marjorie. "The Writer and Her Roots," in Kintanar, Thelma
B., Ed. *Women Reading* . . . , 15.

NELSON ALGREN

"The Devil Came Down Division Street"
Gladsky, Thomas. *Princes, Peasants* . . . , 145–146.

WOODY ALLEN

"The Kugelmass Episode"
+Charters, Ann, and William E. Sheidley. *Resources for
Teaching* . . . , 3rd ed., 4–5.

ISABEL ALLENDE

"The Judge's Wife"
Spanos, Tony. "Isabel Allende's 'The Judge's Wife': Heroine or
Female Stereotype?" *Encyclia*, 67 (1990), 163–172.

JORGE AMADO

"A morte e a morte de Quincas Berro D'agua"
Chamberlain, Bobby J. *Jorge Amado*, 50–52, 53, 55–60.

KINGSLEY AMIS

"Dear Illusion"
Vickery, John B. "Alternative Worlds: The Short Stories," in Salwak, Dale, Ed. *Kingsley Amis* . . . , 159–161.

"The House on the Headland"
Vickery, John B. "Alternative Worlds . . . ," 164–165.

"I Spy Strangers"
Gindin, James. "Changing Social and Moral Attitudes," in Salwak, Dale, Ed. *Kingsley Amis* . . . , 135.
Vickery, John B. "Alternative Worlds . . . ," 156–158.

"My Enemy's Enemy"
Vickery, John B. "Alternative Worlds . . . ," 154–155.

"Who or What Was It?"
Vickery, John B. "Alternative Worlds . . . ," 163–164, 165.

MARTIN AMIS

"Bujak and the Strong Force"
Head, Dominic. *The Modernist* . . . , 197–199.

HANS CHRISTIAN ANDERSEN

"The Bell"
Greenway, John L. " 'Reason in Imagination is Beauty': Oersted's Acoustics and H. C. Andersen's 'The Bell,' " *Scandinavian Stud*, 63 (1991), 318–325.

"Psychen"
Sanders, Karin. "Nemesis of Mimesis: The Problem of Representation in H. C. Andersen's 'Psychen,' " *Scandinavian Stud*, 64 (1992), 1–25.

"The Shadow"
Herdman, John. *The Double* . . . , 44–46.

JESSICA ANDERSON

"Against the Wall"
Colmer, John. "Solitude and Relationship in Jessica Anderson's Shorter Fiction," in Bardolph, Jacquelin, Ed. *Short Fiction* . . . , 65–66.

"The Aviator"
Colmer, John. "Solitude and Relationship . . . ," 66.

"The Milk"
Colmer, John. "Solitude and Relationship . . . ," 66.

"Outside Friends"
Colmer, John. "Solitude and Relationship . . . ," 67.

"Under the House"
Colmer, John. "Solitude and Relationship . . . ," 64–65.
"The Way to Budjerra Heights"
Colmer, John. "Solitude and Relationship . . . ," 65–66.

SHERWOOD ANDERSON

"Adventure"
Papinchak, Robert A. *Sherwood Anderson* . . . , 24.
"Blackfoot's Masterpiece"
Papinchak, Robert A. *Sherwood Anderson* . . . , 17–18.
"Brother Death"
Papinchak, Robert A. *Sherwood Anderson* . . . , 43–45.
"Death"
Papinchak, Robert A. *Sherwood Anderson* . . . , 26–27.
"Death in the Woods"
+ Charters, Ann, and William E. Sheidley. *Resources for Teaching* . . . , 3rd ed., 7–8.
Miller, William V. "Psychological Stasis or Artistic Process: The Narrator Problem in Sherwood Anderson's 'Death in the Woods,' " *Old Northwest*, 15, i–ii (Spring–Summer, 1990), 34–40.
Papinchak, Robert A. *Sherwood Anderson* . . . , 41–43.
"The Egg"
+ Bohner, Charles H. *Instructor's Manual* . . . , 2–4.
Papinchak, Robert A. *Sherwood Anderson* . . . , 39–41.
"Hands"
+ Charters, Ann, and William E. Sheidley. *Resources for Teaching* . . . , 3rd ed., 9.
Papinchak, Robert A. *Sherwood Anderson* . . . , 7–10, 21.
Weber, Ronald. *The Midwestern* . . . , 104–106.
Wilson, Christopher P. *White Collar Fiction* . . . , 197–199.
"I'm a Fool"
Papinchak, Robert A. *Sherwood Anderson* . . . , 34–35.
"I Want to Know Why"
+ Bohner, Charles H. *Instructor's Manual* . . . , 4–5.
Cassill, R. V. . . . *Instructor's Handbook*, 1–2.
Coulthard, A. R. "Anderson's 'I Want to Know Why,' " *Explicator*, 49, iii (1991), 169–170.
Papinchak, Robert A. *Sherwood Anderson* . . . , 32–34.
"Loneliness"
Papinchak, Robert A. *Sherwood Anderson* . . . , 25–26.
"The Man Who Became a Woman"
Papinchak, Robert A. *Sherwood Anderson* . . . , 35–38.
"Out of Nowhere into Nothing"
Bidney, Martin. "Thinking about Walt and Melville in a Sherwood

Anderson Tale: An Independent Woman's Transcendental Quest,''
Stud Short Fiction, 29 (1992), 517–530.

"The Rabbit Pen"
Papinchak, Robert A. *Sherwood Anderson . . .* , 11–15.

"The Sad Horn-Blowers"
Papinchak, Robert A. *Sherwood Anderson . . .* , 38–39.

"Sister"
Papinchak, Robert A. *Sherwood Anderson . . .* , 15–16.

"Sophistication"
Papinchak, Robert A. *Sherwood Anderson . . .* , 26–27.

"The Story Writers"
Papinchak, Robert A. *Sherwood Anderson . . .* , 16–17.

"That Sophistication"
Papinchak, Robert A. *Sherwood Anderson . . .* , 30–31.

"The Thinker"
Papinchak, Robert A. *Sherwood Anderson . . .* , 24.

"Unlighted Lamps"
Papinchak, Robert A. *Sherwood Anderson . . .* , 47.

"Unused"
Papinchak, Robert A. *Sherwood Anderson . . .* , 45–46.

"Vibrant Life"
Papinchak, Robert A. *Sherwood Anderson . . .* , 16.

"The White Streak"
Papinchak, Robert A. *Sherwood Anderson . . .* , 18–19.

LEONID ANDREEV

"Darkness"
Barratt, Andrew. "Maksim Gorky and Leonid Andreev: At the Heart
of 'Darkness,' " in Luker, Nicholas, Ed. *The Short Story in
Russia . . .* , 73–97.

ANONYMOUS

"Life Insurance"
Peterson, Brent O. *Popular Narratives . . .* , 174–177.

MAX APPLE

"The Oranging of America"
Klinkowitz, Jerome. *Structuring the Void . . .* , 75–78.

REINALDO ARENAS

"Adiós a mamá"
Hernández Miyares, Julio E. " 'Adiós a mamá': Un libro inédito de
Reinaldo Arenas," *Círculo*, 21 (1992), 80–81.

"Algo sucede en el último balcón"
Hernández Miyares, Julio E. " 'Adiós . . . ," 79–80.
"*El Cometa Halley*"
Hernández Miyares, Julio E. " 'Adiós . . . ," 83.
"Final de un cuento"
Hernández Miyares, Julio E. " 'Adiós . . . ," 84–85.
"La Gran Fuerza"
Hernández Miyares, Julio E. " 'Adiós . . . ," 78–79.
"Memorias de la tierra"
Hernández Miyares, Julio E. " 'Adiós . . . ," 85–86.
"La Torre de Cristal"
Hernández Miyares, Julio E. " 'Adiós . . . ," 83–84.
"Traidor"
Hernández Miyares, Julio E. " 'Adiós . . . ," 81–83.

RAFAEL ARÉVALO MARTÍNEZ

"The Man Who Looked Like a Horse"
Foster, David W. *Gay and Lesbian Themes* . . . , 45–50.

INÉS ARREDONDO

"El amigo"
Flores Grajales, Guadalupe. "Las sociedades narrativas de Inés
Arredondo. Una posibilidad del encuentro amoroso total," *La
Palabra y el Hombre*, 79 (1991), 221–223.
"Las mariposas nocturnas"
Flores Grajales, Guadalupe. "Las sociedades . . . ," 223–225.
"Sombra entre sombras"
Flores Grajales, Guadalupe. "Las sociedades . . . ," 225–227.

JUAN JOSÉ ARREOLA

"Tres días y un cenicero"
Pellicer, Rosa. "La con-fabulación de Juan José Arreola," *Revista
Iberoamericana*, 58 (1992), 544–545, 546.

JOSÉ MARÍA ARGUEDAS

"Diamantes y pedernales"
Cornejo-Polar, Antonio. " 'Diamantes y pedernales': elogio de la
música indígena," *Anthropos R*, 128 (January, 1992), 49–52.

MIKHAIL ARTSYBASHEV

"The Doctor"
  Luker, Nicholas. "Studies in Instability: Artsybashev's *Etiudy*
  (1910)," in Luker, Nicholas, Ed. *The Short Story in Russia* . . . ,
  121–124.
"From the Life of a Little Woman"
  Luker, Nicholas. "Studies in Instability . . . ," 106–108.
"Happiness"
  Luker, Nicholas. "Studies in Instability . . . ," 104–106.
"In the Village"
  Luker, Nicholas. "Studies in Instability . . . ," 113–115.
"On the White Snow"
  Luker, Nicholas. "Studies in Instability . . . ," 117–119.
"One Day"
  Luker, Nicholas. "Studies in Instability . . . ," 115–117.
"Peasant and Master"
  Luker, Nicholas. "Studies in Instability . . . ," 111–113.
"The Thought"
  Luker, Nicholas. "Studies in Instability . . . ," 109–111.
"The Villain"
  Luker, Nicholas. "Studies in Instability . . . ," 119–121.
"The Wife"
  Luker, Nicholas. "Studies in Instability . . . ," 108–109.

MIGUEL ANGEL ASTURIAS

"Torotumbo"
  Ortiz Guzmán, Rosaura. " 'Torotumbo': Una posible
  interpretación," *Cupey*, 1, ii (July–December, 1984), 53–60.

MARGARET ATWOOD

"Death by Landscape"
  Surette, Leon. "Creating the Canadian Canon," in Lecker, Robert,
  Ed. *Canadian Canons* . . . , 201–202.
"Giving Birth"
  Carrera, Isabel. "Metalinguistic Features in Short Fiction by Lessing
  and Atwood: From Sign and Subversion to Symbol and
  Deconstruction," in Bardolph, Jacquelin, Ed. *Short Fiction* . . . ,
  161–163.
  Divasson, Lourdes. "The Short Stories of Margaret Atwood: A
  Visible Link Between Her Poetry and Longer Fiction," in
  Bardolph, Jacquelin, Ed. *Short Fiction* . . . , 154.

"Happy Endings"
    Charters, Ann, and William E. Sheidley. *Resources for Teaching* . . . ,
    3rd ed., 11.
"Lives of the Poets"
    Divasson, Lourdes. "The Short Stories . . . ," 155.
"Rape Fantasies"
    +Bohner, Charles H. *Instructor's Manual* . . . , 5–6.
    +Cassill, R. V. . . . *Instructor's Handbook*, 2–3.
"Walking on Water"
    Carrington, Ildikó de Papp. "Definitions of a Fool: Alice Munro's
    'Walking on Water' and Margaret Atwood's *Two Stories About
    Emma*: 'The Whirlpool Rapids' and 'Walking on Water,' " *Stud
    Short Fiction*, 28 (1991), 138–139, 141, 142, 143–146.
"The War in the Bathroom"
    Divasson, Lourdes. "The Short Stories . . . ," 153–154.
"The Whirlpool Rapids"
    Carrington, Ildikó de Papp. "Definitions . . . ," 137–138, 141.

LOUIS AUCHINCLOSS

"The 'Fulfillment' of Grace Eliot"
    Tintner, Adeline R. "Punishing Morton Fullerton: Louis
    Auchincloss's 'The "Fulfillment" of Grace Eliot,' " *Twentieth
    Century Lit*, 38, i (1992), 44–53.

WILLIAM AUSTIN

"Peter Rugg, the Missing Man"
    Mathews, James W. "Peter Rugg and Cheever's Swimmer:
    Archetypal Missing Men," *Stud Short Fiction*, 29 (1992), 95–97.

FRANCISCO AYALA

"Susana saliendo del baño"
    Navarro Durán, Rosa. "Una miniatura literaria: 'Susana saliendo del
    baño' de Francisco Ayala," *Castilla*, 9–10 (1985), 103–113.
"Un quid pro quo or Who Is Who"
    Altisent, Marta E. "Periodismo y ficción en un cuento de Francisco
    Ayala," *Revista de temas hispánicos*, 6 (1988), 99–112.

MARIANO AZUELA

"The Underdogs"
    Fuentes, Carlos. "The Barefoot Iliad," in Azuela, Mariano, *The
    Underdogs*, 123–140.

Menton, Seymour. "Epic Textures of 'Los de abajo,' " in Azuela Mariano, *The Underdogs*, 141–155.

ISAAC BABEL

"Continuation of Story of a Horse"
Kornblatt, Judith D. *The Cossack Hero* . . . , 124–125.
"Crossing the Zbruch"
Kornblatt, Judith D. *The Cossack Hero* . . . , 111–114, 118–119.
"Di Grasso"
Nakhimovsky, Alice S. *Russian-Jewish Literature* . . . , 72–73.
"First Love"
Nakhimovsky, Alice S. *Russian-Jewish Literature* . . . , 103–105.
"How It Was Done in Odessa"
Nakhimovsky, Alice S. *Russian-Jewish Literature* . . . , 98–100.
"The Life and Adventures of Marvey Pavlichenko"
Danow, David K. "A Poetics of Inversion: The Non-Dialogic Aspect of Isaac Babel's *Red Cavalry*," *Mod Lang R*, 86 (1991), 948–950.
Kornblatt, Judith D. *The Cossack Hero* . . . , 118, 119.
"My First Goose"
Cassill, R. V. . . . *Instructor's Handbook*, 4.
+Charters, Ann, and William E. Sheidley. *Resources for Teaching* . . . , 3rd ed., 12–13.
"Pan Apolek"
Kornblatt, Judith D. *The Cossack Hero* . . . , 120–121.
"Prishchepa's Vengeance"
Danow, David K. "A Poetics of Inversion . . . ," 950–951.
"The Rebbe"
Nakhimovsky, Alice S. *Russian-Jewish Literature* . . . , 94–96.
"The Rebbe's Son"
Nakhimovsky, Alice S. *Russian-Jewish Literature* . . . , 96–97.
"The Story of My Dovecot"
+Bohner, Charles H. *Instructor's Manual* . . . , 7–8.
"Story of a Horse"
Kornblatt, Judith D. *The Cossack Hero* . . . , 122–124.

MURRAY BAIL

"The Drover's Wife"
Thieme, John. "Drover's Wives," in Bardolph, Jacquelin, Ed. *Short Fiction* . . . , 71–72.

JAMES BALDWIN

"Sonny's Blues"
+Bohner, Charles H. *Instructor's Manual* . . . , 8–9.

+Cassill, R. V. . . . *Instructor's Handbook*, 5–6.
Charters, Ann, and William E. Sheidley. *Resources for Teaching* . . . ,
    3rd ed., 14.
Keating, Helane L., and Walter Levy. *Instructor's Manual: Lives
    Through Literature* . . . , 31–32.
Robertson, Patricia R. "Baldwin's 'Sonny's Blues': The Scapegoat
    Metaphor," *Univ Mississippi Stud Engl*, 9 (1991), 189–198.
Savery, Pancho. "Baldwin, Bebop, and 'Sonny's Blues,' " in
    Trimmer, Joseph, and Tilly Warnock, Eds. *Understanding
    Others* . . . , 166–168, 171–174.

JOHN BALLEM

"Death on Horseback"
Škvorecký, Josef. "Detective Stories: Some Notes on *Fingerprint*,"
    in Friedland, M. L., Ed. *Rough Justice* . . . , 242–243.

HONORÉ DE BALZAC

"Adieu"
Hutton, Margaret-Anne. "Know Thyself vs Common Knowledge:
    Bleich's Epistemology Seen Through Two Short Stories by
    Balzac," *Mod Lang R*, 86 (1991), 53–56.
"Le Colonel Chabert"
Hutton, Margaret-Anne. "Know Thyself . . . ," 51–53.
"The Duchess of Langeais"
Vanoncini, André, " 'La Duchesse de Langeais' ou la mise à mort de
    l'objet textuel," *Travaux de Littérature*, 4 (1991), 209–215.
"L'Elixir de longue vie"
Cummiskey, Gary. *The Changing* . . . , 79–83.
"Facino Cane"
Fischler, Alexander. "Distance and Narrative Perspective in Balzac's
    'Facino Cane' " *L'Esprit Créateur*, 31, iii (1991), 15–25.
Rashkin, Esther. *Family Secrets* . . . , 81–92.
Rignall, John. *Realist Fiction* . . . , 11, 12, 44–48.
"Melmoth réconcilié"
Cummiskey, Gary. *The Changing* . . . , 83–87.
"A Passion in the Desert"
+Cassill, R. V. . . . *Instructor's Handbook*, 6–7.
"Sarrasine"
Jullien, Dominique. "Of Stories and Women," *SubStance*, 20, ii
    (1991), 78–83.
Tambling, Jeremy. *Narrative and Ideology*, 94–95.
"Les Secrets de la princesse"
Jullien, Dominique. "Of Stories and Women," 83–87.

TONI CADE BAMBARA

"The Apprentice"
Lyles, Lois F. "Time, Motion, Sound and Fury in *The Sea Birds Are Still Alive*," *Coll Lang Assoc J*, 36 (1992), 135, 139, 142.

"Broken Field Running"
Lyles, Lois F. "Time, Motion . . . ," 137–139, 140.

"The Hammer Man"
+ Charters, Ann, and William E. Sheidley. *Resources for Teaching* . . . , 3rd ed., 16.

"The Lesson"
+ Bohner, Charles H. *Instructor's Manual* . . . , 9–10.
Keating, Helane L., and Walter Levy. *Instructor's Manual: Lives Through Literature* . . . , 69.

"The Long Night"
Lyles, Lois F. "Time, Motion . . . ," 142–143.

"The Organizer's Wife"
Lyles, Lois F. "Time, Motion . . . ," 135–137, 140–142.

"The Sea Birds Are Still Alive"
Lyles, Lois F. "Time, Motion . . . ," 139.

RUSSELL BANKS

"My Mother's Memoirs, My Father's Lie, and Other True Stories"
Bohner, Charles H. *Instructor's Manual* . . . , 10–11.

HARRY BARBA

"The Armenian Cowboy"
Bedrosian, Margaret. "Transplantation," in Bedrosian, Margaret, Ed. *The Magic Pine Ring*, 76–77.

JULES-AMÉDÉE BARBEY D'AUREVILLY

"At a Dinner Party of Atheists"
Stivale, Charles J. " 'Like the Sculptor's Chisel': Voices 'On' and 'Off' in Barbey d'Aurevilly's *Les Diaboliques*," *Romanic R*, 82 (1991), 326.

"Le Bonheur dans le crime"
Stivale, Charles J. " 'Like the Sculptor's Chisel' . . . ," 326.

"Le dessous de cartes d'une partie de whist"
Stivale, Charles J. " 'Like the Sculptor's Chisel' . . . ," 327.

"Le plus bel amour de Don Juan"
Stivale, Charles J. " 'Like the Sculptor's Chisel' . . . ," 326–327.

"Le ridou cramoisi"
Stivale, Charles J. " 'Like the Sculptor's Chisel' . . . ," 321–325.

"A Woman's Vengeance"
Stivale, Charles J. " 'Like the Sculptor's Chisel' . . . ," 328–329.

ARTURO BAREA

"Coñac"
  Percival, Anthony. "El cuento de la Guerra Civil Española: Del neo-
  realismo al 'posmodernismo' (*Valor y miedo* de Arturo Barea y
  Largo noviembre de Madrid de Juan Eduardo Zúñiga)," in Boland,
  Roy, and Alun Kenwood, Eds. *War and Revolution* . . . , 146–147.
"Servicio de noche"
  Percival, Anthony. "El cuento de la Guerra . . . ," 144–145.

RUBÉN BAREIRO SAGUIER

"Anniversary"
  Weldt, Helene. "Cases of Ambiguity in Rubén Bareiro Saguier's *Ojo
  por diente*," *Hispano*, 36, i (1992), 44–45.
"Blood Pact"
  Weldt, Helene. "Cases of Ambiguity . . . ," 42–44, 45, 51–52
"Browning 45"
  Weldt, Helene. "Cases of Ambiguity . . . ," 50–51, 53–54.
"Eye for Eye"
  Weldt, Helene. "Cases of Ambiguity . . . ," 47–48, 49–50, 51.
"Nocturnal Patrol"
  Weldt, Helene. "Cases of Ambiguity . . . ," 50, 52.
"North Wind"
  Weldt, Helene. "Cases of Ambiguity . . . ," 45–46.
"Only a Moment"
  Weldt, Helene. "Cases of Ambiguity . . . ," 42.
"The Operation"
  Weldt, Helene. "Cases of Ambiguity . . . ," 52–53.
"Salmon and Dorado"
  Weldt, Helene. "Cases of Ambiguity . . . ," 48.
"Tooth for Tooth"
  Weldt, Helene. "Cases of Ambiguity . . . ," 47.

DJUNA BARNES

"Cassation" [Originally "A Little Girl Tells a Story to a Lady"]
  Allen, Carolyn. "Writing toward *Nightwood*: Djuna Barnes'
  Seduction Stories," in Broe, Mary L., Ed. *Silence and
  Power* . . . , 58–62.
"Dusie"
  Allen, Carolyn. "Writing toward *Nightwood* . . . ," 64–65.
"The Grand Malade" [Originally "The Little Girl Continues"]
  Allen, Carolyn. "Writing toward *Nightwood* . . . ," 62–63.

JOHN BARTH

"Bellerophoniad"
Raper, Julius R. *Narcissus from Rubble* . . . , 113–118.

"Dunyazadiad"
Raper, Julius R. *Narcissus from Rubble* . . . , 118–126.

"Lost in the Funhouse"
Adams, Alice. "The American Short Story in the Cybernetic Age,"
J Short Story Engl, 17 (Autumn, 1991), 16–17.
+ Bohner, Charles H. *Instructor's Manual* . . . , 11–13.
+ Charters, Ann, and William E. Sheidley. *Resources for Teaching* . . . , 3rd ed., 18–19.

"Perseid"
Raper, Julius R. *Narcissus from Rubble* . . . , 106–113.

DONALD BARTHELME

"Abduction from the Seraglio"
Roe, Barbara L. *Donald Barthelme* . . . , 131–132.

"At the Tolstoy Museum"
Roe, Barbara L. *Donald Barthelme* . . . , 51–54.

"The Balloon"
Head, Dominic. *The Modernist* . . . , 200–204.
Maltby, Paul. *Dissident Postmodernists* . . . , 44–46.
Roe, Barbara L. *Donald Barthelme* . . . , 8–11.

"Basil from Her Garden"
Roe, Barbara L. *Donald Barthelme* . . . , 62–63.

"Bluebeard"
Roe, Barbara L. *Donald Barthelme* . . . , 18–20.

"Bone Bubbles"
Roe, Barbara L. *Donald Barthelme* . . . , 48–49.

"Brain Damage"
Roe, Barbara L. *Donald Barthelme* . . . , 56–58.

"Captain Blood"
Roe, Barbara L. *Donald Barthelme* . . . , 21–23.

"The Captured Woman"
Roe, Barbara L. *Donald Barthelme* . . . , 46–47.

"Chablis"
Roe, Barbara L. *Donald Barthelme* . . . , 73–74.

"A City of Churches"
+ Bohner, Charles H. *Instructor's Manual* . . . , 13–14.
Roe, Barbara L. *Donald Barthelme* . . . , 65–66.

"Critique de la Vie Quotidienne"
Maltby, Paul. *Dissident Postmodernists* . . . , 63–64.
Roe, Barbara L. *Donald Barthelme* . . . , 69–71.

"Daumier"
Roe, Barbara L. *Donald Barthelme* . . . , 42–44.

"The Dolt"
Roe, Barbara L. *Donald Barthelme* . . . , 7–8.

"The Emerald"
Roe, Barbara L. *Donald Barthelme* . . . , 79–80.

"Engineer-Private Paul Klee Misplaces an Aircraft Between Milbertshofen and Cambrai, March 1916"
Roe, Barbara L. *Donald Barthelme* . . . , 27–29.

"Eugénie Grandet"
Maltby, Paul. *Dissident Postmodernists* . . . , 70–74.
Roe, Barbara L. *Donald Barthelme* . . . , 13–16.

"The Explanation"
Adams, Alice. "The American Short Story in the Cybernetic Age," *J Short Story Engl*, 17 (Autumn, 1991), 16–17.

"The Falling Dog"
Maltby, Paul. *Dissident Postmodernists* . . . , 68–70.

"The Flight of the Pigeons from the Palace"
Roe, Barbara L. *Donald Barthelme* . . . , 54–56.

"Game"
Roe, Barbara L. *Donald Barthelme* . . . , 67–68.

"The Glass Mountain"
Roe, Barbara L. *Donald Barthelme* . . . , 11–13.

"I am, at the moment . . ."
Roe, Barbara L. *Donald Barthelme* . . . , 82–83.

"The Indian Uprising"
McHale, Brian, and Moshe Ron. "On Not-Knowing How to Read Barthelme's 'The Indian Uprising,' " *R Contemp Fiction*, 11, ii (1991), 50–68.
Maltby, Paul. *Dissident Postmodernists* . . . , 78–81.

"Kierkegaard Unfair to Schlegel"
Roe, Barbara L. *Donald Barthelme* . . . , 60–62.

"A Manual for Sons"
Roe, Barbara L. *Donald Barthelme* . . . , 71–72.

"Me and Miss Mandible"
Maltby, Paul. *Dissident Postmodernists* . . . , 46–48.

"Morning"
Roe, Barbara L. *Donald Barthelme* . . . , 76–77.

"A Nation of Wheels"
Roe, Barbara L. *Donald Barthelme* . . . , 51, 53.

"The New Music"
Roe, Barbara L. *Donald Barthelme* . . . , 77–79.

"Now that I am older . . ."
Roe, Barbara L. *Donald Barthelme* . . . , 82.

"On the Deck"
  Roe, Barbara L. *Donald Barthelme* . . . , 36–37.

"Our Work and Why We Do It"
  Roe, Barbara L. *Donald Barthelme* . . . , 33–35.

"Overnight to Many Distant Cities"
  Roe, Barbara L. *Donald Barthelme* . . . , 83–85.

"Paraguay"
  Maltby, Paul. *Dissident Postmodernists* . . . , 76–78.

"The Phantom of the Opera's Friend"
  Roe, Barbara L. *Donald Barthelme* . . . , 26–27.

"The President"
  Maltby, Paul. *Dissident Postmodernists* . . . , 50–52.
  Roe, Barbara L. *Donald Barthelme* . . . , 66–67.

"Rebecca"
  Piwinski, David J. "Country-Western Music and the Bible: An
    Allusion in Donald Barthelme's 'Rebecca,' " *Notes Contemp Lit*,
    21, i (1991), 3–4.

"Report"
  Maltby, Paul. *Dissident Postmodernists* . . . , 54–55.
  Roe, Barbara L. *Donald Barthelme* . . . , 68.

"The Rise of Capitalism"
  Maltby, Paul. *Dissident Postmodernists* . . . , 64–67.

"Robert Kennedy Saved from Drowning"
  Maltby, Paul. *Dissident Postmodernists* . . . , 52–54.
  Roe, Barbara L. *Donald Barthelme* . . . , 44–46.

"The School"
  Charters, Ann, and William E. Sheidley. *Resources for Teaching* . . . ,
    3rd ed., 21–22.
  Roe, Barbara L. *Donald Barthelme* . . . , 64–65.

"The Sea of Hesitation"
  Roe, Barbara L. *Donald Barthelme* . . . , 80–81.

"A Shower of Gold"
  Maltby, Paul. *Dissident Postmodernists* . . . , 48–50.
  Roe, Barbara L. *Donald Barthelme* . . . , 16–18.

"Sindbad"
  Roe, Barbara L. *Donald Barthelme* . . . , 23–24.

"The Temptation of St. Anthony"
  Roe, Barbara L. *Donald Barthelme* . . . , 25–26.

"Tickets"
  Roe, Barbara L. *Donald Barthelme* . . . , 86–88.

"To London and Rome"
  Roe, Barbara L. *Donald Barthelme* . . . , 31–32.

"Views of My Father Weeping"
  Roe, Barbara L. *Donald Barthelme* . . . , 39–42, 55–56.

"Visitors"
    Roe, Barbara L. *Donald Barthelme* . . . , 74–75.
"What to Do Next"
    Roe, Barbara L. *Donald Barthelme* . . . , 47–48.
"A Woman seated on a plain wooden chair . . ."
    Roe, Barbara L. *Donald Barthelme* . . . , 37–39.
"The Wound"
    Roe, Barbara L. *Donald Barthelme* . . . , 32–33.

FREDERICK BARTHELME

"Box Step"
    Aldridge, John W. *Talents and Technicians* . . . , 75–76.
"Monster Deal"
    Aldridge, John W. *Talents and Technicians* . . . , 76–77.

CHARLES BAUDELAIRE

"La Fanfarlo"
    Lloyd, Rosemary. "Introduction," *The Prose Poems* . . . [by Charles
    Baudelaire], vii–x.

BARBARA BAYNTON

"The Chosen Vessel"
    Walker, Shirley. "The Deconstruction of the Bush: Australian
    Women Short Story Writers," in Bardolph, Jacquelin, Ed. *Short
    Fiction* . . . , 78–79.
"Squeaker's Mate"
    Walker, Shirley. "The Deconstruction . . . ," 78.

ANN BEATTIE

"Eric Clapton's Lover"
    Aldridge, John W. *Talents and Technicians* . . . , 63–65.
"Jacklighting"
    Story, Kenneth E. "Throwing a Spotlight on the Past: Narrative
    Method in Ann Beattie's 'Jacklighting,' " *Stud Short Fiction*, 27
    (1990), 106–109.
"Janus"
    Cassill, R. V. . . . *Instructor's Handbook*, 8.
"Skeletons"
    Hornby, Nick. *Contemporary American Fiction*, 8–9.
"Vermont"
    Aldridge, John W. *Talents and Technicians* . . . , 65–66.

"A Vintage Thunderbird"
Plath, James. "My Lover the Car: Ann Beattie's 'A Vintage Thunderbird' and Other Vehicles," *Kansas Q*, 21, iv (1990), 113–119.

SAMUEL BECKETT

"Afar a Bird"
Cochran, Robert. *Samuel Beckett* . . . , 63–64.

"Assumption"
Cochran, Robert. *Samuel Beckett* . . . , 3–5.

"The Calmative"
Cochran, Robert. *Samuel Beckett* . . . , 32–35.
DiBattista, Maria. *First Love* . . . , 213–216.

"A Case in a Thousand"
Cochran, Robert. *Samuel Beckett* . . . , 18–20.
Harrington, John P. *The Irish Beckett*, 70–72.

"Company"
Cochran, Robert. *Samuel Beckett* . . . , 70–74.

"Dante and the Lobster"
Carey, Phyllis. "Stephen Dedalus, Belacqua Shuah, and Dante's *Pietà*," in Carey, Phyllis, and Ed Jewinski, Eds. *RE: Joyce 'n Beckett*, 108–144.
Cochran, Robert. *Samuel Beckett* . . . , 5–9.
Gillespie, Michael P. "Textually Uninhibited: The Playfulness of Joyce and Beckett," in Carey, Phyllis, and Ed Jewinski, Eds. *RE: Joyce 'n Beckett*, 94–96.
Welch, Robert. *Irish Writers* . . . , 171.
Cochran, Robert. *Samuel Beckett* . . . , 5–9.

"Ding-Dong"
Cochran, Robert. *Samuel Beckett* . . . , 9–10.

"Draff"
Cochran, Robert. *Samuel Beckett* . . . , 16–17.

"The End"
Cochran, Robert. *Samuel Beckett* . . . , 21–27.

"Enough"
Catanzaro, Mary F. "Enough or Too Little? Voicings of Desire and Discontent in Beckett's 'Enough,' " in Smith, Joseph H., Ed. *The World* . . . , 16–28.
Cochran, Robert. *Samuel Beckett* . . . , 52–54.

"The Expelled"
Cochran, Robert. *Samuel Beckett* . . . , 27–29.
DiBattista, Maria. *First Love* . . . , 212–213.
Shillony, Helena. " 'L'Expulsé' de Beckett: La naissance d'une écriture," *Lettres Romanes*, 45, iii (1991), 207–214.

"Fingal"
  Cochran, Robert. *Samuel Beckett* . . . , 9.
"First Love"
  Cochran, Robert. *Samuel Beckett* . . . , 29–32.
  DiBattista, Maria. *First Love* . . . , 213, 224–231.
"Fizzle 1"
  Rabinovitz, Rubin. *Innovation* . . . , 138–139.
"Fizzle 2"
  Rabinovitz, Rubin. *Innovation* . . . , 139–140.
"Fizzle 3"
  Rabinovitz, Rubin. *Innovation* . . . , 141, 142–143.
"Fizzle 4"
  Rabinovitz, Rubin. *Innovation* . . . , 143.
"Fizzle 7"
  Rabinovitz, Rubin. *Innovation* . . . , 145–146.
"Fizzle 8"
  Rabinovitz, Rubin. *Innovation* . . . , 121–122, 147–148, 149–150.
"For to End Yet Again"
  Cochran, Robert. *Samuel Beckett* . . . , 66–68.
"From an Abandoned Work"
  Cochran, Robert. *Samuel Beckett* . . . , 44–46.
"Ping"
  Doherty, Francis. "Paf, Hop, Bing, and Ping," *J Short Story Engl*,
    17 (Autumn, 1991), 23–41.
"Texts for Nothing"
  Wolosky, Shira. "The Negative Way Negated: Samuel Beckett's
    'Texts for Nothing,' " *New Lit Hist*, 22 (1991), 220–228.
"Yellow"
  Welch, Robert. *Irish Writers* . . . , 170–171.

GUSTAVO ADOLFO BÉCQUER

"La ajorca de oro"
  Baker, Armand F. "Self Realization in the *Leyendas* of Gustavo
    Adolfo Bécquer," *Revista Hispánica Moderna*, 42 (1991), 194–196.
"El Caudillo de las manos rojas"
  Baker, Armand F. "Self Realization . . . ," 198–199.
"Creed en Dios"
  Baker, Armand F. "Self Realization . . . ," 204–206.
"El Cristo de la calavera"
  Baker, Armand F. "Self Realization . . . ," 202.
"La cruz del diablo"
  Marcone, Jorge. "La tradición oral y el cuento fantástico en 'La cruz
    del diablo' de G. A. Bécquer," *Mester*, 19, ii (1990), 50–57.

"La cueva de la mora"
Baker, Armand F. "Self Realization . . . ," 199–200.

"El gnomo"
Baker, Armand F. "Self Realization . . . ," 200–202.

"Los ojos verdes"
Baker, Armand F. "Self Realization . . . ," 196.

"La promesa"
Baker, Armand F. "Self Realization . . . ," 202–204.

"El rayo de luna"
Baker, Armand F. "Self Realization . . . ," 196–198.
Romain, Bella. "The 'Landscape of the Subconscious' as Revealed in Bécquer's 'El rayo de luna' ('The Moonbeam')," *West Georgia Coll R*, 22 (May, 1992), 23–26.

"Tres fechas"
Baker, Armand F. "Self Realization . . . ," 194.

MAX BEERBOHM

"A. V. Laider"
Maner, Martin. "Beerbohm's Seven Men and the Power of the Press," *Engl Lit Transition*, 34, ii (1991), 141, 143–145.

"Enoch Soames"
Maner, Martin. "Beerbohm's Seven . . . ," 139–140, 142, 143, 145–146, 147–148.

"Felix Argallo and Walter Ledgett"
Maner, Martin. "Beerbohm's Seven . . . ," 137–138, 142–143.

"Hilary Maltby and Stephen Braxton"
Maner, Martin. "Beerbohm's Seven . . . ," 138–139, 141–142, 143.

"Savonarola Brown"
Maner, Martin. "Beerbohm's Seven . . . ," 141, 146–147.

SAUL BELLOW

"Cousins"
Hyland, Peter. *Saul Bellow*, 124–125.

"Dora"
Lelchuk, Alan. "Recent Adventures of Saul Bellow: Reflections on 'What Kind of Day Did You Have?' " in Goldman, L. H., Gloria L. Cronin, and Ada Aharoni, Eds. *Saul Bellow . . .* , 74–77.

"A Father-to-Be"
Hyland, Peter. *Saul Bellow*, 120.

"Him with His Foot in His Mouth"
Hyland, Peter. *Saul Bellow*, 124.

"Leaving the Yellow House"
+Cassill, R. V. . . . *Instructor's Handbook*, 9–10.

Hyland, Peter. *Saul Bellow*, 121.
Lelchuk, Alan. "Recent Adventures . . . ," 78–85.
"Looking for Mr. Green"
Hyland, Peter. *Saul Bellow*, 119.
"Mosby's Memoirs"
Hyland, Peter. *Saul Bellow*, 122.
"The Old System"
Hyland, Peter. *Saul Bellow*, 121–122.
"Seize the Day"
Hyland, Peter. *Saul Bellow*, 40–47.
Miller, Ruth. *Saul Bellow* . . . , 93–98.
Kremer, S. Lillian. "An Intertextual Reading of 'Seize the Day':
    Absorption and Revision," *Saul Bellow J*, 10, i (1991), 46–56.
Raper, Julius R. *Narcissus from Rubble* . . . , 12–26.
Shiels, Michael. "Space, Place, and Pace: A Cinematic Reading of
    'Seize the Day,' " in Bach, Gerhard, Ed. *Saul Bellow* . . . , 55–62.
"A Silver Dish"
Hyland, Peter. *Saul Bellow*, 123–124.
"What Kind of Day Did You Have?"
Hyland, Peter. *Saul Bellow*, 125–127.
Lelchuk, Alan. "Recent Adventures . . . ," 59–71.
"Zetland: By a Character Witness"
Hyland, Peter. *Saul Bellow*, 123.

MARIO BENEDETTI

"Sábado de Gloria"
Dehennin, Elsa. "A propósito del realismo de Mario Benedetti,"
    Revista Iberoamericana, 58 (1992), 1085–1090.

JOAQUÍN BESTARD VÁSQUEZ

"De la misma herida"
Huck, George A. "La obra de Bestard: Voces del tercer mundo,"
    Plural, 186 (1987), 17–30.

JOSÉ BIANCO

"Sombras suele vestir"
Domínguez, Mignon. "El discurso fantasmal y la 'mise en abyme' en
    'Sombras suele vestir' de José Bianco," in Domíguez, Mignon, Ed.
    Estudios de narratología, 99–122.

AMBROSE BIERCE

"The Affair at Coulter's Notch"
Conlogue, William. "A Haunting Memory: Ambrose Bierce and the
    Ravine of the Dead," *Stud Short Fiction*, 28 (1991), 26–27.

"The Coup de Grâce"
   Conlogue, William. "A Haunting Memory . . . ," 26–27.
"The Haunted Valley"
   Conlogue, William. "A Haunting Memory . . . ," 22–24.
"The Hypnotist"
   Wolotkiewicz, Diana A. "Ambrose Bierce's Use of the Grotesque
   Mode: The Pathology of Society," *J Short Story Engl*, 16 (Spring,
   1991), 88–89.
"An Imperfect Conflagration"
   Wolotkiewicz, Diana A. ". . . Pathology of Society," 86–87.
"Killed at Resaca" [Originally "The Coward"]
   Conlogue, William. "A Haunting Memory . . . ," 24–26.
"My Favorite Murder"
   Wolotkiewicz, Diana A. ". . . Pathology of Society," 87–88.
"An Occurrence at Owl Creek Bridge"
   + Bohner, Charles H. *Instructor's Manual* . . . , 14–15.
   + Cassill, R. V. . . . *Instructor's Handbook*, 11–12.
   + Charters, Ann, and William E. Sheidley. *Resources for
   Teaching* . . . , 3rd ed., 24–25.

ADOLFO BIOY CASARES

"De los dos lados"
   Barrera, Trinidad. "Adolfo Bioy Casares, la aventura de vivir,"
   Revista Iberoamericana, 58 (1992), 345–346.
"Encrucijada"
   Barrera, Trinidad. "Adolfo Bioy Casares . . . ," 347.
"Máscaras venecianas"
   Domínguez, María L. "Del espacio americano al espacio europeo.
   La espacialidad fantástica en un relato de Adolfo Bioy Casares,"
   Anthropos R, 127 (1991), 57–61.

ELIZABETH BISHOP

"Memories of Uncle Neddy"
   Wallace, Patricia. "Erasing the Maternal: Rereading Elizabeth
   Bishop," *Iowa R*, 22, ii (1992), 82, 83–85, 93–99.

NEIL BISSOONDATH

"The Cage"
   Boxill, Anthony. "Women and Migration in Some Short Stories of
   Bharati Mukherjee and Neil Bissoondath," *Literary Half-Yearly*,
   32, ii (1991), 47–48.
"Dancing"
   Boxill, Anthony. "Women and Migration . . . ," 48–49.

JÓHANN MAGNÚS BJARNASON

"An Icelandic Giant"
  Wolf, Kirsten. "Heroic Past—Heroic Present: Western Icelandic
  Literature," *Scandinavian Stud*, 63 (1991), 439–440.

MAURICE BLANCHOT

"La Folie du jour"
  Assali, N. Donald. "Vers un nouveau récit: 'La Folie du jour' de
  Maurice Blanchot," *Francographies*, 1 (1992), 129–134.

NORBERT BLEI

"The Chair Trick"
  Shereikis, Richard. "Scenes from the South Side: The Chicago
  Fiction of Norbert Blei," *Midamerica*, 18 (1991), 140.
"The Ghost of Sandburg's Phizzog"
  Shereikis, Richard. "Scenes . . . ," 141–142.
"The Secret Places of the Stairs"
  Shereikis, Richard. "Scenes . . . ," 139–140.
"Skarda"
  Shereikis, Richard. "Scenes . . . ," 136–137, 138.
"Stars"
  Shereikis, Richard. "Scenes . . . ," 139, 142.
"This Horse of a Body of Mine"
  Shereikis, Richard. "Scenes . . . ," 140–141.

CECIL BØDKER

"The Ram"
  Skydsgaard, Niels J. "Literary Form and Cultural
  Norm—Preliminary Investigations for a Study of Reader
  Experience of a Fictitious Character," *Orbis Litterarum*, 47 (1992),
  342–345, 352.

HEINRICH BÖLL

"Christmas Not Just Once a Year"
  Conrad, Robert. *Understanding Heinrich Böll*, 37–43.
"Like a Bad Dream"
  +Bohner, Charles H. *Instructor's Manual . . .* , 15–16.
  +Charters, Ann, and William E. Sheidley. *Resources for
  Teaching . . .* , 3rd ed., 25–26.

"The Thrower-Away"
Conrad, Robert. *Understanding Heinrich Böll*, 43–51.

"Traveler, You Will Come to a Spa"
Berman, Russell A. "The Rhetoric of Citation and the Ideology of War in Heinrich Böll's Short Stories," *Germ R*, 66 (1991), 156–158.

"When War Broke Out"
Berman, Russell A. "The Rhetoric of Citation . . . ," 158–159.

MARÍA LUISA BOMBAL

"The Tree"
Schulz, Bárbara. "La visión andrógina en 'El árbol,' de María Luisa Bombal," *Estudios Filológicos*, 27 (1992), 113–122.

"The New Islands"
Smith, Verity. "Dwarfed by Snow White: Feminist Revisions of Fairy Tale Discourse in the Narrative of María Luisa Bombal and Dulce María Loynaz," in Condé, L. P., and S. M. Hart, Eds. *Feminist Readings* . . . , 143–146.

"La última niebla"
Manriquez de Cugniet, María del Valle. "La descripción en 'La última niebla': Modalidades y motivación," in Domíguez, Mignon, Ed. *Estudios de narratología*, 81–98.

JORGE LUIS BORGES

"Abenjacán the Bojari, Dead in His Labyrinth"
Gutiérrez Carbajo, Francisco. "El relato policial en Borges," *Cuadernos Hispanoamericanos*, 505–507 (July–September, 1992), 383.

"The Aleph"
Brodzki, Bella. "Borges and the Idea of Woman," *Discurso*, 10, ii (1992), 38–40.
Fernández Ferrer, Antonio. "El Aleph de 'El Aleph,' " *Cuadernos Hispanoamericanos*, 505–507 (July–September, 1992), 481–493.
Merrell, Floyd. *Unthinking Thinking* . . . , 7–9, 145–154.
Rodríguez-Luis, Julio. *The Contemporary* . . . , 39–41.

"The Approach to Almotásim"
Gutiérrez Carbajo, Francisco. "El relato policial . . . ," 382.
Rodríguez-Luis, Julio. *The Contemporary* . . . , 45–46.

"Averroes' Search"
Merrell, Floyd. *Unthinking Thinking* . . . , 74–76.

"The Babylonian Lottery"
Merrell, Floyd. *Unthinking Thinking* . . . , 173–177.

"The Book of Sand"
Rodríguez-Luis, Julio. *The Contemporary* . . . , 54–55.

"Borges and I"
Tambling, Jeremy. *Narrative and Ideology*, 45–47.
"The Circular Ruins"
Fleming, Leonor. "Un dios múltiple: Una lectura de 'Las ruinas circulares,' " *Cuadernos Hispanoamericanos*, 505–507 (July–September, 1992), 467–472.
Gutiérrez Carbajo, Francisco. "El relato policial . . . ," 380–381.
Merrell, Floyd. *Unthinking Thinking* . . . , 33–38.
"The Congress"
Brodzki, Bella. "Borges and the Idea . . . ," 46–48.
"Death and the Compass"
Gutiérrez Carbajo, Francisco. "El relato policial . . . ," 378–380.
Liberman, Arnoldo. "Borges, el judío blanco," *Cuadernos Hispanoamericanos*, 505–507 (July–September, 1992), 149–150.
Major, René. "La parabole de la lettre volée: de la direction de la curé et de son récit," *Études Freudiennes*, 30 (October, 1987), 103–107, 110; rpt. "The Parable of the Purloined Letter: The Direction of the Curé and Its Telling," trans. John Forrester, *Stanford Lit R*, 8, i–ii (Spring-Fall, 1991), 72–77, 81.
Merrell, Floyd. *Unthinking Thinking* . . . , 46–48, 203–205.
Miller, J. Hillis. *Adriadne's Thread* . . . , 229–256.
Williams, Gareth. "Lectura intertextual en 'La muerte y la brújula,' " *Revista Canadiense*, 15 (1991), 295–304.
"Deutsches Requiem"
Liberman, Arnoldo. "Borges, el judío blanco," 145.
"Diálogo de muertos"
Murad, Timothy. "Una biografía poética de Juan Facundo Quiroga," *Mundi/Crítica/Literatura*, 2, iv (1988), 70–72.
"Doctor Brodie's Report"
Malekin, Peter. "Knowing about Knowing: Paradigms of Knowledge in the Postmodern Fantastic," in Ruddick, Nicholas, Ed. *State* . . . , 42.
"The Duel"
Brodzki, Bella. "Borges and the Idea . . . ," 44–45.
"Emma Zunz"
Gutiérrez Carbajo, Francisco. "El relato policial . . . ," 386.
Ludmer, Josefina. "Las justicias de Emma," *Cuadernos Hispanoamericanos*, 505–507 (July–September, 1992), 473–480.
McGuirk, Bernard. "Z/Z," in *Coloquio internacional* . . . , 207–231.
"The End of the Duel"
+ Bohner, Charles H. *Instructor's Manual* . . . , 16–17.
"Funes the Memorious"
Merrell, Floyd. *Unthinking Thinking* . . . , 78–80.
Stavans, Ilán. "El arte de la memoria," *Mester*, 19, ii (1990), 79–108.
"The Garden of Forking Paths"
Charters, Ann, and William E. Sheidley. *Resources for Teaching* . . . , 3rd ed., 27–28.

Elmajdoub, Aburawi A., and Mary K. Miller. "The 'Eternal Now' in Borges' 'The Garden of Forking Paths' and 'Pierre Menard, author of *Don Quixote*,' " *Durham Univ J*, 83 (1991), 249–250.

Gutiérrez Carbajo, Francisco. "El relato policial . . . ," 383–385.

Kushigian, Julia A. *Orientalism* . . . , 25–27.

Merrell, Floyd. *Unthinking Thinking* . . . , 177–182.

Weissert, Thomas P. "Representation and Bifurcation: Borges's Garden of Chaos Dynamics," in Hayles, N. Katherine, Ed. *Chaos and Order* . . . , 223–243.

"God's Script" [same as "The Writing of the Lord"]

Balderston, Daniel. "Cuento (corto) y cuentas (largas) en 'La escritura del dios,' " *Cuadernos Hispanoamericanos*, 505–507 (July–September, 1992), 445–454.

Merrell, Floyd. *Unthinking Thinking* . . . , 65–66.

Rodríguez-Luis, Julio. *The Contemporary* . . . , 43–44.

Schuessler, Michael K. "Un espejo en la oscuridad: 'La escritura del Dios' y la ontología del Verbo," *Mester*, 19, ii (1990), 83–95.

Tyler, Joseph. "The Image of the Tiger in Borges' Fiction," in Tyler, Joseph, Ed. *Borges' Craft* . . . , 59–62.

"The Gospel According to Mark"

Malekin, Peter. "Knowing about Knowing . . . ," 42.

"The House of Asterion"

Alvarez, Nicolás E. "Lectura y re-escritura: La mitopoiesis de 'La casa de Asterión' de Borges," *Revista Iberoamericana*, 57 (1991), 507–518.

Bennett, Maurice. "Borges's 'The House of Asterion,' " *Explicator*, 50, iii (1992), 166–169.

Merrell, Floyd. *Unthinking Thinking* . . . , 62–63.

"The Immortal"

Batista Rodríguez, José J. "Notas sobre el tratamiento de la inmortalidad en Borges y Luciano," *Revista Filología*, 10 (1991), 15–20.

Crumb, Michael. "Image Strategies in Postmodernism: Borges' 'The Immortal,' " in Tyler, Joseph, Ed. *Borges' Craft* . . . , 27–42.

Kushigian, Julia A. *Orientalism* . . . , 29–32.

Merrell, Floyd. *Unthinking Thinking* . . . , 229–233.

"The Intruder"

Brodzki, Bella. "Borges and the Idea . . . ," 41–44.

"El juez Lu"

Jiménez Emán, Gabriel. "Un Borges oriental," *Escritura*, 15 (1990), 51, 52–53.

"The Library of Babel"

Merrell, Floyd. *Unthinking Thinking* . . . , 69–71.

"The Meeting"

Rodríguez-Luis, Julio. *The Contemporary* . . . , 49–50.

"The Other"

Merrell, Floyd. *Unthinking Thinking* . . . , 93–94.

"The Other Death"
Rodríguez-Luis, Julio. *The Contemporary* . . . , 41–43.

"Pierre Menard, Author of *Don Quixote*"
+ Cassill, R. V. . . . *Instructor's Handbook*, 12–13.
Elmajdoub, Aburawi A., and Mary K. Miller. "The 'Eternal
    Now' . . . ," 250–251.
Gutiérrez Girardot, Rafael. "Pierre Menard o Paul Mallarmé,"
    Quimera, 105 (1991), 54–61.
Irwin, Joan T. "The Journey to the South: Poe, Borges, and
    Faulkner," *Virginia Q R*, 67 (1991), 420–424.
Rabell, Carmen, R. "Lenguaje y escrilectura en 'Pierre Menard,
    autor del *Quijote*,' " *Hispanic R*, 13 (1992), 27–36.
Rodríguez, Marta. " 'Pierre Menard, autor del *Quijote*': Esquema
    semántico del tópico de la crítica literaria," *Cuadernos
    Hispanoamericanos*, 505–507 (July–September, 1992), 439–444.
Rodríguez-Luis, Julio. *The Contemporary* . . . , 35–37.

"The Secret Miracle"
Merrell, Floyd. *Unthinking Thinking* . . . , 41–42.
Rodríguez-Luis, Julio. *The Contemporary* . . . , 38–39.
Tijeras, Eduardo. "Conjeturar a Borges," *Cuadernos
    Hispanoamericanos*, 505–507 (July–September, 1992), 135–136.

"El sendero mágico"
Jiménez Emán, Gabriel. "Un Borges . . . ," 51–52.

"The Shape of the Sword"
Gutiérrez Carbajo, Francisco. "El relato policial . . . ," 385.

"The South"
Frisch, Mark F. "Self-Definition and Redefinition in the New World:
    Coover's *The Universal Baseball Association* and Borges,"
    Confluencia, 4, ii (1989), 15–16.
González-Casanovas, Roberto J. "Borges's Argentinian South:
    Legend, Fiction, and Myth in 'El sur,' " *West Virginia Univ. Philol
    Papers*, 37 (1991), 151–157.
Irwin, Joan T. "The Journey . . . ," 427–429.
Neustadt, Bob. "Borges y García Márquez: Paralelismos
    narrativos," *Confluencia*, 7, i (1991), 82, 83, 84, 85–86.

"Tlön, Uqbar, Orbis Tertius"
Duncan, Cynthia K. "Hacia una interpretación de lo fantástico en el
    contexto de la literatura hispanoamericana," *Texto Crítico*, 16
    (January–December, 1990), 57–58.
Kason, Nancy M. "The Mirror or Utopia: 'Tlön, Uqbar, Orbis
    Tertius,' " in Tyler, Joseph, Ed. *Borges' Craft* . . . , 7–16.
Merrell, Floyd. *Unthinking Thinking* . . . , 158–161.
Rodríguez-Luis, Julio. *The Contemporary* . . . , 36–37.
Zanelli, Carmela. "Las aspiraciones de Tlön," *Mester*, 19, ii (1990),
    109–122.

"Ulrike"
Brodzki, Bella. "Borges and the Idea . . . ," 45–46.

"Utopia of a Tired Man"
  Rodríguez-Luis, Julio. *The Contemporary* . . . , 51–53.
"The Zahir"
  Brodzki, Bella. "Borges and the Idea . . . ," 37, 40.
  Kushigian, Julia A. *Orientalism* . . . , 33–35.
  Merrell, Floyd. *Unthinking Thinking* . . . , 5–8.
  Rodríguez-Luis, Julio. *The Contemporary* . . . , 41.

TADEUSZ BOROWSKI

"This Way for the Gas, Ladies and Gentlemen"
  Charters, Ann, and William E. Sheidley. *Resources for Teaching* . . . ,
  3rd ed., 29–30.

ELIZABETH BOWEN

"Daffodils"
  Keating, Helane L., and Walter Levy. *Instructor's Manual: Lives
  Through Literature* . . . , 70.
"The Demon Lover"
  Greene, George. "Elizabeth Bowen: The Sleuth Who Bugged Tea
  Cups," *Virginia Q R*, 67 (1991), 614–616.
"Ivy Gripped the Steps"
  Greene, George. "Elizabeth Bowen . . . ," 610–612.
"Look at All Those Roses"
  Greene, George. "Elizabeth Bowen . . . ," 608–609.
"Reduced"
  Greene, George. "Elizabeth Bowen . . . ," 607–608.
"Sunday Afternoon"
  Greene, George. "Elizabeth Bowen . . . ," 612–614.

PAUL BOWLES

"A Distant Episode"
  Charters, Ann, and William E. Sheidley. *Resources for Teaching* . . . ,
  3rd ed., 31.
"The Fqih"
  Al-Ghalith, Asad. "Paul Bowles's Portrayal of Islam in His Moroccan
  Short Stories," *Int'l Fiction R*, 19, ii (1992), 107–108.
"The Story of Lachcen and Idir"
  Al-Ghalith, Asad. "Paul Bowles's Portrayal . . . ," 105, 107.
"The Waters of Isli"
  Al-Ghalith, Asad. "Paul Bowles's Portrayal . . . ," 108.
"The Wind at Beni Midar"
  Al-Ghalith, Asad. "Paul Bowles's Portrayal . . . ," 105, 106, 107.

KAY BOYLE

"Anschluss"
  Bell, Elizabeth S. *Kay Boyle* . . . , 75–77.
"Art Colony"
  Bell, Elizabeth S. *Kay Boyle* . . . , 27–28.
  Cassill, R. V. . . . *Instructor's Handbook*, 14–15.
"The Ballet of Central Park"
  Bell, Elizabeth S. *Kay Boyle* . . . , 69–72.
"Begin Again"
  Bell, Elizabeth S. *Kay Boyle* . . . , 59–60.
"Black Boy"
  Bell, Elizabeth S. *Kay Boyle* . . . , 21–22.
  Loeffelholz, Mary. *Experimental Lives* . . . , 142–143.
"The Canals of Mars"
  Bell, Elizabeth S. *Kay Boyle* . . . , 52–53.
"Count Lothar's Heart"
  Bell, Elizabeth S. *Kay Boyle* . . . , 34–35.
"Dear Mr. Walrus"
  Bell, Elizabeth S. *Kay Boyle* . . . , 37–38.
"Defeat"
  Bell, Elizabeth S. *Kay Boyle* . . . , 47–48.
"A Disgrace to the Family"
  Bell, Elizabeth S. *Kay Boyle* . . . , 80–82.
"Effigy of War"
  Bell, Elizabeth S. *Kay Boyle* . . . , 48–49.
"Episode in the Life of an Ancestor"
  Clark, Suzanne. *Sentimental Modernism* . . . , 130–132.
  Loeffelholz, Mary. *Experimental Lives* . . . , 141–142.
"The First Lover"
  Bell, Elizabeth S. *Kay Boyle* . . . , 20–21.
"His Idea of a Mother"
  Bell, Elizabeth S. *Kay Boyle* . . . , 23–25.
"Home"
  Bell, Elizabeth S. *Kay Boyle* . . . , 65, 66.
"I Can't Get Drunk"
  Bell, Elizabeth S. *Kay Boyle* . . . , 26–27.
"Keep Your Pity"
  Bell, Elizabeth S. *Kay Boyle* . . . , 35–37.
"The Loneliest Man in the U.S. Army"
  Bell, Elizabeth S. *Kay Boyle* . . . , 51–52.
"The Lost"
  Bell, Elizabeth S. *Kay Boyle* . . . , 63–65.
"The Lovers of Gain"
  Bell, Elizabeth S. *Kay Boyle* . . . , 60–61.

"Luck for the Road"
Bell, Elizabeth S. *Kay Boyle* . . . , 77–78.

"Major Engagement in Paris"
Bell, Elizabeth S. *Kay Boyle* . . . , 45–47.

"The Man Who Died Young"
Bell, Elizabeth S. *Kay Boyle* . . . , 22–23.

"Nothing Ever Breaks Except the Heart"
Bell, Elizabeth S. *Kay Boyle* . . . , 78–79.

"On the Run"
Bell, Elizabeth S. *Kay Boyle* . . . , 16–17.
Clark, Suzanne. *Sentimental Modernism* . . . , 134–136.

"Polar Bears and Others"
Bell, Elizabeth S. *Kay Boyle* . . . , 13–14.

"Rest Cure"
Bell, Elizabeth S. *Kay Boyle* . . . , 25–26.

"Security"
Bell, Elizabeth S. *Kay Boyle* . . . , 39–40.

"The Soldier Ran Away"
Bell, Elizabeth S. *Kay Boyle* . . . , 82–83.

"Episode in the Life of an Ancestor"
Loeffelholz, Mary. *Experimental Lives* . . . , 141–142.

"Summer Evening"
Bell, Elizabeth S. *Kay Boyle* . . . , 61–63.

"Their Name Is Macaroni"
Bell, Elizabeth S. *Kay Boyle* . . . , 49–51.

"Three Little Men"
Bell, Elizabeth S. *Kay Boyle* . . . , 19–20.

"Vacation Time"
Bell, Elizabeth S. *Kay Boyle* . . . , 15–16.

"Wedding Day"
Bell, Elizabeth S. *Kay Boyle* . . . , 9–11.
Clark, Suzanne. *Sentimental Modernism* . . . , 132–134.

"White as Snow"
Bell, Elizabeth S. *Kay Boyle* . . . , 38–39.

"The White Horses of Vienna"
Bell, Elizabeth S. *Kay Boyle* . . . , 30–33.
Loeffelholz, Mary. *Experimental Lives* . . . , 143–144.

"Winter in Italy"
Bell, Elizabeth S. *Kay Boyle* . . . , 42.

"Winter Night"
Bell, Elizabeth S. *Kay Boyle* . . . , 53–54.

"Your Body Is a Jewel Box"
Bell, Elizabeth S. *Kay Boyle* . . . , 41–42.

RAY BRADBURY

"The Jar"
   Burleson, Donald R. "Connings: Bradbury/Oats," *Stud Weird Fiction*, 11 (Spring, 1992), 24–25, 26–27, 28, 29.

"The Kilimanjaro Device"
   Logsdon, Loren. "Ray Bradbury's 'The Kilimanjaro Device': The Need to Correct the Errors of Time," *Midwestern Miscellany*, 20 (1992), 28–39.

"The Night"
   Stockwell, Peter. "Language, Knowledge, and the Stylistics of Science Fiction," in Shaw, Philip, and Peter Stockwell, Eds. *Subjectivity and Literature* . . . , 101–112.

"The Veld"
   Cassill, R. V. . . . *Instructor's Handbook*, 15–16.

LEO BRADLEY

"The Sea and the Old Man"
   McLeod, Alan. "The Short Fiction of Belize," in Bardolph, Jacquelin, Ed. *Short Fiction* . . . , 97.

JOHANNA and GÜNTER BRAUN

"Transparentia Okularia"
   Mabee, Barbara. "Astronauts, Angels, and Time Machines: The Fantastic in Recent German Democratic Republic Literature," in Morse, Donald E., Marshall B. Tymn, and Csilla Bertha, Eds. *The Celebration* . . . , 229–230.

"The X-Times Reproduced Hero"
   Mabee, Barbara. "Astronauts, Angels . . . ," 227–228.

CLEMENS BRENTANO

"Märchen von Gockel und Hinkel"
   Simon, Ralf. "Autormasken, Schriftcharakter und Textstruktur in Brentanos Spätfassung des 'Gockel'-Märchens," *Zeitschrift für Deutsche Philologie*, 111, ii (1992), 201–231.

GREGORIO BRILLANTES

"The Blue Piano"
   Grow, L. M. "Expulsion from Eden in Gregorio Brillantes," *Philippine Stud*, 39 (1991), 498–499, 508, 513, 515, 518.

"The Distance to Andromeda"
   Grow, L. M. "Expulsion . . . ," 494, 504, 508, 515, 518.

"The Exiles"
Grow, L. M. "Expulsion . . . ," 498, 506–507.

"Faith, Love, Time and Dr. Lazaro"
Grow, L. M. "Expulsion . . . ," 492, 494, 502, 507, 513, 518.

"Flood in Tarlac"
Lucero, Rosario Cruz. "The Philippine Short Story, 1981–1990: The Voice of the Self-Authenticating Other," *Tenggara*, 26 (1990), 82–83.

"The Girl Elena"
Grow, L. M. "Expulsion . . . ," 514–515.

"The Light and Shadow of the Leaves"
Grow, L. M. "Expulsion . . . ," 510, 513, 514, 517.

"The Living and the Dead"
Grow, L. M. "Expulsion . . . ," 501, 502, 509.

"The Mountains"
Grow, L. M. "Expulsion . . . ," 500–501, 508–509.

"The Radio and the Green Meadows"
Grow, L. M. "Expulsion . . . ," 498, 514, 516.

"What Shall We Do When We All Go Out"
Grow, L. M. "Expulsion . . . ," 496, 503–504, 512, 516.

"The World of the Moon"
Grow, L. M. "Expulsion . . . ," 492–493, 496, 504, 505, 514, 517.

LARRY BROWN

"Waiting for the Ladies"
Farmer, Joy A. "The Sound and the Fury of Larry Brown's 'Waiting for the Ladies,' " *Stud Short Fiction*, 29 (1992), 315–322.

GAÉTAN BRULOTTE

"Plagiaire"
Fisher, Claudine G. "Sensibilités française et québécoise dan *Plages*," *Revue Francophone de Louisiane*, 5, i (Spring, 1990), 64–67.

HERMINIA BRUMANA

"Las desorientadas"
Masiello, Francine. *Between Civilizations* . . . , 181.

ALFREDO BRYCE ECHENIQUE

"Anorexia y tijerita"
Parsons, Robert A. " 'Watches Without Owners': Variations on a

Spanish American Satirical Theme," *Confluencia*, 7, i (1991),
56–57, 58, 59, 60, 61.

"Con Jimmy, en Paracas"
Mora, Gabriela. *"Huerto cerrado* de Alfredo Bryce Echenique,
colección integrada, cíclica y secuencial de cuentos," *Revista
Canadiense*, 16, ii (1992), 322–323.

"El descubrimiento de América"
Mora, Gabriela. *"Huerto . . . ,"* 324–325.

"Dos indios"
Mora, Gabriela. *"Huerto . . . ,"* 321–322.

"Extraña diversión"
Mora, Gabriela. *"Huerto . . . ,"* 325–326.

"Las notas que duermen en las cuerdas"
Mora, Gabriela. *"Huerto . . . ,"* 323–324.

ANTHONY BUKOSKI

"A Chance of Snow"
Gladsky, Thomas S. *Princes, Peasants . . .* , 267–268.

"The Children of Strangers"
Gladsky, Thomas S. *Princes, Peasants . . .* , 265.

"A Concert in Minor Pieces"
Gladsky, Thomas S. *Princes, Peasants . . .* , 264–265.

"The Eve of the First"
Gladsky, Thomas S. *Princes, Peasants . . .* , 263–264.

"The Pulaski Guards"
Gladsky, Thomas S. *Princes, Peasants . . .* , 266–267.

"The River of the Flowering Banks"
Gladsky, Thomas S. *Princes, Peasants . . . .,* 269–270.

CARLOS BULOSAN

"The Story of a Letter"
Campomanes, Oscar V. "Filipinos in the United States and Their
Literature of Exile," in Lim, Shirley G., and Amy Ling, Eds.
Reading the Literatures . . . , 63–65.

EDWARD GEORGE BULWER-LYTTON

"The Haunted and the Haunters; or, The House and the Brain"
Waddington, Patrick. "Two Authors of Strange Stories: Bulwer-
Lytton and Turgenev," *New Zealand Slavonic J*, [n.v.] (1992),
39, 44.

ANTHONY BURGESS

"The Eve of St. Venus"
Stinson, John J. *Anthony Burgess Revisited*, 80–81.

ANTONIA BYATT

"Precipice-Encurled"
Campbell, Jane. " 'The Somehow May Be Thishow': Fact, Fiction, and Intertextuality in Antonia Byatt's 'Precipice-Encurled,' " *Stud Short Fiction*, 28 (1991), 115–123.

GEORGE WASHINGTON CABLE

"Jean-Ah Poquelin"
Gaudet, Marcia. "Folklore and Compassion: The Treatment of Leprosy in George Washington Cable's 'Jean-Ah Poquelin,' " *Louisiana Literature*, 1, ii (1984), 20–23.

"Salome Müller"
Petry, Alice H. "The Limits of Truth in Cable's 'Salome Müller,' " *Papers Lang & Lit*, 27 (1991), 20–31.

LYDIA CABRERA

"La excelente doña Jicotea Concha"
Romeu, Raquel. "Dios, animal, hombre o mujer: Jicotea, un personaje de Lydia Cabrera," *Letras Femeninas*, 15, i–ii (1989), 30, 34–35.

"Jicotea era un buen hijo"
Romeu, Raquel. "Dios, animal . . . ," 32.

"La tesorera del Diablo"
Romeu, Raquel. "Dios, animal . . . ," 33–34.

"El vuelo de Jicota"
Romeu, Raquel. "Dios, animal . . . ," 33.

ERSKINE CALDWELL

"Blue Boy"
Cook, Sylvia J. *Erskine Caldwell . . .* , 73–75.

"The Cold Winter"
Cook, Sylvia J. *Erskine Caldwell . . .* , 71–72.

"Country Full of Swedes"
Cook, Sylvia J. *Erskine Caldwell . . .* , 65–66.

"The Fly in the Coffin"
Cook, Sylvia J. *Erskine Caldwell . . .* , 82–83.

"Kneel to the Rising Sun"
  Cook, Sylvia J. *Erskine Caldwell . . .* , 72–73.
"Masses of Men"
  Cook, Sylvia J. *Erskine Caldwell . . .* , 73–74, 75–76.
"Midsummer Passion"
  Cook, Sylvia J. *Erskine Caldwell . . .* , 58–59.
"Nine Dollars' Worth of Mumble"
  Cook, Sylvia J. *Erskine Caldwell . . .* , 82–83.
"The People's Choice"
  Cook, Sylvia J. *Erskine Caldwell . . .* , 65–66.
"The Picture"
  Cook, Sylvia J. *Erskine Caldwell . . .* , 65.
"Saturday Afternoon"
  Cook, Sylvia J. *Erskine Caldwell . . .* , 57–58.
"Slow Death"
  Cook, Sylvia J. *Erskine Caldwell . . .* , 70–71.

MORLEY CALLAGHAN

"Now That April's Here"
  Cassill, R. V. *. . . Instructor's Handbook*, 17.

ITALO CALVINO

"The Adventure of a Photographer"
  Hume, Kathryn. *Calvino's Fictions . . .* , 50.
"The Distance of the Moon"
  Cassill, R. V. *. . . Instructor's Handbook*, 17–18.
  Charters, Ann, and William E. Sheidley. *Resources for Teaching . . .* ,
    3rd ed., 33–34.
  Hume, Kathryn. "Sensuality and the Senses in Calvino's Fiction,"
    Modern Lang Notes, 107 (1992), 163–164.
"L'implosione"
  Hume, Kathryn. "Sensuality and the Senses . . . ," 165–166.
"In a Network of Lines that Intersect"
  Hume, Kathryn. *Calvino's Fictions . . .* , 120–121.
"Il nome, il naso"
  Hume, Kathryn. "Sensuality and the Senses . . . ," 171–172.
"The Nonexistent Knight"
  Barrett, Tracy. "The Narrator of Italo Calvino's 'Il cavaliere
    inesistente,' " *Quaderni d'Italianistica*, 13, i (1992), 57–70.
"The Origin of the Birds"
  Hume, Kathryn. *Calvino's Fictions . . .* , 36, 50–52, 66, 162.

"Sotto il sole giaguaro" ["Under the Jaguar Sun"]
  Hume, Kathryn. *Calvino's Fictions* . . . , 17–32.
  ———. "Sensuality and the Senses . . . ," 172–175.

JULIO IGLESIAS CALVIÑO

"Argumento ontológíco"
  Crespillo, M. "Julio Calviño, fabulador del vacío," *Analecta Malacitana*, 10, ii (1987), 383–384.
"Cero"
  Crespillo, M. "Julio Calviño . . . ," 374–375, 376.
"Le Chat"
  Crespillo, M. "Julio Calviño . . . ," 397.
"La Cosa"
  Crespillo, M. "Julio Calviño . . . ," 377.
"El devorador de gestos"
  Crespillo, M. "Julio Calviño . . . ," 385.
"El fin del mundo"
  Crespillo, M. "Julio Calviño . . . ," 373–374.
"Los fusilados"
  Crespillo, M. "Julio Calviño . . . ," 385.
"Medusa"
  Crespillo, M. "Julio Calviño . . . ," 396–397.
"Las meninas"
  Crespillo, M. "Julio Calviño . . . ," 381.
"La mirada"
  Crespillo, M. "Julio Calviño . . . ," 382.
"Orangután"
  Crespillo, M. "Julio Calviño . . . ," 377–378.
"La prosa del mundo"
  Crespillo, M. "Julio Calviño . . . ," 379.
"El semáforo"
  Crespillo, M. "Julio Calviño . . . ," 378.
"El sistema"
  Crespillo, M. "Julio Calviño . . . ," 391.

ALBERT CAMUS

"The Adulterous Woman"
  Amoia, Alba. "Albert Camus's 'Exile' and 'The Kingdom,' " *Dalhousie French Stud*, 19 (Fall–Winter, 1990), 46–47.
  Lynch, Martha. "L'Image du colon dans 'La Femme adultère,' " *La Revue des Lettres Modernes*, 985–992 (1991), 139–152.
  McCarthy, Patrick. "Camus, Orwell and Greene: The Impossible

Fascination of the Colonised," in King, Adele, Ed. *Camus's "L'Etranger"* . . . , 228–230.

Morot-Sir, Edouard. "La Double transcendance du féminin et du masculin dans 'La femme adultère' d'Albert Camus," *Dalhousie French Stud*, 19 (Fall–Winter, 1990), 51–60.

Waters, Valerie. "Camus's 'La Femme adultère': Janine's Dream," *Romance Stud*, 18 (Summer, 1991), 65–73.

"The Artist at Work"

Amoia, Alba. "Albert Camus's . . . ," 49.

"The Fall"

Amoia, Alba. "Albert Camus's . . . ," 45.

"The Guest"

Grimaud, Michel. "Humanism and the 'White Man's Burden': Camus, Daru, Meursault, and the Arabs," in King, Adele, Ed. *Camus's "L'Etranger"* . . . , 170–171, 175–180.

McCarthy, Patrick. "Camus, Orwell . . . ," 230–231.

"The Growing Stone"

Amoia, Alba. "Albert Camus's . . . ," 49–50.

Mellon, Linda F. "An Archetypal Analysis of Camus's 'La Pierre qui pousse': The Hero Quest as Process of Individuation," *French R*, 64 (1991), 934–947.

Venesoen, Constant. "Une Symbolique de 'La Pierre qui pousse,' d'Albert Camus," *L'Information Littéraire*, 44, iii (1992), 35–37.

"The Renegade"

Amoia, Alba. "Albert Camus's . . . ," 47.

"The Stranger"

Chaitin, Gilbert D. "Confession and Desire in 'L'Etranger,' " *Symposium*, 46 (1992), 163–174.

———. "Narrative Desire in 'L'Etranger,' " in King, Adele, Ed. *Camus's "L'Estranger"* . . . , 125–138.

Curtis, Jerry L. "Cultural Alienation: A New Look at the Hero of 'The Stranger,' " *J Am Culture*, 15, ii (1992), 31–38.

Favre, Frantz. " 'L'Etranger' and 'Metaphysical Anxiety,' " in King, Adele, Ed. *Camus's "L'Etranger"* . . . , 36–44.

Fletcher, John. " 'L'Etranger' and the New Novel," in King, Adele, Ed. *Camus's "L'Etranger"* . . . , 211–213, 216–218.

Grimaud, Michel. "Humanism . . . ," 171–175.

Kaplan, Alice Y. "The American Stranger," *So Atlantic Q*, 91 (1992), 85–110.

Leov, Nola M. " 'Il faut comprendre': Communication and Non-Communication in 'L'Etranger,' " *New Zealand J French Stud*, 12, i (1991), 15–29.

Lewin, Philip. "Affective Schemas in the Appropriation of Narrative Texts," *Metaphor and Symbolic Activity*, 7, i (1992), 11–34.

McBride, Joseph. *Albert Camus* . . . , 8–14, 48–56.

McGuire, Kathryn B. "Camus's 'The Stranger,' " *Explicator*, 50, i (1991), 50–52.

Mistacco, Vicki. "Mama's Boy: Reading Woman in 'L'Etranger,' "
in King, Adele, Ed. *Camus's "L'Etranger"* . . . , 152–169.

Murray, Jack. "Closure and Anticlosure in Camus's 'L'Etranger':
Some Ideological Considerations," *Symposium*, 46 (1992),
225–228.

Pabst, Walter. "Un Héros absurde: Meursault et ses ancêtres,"
Lettres Romanes, 45, iii (1991), 195–200.

Rigaud, Jan. "Depiction of Arabs in 'L'Etranger,' " in King, Adele,
Ed. *Camus's "L'Etranger"* . . . , 183–192.

Riggs, Larry W., and Paula Willoquet-Maricondi. "Colonialism,
Enlightenment, Castration: Writing, Narration, and Legibility in
'L'Etranger,' " *Stud Twentieth-Century Lit*, 16 (1992), 265–288.

Schofer, Peter. "The Rhetoric of the Text: Causality, Metaphor, and
Irony," in King, Adele, Ed. *Camus's "L'Etranger"*. . . , 139–151.

Simon, Ernest. "Palais de Justice and Poetic Justice in Albert Camus'
'The Stranger,' " *Cardozo Stud Law & Lit*, 3, i (1991), 111–125.

ROBERT CANTWELL

"Hills Around Centralia"
Hanley, Lawrence F. "Cultural Work and Class Politics: Rereading
and Remaking Proletarian Literature in the United States," *Mod
Fiction Stud*, 38 (1992), 723.

JOSÉ CARDOSO PIRES

"Amanhã, Se Deus Quiser"
Warner, Robin. "Narration as Critique in Some Short Stories of José
Cardoso Pires," *Romance Q*, 39, iii (1992), 361–365.

"Os Caminheiros"
Warner, Robin. "Narration . . . ," 365–367.

PETER CAREY

"Do You Love Me?"
Adam, Ian. "Breaking the Chain: Anti-Saussurean Resistance in
Birney, Carey and C. S. Peirce," in Adam, Ian, and Helen Tiffin,
Eds. *Past the Last Post* . . . , 79–90.

"The Last Day of a Famous Mime"
Ryan-Fazilleau, Suzan. "One-Upmanship in Peter Carey's Short
Stories," *J Short Story Engl*, 16 (Spring, 1991), 51–52.

"The Puzzling Nature of Blue"
Ryan-Fazilleau, Suzan. "One-Upmanship . . . ," 56–58.

"Room No. 5 (Escribo)"
Ryan-Fazilleau, Suzan. "One-Upmanship . . . ," 52–56.

"War Crimes"
Ryan-Fazilleau, Suzan. "One-Upmanship . . . ," 58–62.

WILLIAM CARLETON

"The Lough Derg Pilgrim"
O'Brien, Margaret. "William Carleton: The Lough Derg Exile," in
Hyland, Paul, and Neil Sammells, Eds. *Irish Writing* . . . , 82–97.

ANGELA CARTER

"Black Venus"
Matus, Jill. "Blond, Black and Hottentot Venus: Contest and Critique
in Angela Carter's 'Black Venus,' " *Stud Short Fiction*, 28 (1991),
467–476.

"Our Lady of the Massacre"
Black, Joel. *The Aesthetics of Murder* . . . , 173–174.

"Lady of the House of Love"
Wilson, Robert R. "Slip Page: Angela Carter, In/Out/In the Post-
Modern Nexus," in Adam, Ian, and Helen Tiffin, Eds. *Past the
Last Post* . . . , 115–121.

"The Werewolf"
Charters, Ann, and William E. Sheidley. *Resources for Teaching* . . . ,
3rd ed., 34–35.

ADA JACK CARVER

"The Old One"
Meese, Elizabeth. "What the Old Ones Know: Ada Jack Carver's
Cane River Stories," in Brown, Dorothy H., and Barbara C. Ewell,
Eds. *Louisiana Women* . . . , 147–148.

"The Raspberry Dress"
Meese, Elizabeth. "What the Old Ones . . . ," 148–149.

RAYMOND CARVER

"After the Denim"
Runyon, Randolph P. *Reading Raymond Carver* . . . , 114–120.

"Are You a Doctor?"
Nesset, Kirk. " 'This Word Love': Sexual Politics and Silence in
Early Raymond Carver," *Am Lit,* 63 (1991), 301–304.

"The Bath"
Campbell, Ewing. "Raymond Carver's Therapeutics of Passion," *J
Short Story Engl,* 16 (Spring, 1991), 11–13.
Lehman, Daniel W. "Raymond Carver's Management of Symbol," *J
Short Story Engl,* 17 (Autumn, 1991), 51–52.
Runyon, Randolph P. *Reading Raymond Carver* . . . , 107–110,
113–114.

"Bicycles, Muscles, Cigarettes"
Hornby, Nick. *Contemporary American Fiction*, 35–36.
Runyon, Randolph P. *Reading Raymond Carver . . .* , 72–77.

"Blackbird Pie"
Hornby, Nick. *Contemporary American Fiction*, 47–48.
Runyon, Randolph P. *Reading Raymond Carver . . .* , 194–204, 207.

"Boxes"
Runyon, Randolph P. *Reading Raymond Carver . . .* , 190–191, 204.

"The Bridle"
Runyon, Randolph P. *Reading Raymond Carver . . .* , 178–182.

"The Calm"
Runyon, Randolph P. *Reading Raymond Carver . . .* , 126–128.

"Careful"
Donahue, Peter J. "Alcoholism as Ideology in Raymond Carver's
'Careful' and 'Where I'm Calling From,' " *Extrapolation*, 32
(1991), 54–63.
Runyon, Randolph P. *Reading Raymond Carver . . .* , 161–169.

"Cathedral"
+ Bohner, Charles H. *Instructor's Manual . . .* , 17–18.
Engel, Monroe. "Knowing More Than One Imagines; Imagining
More Than One Knows," *Agni*, 31–32 (1990), 167–169, 170, 171,
172, 173, 174, 175.
Hathcock, Nelson. " 'The Possibility of Resurrection': Re-Vision in
Carver's 'Feathers' and 'Cathedral,' " *Stud Short Fiction,* 28
(1991), 37–39.
Hornby, Nick. *Contemporary American Fiction*, 44.
Keating, Helane L., and Walter Levy. *Instructor's Manual: Lives
Through Literature . . .* , 67–68.
Runyon, Randolph P. *Reading Raymond Carver . . .* , 181–185.

"Chef's House"
Lehman, Daniel W. ". . . Management of Symbol," 46.
Runyon, Randolph P. *Reading Raymond Carver . . .* , 140–143.

"Collectors"
Runyon, Randolph P. *Reading Raymond Carver . . .* , 34–38.

"The Compartment"
Clark, Miriam M. "Raymond Carver's Monologic Imagination," *Mod
Fiction Stud,* 37 (1991), 243–244.
Runyon, Randolph P. *Reading Raymond Carver . . .* , 144–148,
160–161.

"Distance"
Hornby, Nick. *Contemporary American Fiction*, 38–39.

"The Ducks"
Runyon, Randolph P. *Reading Raymond Carver . . .* , 66–72.

"Elephant"
Runyon, Randolph P. *Reading Raymond Carver . . .* , 189–190.

"Errand"
Boddy, Kasia. "Companion-Souls of the Short Story: Anton Chekhov and Raymond Carver," *Scottish Slavonic R*, 18 (Spring, 1992), 106–109.
Hornby, Nick. *Contemporary American Fiction*, 49–50.
Runyon, Randolph P. *Reading Raymond Carver . . .*, 192–194.

"Everything Stuck to Him"
Hornby, Nick. *Contemporary American Fiction*, 38–39.
Runyon, Randolph P. *Reading Raymond Carver . . .*, 129–130.

"Fat"
Nesset, Kirk. " 'This Word Love' . . . ," 298–301.
Runyon, Randolph P. *Reading Raymond Carver . . .*, 11–15, 17.
Szporer, Michael. "Minimalism and the Collapse of the Soviet Empire Style," *Mosaic*, 25, iv (1992), 132–133.

"The Father"
Runyon, Randolph P. *Reading Raymond Carver . . .*, 21–22.

"Feathers"
Hathcock, Nelson. " 'The Possibility of Resurrection' . . . ," 34–37.
Lehman, Daniel W. ". . . Management of Symbol," 54–55.
Runyon, Randolph P. *Reading Raymond Carver . . .*, 137–142.

"Fever"
Hornby, Nick. *Contemporary American Fiction*, 43–44.
Runyon, Randolph P. *Reading Raymond Carver . . .*, 174–178.

"Gazebo"
Aldridge, John W. *Talents and Technicians . . .*, 52–54.
Runyon, Randolph P. *Reading Raymond Carver . . .*, 99–103.

"How About This?"
Runyon, Randolph P. *Reading Raymond Carver . . .*, 69–72, 76.

"I Could See the Smallest Things"
Runyon, Randolph P. *Reading Raymond Carver . . .*, 101–103, 106–107.

"The Idea"
Runyon, Randolph P. *Reading Raymond Carver . . .*, 15–18.

"Intimacy"
Hornby, Nick. *Contemporary American Fiction*, 46–47.

"Jerry and Molly and Sam"
Runyon, Randolph P. *Reading Raymond Carver . . .*, 54–59, 64–66.

"Menudo"
Runyon, Randolph P. *Reading Raymond Carver . . .*, 191–192.

"Mr. Coffee and Mr. Fixit"
Runyon, Randolph P. *Reading Raymond Carver . . .*, 90–101.

"Neighbors"
Nesset, Kirk. " 'This Word Love' . . . ," 295–298.
Runyon, Randolph P. *Reading Raymond Carver . . .*, 13–16.

"Night School"
   Runyon, Randolph P. *Reading Raymond Carver* . . . , 31–34.
"Nobody Said Anything"
   Runyon, Randolph P. *Reading Raymond Carver* . . . , 22–29.
"One More Thing"
   Runyon, Randolph P. *Reading Raymond Carver* . . . , 134–135.
"Popular Mechanics"
   Lehman, Daniel W. ". . . Management of Symbol," 47.
   Runyon, Randolph P. *Reading Raymond Carver* . . . , 128–130.
"Preservation"
   Lehman, Daniel W. ". . . Management of Symbol," 45–46.
   Runyon, Randolph P. *Reading Raymond Carver* . . . , 142–144.
"Put Yourself in My Shoes"
   Runyon, Randolph P. *Reading Raymond Carver* . . . , 43–57.
"Sacks"
   Runyon, Randolph P. *Reading Raymond Carver* . . . , 104–109, 113.
"A Serious Talk"
   Runyon, Randolph P. *Reading Raymond Carver* . . . , 124–128.
"Signals"
   Runyon, Randolph P. *Reading Raymond Carver* . . . , 77–80.
"Sixty Acres"
   Runyon, Randolph P. *Reading Raymond Carver* . . . , 28–29.
"A Small, Good Thing"
   Campbell, Ewing. ". . . Therapeutics of Passion," 13–16.
   Hornby, Nick. *Contemporary American Fiction*, 40–42.
   Lehman, Daniel W. ". . . Management of Symbol," 52–53.
   Runyon, Randolph P. *Reading Raymond Carver* . . . , 146–161.
   Szporer, Michael. "Minimalism . . . ," 132–133.
"So Much Water So Close to Home"
   Runyon, Randolph P. *Reading Raymond Carver* . . . , 119–123.
"The Student's Wife"
   Runyon, Randolph P. *Reading Raymond Carver* . . . , 41–44, 53.
"Tell the Women We're Going"
   Runyon, Randolph P. *Reading Raymond Carver* . . . , 110–117.
"They're Not Your Husband"
   Runyon, Randolph P. *Reading Raymond Carver* . . . , 16–18, 20.
"The Third Thing That Killed My Father Off"
   Runyon, Randolph P. *Reading Raymond Carver* . . . , 122–126.
"The Train"
   Runyon, Randolph P. *Reading Raymond Carver* . . . , 171–178.
"Viewfinder"
   Lehman, Daniel W. ". . . Management of Symbol," 49–50.
   Runyon, Randolph P. *Reading Raymond Carver* . . . , 87–90, 92–93,
      95–98, 111–113.

"Vitamins"
 Runyon, Randolph P. *Reading Raymond Carver* . . . , 151–161.
 Szporer, Michael. "Minimalism . . . ," 132–133.
"What Do You Do in San Francisco?"
 Runyon, Randolph P. *Reading Raymond Carver* . . . , 37–43.
"What Is It?"
 Nesset, Kirk. " 'This Word Love' . . . ," 304–307.
 Runyon, Randolph P. *Reading Raymond Carver* . . . , 75–78.
"What's in Alaska?"
 Runyon, Randolph P. *Reading Raymond Carver* . . . , 29–31, 32–33.
"What We Talk About When We Talk About Love"
 +Charters, Ann, and William E. Sheidley. *Resources for
  Teaching* . . . , 3rd ed., 35–36.
 Lehman, Daniel W. ". . . Management of Symbol," 47–48.
 Runyon, Randolph P. *Reading Raymond Carver* . . . , 131–135.
"Where I'm Calling From"
 +Cassill, R. V. . . . *Instructor's Handbook*, 19–20.
 Donahue, Peter J. "Alcoholism as Ideology . . . ," 54–63.
 Haslam, Thomas J. " 'Where I'm Calling From': A Textual and
  Critical Study," *Stud Short Fiction,* 29 (1992), 61–64.
 Malamet, Elliott. "Raymond Carver and the Fear of Narration," *J
  Short Story Engl,* 17 (Autumn, 1991), 61–69.
 Runyon, Randolph P. *Reading Raymond Carver* . . . , 167–172.
"Whoever Was Using This Bed"
 Runyon, Randolph P. *Reading Raymond Carver* . . . , 192–194.
"Why Don't You Dance?"
 Lehman, Daniel W. ". . . Management of Symbol," 48.
 Runyon, Randolph P. *Reading Raymond Carver* . . . , 86–90.
"Why, Honey?"
 Runyon, Randolph P. *Reading Raymond Carver* . . . , 58–69, 83.
"Will You Please Be Quiet, Please?"
 Clark, Miriam M. ". . . Monologic Imagination," 244–245.
 Nesset, Kirk. " 'This Word Love' . . . ," 307–312.
 Runyon, Randolph P. *Reading Raymond Carver* . . . , 79–83.

R. V. CASSILL

"The Father"
 Cassill, R. V. . . . *Instructor's Handbook*, 20–21.

ROSARIO CASTELLANOS

"Aceite guapo"
 Gómez Parham, Mary. "Alienation in Rosario Castellanos' *Ciudad
  real*," *Letras Femeninas*, 15, i–ii (1989), 23–24.

"El advenimiento del águila"
Gómez Parham, Mary. "Alienation . . . ," 25.

"Album de familia"
Geldrich-Leffman, Hanna. "Marriage in the Short Stories of Rosario Castellanos," *Chasqui,* 21, i (1992), 30.

"Las amistades efímeras"
Geldrich-Leffman, Hanna. "Marriage . . . ," 30.

"Arthur Smith salva sin alma"
Gómez Parham, Mary. "Alienation . . . ," 26–27.

"Cabecita blanca"
Geldrich-Leffman, Hanna. "Marriage . . . ," 35.

"Domingo"
Geldrich-Leffman, Hanna. "Marriage . . . ," 34–35.

"Lección de cocina"
Geldrich-Leffman, Hanna. "Marriage . . . ," 33–34.

"Modesta Gómez"
Gómez Parham, Mary. "Alienation . . . ," 24–25.

"La muerte del tigre"
Gómez Parham, Mary. "Alienation . . . ," 22–23.

"La rueda del hambriento"
Gómez Parham, Mary. "Alienation . . . ," 25–26.

"La suerte de Teodoro Méndez Acubal"
Gómez Parham, Mary. "Alienation . . . ," 24.

"La tregua"
Duncan, Cynthia. "Language as a Barrier to Communication Between the Classes in Rosario Castellanos's 'La tregua' and José Revueltas's 'El lenguaje de nadie,' " *Hispania*, 74 (1991), 869–871.

"Tres nudos en la red"
Geldrich-Leffman, Hanna. "Marriage . . . ," 32–33.

"El viudo Román"
Geldrich-Leffman, Hanna. "Marriage . . . ," 31.

WILLA CATHER

"Before Breakfast"
Wasserman, Loretta. *Willa Cather* . . . , 17–20.

"The Best Years"
Blanch, Mae. "Joy and Terror: Figures of Grace in Cather and O'Connor Stories," *Lit & Belief*, 8 (1988), 111–113.
Romines, Ann. *The Home Plot* . . . , 170–171.
Wasserman, Loretta. *Willa Cather* . . . , 121–123.

"The Bohemian Girl"
Levy, Helen F. *Fiction of the Home Place* . . . , 66, 71–74, 81.
Romines, Ann. *The Home Plot* . . . , 135–139, 140, 143, 144.
Wasserman, Loretta. *Willa Cather* . . . , 44–46.

"Coming, Aphrodite!"
   Messitt, Holly. "The Internal Gaze: 'Coming, Aphrodite!' and the
   Panopticon," *Willa Cather Pioneer Memorial Newsletter*, 36, iii
   (1992), 34–37.
   +Petry, Alice H. "Caesar and the Artist in Willa Cather's 'Coming,
   Aphrodite!' " in Wasserman, Loretta. *Willa Cather . . .* , 128–135.
   Wasserman, Loretta. *Willa Cather . . .* , 37–41.

"The Diamond Mine"
   Wasserman, Loretta. *Willa Cather . . .* , 33–34.

"The Enchanted Bluff"
   Wasserman, Loretta. *Willa Cather . . .* , 14–17.

"Eric Hermannson's Soul"
   Baker, Bruce. "Nebraska's Cultural Desert: Willa Cather's Early
   Short Stories," *Midamerica*, 14 (1987), 14–15.
   Wasserman, Loretta. *Willa Cather . . .* , 42–44.
   Weber, Ronald. *The Midwestern . . .* , 124–125.

"The Garden Lodge"
   Wasserman, Loretta. *Willa Cather . . .* , 26–27.

"The Golden Slipper"
   Wasserman, Loretta. *Willa Cather . . .* , 34–36.

"Jack-a-Boy"
   Blanch, Mae. "Joy and Terror . . . ," 105–108.
   Wasserman, Loretta. *Willa Cather . . .* , 72–73.

"The Joy of Nelly Deane"
   Levy, Helen F. *Fiction of the Home Place . . .* , 66, 71–74, 81.
   Wasserman, Loretta. *Willa Cather . . .* , 45–46.

"Neighbour Rosicky"
   Romines, Ann. *The Home Plot . . .* , 163–164.
   +Rosowski, Susan J. "*Obscure Destinies*: Unalterable Realities," in
   Wasserman, Loretta. *Willa Cather . . .* , 147–152.
   Wasserman, Loretta. *Willa Cather . . .* , 52–55.
   Weber, Ronald. *The Midwestern . . .* , 142–144.

"The Old Beauty"
   Wasserman, Loretta. *Willa Cather . . .* , 64–72.

"Old Mrs. Harris"
   Carlin, Deborah. *Cather, Canon . . .* , 89–115.
   Romines, Ann. *The Home Plot . . .* , 164–174, 189.
   +Rosowski, Susan J. "*Obscure Destinies . . .* , 152–156.
   Wasserman, Loretta. *Willa Cather . . .* , 55–59.

"On the Divide"
   Weber, Ronald. *The Midwestern . . .* , 122–123.

"Paul's Case"
   +Bohner, Charles H. *Instructor's Manual . . .* , 18–19.
   Cassill, R. V. *. . . Instructor's Handbook*, 21–23.
   +Charters, Ann, and William E. Sheidley. *Resources for
   Teaching . . .* , 3rd ed., 37–38.

Page, Phillip. "The Theatricality of Willa Cather's 'Paul's Case,' "
Stud Short Fiction, 28 (1991), 553–557.
Pitcher, Edward W. "Willa Cather's 'Paul's Case' and the Faustian
Temperament," *Stud Short Fiction*, 28 (1991), 547–550.
Salda, Michael N. "What Really Happens in Cather's 'Paul's Case'?"
Stud Short Fiction, 29 (1992), 113–119.
Wasserman, Loretta. *Willa Cather . . .* , 21–26.

"Peter"
Baker, Bruce. ". . . Cather's Early Short Stories," 12–14.

"A Resurrection"
Harris, Jeane. "Aspects of Athene in Willa Cather's Short Fiction,"
Stud Short Fiction, 28 (1991), 180–181.

"The Sculptor's Funeral"
Wasserman, Loretta. *Willa Cather . . .* , 27–29.
Weber, Ronald. *The Midwestern . . .* , 126–127.

"Tommy the Unsentimental"
Harris, Jeane. "Aspects of Athene . . . ," 179–180.

"The Treasure of Far Island"
Harris, Jeane. "Aspects of Athene . . . ," 181–182.

"Two Friends"
Romines, Ann. *The Home Plot . . .* , 163, 164.
Sherf, Mark. "The Unreliable Narrator and Political Reality in 'Two
Friends,' " *Willa Cather Pioneer Memorial Newsletter,* 36, iii
(1992), 40–42.
Wasserman, Loretta. *Willa Cather . . .* , 156–160.

"Uncle Valentine"
+ Arnold, Marilyn. "Pittsburgh and the Conflict of Values: Mixed
Melody," in Wasserman, Loretta. *Willa Cather . . .* , 138–145.
Wasserman, Loretta. *Willa Cather . . .* , 46–51.

"A Wagner Matinée"
Baker, Bruce. ". . . Cather's Early Short Stories," 15–17.
Romines, Ann. *The Home Plot . . .* , 128–134, 139, 143–144.
Wasserman, Loretta. *Willa Cather . . .* , 29–31.
Weber, Ronald. *The Midwestern . . .* , 125–126.

CAMILO JOSÉ CELA

"La insólita y gloriosa hazaña del Cipote de Archidona"
Pérez, Janet. "Euphemism, Euphuism, Euchologue: Cela and the
Poetics of Polite Obscenity," *Antípodas*, 4 (1992), 68–72.

ROSA CHACEL

"Icada, Nevda, Diada"
Holdsworth, Carole A. "Chacel's Myth of the Viviparous Zero,"
Monographic R, 8 (1992), 70–78.

ADELBERT VON CHAMISSO

"Peter Schlemihls Wundersame Geschichte"
 Herdman, John. *The Double* . . . , 41–44.
 Weissberg, Liliane. "Literatur als Representationsform. Zur Lektüre
 von Lektüre," in Dannenberg, Lutz, and Friedrich Vollhardt, Eds.,
 Vom Umgang mit Literatur . . . , 304–307.
 White, Ann, and John White. "The Devil's Devices in Chamisso's
 'Peter Schlemihl': An Article in Seven-League Boots," *Germ Life
 and Letters*, 45, iii (1992), 220–225.

RAYMOND CHANDLER

"The Bronze Door"
 Larsen, Michael J. "Miracles and Murder: Raymond Chandler's
 Fantastic Stories," in Saciuk, Olena H., Ed. *The Shape* . . . ,
 166–167.
"The Curtain"
 Priestman, Martin. *Detective Fiction* . . . , 172–176.
"Killer in the Rain"
 Priestman, Martin. *Detective Fiction* . . . , 172–176.
"Pearls Are a Nuisance"
 Tate, J. O. "Raymond Chandler's Pearl," *Clues*, 13, ii (1992),
 177–195.
"Professor Bingo's Snuff"
 Larsen, Michael J. "Miracles and Murder . . . ," 167–170.

FRANÇOIS-RENÉ DE CHATEAUBRIAND

"Atala"
 Becker-Theye, Betty. "Cooper and Chateaubriand: The American
 Wilderness as Simple/More Complex World," *Platte Valley R*, 19,
 ii (1991), 45–46, 47, 48–49, 50–52.
"René"
 Le Hir, Marie-Pierre. "Landscapes of Brittany in Chateaubriand,
 Balzac, and Flaubert," *West Virginia Univ Philol Papers*, 37
 (1991), 20–23.

ALEXANDRE CHATRIAN

"L'Esquisse mystérieuse" [co-author Emile Erckmann]
 Cummiskey, Gary. *The Changing Face* . . . , 102–108.

JOHN CHEEVER

"The Brigadier and the Golf Widow"
 Castronovo, David. *The American Gentleman* . . . , 84.

"The Bus to St. James's"
Castronovo, David. *The American Gentleman* . . . , 83.

"The Country Husband"
Chandler, Marilyn R. *Dwelling in the Text* . . . , 286–288.

"The Enormous Radio"
+ Bohner, Charles H. *Instructor's Manual* . . . , 20–21.
Cassill, R. V. . . . *Instructor's Handbook*, 23–24.
Castronovo, David. *The American Gentleman* . . . , 82–83.

"The Five-Forty-Eight"
Cassill, R. V. . . . , *Instructor's Handbook*, 25–26.

"Goodbye, My Brother"
Mayo, Wendell. " 'I' and 'Not-I': Rhetoric and Difference in John
Cheever's 'Goodbye, My Brother,' " *J Short Story Engl,* 17
(Autumn, 1991), 91–102.

"The Housebreaker of Shady Hill"
Castronovo, David. *The American Gentleman* . . . , 85.

"The Lowboy"
Castronovo, David. *The American Gentleman* . . . , 111–112.

"The Pot of Gold"
Fishman, Ethan. "Images of Lockean America in Contemporary
American Fiction," in Whitebrook, Maureen, Ed. *Reading
Political Stories,* 176–177.

"The Swimmer"
Blythe, Hal, and Charlie Sweet. "Alcoholism and 'The Swimmer,' "
Notes Contemp Lit, 22, iv (1992), 9–10.
———. "Cheever's Dark Knight of the Soul: The Failed Quest,"
Stud Short Fiction, 29 (1992), 347–351.
———. "The Ironic Return to the Womb in Cheever's 'The
Swimmer,' " *Notes Contemp Lit,* 22, i (1992), 8–9.
———. "Neddy Merrill: Cheever's Failed Adam," *Notes Contemp
Lit,* 22, iv (1992), 10–11.
+ Bohner, Charles H. *Instructor's Manual* . . . , 21–22.
Cervo, Nathan. "Cheever's 'The Swimmer,' " *Explicator,* 50, i
(1991), 49–50.
+ Charters, Ann, and William E. Sheidley. *Resources for
Teaching* . . . , 3rd ed., 40–41.
Mathews, James W. "Peter Rugg and Cheever's Swimmer:
Archetypal Missing Men," *Stud Short Fiction,* 29 (1992), 95,
97–101.

ANTON CHEKHOV

"The Bishop"
McVay, Gordon. "Chekhov's Last Two Stories: Dreaming of
Happiness," in Luker, Nicholas, Ed. *The Short Story in
Russia* . . . , 1–7.

Turner, C. J. G. "Time in Chekhov's 'The Bishop,' " *Mod Lang R*,
86 (1991), 131–136.

"The Black Monk"
Herdman, John. *The Double* . . . , 148–151.

"The Bride"
McVay, Gordon. "Chekhov's Last Two . . . ," 7–12.

"The Darling"
+ Bohner, Charles H. *Instructor's Manual* . . . , 22–23.
Charters, Ann, and William E. Sheidley. *Resources for Teaching* . . . ,
3rd ed., 42–43.
Peterson, Nadya. "The Languages of 'Darling,' " *Canadian-
American Slavic Stud*, 24, ii (1990), 199–200, 203–215.

"The Duel"
Robinson, Fred M. *Comic Moments*, 160–169.

"Dushechka"
Cassill, R. V. . . . *Instructor's Handbook*, 30–31.

"Gooseberries"
+ Bohner, Charles H. *Instructor's Manual* . . . , 23–24.

"His Wife"
Conrad, Joseph L. "Studies in Deception: Anton Chekov's Short
Story 'His Wife,' " *Scottish Slavonic R*, 16 (Spring, 1991), 47–62.

"The Lady with the Dog" [same as "The Lady with the Lapdog," "The
Lady with the Pet Dog," "The Lady with the Small Dog"]
+ Bohner, Charles H. *Instructor's Manual* . . . , 24–26.
+ Cassill, R. V. . . . *Instructor's Handbook*, 27–28.
+ Charters, Ann, and William E. Sheidley. *Resources for
Teaching* . . . , 3rd ed., 44–45.
Keating, Helane L., and Walter Levy. *Instructor's Manual: Lives
Through Literature* . . . , 87–88.

"A Visit to Friends"
+ Cassill, R. V. . . . *Instructor's Handbook*, 29–30.

CHARLES W. CHESNUTT

"Baxter's Procrustes"
Werner, Craig. "The Framing of Charles W. Chesnutt: Practical
Deconstruction in the Afro-American Tradition," *Univ Mississippi
Stud Engl*, 9 (1991), 19–21.

"The Conjurer's Revenge"
Scott, Joyce H. "Who 'Goophered' Whom: The Afro-American
Fabulist and His Tale in Charles Chesnutt's *The Conjure Woman*,"
Bestia, 2 (May, 1990), 52–56.

"Dave's Neckliss"
Patton, Richard J. "Studyin' 'Bout Ole Julius: A Note on Charles W.
Chesnutt's Uncle Julius McAdoo," *Am Lit Realism*, 24, iii (1992),
74–75, 76, 77.

"A Deep Sleeper"
   Patton, Richard J. "Studyin' . . . ," 73, 74, 75.

"The Goophered Grapevine"
   Werner, Craig. "The Framing . . . ," 13–14, 17.

"The Gray Wolf's Ha'nt"
   Scott, Joyce H. "Who 'Goophered' . . . ," 58–61.
   Selinger, Eric. "Aunts, Uncles, Audience: Gender and Genre in
      Charles Chesnutt's *The Conjure Woman*," *Black Am Lit*, 25
      (1991), 680–683.

"Hot-Foot Hannibal"
   Selinger, Eric. "Aunts, Uncles . . . ," 683–685.

"Lonesome Ben"
   Patton, Richard J. "Studyin' . . . ," 76, 77.

"Mars Jeem's Nightmare"
   Selinger, Eric. "Aunts, Uncles . . . ," 673–676.
   Werner, Craig. "The Framing . . . ," 14–15, 16–17.

"Po' Sandy"
   Selinger, Eric. "Aunts, Uncles . . . ," 671–672.

"Sis' Becky's Pickaninny"
   Scott, Joyce H. "Who 'Goophered' . . . ," 56–58.
   Selinger, Eric. "Aunts, Uncles . . . ," 676–678.

"The Wife of His Youth"
   Wardley, Lynn. "Relic, Fetish, Femmage: The Aesthetics of
      Sentiment in the Work of Stowe," in Samuels, Shirley, Ed. *The
      Culture of Sentiment* . . . , 217–218.

GILBERT KEITH CHESTERTON

"The Blue Cross"
   Priestman, Martin. *Detective Fiction* . . . , 124–128.

"The Flying Stars"
   Priestman, Martin. *Detective Fiction* . . . , 132–134.

"The Invisible Man"
   Trotter, David. "Theory and Detective Fiction," *Critical Q*, 33, ii
      (1991), 72.

"The Mask of Midas"
   Christopher, Joe R. "Father Brown's Final Adventure," *Mystery
      Fancier*, 13, iv (1992), 33–41.

"The Queer Feet"
   Priestman, Martin. *Detective Fiction* . . . , 130–133.

"The Secret Garden"
   Cervo, Nathan A. "The Pleonastic Suicide of Aristide Valentin in
      Chesterton's 'The Secret Garden,' " *Chesterton R*, 18, iii (1992),
      391–394.

Priestman, Martin. *Detective Fiction . . . ,* 128–130.
Trotter, David. "Theory and Detective Fiction," 72.

LYDIA MARIA CHILD

"Slavery's Pleasant Homes"
    Karcher, Carolyn L. "Rape, Murder, and Revenge in 'Slavery's
    Pleasant Homes': Lydia Maria Child's Antislavery Fiction and the
    Limits of Genre," in Samuels, Shirley, Ed. *The Culture of
    Sentiment. . . ,* 64–72.

FRANK CHIN

"Confessions of the Chinatown Cowboy"
    Li, David L. "The Production of Chinese American Tradition:
    Displacing American Orientalist Discourse," in Lim, Shirley G.,
    and Amy Ling, Eds. *Reading the Literatures . . . ,* 324–326.

LOUISE E. CHOLLET

"Tom Lodowne"
    Diffley, Kathleen. *Where My Heart . . . ,* 23–25.

KATE CHOPIN

"After the Winter"
    Ellis, Nancy S. "Insistent Refrains and Self-Discovery: Accompanied
    Awakenings in Three Stories by Kate Chopin," in Boren, Lynda
    S., and Sara D. Davis, Eds. *Kate Chopin Reconsidered*, 217–220.
"Alexandre's Wonderful Experiment"
    Thomas, Heather K. " 'What Are the Prospects for the Book?':
    Rewriting a Woman's Life," in Boren, Lynda S., and Sara D.
    Davis, Eds. *Kate Chopin Reconsidered*, 49–50.
"At Cheniere Caminada"
    Ellis, Nancy S. "Insistent Refrains . . . ," 220–223.
"Athénaïse"
    Toth, Emily. "Kate Chopin Thinks Back Through Her Mothers:
    Three Stories by Kate Chopin," in Boren, Lynda S., and Sara D.
    Davis, Eds. *Kate Chopin Reconsidered*, 18–21, 24.
"Charlie"
    Blythe, Anne M. "Kate Chopin's 'Charlie,' " in Boren, Lynda S.,
    and Sara D. Davis, Eds. *Kate Chopin Reconsidered*, 207–215.
    Thomas, Heather K. " 'What Are . . . ," 50–51.
"Désirée's Baby"
    Foy, Roslyn R. "Chopin's 'Désirée's Baby,' " *Explicator*, 49, iv
    (1991), 222–223.

Peel, Ellen. "Semiotic Subversion in 'Désirée's Baby,' " in Brown,
Dorothy H., and Barbara C. Ewell, Eds. *Louisiana Women* . . . ,
57–73.

"An Egyptian Cigarette"
Davis, Sara D. "Chopin's Movement Toward Universal Myth," in
Boren, Lynda S., and Sara D. Davis, Eds. *Kate Chopin
Reconsidered*, 202–203.

"Regret"
+ Charters, Ann, and William E. Sheidley. *Resources for
Teaching* . . . , 3rd ed., 46–47.

"The Storm"
Keating, Helane L., and Walter Levy. *Instructor's Manual: Lives
Through Literature* . . . , 111.

"The Story of an Hour"
+ Bohner, Charles H. *Instructor's Manual* . . . , 26–27.
Cassill, R. V. . . . *Instructor's Handbook*, 32.
Charters, Ann, William E. Sheidley, and Martha Ramsey.
Instructor's Manual . . . , 2nd ed., 36; rpt. Charters, Ann, and
William E. Sheidley. *Resources for Teaching* . . . , 3rd ed., 48.
Mitchell, Angelyn. "Feminine Double Consciousness in Kate
Chopin's 'The Story of an Hour,' " *CEAMAG*, 5, i (1992), 59–64.

"A Vocation and a Voice"
Ellis, Nancy S. "Insistent Refrains . . . ," 224–229.

"The White Eagle"
Thomas, Heather K. " 'What Are . . . ," 51–52.

SANDRA CISNEROS

"The House on Mango Street"
Ricard, Serge. "La Désespérance d'Esperanza: Espace rêvé, espace
vécu dans 'The House on Mango Street' de Cisneros," in Béranger,
Jean, Ed. *L'Ici et* . . . , 175–187.
Rosaldo, Renato. "Fables of the Fallen Guy," in Calderón, Héctor,
and José D. Saldívar, Eds. *Criticism* . . . , 85, 92–93.
Valdés, María Elena de. "In Search of Identity in Cisneros' 'The
House on Mango Street,' " *Canadian R Am Stud*, 23, i (1992),
55–72.

CLARÍN [LEOPOLDO ALAS]

"El cura de Vericueto"
Miller, Stephen. "Intertexts, Contexts, and Clarinian Canon: The
Place of 'El cura de Vericueto,' " *Bull Hispanic Stud,* 68 (1991),
463–477.

ARTHUR C. CLARKE

"The Star"
+Cassill, R. V. . . . *Instructor's Handbook*, 33.

AUSTIN CLARKE

"Canadian Experience"
Ramraj, Victor. "Temporizing Laughter: The Later Stories of Austin
Clarke," in Bardolph, Jacquelin, Ed. *Short Fiction* . . . , 128–129.

"Coll. SS Tins. Ap. Toron.—A Fable"
Ramraj, Victor. "Temporizing Laughter . . . ," 128–129.

"A Funeral"
Ramraj, Victor. "Temporizing Laughter . . . ," 129.

"The Smell"
Ramraj, Victor. "Temporizing Laughter . . . ," 130.

JACK FLETCHER COBB

"Polak Joe's Finish"
Gladsky, Thomas S. *Princes, Peasants* . . . , 48–49.

SIDONIE-GABRIELLE COLETTE

"Chance Acquaintances"
Strand, Dana. "The 'Third Woman' in Colette's 'Chance
Acquaintances,' " *Stud Short Fiction*, 29 (1992), 499–508.

"The Hidden Woman"
Cassill, R. V. . . . *Instructor's Handbook*, 36.

"The Hollow Nut"
Charters, Ann, and William E. Sheidley. *Resources for Teaching* . . . ,
3rd ed., 50.

"The Rivals"
Keating, Helane L., and Walter Levy. *Instructor's Manual: Lives
Through Literature* . . . , 45–46.

WILKIE COLLINS

"A Terribly Strange Bed"
Rance, Nicholas. . . . *Walking the Moral Hospital*, 54–57.

JOSEPH CONRAD

"Amy Foster"
Epstein, Hugh. " 'Where He Is Not Wanted': Impression and

Articulation in 'The Idiots' and 'Amy Foster,' " *Conradiana,* 23 (1991), 226–231.

Griem, Eberhard. "Physiological Possibility in Conrad's 'Amy Foster': The Problem of Narrative Technique," *Conradiana,* 24 (1992), 126–134.

Maisonnat, Claude. "Exile, Betrayal and the Foreclosure of the Name-of-the-Father in 'Amy Foster,' " *L'Epoque Conradienne,* 18 (1992), 103–124.

"The End of the Tether"

Lombard, François. "Joseph Conrad et la Mer dans 'The End of the Tether,' " *L'Epoque Conradienne,* [n.v.] (1989), 23–32.

McLauchlan, Juliet. " 'The Empty Heavens': A Reading of 'The End of the Tether,' " *L'Epoque Conradienne,* [n.v.] (1988), 47–61.

Stape, J. H. "Conrad's 'Unreal City': Singapore in 'The End of the Tether,' " in Moore, Gene M., Ed. *Conrad's Cities . . . ,* 85–96.

"Falk"

Curreli, Mario, and Fausto Ciompi. "A Socio-Semiotic Reading of Conrad's 'Falk,' " *L'Epoque Conradienne,* [n.v.] (1988), 35–45.

"Freya of the Seven Isles"

Erdinast-Vulcan, Daphna. "Narrateur, Voyeur, Voyageur: Anti-Romance in 'Freya of the Seven Isles,' " *L'Epoque Conradienne,* 17 (1991), 23–33.

"Heart of Darkness"

Ambrosini, Richard. *Conrad's Fiction . . . ,* 84–115.

Arneson, Richard J. "Marlow's Skepticism in 'Heart of Darkness,' " *Ethics* (April, 1984), 420–440.

Bennett, Carl D. *Joseph Conrad,* 75–83.

Bongie, Chris. "Exotic Nostalgia: Conrad and the New Imperialism," in Arac, Jonathan, and Harriet Ritvo, Eds. *Macropolitics . . . ,* 277–285.

Brink, André. "Woman and Language in Darkest Africa: The Quest for Articulation in Two Postcolonial Novels," *Literator,* 13, i (1992), 1–8.

+ Cassill, R. V. . . . *Instructor's Handbook,* 37–41.

+ Charters, Ann, and William E. Sheidley. *Resources for Teaching . . . ,* 3rd ed., 51–52.

De Koven, Marianne. *Rich and Strange . . . ,* 89–100.

Erdinast-Vulcan, Daphna. *Joseph Conrad . . . ,* 91–108.

Goonetilleke, D. C. R. A. "Ironies of Progress: Conrad and Imperialism in Afrika," in Giddings, Robert, Ed. *Literature and Imperialism,* 75–111.

Hampson, Robert. *Joseph Conrad . . . ,* 106–116.

———. " 'Heart of Darkness' and 'The Speech that Cannot be Silenced,' " *English,* 39 (Spring, 1990), 15–32.

Hawkins, Hunt. "Conrad's 'Heart of Darkness': Politics and History," *Conradiana,* 24 (1992), 217.

Hay, Eloise K. "Cities Like Whited Sepulchres," in Moore, Gene M., Ed. *Conrad's Cities . . . ,* 125–137.

————. "Rattling Talkers and Silent Sooth-Sayers: The Race for 'Heart of Darkness,' " *Conradiana*, 24 (1992), 167–178.

Henricksen, Bruce. *Nomadic Voices* . . . , 47–80.

Hooper, Myrthe. "The Heart of Light: Silence in Conrad's 'Heart of Darkness,' " *L'Epoque Conradienne*, [n.v.] (1990), 109–113.

Humphries, Reynold. "Restraint, Cannibalism and the 'Unspeakable Rites' in 'Heart of Darkness,' " *L'Epoque Conradienne*, [n.v.] (1990), 51–78.

Hynes, Samuel. "Introduction," *The Complete Short Fiction* . . . [by Joseph Conrad], xv–xvi.

Knapp, Bettina L. *Exile and the Writer* . . . , 49–74.

Leondopoulos, Jordan. *Still the Moving World* . . . , 21–35.

Mansell, Darrel. "Trying to Bring Literature Back Alive: The Ivory in Joseph Conrad's 'Heart of Darkness,' " *Criticism,* 33 (1991), 205–215.

Parrinder, Patrick. " 'Heart of Darkness': Geography as Apocalypse," in Stokes, John, Ed. *Fin de Siècle* . . . , 85–101.

Pecora, Vincent P. "Metropolitan Ironies: Conrad's 'Heart of Darkness,' " *Conradiana,* 24 (1992), 179–189.

Saha, P. K. "Conrad's 'Heart of Darkness,' " *Explicator*, 50, iii (1992), 155–159.

Schwarz, Daniel R. "Teaching 'Heart of Darkness': Towards a Pluralistic Perspective," *Conradiana,* 24 (1992), 194–205.

Shaffer, Brian W. " 'Progress and Civilization and all the Virtues': Teaching 'Heart of Darkness' via 'An Outpost of Progress,' " *Conradiana*, 24 (1992), 221, 222, 223, 224, 225, 226, 227.

Stampfl, Barry. "Marlow's Rhetoric of (Self-) Deception in 'Heart of Darkness,' " *Mod Fiction Stud,* 37 (1991), 183–196.

————. "Conrad's 'Heart of Darkness,' " *Explicator,* 49, iii (1991), 162–165.

Stéphane, Nelly. "La Morale au coeur de Ténèbres," *Europe*, 70 (June–July, 1992), 64–68.

Watts, Cedric. "Conrad and the Myth of the Monstrous Town," in Moore, Gene M., Ed. *Conrad's Cities* . . . , 22–23, 24.

West, Roger. "Conrad's 'Heart of Darkness,' " *Explicator*, 50, iv (1992), 222–223.

"The Idiots"

Epstein, Hugh. " 'Where He is Not Wanted' . . . ," 218–226.

"The Informer"

Hepburn, Allan. "Collectors in Conrad's 'The Informer,' " *Stud Short Fiction*, 29 (1992), 103–112.

"Karain"

Ambrosini, Richard. *Conrad's Fiction* . . . , 70–79.

Drouart, Michele. " 'Gunrunning,' Theatre, and Cultural Attitude in Conrad's 'Karain,' " *J South Pacific Assn Commonwealth Lit Lang Stud*, 33 (May, 1992), 137–149.

Erdinast-Vulcan, Daphna. *Joseph Conrad* . . . , 31–33.

Gogwilt, Christopher. "The Charm of Empire: Joseph Conrad's 'Karain: A Memory,' " *Mosaic,* 24, i (1991), 77–91.

Hampson, Robert. " 'Topographical Mysteries': Conrad and London," in Moore, Gene M., Ed. *Conrad's Cities* . . . , 161–162.

McLauchlan, Juliet. "Conrad's 'Decivilized' Cities," in Moore, Gene M., Ed. *Conrad's Cities* . . . ," 61–62.

Watts, Cedric. "Conrad . . . ," 21–22.

"An Outcast of the Islands"

McLauchlan, Juliet. "Conrad's 'Decivilized'. . . ," 60.

"An Outpost of Progress"

D'Elia, Gaetano. "Sucre et Ivoire: 'Un Avant-Poste du Progrès,' " *L'Epoque Conradienne*, [n.v.] (1988), 25–34.

Rising, Katherine. "The Complex Death of Kayerts," *Conradiana*, 23 (1991), 157–169.

Shaffer, Brian W. " 'Progress . . . ," 220, 222, 223, 224, 225, 226.

"The Planter of Malata"

McLauchlan, Juliet. "Conrad's 'Decivilized'. . . ," 64–66.

"The Rescue"

McLauchlan, Juliet. "Conrad's 'Decivilized'. . . ," 66–69.

"The Return"

McLauchlan, Juliet. "Conrad's 'Decivilized'. . . ," 62–64.

"The Secret Sharer"

Bennett, Carl D. *Joseph Conrad,* 113–115.

Bohner, Charles H. *Instructor's Manual* . . . , 28–30.

Hampson, Robert. *Joseph Conrad* . . . , 191–195.

Keating, Helane L., and Walter Levy. *Instructor's Manual: Lives Through Literature* . . . , 48–49.

Quinones, Ricardo J. *The Changes of Cain* . . . , 109–121.

Rashkin, Esther. *Family Secrets* . . . , 49–63.

"The Shadow Line"

Erdinast-Vulcan, Daphna. *Joseph Conrad* . . . , 127–138.

"The Tale"

Rundle, Vivienne. " 'The Tale' and the Ethics of Interpretation," *Conradian*, 17, i (1992), 17–35.

"Typhoon"

Bennett, Carl D. *Joseph Conrad,* 54–57.

Brown, Carolyn B. "Creative Combat in 'Typhoon,' " *Conradian*, 17, i (1992), 1–16.

Chareyre-Méjan, Alain. "L'Annulation par la tempéte," *Europe*, 70 (June–July, 1992), 99–110.

Griem, Eberhard. "Rhetoric and Reality in Conrad's 'Typhoon,' " *Conradiana*, 24 (1992), 21–32.

Luyat, Anne. "Voyage to the End of Strangeness in 'Typhoon,' " *L'Epoque Conradienne*, 17 (1991), 35–45.

"Youth"

Ambrosini, Richard. *Conrad's Fiction* . . . , 79–83.

Caraher, Brian G. "A Modernist Allegory of Narration: Joseph Conrad's 'Youth' and the Ideology of the Image," in Downing, David B., and Susan Bazargan, Eds. *Image* . . . , 47–68.

JACK CONROY

"A Coal Miner's Widow"
    Hanley, Lawrence F. "Cultural Work and Class Politics: Re-reading
    and Remaking *Proletarian Literature in the United States*," *Mod
    Fiction Stud*, 38 (1992), 725–726, 727.

BENJAMIN CONSTANT

"Adolphe"
    Fontana, Biancamaria. *Benjamin Constant* . . . , 118–133.

SUSANA CONSTANTE

"El Jardín"
    Pérez, Janet. "Characteristics of Erotic Brief Fiction by Women in
    Spain," *Monographic R*, 7 (1991), 179–181.

J. CALIFORNIA COOPER

"Living"
    Marshall, Barbara J. "Kitchen Table Talk: J. California Cooper's Use
    of Nommo—Female Bonding and Transcendence," in Blacksire-
    Belay, Carol A., Ed. *Language and Literature* . . . , 97–98.

"Sisters of the Rain"
    Marshall, Barbara J. "Kitchen Table . . . ," 99–100.

ROBERT COOVER

"After Lazarus"
    Kennedy, Thomas E. *Robert Coover* . . . , 76–79.

"The Babysitter"
    +Cassill, R. V. . . . *Instructor's Handbook*, 42–43.
    Gass, William H. "Pricksongs & Descants," in *Fiction &
    Figures* . . . , 105–106; rpt. Kennedy, Thomas E., *Robert
    Coover* . . . , 128–129.
    Kennedy, Thomas E. *Robert Coover* . . . , 62–64.

"Beginnings"
    Kennedy, Thomas E. *Robert Coover* . . . , 71–72.

"The Brother"
    Keating, Helane L., and Walter Levy. *Instructor's Manual: Lives
    Through Literature* . . . , 32–33.
    Kennedy, Thomas E. *Robert Coover* . . . , 36–38, 42–43.

"Cartoon"
    Kennedy, Thomas E. *Robert Coover* . . . , 85–86.

"Charlie in the House of Rue"
Gabert, Charla. "The Metamorphosis of Charlie," *Chicago Review*, 32, ii (Autumn, 1980), 60–64; rpt. Kennedy, Thomas E. *Robert Coover* . . . , 135–139.
Kennedy, Thomas E. *Robert Coover* . . . , 83–84.
Zonderman, Jon. Rev. of "Charlie in the House of Rue," by Robert Coover, *American Book Review*, 4, ii (January–February, 1982), 24; rpt. Kennedy, Thomas E. *Robert Coover* . . . , 134–135.

"The Convention"
Kennedy, Thomas E. *Robert Coover* . . . , 70–71.

"The Door: A Prologue of Sorts"
Kennedy, Thomas E. *Robert Coover* . . . , 12–15, 31.

"The Elevator"
Kennedy, Thomas E. *Robert Coover* . . . , 46–50.

"The Fallguy's Faith"
Kennedy, Thomas E. *Robert Coover* . . . , 69–70.

"Gilda's Dream"
Kennedy, Thomas E. *Robert Coover* . . . , 81–82.

"The Gingerbread House"
Charters, Ann, and William E. Sheidley. *Resources for Teaching* . . . , 3rd ed., 54–55.
Kennedy, Thomas E. *Robert Coover* . . . , 26–32.

"The Hat Act"
Kennedy, Thomas E. *Robert Coover* . . . , 64–67.

"In a Train Station"
Kennedy, Thomas E. *Robert Coover* . . . , 38–39.

"Intermission"
Kennedy, Thomas E. *Robert Coover* . . . , 84–85.

"J's Marriage"
Kennedy, Thomas E. *Robert Coover* . . . , 40–44.

"Klee Dead"
Kennedy, Thomas E. *Robert Coover* . . . , 39–40.

"The Leper's Helix"
Kennedy, Thomas E. *Robert Coover* . . . , 59–60.

"The Magic Poker"
+Bohner, Charles H. *Instructor's Manual* . . . , 30–31.
Kennedy, Thomas E. *Robert Coover* . . . , 15–24.

"The Marker"
Kennedy, Thomas E. *Robert Coover* . . . , 34–36.

"The Milkmaid of Salmaniego"
Kennedy, Thomas E. *Robert Coover* . . . , 57–59.

"Morris in Chains"
Kennedy, Thomas E. *Robert Coover* . . . , 24–26.
Maltby, Paul. *Dissident Postmodernists* . . . , 86–88.

"Panel Game"
Kennedy, Thomas E. *Robert Coover* . . . , 33–34.
Maltby, Paul. *Dissident Postmodernists* . . . , 82–84.

"A Pedestrian Accident"
Kennedy, Thomas E. *Robert Coover* . . . , 60–62.

"The Phantom of the Movie Palace"
Kennedy, Thomas E. *Robert Coover* . . . , 73–76.

"Prologue"
Kennedy, Thomas E. *Robert Coover* . . . , 32–33.

"Quenby and Ola, Swede and Carl"
Kennedy, Thomas E. *Robert Coover* . . . , 52–55.

"The Romance of the Thin Man and the Fat Lady"
Kennedy, Thomas E. *Robert Coover* . . . , 50–52.

"Scene for Winter"
Kennedy, Thomas E. *Robert Coover* . . . , 55–57.

"Selected Short Subjects"
Kennedy, Thomas E. *Robert Coover* . . . , 81–83.

"The Sentient Lens"
Kennedy, Thomas E. *Robert Coover* . . . , 55–62.

"Shootout at Gentry's Junction"
Kennedy, Thomas E. *Robert Coover* . . . , 79–81.

"The Wayfarer"
Kennedy, Thomas E. *Robert Coover* . . . , 44–46.
Maltby, Paul. *Dissident Postmodernists* . . . , 84–86.

"You Must Remember This"
Kennedy, Thomas E. *Robert Coover* . . . , 87–89.

GILDA CORDERO-FERNANDO

"The Eye of the Needle"
Arambulo, Thelma E. "The Filipina as Writer: Against All Odds," in
Kintanar, Thelma B., Ed. *Women Reading* . . . , 179–180.

"High Fashion"
Arambulo, Thelma E. "The Filipina . . . ," 177.

"Hothouse"
Arambulo, Thelma E. "The Filipina . . . ," 180.

"The Level of Each Day's Needs"
Arambulo, Thelma E. "The Filipina . . . ," 177–178.

"Magnanimity"
Arambulo, Thelma E. "The Filipina . . . ," 177.

"The People in War"
Arambulo, Thelma E. "The Filipina . . . ," 178–179.

JULIO CORTÁZAR

"Apocalipsis de Solentiname"
Cruz, Julia. "Revolución y literatura en un cuento de Julio Cortázar,"
in Boland, Roy, and Alun Kenwood, Eds. *War and
Revolution* . . . , 89–95.

"La autopista"
Rodríguez-Luis, Julio. *The Contemporary* . . . , 84–85.

"Axolotl"
Hahn, Hannelore. "Comparación de 'Axolotl' de Julio Cortázar y
'La metamorfosis' de Franz Kafka," *Nuez*, 4, x–xi (1992), 26–27,
28.

"La banda"
McCard, Victoria. "El subalterno en Cortázar," *Revista de Estudios
Hispánicos*, 17–18 (1990–1991), 252–254.

"Bestiario"
González, Eduardo. *The Monstered Self* . . . , 143–155.
King, Sarah E. *The Magical* . . . , 19, 27, 32–35, 45, 46, 48.
Rodríguez-Luis, Julio. *The Contemporary* . . . , 68–71.

"Blow-Up" [originally "Las babas del diablo"]
Charters, Ann, and William E. Sheidley. *Resources for Teaching* . . . ,
3rd ed., 55–56.

"Casa tomada"
Martínez, Renato. "El 'Otro' y el proceso a la escritura: El caso del
'Boom,' " in Crafton, John M., Ed. *Selected Essays* . . . ,
129–131, 137–138.
Rodríguez-Luis, Julio. *The Contemporary* . . . , 63–64.

"Cefalea"
González, Eduardo. *The Monstered Self* . . . , 99–117.
Rodríguez-Luis, Julio. *The Contemporary* . . . , 62–63.

"Clippings"
Rodríguez-Luis, Julio. *The Contemporary* . . . , 91–92.

"Continuidad de los parques"
Duncan, Cynthia K. "Hacia una interpretación de lo fantástico en el
contexto de la literatura hispanoamericana," *Texto Crítico*, 16
(January–December, 1990), 56.
González, Eduardo. *The Monstered Self* . . . , 122–126.
Juan-Navarro, Santiago. "79 O 99/Modelos para desarmar: claves
para una lectura morelliana de 'Continuidad de los parques' de
Julio Cortázar," *Hispanic J*, 13 (1992), 241–249.

"Deshoras"
King, Sarah E. *The Magical* . . . , 21–22, 29, 49, 50, 54–55.

"Después del almuerzo"
King, Sarah E. *The Magical* . . . , 24, 27, 39–41, 46.

"Diario para un cuento"
Knickerbocker, Dale. "La teoría literaria implícita en 'Diario para un

cuento' de Julio Cortázar,'' *Inti*, 34–35 (Fall, 1991–Spring, 1992), 151–158.

"En nombre de Boby"
King, Sarah E. *The Magical* . . . , 26–27, 45.

"La escuela de la noche"
Kason, Nancy M. "El compromiso político en 'La escuela de noche' de Cortázar," *Cuadernos Americanos*, 6, i (January–February, 1992), 233–238.

"Fin de etapa"
Morell, Hortensia R. " 'Fin de etapa': Los peligros liminares del arte," *Discurso Literario*, 6, i (1988), 35–44.

"The Gates of Heaven"
Rodríguez-Luis, Julio. *The Contemporary* . . . , 66–67.

"Graffiti"
Tyler, Joseph. "Repression and Violence in Selected Contemporary Argentine Stories," *Discurso*, 9, ii (1992), 92–93.
———. "Tales of Repression and 'Desaparecidos' in Valenzuela and Cortázar," *Romance Lang Annual*, 3 (1991), 604.

"The Idol of the Cyclades"
Rodríguez-Luis, Julio. *The Contemporary* . . . , 75–77.

"Instrucciones para John Howell"
Juan-Navarro, Santiago. "El lector se rebela: 'Instrucciones para John Howell' de Julio Cortázar o la estética de la subversión," *Mountain Interstate Foreign Lang Conference R* (October, 1991), 149–158.
Rodríguez-Luis, Julio. *The Contemporary* . . . , 85–86.

"The Island at Noon"
Cruz, Julia. "Todorov's Pure Fantastic in a Story by Julio Cortázar," in Saciuk, Olena H. *The Shape* . . . , 75–83.
Rodríguez-Luis, Julio. *The Contemporary* . . . , 83.

"Lejana"
Martínez, Renato. "El 'Otro' . . . ," 134–135, 138.
McCard, Victoria. "El subalterno . . . ," 248–250.
Pita, Beatrice. "Manipulaciones del discurso femenino: 'Yo y La Otra' en *Usurpación* de Beatriz Guido y 'Lejana' de Julio Cortázar," *Crítica*, 2, ii (1990), 79–80, 81, 82, 83.
Rodríguez-Luis, Julio. *The Contemporary* . . . , 67–68.

"Letter to a Young Lady in Paris"
Rodríguez-Luis, Julio. *The Contemporary* . . . , 64–66.

"Las Ménades"
McCard, Victoria. "El subalterno . . . ," 252–253.

"The Other Heaven"
Rodríguez-Luis, Julio. *The Contemporary* . . . , 80–82.
Young, Richard A. "La poética de la flor en 'El otro cielo,' de Julio Cortázar," *Romance Q*, 39 (1992), 347–354.

"El perseguidor"
 McCard, Victoria. "El subalterno . . . ," 254–257.

"Pesadillas"
 Terramorsi, Bernard. " 'Pesadillas' de Julio Cortázar: De l'histoire
 de spectre au spectre de l'histoire," *Sociocriticism*, 6 (1990),
 133–146.

"A Place Called Kindberg"
 Young, Richard A. "Prefabrication in Julio Cortázar's 'Lugar llamado
 Kindberg,' " *Stud Short Fiction*, 28 (1991), 521–534.

"Las puertas del cielo"
 Martínez, Renato. "El 'Otro' . . . ," 136–137, 138.
 McCard, Victoria. "El subalterno . . . ," 250, 251.

"La salud de los enfermos"
 Trastoy, Beatriz. " 'La salud de los enfermos' de Cortázar: Notas
 sobre la ficción teatral," *Latin Am Theater R*, 26, i (1992), 103–110.

"The Second Time Around"
 Tyler, Joseph. "Repression . . . ," 89–92.
 ———. "Tales . . . ," 603.

"Secret Weapons"
 González, Eduardo. *The Monstered Self* . . . , 155–162.
 Rodríguez-Luis, Julio. *The Contemporary* . . . , 79–80.

"Severo's Phrases"
 Rodríguez-Luis, Julio. *The Contemporary* . . . , 86–87.

"Silvia"
 Callan, Richard. "Cortázar's Story 'Silvia': The Hero and the Golden
 Hoard," *Chasqui*, 20, ii (1991), 46–53.
 González, Eduardo. *The Monstered Self* . . . , 126–129.
 King, Sarah E. *The Magical* . . . , 26, 28, 49, 50, 51–53, 55.

"Torito"
 McCard, Victoria. "El subalterno . . . ," 254.

"Los venenos"
 King, Sarah E. *The Magical* . . . , 24, 27, 35–39.
 Stavans, Ilan. "Kafka, Cortázar, Gass," *R Contemp Fiction*, 11, iii
 (1991), 132–133.

"Verano"
 King, Sarah E. *The Magical* . . . , 25, 48.

LOUIS MARIE ANNE COUPERUS

"The Binoculars"
 Francken, Eep. "As the Brains Splattered: J. Fontijn's Psychological
 Interpretation of 'The Binoculars,' by Louis Couperus," *Dutch
 Crossing*, 47 (1992), 87–94.

STEPHEN CRANE

"The Blue Hotel"
+ Bohner, Charles H. *Instructor's Manual . . .* , 31–32.
+ Cassill, R. V. *. . . Instructor's Handbook*, 46–47.
Feaster, John. "Violence and the Ideology of Capitalism: A Reconsideration of Crane's 'The Blue Hotel,' " *Am Lit Realism*, 25, i (1992), 80–94.
Juan-Navarro, Santiago. "Reading Reality: The Tortuous Path to Perception in Stephen Crane's 'The Open Boat' and 'The Blue Hotel,' " *Revista Canaria de Estudios Ingleses*, [n.v.] (November, 1989), 43–48.
Oriard, Michael. *Sporting with the Gods . . .* , 246–248.
Quinn, Brian T. "A Contrastive Look at Stephen Crane's Naturalism as Depicted in 'The Open Boat' and 'The Blue Hotel,' " *Stud Engl Lang & Lit*, 42 (1992), 55–61.

"The Bride Comes to Yellow Sky"
Zanger, Jules. "Stephen Crane's 'Bride' as Countermyth of the West," *Great Plains Q*, 11 (1991), 157–165.

"Death and the Child"
Holton, Milne. "Stephen Crane's 'Death and the Child': The Context of the Text," *Stephen Crane Stud*, 1, ii (1992), 1–8.

"Killing His Bear"
Benfey, Christopher. *The Double Life . . .* , 56–58.

"Maggie: A Girl of the Streets"
Benfey, Christopher. *The Double Life . . .* , 61–73.
Hapke, Laura. "The American Working Girl and the New York Tenement Tale of the 1890s," *J Am Culture*, 15, ii (1992), 48–49.
Novotny, George T. "Crane's 'Maggie, A Girl of the Streets,' " *Explicator*, 50, iv (1992), 225–227.
Sweeney, Gerald M. "The Syphilitic World of Stephen Crane's 'Maggie,' " *Am Lit Realism*, 24 (1991), 79–85.

"Manacled"
Benfey, Christopher. *The Double Life . . .* , 263–264.

"The Monster"
Benfey, Christopher. *The Double Life . . .* , 258–260.
Giles, Ronald K. "Responding to Crane's 'The Monster,' " *So Atlantic R*, 57, ii (1992), 45–55.

"A Mystery of Heroism"
Steffelbauer, Berta. "Stephen Crane's Short Story 'A Mystery of Heroism,' " *Moderne Sprachen*, 35, iv (1991), 23–31.

"The Octopush"
Church, Joseph. "Reading, Writing, and the Risk of Entanglement in Crane's 'Octopush,' " *Stud Short Fiction*, 29 (1992), 341–346.

"An Ominous Baby"
Benfey, Christopher. *The Double Life . . .* , 87–89.

"The Open Boat"
  Benfey, Christopher. *The Double Life* . . . , 194–198.
  + Bohner, Charles H. *Instructor's Manual* . . . , 33–34.
  + Cassill, R. V. . . . *Instructor's Handbook*, 44–45.
  + Charters, Ann, and William E. Sheidley. *Resources for
    Teaching* . . . , 3rd ed., 57–58.
  Juan-Navarro, Santiago. "Reading Reality . . . ," 38–43.
  Metress, Christopher. "From Indifference to Anxiety: Knowledge
    and the Reader in 'The Open Boat,' " *Stud Short Fiction,* 28
    (1991), 47–53.
  Quinn, Brian T. "A Contrastive Look . . . ," 50–55.
  Rath, Sura P., and Mary N. Shaw. "The Dialogic Narrative of 'The
    Open Boat,' " *Lit Theory Classroom,* 18, ii (1991), 94–106.

"The Third Violet"
  Benfey, Christopher. *The Double Life* . . . , 148–156.

"This Majestic Lie"
  Benfey, Christopher. *The Double Life* . . . , 254–256.

"The Upturned Face"
  Benfey, Christopher. *The Double Life* . . . , 264–267.

ALEXIS CURVERS

"Entre deux anges"
  De Blauwe, Christiane. "A propos de 'Entre deux anges' d'Alexis
    Curvers," *Le Ragioni Critiche*, 17 (1988), 195–201.

EUGÈNE DABIT

"Une aventure de printemps"
  Lachasse, Pierre. "Réalisme et subjectivité chez Eugène Dabit:
    Analyse de la nouvelle 'Une aventure de printemps' (1935),"
    Littératures, 24 (Spring, 1991), 127–142.

ROALD DAHL

"The Way up to Heaven"
  Bohner, Charles H. *Instructor's Manual* . . . , 34–35.

CAROLINE WELLS HEALEY DALL

"Amy"
  Sánchez-Eppler, Karen. "Bodily Bonds: The Intersecting Rhetorics
    of Feminism and Abolition," in Samuels, Shirley, Ed. *The Culture
    of Sentiment* . . . , 104–106.

RUBÉN DARÍO

"Palomas blancas y garzas morenas"
Salgado, María A. "En torno a Rubén Darío, la literatura intimista y el preciosismo verbal," *Explicación de Textos Literarios*, 19, i (1990–1991), 95–111.

ALPHONSE DAUDET

"La Chèvre de M. Seguin"
Araujo, Norman. "Prosaic Licence and the Use of the Literary Past in Daudet's 'La Chèvre de M. Seguin,' " *Forum Mod Lang Stud*, 27, iii (1991), 195–207.

AMPARO DÁVILA

"La Celda"
Froumann-Smith, Erica. "Patriarchy and Madness: The Dilemma of Female Characters in Three Short Stories by Amparo Dávila," *Discurso*, 8, ii (1991), 140–141.

"Detrás de reja"
Froumann-Smith, Erica. "Patriarchy and Madness . . . ," 141–143.

"La Señorita Julia"
Froumann-Smith, Erica. "Partriarchy and Madness . . . ," 138–139.

REBECCA HARDING DAVIS

"Across the Gulf"
Harris, Sharon M. *Rebecca Harding Davis* . . . , 209–210.

"Anne"
Harris, Sharon M. *Rebecca Harding Davis* . . . , 227–229.

"The Coming of the Night"
Harris, Sharon M. *Rebecca Harding Davis* . . . , 304–305.

"The End of the Vendetta"
Harris, Sharon M. *Rebecca Harding Davis* . . . , 249–250.

"A Faded Leaf of History"
Harris, Sharon M. *Rebecca Harding Davis* . . . , 168–170.

"An Ignoble Martyr"
Harris, Sharon M. *Rebecca Harding Davis* . . . , 242–244.

"In the Market"
Harris, Sharon M. "Redefining the Feminine: Women and Work in Rebecca Harding Davis's 'In the Market,' " *Legacy*, 8, ii (1991), 118–121.

"Jane Murray's Thanksgiving"
Harris, Sharon M. *Rebecca Harding Davis* . . . , 295–296.

"John Lamar"
Harris, Sharon M. *Rebecca Harding Davis* . . . , 76–81.

"Life in the Iron-Mills"
Shurr, William H. " 'Life in the Iron-Mills': A Nineteenth-Century Conversion Narrative," *Am Transcendental Q*, N.S., 5 (1991), 245–257.

"Marcia"
Harris, Sharon M. *Rebecca Harding Davis* . . . , 252–253.

"Out of the Sea"
Harris, Sharon M. *Rebecca Harding Davis* . . . , 123–125.

"Paul Blecker" [originally "The Gurney"]
Harris, Sharon M. *Rebecca Harding Davis* . . . , 104–105.

"Tirar y Soult"
Harris, Sharon M. *Rebecca Harding Davis* . . . , 226–227.

"Two Women"
Harris, Sharon M. *Rebecca Harding Davis* . . . , 160–161.

"Walhalla"
Harris, Sharon M. *Rebecca Harding Davis* . . . , 204–206.

"A Wayside Episode"
Harris, Sharon M. *Rebecca Harding Davis* . . . , 213–215.

"The Wife's Story"
Boudreau, Kristin. " 'The Woman's Flesh of Me': Rebecca Harding Davis's Response to Self-Reliance," *Am Transcendental Q*, N.S., 6 (1992), 132–140.
Harris, Sharon M. *Rebecca Harding Davis* . . . , 108–114.

"The Yares of Black Mountain"
Harris, Sharon M. *Rebecca Harding Davis* . . . , 250–252.

SIDONIE DE LA HOUSSAYE

"Expenditure for a Sign"
Parker, Alice. "Evangeline's Darker Daughters: Crossing Racial Boundaries in Postwar Louisiana," in Brown, Dorothy H., and Barbara C. Ewell, Eds. *Louisiana Women Writers* . . . , 92.

MIGUEL DELIBES

"El sol"
Moreno Martínez, Matilde. "Análisis de 'El sol' (cuento de Miguel Delibes) según una lingüística del hablar," in Cuevas García, Cristóbal, Ed. *Miguel Delibes* . . . , 225–258.

MARCIA DENSER

"Ladies First"
Foster, David W. *Gay and Lesbian Themes* . . . , 94–97.

PALOMA DÍAZ-MAS

"La discreta pecadora, o ejemplo de doncellas recogidas"
Pérez, Janet. "Characteristics of Erotic Brief Fiction by Women in
Spain," *Monographic R*, 7 (1991), 181–183.

JESÚS DÍAZ RODRÍGUEZ

"Con la punta de una piedra"
Cachan, Manuel. "*Los años duros*: La Revolución del discurso y el
discurso de la Revolución cubana," *Explicación de Textos
Literarios*, 19, i (1990–1991), 88–89.

"¡No hay dios que resista esto!"
Cachan, Manuel. "*Los años duros* . . . ," 89–90.

"El polvo a la mitad"
Cachan, Manuel. "*Los años duros* . . . ," 89.

CHARLES DICKENS

"The Boarding-House"
Schiefelbein, Michael E. "Narrative Experience and Specificity:
Reading Dickens's 'Boarding-House,' " *Dickens Q*, 8, ii (1991),
57–67.

"A Christmas Carol"
Burleson, Donald R. "Dickens's 'A Christmas Carol,' " *Explicator*,
50, iv (1992), 211–212.

"The Four Sisters"
Ingham, Patricia. *Dickens, Women* . . . , 26–27.

"Hunted Down"
Allingham, Phillip V. "Dickens's Unreliable Narrator in 'Hunted
Down,' " *Stud Short Fiction*, 29 (1992), 85–93.

"The Perils of Certain English Prisoners"
Nayder, Lillian. "Class Consciousness and the Indian Mutiny in
Dickens's 'The Perils of Certain English Prisoners,' " *Stud Engl
Lit*, 32 (1992), 689–705.

ISAK DINESEN [BARONESS KAREN BLIXEN]

"The Blank Page"
Gubar, Susan. *Writing and Sexual Difference*, ed. Elizabeth Abel,
Chicago: Univ. of Chicago Press, 1982, 73–93; rpt. " 'La página en
blanco' y las formas de creatividad femenina," trans. Paula
Brudny, *Feminaria*, 1, i (1988), 6–16.

"The Blue Jar"
+Charters, Ann, and William E. Sheidley. *Resources for
Teaching* . . . , 3rd ed., 60.

"The Blue Stone"
+Charters, Ann, and William E. Sheidley. *Resources for
Teaching* . . . , 3rd ed., 62.

"The Cardinal's First Tale"
Blackwell, Marilyn J. "The Transforming Gaze: Identity and
Sexuality in the Works of Isak Dinesen," *Scandinavian Stud*, 63, i
(1991), 57–58.

"The Cardinal's Third Tale"
Blackwell, Marilyn J. "The Transforming Gaze . . . ," 56–57.

"The Deluge at Norderney"
Blackwell, Marilyn J. "The Transforming Gaze . . . ," 54–55.

"Ehrengard"
Anderson, Kristine J. "Stories of Blushes: 'Ehrengard' and *Le
Chevalier des Touches*," *Symposium*, 46, ii (1992), 83–93.

"In the Menagerie"
Blackwell, Marilyn J. "The Transforming Gaze . . . ," 53–54.

"The Monkey"
Lokke, Kari. " 'A Whirlpool of Change': Isak Dinesen's 'The
Monkey' as a Beast Fable," *Bestia*, 2 (May, 1990), 87–100.
Masse, Michelle A. *In the Name of Love* . . . , 242–243.

"The Ring"
Dollerup, Cay. "The Perception of Fiction," in Jacobson, Eric,
Jorgen E. Nielsen, Bruce C. Ross, and James Stewart, Eds. *Studies
in* . . . , 131–139.

"The Roads Round Pisa"
Blackwell, Marilyn J. "The Transforming Gaze . . . ," 50–52.

"Sorrow Acre"
+Cassill, R. V. . . . *Instructor's Handbook*, 48–49.

STEPHEN DIXON

"The Sub"
Klinkowitz, Jerome. *Structuring the Void* . . . , 10–11.

ASSIA DJEBAR

"The Dead Speak"
Zimra, Clarisse. "Afterword," in Djebar, Assia. *Women of
Algiers* . . . ," 207–208.

"Women of Algiers in Their Apartment"
Zimra, Clarisse. "Afterword," 198–200, 204–207.

E. L. DOCTOROW

"The Ballads of W. C. Fields (2:20)"
Morris, Christopher D. *Models of Misrepresentation* . . . , 77–78.

"Billy's Dream of a Dead Friend (3:40)"
  Morris, Christopher D. *Models of Misrepresentation* . . . , 76–77.
"Even and Odd in the Garden of Adding (5:15)"
  Morris, Christopher D. *Models of Misrepresentation* . . . , 74–76.
"The Foreign Legation"
  Fowler, Douglas. *Understanding E. L. Doctorow*, 113–115.
  Morris, Christopher D. *Models of Misrepresentation* . . . , 146–149.
"The Hunter"
  Fowler, Douglas. *Understanding E. L. Doctorow*, 117–120.
  Morris, Christopher D. *Models of Misrepresentation* . . . , 145–146.
"The Leather Man"
  Fowler, Douglas. *Understanding E. L. Doctorow*, 115–117.
  Morris, Christopher D. *Models of Misrepresentation* . . . , 149–152.
"Lives of the Poets"
  Fowler, Douglas. *Understanding E. L. Doctorow*, 120–124.
  Morris, Christopher D. *Models of Misrepresentation* . . . , 144–152.
"She's Too Good for Me (2:04)"
  Morris, Christopher D. *Models of Misrepresentation* . . . , 72–73.
"Short Order Cook (2:35)"
  Morris, Christopher D. *Models of Misrepresentation* . . . , 70–72.
"Song to the Leaders of the World (3:26)"
  Morris, Christopher D. *Models of Misrepresentation* . . . , 73–74.
"The Water Works"
  Morris, Christopher D. *Models of Misrepresentation* . . . , 140–142.
"Willi"
  Fowler, Douglas. *Understanding E. L. Doctorow*, 110–112.
  Morris, Christopher D. *Models of Misrepresentation* . . . , 142–145.
"The Writer in the Family"
  Fowler, Douglas. *Understanding E. L. Doctorow*, 112–113.
  Morris, Christopher D. *Models of Misrepresentation* . . . , 138–139.

JOSÉ DONOSO

"China"
  King, Sarah E. *The Magical* . . . , 63–64.
"Gaspard de la nuit"
  Callan, Richard J. " 'Gaspard de la nuit': Crucial Breakthrough in
    the Growth of Personality," in Castillo-Feliú, Guillermo I., Ed.
    The Creative . . . , 129–139.
"El güero"
  King, Sarah E. *The Magical* . . . , 70–72.
"El hombrecito"
  King, Sarah E. *The Magical* . . . , 64–66.
"Paseo"
  King, Sarah E. *The Magical* . . . , 66–68.

Martínez, Renato. "El 'Otro' y el proceso a la escritura: El caso del 'Boom,' " in Crafton, John M., Ed. *Selected Essays* . . . , 131–133.
"Veraneo"
King, Sarah E. *The Magical* . . . , 68–70.

EDWARD O. DORIAN

"The Silk Tie"
Bedrosian, Margaret. "Transplantation," in Bedrosian, Margaret, Ed. *The Magic Pine Ring,* 62–63.

FYODOR DOSTOEVSKY

"The Double"
Head, Dominic. *The Modernist* . . . , 98.
Herdman, John. *The Double* . . . , 100–112.

"The Dream of a Ridiculous Man"
Naiman, Eric. "Of Crime, Utopia, and Repressive Complements: The Further Adventures of the Ridiculous Man," *Slavic R*, 50 (1991), 512–520.

"Notes from Underground"
Bernstein, Michael A. *Bitter Carnival* . . . , 102–108.
Kraeger, Linda, and Joe Barnhart. *Dostoevsky* . . . , 127, 132, 145, 149–150, 153–154, 155.
Terras, Victor. *A History of Russian Literature,* 347–348.

ARTHUR CONAN DOYLE

"The Adventure of the Beryl Coronet"
Priestman, Martin. *Detective Fiction* . . . , 83–85.

"The Adventure of the Brice-Partington Plan"
Ludwig, James. "Who Is Cadogan West and What Is He to Mycroft?" *Baker Street J*, 39, ii (1989), 102–107.

"The Adventure of the Cardboard Box"
Priestman, Martin. *Detective Fiction* . . . , 7–8.

"The Adventure of the Dancing Men"
Fowler, Alastair. "Sherlock Holmes and the Adventure of the Dancing Men and Women," in Tudeau-Clayton, Margaret, and Martin Warner, Eds. *Addressing Frank Kermode* . . . , 154–168.
Torrese, Dante M. "Firearms in the Canon: 'The Adventure of the Dancing Men,' " *Baker Street J*, 41, i (1991), 39–43.

"The Adventure of the Devil's Foot"
Jones, Bob. "A Missed Clue in 'The Devil's Foot,' " *Baker Street J*, 41, iv (1991), 215–217.
Roszell, Calvert. " 'The Devil's Foot' and the Dweller at the Threshold," *Baker Street J*, 41, ii (1991), 100–103.

"The Adventure of the Empty House"
    Cochran, William R. "Re: Murray," *Baker Street J*, 39, ii (1989),
        76–78.
    Kamil, Irving. "The Search for Oscar Meunier," *Baker Street J*, 38,
        iv (1988), 209–214.
    Priestman, Martin. *Detective Fiction . . .* , 96–97.
"The Adventure of the Naval Treaty"
    Walters, Lee R. "The Great Experiment," *Baker Street J*, 38, ii
        (1988), 94–95.
"The Adventure of the Noble Bachelor"
    Kramer, Fred. "A Revealing Buffet on Baker Street," *Baker Street
        J*, 41, iii (1991), 158–160.
"The Adventure of the Priory School"
    Pasley, Robert S. "Breaking the Entail," *Baker Street J*, 39, ii
        (1989), 96–98.
"The Adventure of the Speckled Band"
    Hodgson, John A. "Recoil of 'The Speckled Band': Detective Story
        and Detective Discourse," *Poetics Today*, 13 (1992), 309–324.
"The Blue Carbuncle"
    Priestman, Martin. *Detective Fiction . . .* , 91–92.
"The Boscombe Valley Mystery"
    Burr, Robert C. "But What About the Blood, Holmes?" *Baker Street
        J*, 39, ii (1989), 75, 78.
"A Case of Identity"
    Priestman, Martin. *Detective Fiction . . .* , 9–10.
"The Final Problem"
    Atkinson, Michael. "Staging the Disappearance of Sherlock Holmes:
        The Aesthetics of Absence in 'The Final Problem,' " *Baker Street
        J*, 41, ii (1991), 206–214.
    Dundas, Zachary. "A Look at 'The Final Problem,' " *Baker Street
        J*, 38, ii (1988), 233–236.
    Priestman, Martin. *Detective Fiction . . .* , 94–96.
"His Law Bow"
    Benton, John L. "Dr. Watson's Automobile," *Baker Street J*, 39, ii
        (1989), 79–80.
"The Man with the Twisted Lip"
    Jaffe, Audrey. "Detecting the Beggar: Arthur Conan Doyle, Henry
        Mayhew, and 'The Man with the Twisted Lip,' " *Representations*,
        31 (1990), 96–117.
"The Red-Headed League"
    +Bohner, Charles H. *Instructor's Manual . . .* , 35–36.
    Priestman, Martin. *Detective Fiction . . .* , 86–90.
"A Scandal in Bohemia"
    Priestman, Martin. *Detective Fiction . . .* , 81–83.
"The Solitary Cyclist"
    Hall, Jasmine Y. "Ordering the Sensational: Sherlock Holmes and
        the Female Gothic," *Stud Short Fiction*, 28 (1991), 297–299, 301.

"The Speckled Band"
Hall, Jasmine Y. "Ordering . . . ," 299–300, 301.

"A Study in Scarlet"
Stetak, Ruthann H. "Jefferson Hope: A Fairly Good Dispenser,"
Baker Street J, 39, iii (1989), 144–147.

ROBERT DRAKE

"Amazing Grace"
Folks, Jeffrey J. "A Southern Realist: The Short Stories of Robert
Drake," *Mississippi Q*, 45 (1992), 161–162.

"Mr. Marcus and the Overhead Bridge"
Perkins, James A. "A Sort of Central Fact About Woodville: The
Railroad as Metaphor in the Works of Robert Drake," *Mississippi
Q*, 45 (1992), 146–147.

"A Ticket as Long as Your Arm"
Perkins, James A. "A Sort of . . . ," 147–148.

"The Tower and the Pear Tree"
Perkins, James A. "A Sort of . . . ," 148–149.

NAZLI DRAY

"Monte Kristo"
Bertram, Carel. "Genderized Space in the Modern Turkish Short
Story," *Turkish Stud Assn Bull*, 16 (1992), 30.

ANDRE DUBUS

"Adultery"
Hornby, Nick. *Contemporary American Fiction*, 156–158.

"The Curse"
Charters, Ann, and William E. Sheidley. *Resources for Teaching . . . ,*
3rd ed., 63–64.

"The Doctor"
Bohner, Charles H. *Instructor's Manual . . . ,* 36–37.

"Finding a Girl in America"
Hornby, Nick. *Contemporary American Fiction*, 158–161.

"Voices from the Moon"
Hornby, Nick. *Contemporary American Fiction*, 162–164.

"We Don't Live Here Anymore"
Hornby, Nick. *Contemporary American Fiction*, 152–156.

FERNAND DUMONT

"L'Influence du soleil"
Nicolas, Jérôme. " 'La Région du coeur' ou le désir des mots,"
Ragioni Critiche, 17, lxiii–lxvi (1988), 77, 78, 79, 80.

"La Région du coeur"
Nicolas, Jérôme. " 'La Région . . . ," 76, 78, 79, 80.
"Le Terrain vague"
Nicolas, Jérôme. " 'La Région . . . ," 77, 78, 79, 80.

ALICE DUNBAR-NELSON

"At Eventide"
Bryan, Violet H. "Race and Gender in the Early Works of Alice
Dunbar-Nelson," in Brown, Dorothy H., and Barbara C. Ewell,
Eds. *Louisiana Women Writers* . . . , 131–132.
"Ellen Fenton"
Johnson, Alisa. "Writing Within the Script: Alice Dunbar-Nelson's
'Ellen Fenton,' " *Stud Am Fiction*, 19 (1991), 165–174.
"The Goodness of St. Rocque"
Bryan, Violet H. "Race . . . ," 127–128.
"Hope Deferred"
Bryan, Violet H. "Race . . . ," 133, 134–135.
"Little Miss Sophie"
Bryan, Violet H. "Race . . . ," 125–127.
"Mr. Baptiste"
Bryan, Violet H. "Race . . . ," 133–134.
"Sister Josepha"
Bryan, Violet H. "Race . . . ," 128–129.
"A Story of Vengeance"
Bryan, Violet H. "Race . . . ," 130–131.

SARA JEANNETTE DUNCAN

"An Impossible Ideal"
Albertazzi, Silvia. "Sara Jeannette Duncan's Indian Novellas," in
Bardolph, Jacquelin, Ed. *Short Fiction* . . . , 199.

MARGUERITE DURAS [MARGUERITE DONADIEU]

"L'Amant"
Hellerstein, Nina S. "Family Reflections and the Absence of the
Father in 'L'Amant,' " *Essays French Lit*, 26 (November, 1989),
98–109.

STUART DYBEK

"Blood Soup"
Gladsky, Thomas S. *Princes, Peasants* . . . , 258, 260.

"Chopin in Winter"
  Gladsky, Thomas S. *Princes, Peasants . . .* , 261, 262.
"Hot Ice"
  Gladsky, Thomas S. *Princes, Peasants . . .* , 260–261.
"The Palatski Man"
  Gladsky, Thomas S. *Princes, Peasants . . .* , 259, 260.
"Sauerkraut Soup"
  Gladsky, Thomas S. *Princes, Peasants . . .* , 258, 259, 260.
"The Wake"
  Gladsky, Thomas S. *Princes, Peasants . . .* , 258.

MARIA EDGEWORTH

"The Bracelets"
  Kowaleski-Wallace, Elizabeth. *Their Fathers' Daughters . . .* ,
  118–120.
"The Good French Governess"
  Kowaleski-Wallace, Elizabeth. *Their Fathers' Daughters . . .* ,
  114–117.
"The Purple Jar"
  Kowaleski-Wallace, Elizabeth. *Their Fathers' Daughters . . .* ,
  111–112.

JORGE EDWARDS

"La experiencia"
  Cortínez, Carlos. "El estallido del débil en 'La experiencia' de Jorge
  Edwards," *Confluencia*, 5, ii (1990), 143–147. [See also *Revista
  Chilena Literatura*, 35 (1990), 135–140.]
"Rosaura"
  Cortínez, Carlos. "Eros sin alas: 'Rosaura' de Jorge Edwards,"
  Revista Chilena de Literatura, 38 (1991), 93–99.

JOSEPH VON EICHENDORFF

"The Marble Statue"
  Richter, Simon J. "Under the Sign of Venus: Eichendorff's
  'Marmobild' and the Erotics of Allegory," *So Atlantic R,* 56, ii
  (1991), 59–71.
  Sauter, Michiel. "Marmobilder und Macochismus: Die Venusfiguren
  in Eichendorffs 'Das Marmobild' und Sacher-Masochs 'Venus im
  Pelz,' " *Neophil,* 75, i (1991), 118–127.

GEORGE ELIOT [MARY ANN EVANS]

"Amos Barton"
  Brady, Kristin. *George Eliot,* 60–69.

"Janet's Repentance"
    Brady, Kristin. *George Eliot*, 76–84.
    McSweeney, Kerry. *George Eliot . . .* , 59–61.
"The Lifted Veil"
    Decker, James M. "Interpreting Latimer: Wordsworthian Martyr or Textual Alchemist?" *George Eliot-George Henry Lewes Stud*, 20–21 (September, 1992), 58–62.
    Eagleton, Terry. "Power and Knowledge in 'The Lifted Veil,' " in Newton, K. M., Ed. *George Eliot,* 53–64.
    Kidd, Millie M. "In Defense of Latimer: A Study of Narrative Technique in George Eliot's 'The Lifted Veil,' " *Victorian Newsletter*, 79 (1991), 37–41.
    Taylor, Marcia M. "Born Again: Reviving Bertha Grant," *George Eliot-George Henry Lewes Newsletter*, 18–19 (September, 1991), 46–54.
    Wallace, Anne D. " 'Vague Capricious Memories': 'The Lifted Veil's' Challenge to Wordsworthian Poetics," *George Eliot-George Henry Lewes Newsletter*, 18–19 (September, 1991), 31–45.
"Mr. Gilfil's Love Story"
    Brady, Kristin. *George Eliot*, 69–76.
    DeCuir, André L. "Italy, England, and the Female Artist in George Eliot's 'Mr. Gilfil's Love-Story,' " *Stud Short Fiction*, 29 (1992), 67–75.
    McSweeney, Kerry. *George Eliot . . .* , 58–59.
"The Sad Fortunes of the Reverend Amos Barton"
    Cervetti, Nancy. "The Resurrection of Milly Barton: At the Nexus of Production, Text and Re-production," *Women's Stud*, 21 (1992), 347–359.

SALVADOR ELIZONDO

"En la playa"
    Cabrera, Vicente. "Tortura en camara lenta: Salvador Elizondo 'En la playa' y otras historias," *Revista Interamericana*, 40, iv (1990), 234–399.
    Cluff, Russell M. "La omisión conspicua en Juan Rulfo y Salvador Elizondo," *Palabra y Hombre*, 78 (April–June, 1991), 277–278.

SERGIO ELIZONDO

"Rosa, la Flauta"
    Acosta, Marta. "The Languages of 'Rosa, la Flauta,' " *Confluencia*, 6, ii (1991), 163–168.

GEORGE ELLIOTT

"The Way Back"
    Lynch, Gerald. "The One and the Many: English-Canadian Short Story Cycles," *Canadian Lit*, 130 (Autumn, 1991), 98–110.

HARLAN ELLISON

"I Have No Mouth, and I Must Scream"
Harris-Fain, Darren. "Created in the Image of God: The Narrator
and the Computer in Harlan Ellison's 'I Have No Mouth, and I
Must Scream,' " *Extrapolation, 32* (1991), 143–155.

RALPH ELLISON

"King of the Bingo Game"
+ Bohner, Charles H. *Instructor's Manual . . .* , 37–38.
+ Cassill, R. V. *. . . Instructor's Handbook*, 50–51.
Herman, David J. "Ellison's 'King of the Bingo Game': Finding
Naturalism's Trapdoor," *Engl Lang Notes, 29* (1991), 71–74.
Hoeveler, Diane L. "Game Theory and Ellison's 'King of the Bingo
Game,' " *J Am Culture*, 15, ii (1992), 39–42.

"Battle Royal"
+ Charters, Ann, and William E. Sheidley. *Resources for
Teaching . . .* , 3rd ed., 65–66.

WILLEM ELSSCHOT

"Will-o'-the-Wisp"
Alphen, Ernst van. "Willem Elsschot as Critic of Ideology," *Dutch
Crossing*, 43 (Spring, 1991), 8–22.

EMILE ERCKMANN

"L'Esquisse mystérieuse" [co-author Alexandre Chatrian]
Cummiskey, Gary. *The Changing Face . . .* , 102–108.

LOUISE ERDRICH

"Matchimanito"
Cassill, R. V. *. . . Instructor's Handbook*, 51–52.

"The Red Convertible"
+ Charters, Ann, and William E. Sheidley. *Resources for
Teaching . . .* , 3rd ed., 68.

"Saint Marie"
Medeiros, Paulo. "Cannibalism and Starvation: The Parameters of
Eating Disorders in Literature," in Furst, Lilian R., and Peter W.
Graham, Eds. *Disorderly Eaters . . .* , 21–25.

LINA ESPINA-MOORE

"Nena of the Villa"
Lucero, Rosario Cruz. "The Philippine Short Story, 1981–1990: The
Voice of the Self-Authenticating Other," *Tenggara*, 26 (1990), 86.

FRANCISCO ESPÍNOLA

"El angelito"
Visca, Arturo Sergio. "Francisco Espínola, narrador," *Revista Iberoamericana,* 58 (1992), 287–288.

"Lo inefable"
Visca, Arturo Sergio. "Francisco Espínola . . . ," 990.

"María del Carmen"
Visca, Arturo Sergio. "Francisco Espínola . . . ," 986–987.

"Pedro Iglesias"
Visca, Arturo Sergio. "Francisco Espínola . . . ," 985–986.

"El rapto"
Visca, Arturo Sergio. "Francisco Espínola . . . ," 989–990.

"Las ratas"
Visca, Arturo Sergio. "Francisco Espínola . . . ," 991.

LYGIA FAGUNDES TELLES

"A Janela"
Brown, Richard L. "Lygia Fagundes Telles: Equalizer of the Sexes," *Romance Notes*, 32, ii (1991), 159.

"Antes do Baile Verde"
Brown, Richard L. "Lygia Fagundes Telles . . . ," 160.

"Apenas um Saxofone"
Brown, Richard L. "Lygia Fagundes Telles . . . ," 158.

"Os Objetos"
Brown, Richard L. "Lygia Fagundes Telles . . . ," 158.

"Verde Lagarto Amarelo"
Brown, Richard L. "Lygia Fagundes Telles . . . ," 160.

PHILIP JOSÉ FARMER

"The Henry Miller Dawn Patrol"
Wolf, Gary K. "The Dawn Patrol: Sex, Technology, and Irony in Farmer and Ballard," in Ruddick, Nicholas, Ed. *State . . . ,* 164–165.

WILLIAM FAULKNER

"Ad Astra"
Ferguson, James. *Faulkner's Short Fiction,* 82–83.

"Barn Burning"
Billingslea, Oliver. "Fathers and Sons: The Spiritual Quest in Faulkner's 'Barn Burning,' " *Mississippi Q,* 44 (1991), 287–308.

+ Cassill, R. V. . . . *Instructor's Handbook*, 55–56.

"The Bear"
  Benoit, Raymond. "Archetypes and Ecotones: The Tree in
    Faulkner's 'The Bear' and Irving's 'Rip Van Winkle,' " *Notes
    Contemp Lit*, 22, i (1992), 4–5.
  Burke, Daniel. *Beyond Interpretation* . . . , 103–119.
  Cassill, R. V. . . . *Instructor's Handbook*, 57–65.
  Reesman, Jeanne C. *American Designs* . . . , 170–185.
  Walsh, Timothy. "The Cognitive and Mimetic Function of Absence
    in Art, Music, and Literature," *Mosaic*, 25, ii (1992), 80–81.

"The Big Shot"
  Samway, Patrick. "Intertextual Observations Concerning Faulkner's
    'Mistral,' " *J Short Story Engl*, 16 (Spring, 1991), 73–74.

"Delta Autumn"
  Reesman, Jeanne C. *American Designs* . . . , 183–187.
  Robinson, David W., and Caren J. Town. " 'Who Dealt These
    Cards?': The Excluded Narrators of *Go Down, Moses*," *Twentieth
    Century Lit*, 37 (1991), 199–200.

"Divorce in Naples"
  Ferguson, James. *Faulkner's Short Fiction*, 66.
  Volpe, Edmond L. "A Tale of Ambivalences: Faulkner's 'Divorce in
    Naples,' " *Stud Short Fiction*, 28 (1991), 41–45.

"Dry September"
  + Bohner, Charles H. *Instructor's Manual* . . . , 38–39.
  Griffin, Paul F. "Chances of Being Kind: Rorty, Irony, and Teaching
    Modern Literature," *Lit Theory Classroom*, 18, ii (1991), 113–115.
  Sutton, Brian. "Faulkner's 'Dry September,' " *Explicator*, 49, ii
    (1991), 113–115.

"Dull Tale"
  Samway, Patrick. "Intertextual Observations . . . ," 74–75.

"Evangeline"
  Samway, Patrick. "Intertextual Observations . . . ," 76–77.

"The Fire and the Hearth"
  Clark, Keith. "Man on the Margin: Lucas Beauchamp and the
    Limitations of Space," *Faulkner J*, 6, i (1990), 67–73, 73–75.
  Reesman, Jeanne C. *American Designs* . . . , 158–165.
  Robinson, David W., and Caren J. Town. " 'Who Dealt . . . ,"
    196–197.

"Fox Hunt"
  Ferguson, James. *Faulkner's Short Fiction*, 67–68.

"Go Down Moses"
  Reesman, Jeanne C. *American Designs* . . . , 187–192.
  Robinson, David W., and Caren J. Town. " 'Who Dealt . . . ,"
    202–204.

"Golden Land"
  Kawin, Bruce. "Sharecropping in the Golden Land," in Fowler,
    Doreen, and Ann J. Abadie, Eds. *Faulkner* . . . , 199–201.

"Knight's Gambit"
  Ferguson, James. *Faulkner's Short Fiction,* 145–146.
"Mistral"
  Samway, Patrick. "Intertextual Observations . . . ," 67–71.
"The Old People"
  Reesman, Jeanne C. *American Designs* . . . , 165–170.
  Robinson, David W., and Caren J. Town. " 'Who Dealt . . . ,"
    197–198.
"An Odor of Verbena"
  Donaldson, Susan V. "Dismantling the *Saturday Evening Post*
    Reader: *The Unvanquished* and Changing 'Horizons of
    Expectations,' " in Fowler, Doreen, and Ann J. Abadie, Eds.
    Faulkner . . . , 186–192.
"Pantaloon in Black"
  Reesman, Jeanne C. *American Designs* . . . , 161–165.
  Robinson, David W., and Caren J. Town. " 'Who Dealt . . . ,"
    201–202.
"The Priest"
  Samway, Patrick. "Intertextual Observations . . . ," 67.
"A Return"
  Samway, Patrick. "Intertextual Observations . . . ," 72–73.
"A Rose for Emily"
  +Bohner, Charles H. *Instructor's Manual* . . . , 40–41.
  Burns, Margie. "A Good Rose Is Hard to Find: Southern Gothic as
    Signs of Social Dislocation in Faulkner and O'Connor," in
    Downing, David B., and Susan Bazargan, Eds. *Image* . . . , 107,
    108–113, 114, 115, 117–121.
  +Cassill, R. V. . . . *Instructor's Handbook*, 53–54.
  +Charters, Ann, and William E. Sheidley. *Resources for Teach-
    ing* . . . , 3rd ed., 70–71.
  Doyle, Charles C. "Mute Witnesses: Faulkner's Use of a Popular
    Riddle," *Mississippi Folklore Register*, 24 (1990), 53–55.
  Ferguson, James. *Faulkner's Short Fiction,* 129–130.
  Moore, Gene M. "Of Time and Its Mathematical Progression:
    Problems of Chronology in Faulkner's 'A Rose for Emily,' " *Stud
    Short Fiction*, 29 (1992), 195–204.
  Schwab, Milinda. "A Watch for Emily," *Stud Short Fiction*, 28
    (1991), 215–217.
  Wallace, James M. "Faulkner's 'A Rose for Emily,' " *Explicator*, 50,
    ii (1992), 105–107.
"Snow"
  Samway, Patrick. "Intertextual Observations . . . ," 75–76.
"Spotted Horses"
  Charters, Ann, and William E. Sheidley. *Resources for Teach-
    ing* . . . , 3rd ed., 72–73.
  Ramsey, Allen. " 'Spotted Horses' and Spotted Pups," *Faulkner J*,
    5, ii (1990), 35–38.

"That Evening Sun"
+ Bohner, Charles H. *Instructor's Manual* . . . , 41–42.
"Was"
Robinson, David W., and Caren J. Town. " 'Who Dealt . . . ,"
194–195.

EDNA FERBER

"The Homely Heroine"
Wilson, Christopher P. *White Collar Fiction* . . . , 77–78.
"The Kitchen Side"
Wilson, Christopher P. *White Collar Fiction* . . . , 75–76.
"Sisters Under the Skin"
Wilson, Christopher P. *White Collar Fiction* . . . , 82–83.

CRISTINA FERNÁNDEZ CUBAS

"Los Altillos de Brumal"
Ortega, José. "La dimensión fantástica en los cuentos de Fernández
Cubas," *Monographic R*, 8 (1992), 159–160.
"El ángulo del horror"
Ortega, José. "La dimensión fantástica . . . ," 160–161.
"La Flor de España"
Glenn, Kathleen M. "Gothic Indecipherability and Doubling in the
Fiction of Cristina Fernández Cubas," *Monographic R,* 8 (1992),
130–132.
"Helicón"
Ortega, José. "La dimensión fantástica . . . ," 157–158.
"Lúnula y Violeta"
Glenn, Kathleen M. "Gothic Indecipherability . . . ," 133–134.
Ortega, José. "La dimensión fantástica . . . ," 158–159.
"Mi hermana Elba"
Ortega, José. "La dimensión fantástica . . . ," 161.
"La noche de Jezabel"
Glenn, Kathleen M. "Gothic Indecipherability . . . ," 129–130.
"Omar, amor"
Encinar, Angeles. "Escritoras Españolas actuales: una perspectiva a
través del cuento," *Hispanic J*, 13 (1992), 183–184.
Schaefer, Claudia. "A Simple Question of Symmetry: Women
Writing in Post-Franco Spain," in Erro-Orthmann, Nora, and Juan
Cruz Mendizábal, *La escritora* . . . , 282, 283, 284.
"La ventana del jardín"
Glenn, Kathleen M. "Gothic Indecipherability . . . ," 126–129.

JESÚS FERNÁNDEZ SANTOS

"Los caracoles"
  Reyero, Loló. " 'Los caracoles' de Jesús Fernández Santos, y un par
  de críticos franceses: Vagar divagando," *Inti*, 32–33 (Fall-Spring,
  1990–1991), 53–63.

ROSARIO FERRÉ

"Cuando las mujeres quieren a los hombres"
  Carney, Carmen V. "El amor como discurso político en Ana Lydia
  Vega y Rosario Ferré," *Letras femeninas*, 17, ii (1991), 81.
  Fox-Lockert, Lucía. "El discurso femenino en los cuentos de Rosario
  Ferré y de Elena Garro," in Erro-Orthmann, Nora, and Juan Cruz
  Mendizábal, Eds. *La escritora . . .* , 87–90.

"Isolda's Mirror"
  Castillo, Debra A. *Talking Back . . .* , 155–188.

"Maldito amor"
  Carney, Carmen V. "El amor . . . ," 81–82.
  Cavallo, Susana. "Llevando la contraria: el contracanto de Rosario
  Ferré," *Monographic R*, 8 (1992), 199–203.

"La muñeca menor"
  Carney, Carmen V. "El amor . . . ," 81.

"Sleeping Beauty"
  Netchinsky, Jill. "Madness and Colonization: Ferré's Ballet,"
  Revista de estudios hispánicos, 25 (1991), 103–128.

TIMOTHY FINDLEY

"Stones"
  Regan, Stephen. " 'The Presence of the Past': Modernism and
  Postmodernism in Canadian Short Fiction," in Howells, Coral A.,
  and Lynette Hunter, Eds. *Narrative Strategies . . .* , 113–114.

F. SCOTT FITZGERALD

"Absolution"
  Kuehl, John. *F. Scott Fitzgerald . . .* , 57–64.
  Mangum, Bryant. *A Fortune Yet . . .* , 55–57.

"The Adjuster"
  Kuehl, John. *F. Scott Fitzgerald . . .* , 54–55.
  Mangum, Bryant. *A Fortune Yet . . .* , 69–70.

"An Alcoholic Case"
  Mangum, Bryant. *A Fortune Yet . . .* , 158–159.

"The Ants at Princeton"
  Mangum, Bryant. *A Fortune Yet . . .* , 151–152.

"At Your Age"
  Mangum, Bryant. *A Fortune Yet . . .* , 94, 95.
"An Author's Mother"
  Mangum, Bryant. *A Fortune Yet . . .* , 157–158.
"Babes in the Woods"
  Mangum, Bryant. *A Fortune Yet . . .* , 17, 23–25.
"The Baby Party"
  Mangum, Bryant. *A Fortune Yet . . .* , 67.
"Babylon Revisited"
  +Bohner, Charles H. *Instructor's Manual . . .* , 42–44.
  +Cassill, R. V. *. . . Instructor's Handbook*, 66–67.
  +Charters, Ann, and William E. Sheidley. *Resources for Teaching . . .* , 3rd ed., 73–74.
  Kuehl, John. *F. Scott Fitzgerald . . .* , 80–86.
  Mangum, Bryant. *A Fortune Yet . . .* , 96–98.
"Benediction"
  Mangum, Bryant. *A Fortune Yet . . .* , 25–26.
"The Bowl"
  Mangum, Bryant. *A Fortune Yet . . .* , 105.
"The Bridal Party"
  Mangum, Bryant. *A Fortune Yet . . .* , 82.
"A Change of Class"
  Mangum, Bryant. *A Fortune Yet . . .* , 120–121.
"The Count of Darkness"
  Mangum, Bryant. *A Fortune Yet . . .* , 144–145.
"Crazy Sunday"
  Kuehl, John. *F. Scott Fitzgerald . . .* , 86–93.
  Mangum, Bryant. *A Fortune Yet . . .* , 98–99.
"Dalyrimple Goes Wrong"
  Mangum, Bryant. *A Fortune Yet . . .* , 26–27.
"The Dance"
  Mangum, Bryant. *A Fortune Yet . . .* , 73–74.
"Design in Plaster"
  Mangum, Bryant. *A Fortune Yet . . .* , 161–162.
"Diagnosis"
  Mangum, Bryant. *A Fortune Yet . . .* , 122.
"The Diamond as Big as the Ritz"
  Kuehl, John. *F. Scott Fitzgerald . . .* , 45–51.
  Mangum, Bryant. *A Fortune Yet . . .* , 39–40.
"Discard"
  Mangum, Bryant. *A Fortune Yet . . .* , 172–173.
"The Family Bus"
  Mangum, Bryant. *A Fortune Yet . . .* , 128.
"Family in the Wind"
  Mangum, Bryant. *A Fortune Yet . . .* , 123–124.

"Fate in Her Hands"
Mangum, Bryant. *A Fortune Yet . . .* , 141–142.

"The Fiend"
Mangum, Bryant. *A Fortune Yet . . .* , 152–153.

"Financing Finnegan"
Kuehl, John. *F. Scott Fitzgerald . . .* , 115–117.
Mangum, Bryant. *A Fortune Yet . . .* , 159–160.

"Flight and Pursuit"
Mangum, Bryant. *A Fortune Yet . . .* , 122–123.

"A Freeze-Out"
Mangum, Bryant. *A Fortune Yet . . .* , 121–122.

"The Freshest Boy"
Mangum, Bryant. *A Fortune Yet . . .* , 109–110.

"Gods of Darkness"
Mangum, Bryant. *A Fortune Yet . . .* , 145–146.

"Head and Shoulders"
Mangum, Bryant. *A Fortune Yet . . .* , 31.

"The Hotel Child"
Mangum, Bryant. *A Fortune Yet . . .* , 82–83, 84.

"I Didn't Get Over"
Mangum, Bryant. *A Fortune Yet . . .* , 158.

"I Got Shoes"
Mangum, Bryant. *A Fortune Yet . . .* , 127–128.

"The Ice Palace"
Drushell, Barbara. "Fitzgerald's 'The Ice Palace,' " *Explicator*, 49,
iv (1991), 237–238.
Kuehl, John. *F. Scott Fitzgerald . . .* , 34–39.
Mangum, Bryant. *A Fortune Yet . . .* , 32–33, 42–43.

"In the Darkest Hour"
Mangum, Bryant. *A Fortune Yet . . .* , 144.

"Indecision"
Mangum, Bryant. *A Fortune Yet . . .* , 92–93.

"The Intimate Strangers"
Mangum, Bryant. *A Fortune Yet . . .* , 140–141.

"Jacob's Ladder"
Kuehl, John. *F. Scott Fitzgerald . . .* , 102–103.
Mangum, Bryant. *A Fortune Yet . . .* , 85–86.

"The Jelly-Bean"
Mangum, Bryant. *A Fortune Yet . . .* , 43.

"Last Kiss"
Mangum, Bryant. *A Fortune Yet . . .* , 173–175.

"The Last of the Belles"
Kuehl, John. *F. Scott Fitzgerald . . .* , 74–76.
Mangum, Bryant. *A Fortune Yet . . .* , 119–120.

"Lo, the Poor Peacock"
  Mangum, Bryant. *A Fortune Yet* . . . , 139–140.
"The Lost Decade"
  Mangum, Bryant. *A Fortune Yet* . . . , 162.
"The Love Boat"
  Mangum, Bryant. *A Fortune Yet* . . . , 94, 95.
"Love in the Night"
  Mangum, Bryant. *A Fortune Yet* . . . , 79–80.
"Magnetism"
  Mangum, Bryant. *A Fortune Yet* . . . , 86–88.
"Majesty"
  Mangum, Bryant. *A Fortune Yet* . . . , 80–82.
"A Man in the Way"
  Mangum, Bryant. *A Fortune Yet* . . . , 166.
"May Day"
  Kuehl, John. *F. Scott Fitzgerald* . . . , 39–45.
  Mangum, Bryant. *A Fortune Yet* . . . , 38–39.
"More than Just a House"
  Mangum, Bryant. *A Fortune Yet* . . . , 126–127.
"Myra Meets His Family"
  Mangum, Bryant. *A Fortune Yet* . . . , 31–32.
"A New Leaf"
  Mangum, Bryant. *A Fortune Yet* . . . , 93–94.
"New Types"
  Mangum, Bryant. *A Fortune Yet* . . . , 133–134.
"A Night at the Fair"
  Mangum, Bryant. *A Fortune Yet* . . . , 108–109.
"The Night Before Chancellorsville"
  Mangum, Bryant. *A Fortune Yet* . . . , 150–151.
"No Flowers"
  Mangum, Bryant. *A Fortune Yet* . . . , 132–133.
"Not in the Guidebook"
  Mangum, Bryant. *A Fortune Yet* . . . , 65, 66.
"The Offshore Pirate"
  Mangum, Bryant. *A Fortune Yet* . . . , 33–34.
"On Schedule"
  Mangum, Bryant. *A Fortune Yet* . . . , 94–95.
"One of My Oldest Friends"
  Mangum, Bryant. *A Fortune Yet* . . . , 64–65.
"One Trip Abroad"
  Kuehl, John. *F. Scott Fitzgerald* . . . , 102–109.
  Mangum, Bryant. *A Fortune Yet* . . . , 91–92.
"Outside the Cabinet-Maker's"
  Kuehl, John. *F. Scott Fitzgerald* . . . , 112–114.

"The Passionate Eskimo"
Mangum, Bryant. *A Fortune Yet* . . . , 139.

"Pat Hobby's Christmas Wish"
Mangum, Bryant. *A Fortune Yet* . . . , 165–166.

"A Patriotic Short"
Mangum, Bryant. *A Fortune Yet* . . . , 168.

"A Penny Spent"
Mangum, Bryant. *A Fortune Yet* . . . , 80.

"The Pierian Springs"
Kuehl, John. *F. Scott Fitzgerald* . . . , 21–25.

"Presumption"
Mangum, Bryant. *A Fortune Yet* . . . , 103.

"Reade, Substitute Right Half"
Mangum, Bryant. *A Fortune Yet* . . . , 13–14.

"The Rich Boy"
Castronovo, David. *The American Gentleman* . . . , 69–70.
Kuehl, John. *F. Scott Fitzgerald* . . . , 68–73.
Mangum, Bryant. *A Fortune Yet* . . . , 70–73.

"The Rough Crossing"
Mangum, Bryant. *A Fortune Yet* . . . , 88–89.

"The Rubber Check"
Mangum, Bryant. *A Fortune Yet* . . . , 124–125.

"The Scandal Detectives"
Mangum, Bryant. *A Fortune Yet* . . . , 107–108.

"Send Me In, Coach"
Mangum, Bryant. *A Fortune Yet* . . . , 152.

"The Sensible Thing:
Mangum, Bryant. *A Fortune Yet* . . . , 50–51.

"Shaggy's Morning"
Mangum, Bryant. *A Fortune Yet* . . . , 151.

"A Short Trip Home"
Mangum, Bryant. *A Fortune Yet* . . . , 104.

"Six of One—,"
Mangum, Bryant. *A Fortune Yet* . . . , 74.

"The Smilers"
Mangum, Bryant. *A Fortune Yet* . . . , 27.

"Strange Sanctuary"
Mangum, Bryant. *A Fortune Yet* . . . , 142.

"The Swimmers"
Kuehl, John. *F. Scott Fitzgerald* . . . , 109–112.
Mangum, Bryant. *A Fortune Yet* . . . , 89–90.

"Three Acts of Music"
Mangum, Bryant. *A Fortune Yet* . . . , 151.

"Trouble"
Mangum, Bryant. *A Fortune Yet* . . . , 136–137.
"Two Wrongs"
Kuehl, John. *F. Scott Fitzgerald* . . . , 77–78.
Mangum, Bryant. *A Fortune Yet* . . . , 90–91.
"What a Handsome Pair"
Mangum, Bryant. *A Fortune Yet* . . . , 125–126.
"Winter Dreams"
Kuehl, John. *F. Scott Fitzgerald* . . . , 64–68.
Mangum, Bryant. *A Fortune Yet* . . . , 53–55.
"Your Way and Mine"
Mangum, Bryant. *A Fortune Yet* . . . , 66.

GUSTAVE FLAUBERT

"Herodias"
Erickson, Karen L. "Prophetic Utterance and Irony in *Tres contes*,"
in Cooper, Barbara T., and Mary Donaldson-Evans, Eds.
Modernity and Revolution . . . , 65–66.
"St. Julien"
+Cassill, R. V. . . . *Instructor's Handbook*, 68–70.
Erickson, Karen L. "Prophetic Utterance . . . ," 66–68.
"A Simple Heart"
Chambers, Ross. "Irony and Misogyny: Authority and the
Homosocial in Baudelaire and Flaubert," *Australian J French
Stud*, 26, iii (1989), 283–286.
+Charters, Ann, and William E. Sheidley. *Resources for Teach-
ing* . . . , 3rd ed., 75–76.
Clark, John R. *The Modern Satiric Grotesque* . . . , 97–98.
Erickson, Karen L. "Prophetic Utterance . . . ," 68–71.
Rodríguez, Alfred. " 'Un coeur simple' de Flaubert y dos obras
maestras españolas: *Doña Berta* y *Misericordia*," *Hispano*, 104
(1992), 25–29.

THEODEOR FONTANE

"Schach von Wuthenow"
Guards, Sylvain. " 'Schach von Wuthenow': Ein 'Passionsspiel' in
Fontanescher Manier," *Germ R*, 67 (1992), 59–68.

SHELBY FOOTE

"All Right About That"
Phillips, Robert L. *Shelby Foote* . . . , 45–46.
"Child by Fever"
Phillips, Robert L. *Shelby Foote* . . . , 139–149.

"The Freedom Kick"
Phillips, Robert L. *Shelby Foote* . . . , 149–150.
"The Good Pilgrim: A Fury is Calmed"
Phillips, Robert L. *Shelby Foote* . . . , 43–45.
"The Old Man That Sold Peanuts in New Orleans"
Phillips, Robert L. *Shelby Foote* . . . , 47–48.
"Pillar of Fire"
Phillips, Robert L. *Shelby Foote* . . . , 150–155.
"Rain Down Home"
Phillips, Robert L. *Shelby Foote* . . . , 135–136.
"Ride Out" [revision of "Tell Them Good-By"]
Phillips, Robert L. *Shelby Foote* . . . , 136–139.
"A Tale Untitled"
Phillips, Robert L. *Shelby Foote* . . . , 44–45.

AIDA RIVERA FORD

"The Chieftest Mourner"
Evasco, Marjorie. "The Writer and Her Roots," in Kintanar, Thelma
B., Ed. *Women Reading* . . . , 16.

RICHARD FORD

"Optimists"
Hornby, Nick. *Contemporary American Fiction*, 106–108.

THELMA FORESHAW

"The Mateship Syndrome"
Walker, Shirley. "The Deconstruction of the Bush: Australian
Women Short Story Writers," in Bardolph, Jacquelin, Ed. *Short
Fiction* . . . , 81–82.

E. M. FORSTER

"Ansell"
Heldreth, Leonard G. "Fantasy as Criticism in Forster's Short
Fiction," in Saciuk, Olena H., *The Shape* . . . , 10–11.
"Arthur Snatchfold"
Heldreth, Leonard G. "Fantasy as Criticism . . . ," 11.
"The Celestial Omnibus"
Heldreth, Leonard G. "Fantasy as Criticism . . . ," 12–13.
"Other Kingdom"
Heldreth, Leonard G. "Fantasy as Criticism . . . ," 17.

"The Road from Colonus"
  + Cassill, R. V. . . . *Instructor's Handbook*, 70–72.
  Heldreth, Leonard G. "Fantasy as Criticism . . . ," 14–16.
  Storey, Michael L. "Forster's 'The Road from Colonus,' "
    Explicator, 49, iii (1991), 170–173.
"The Story of a Panic"
  Heldreth, Leonard G. "Fantasy as Criticism . . . ," 13–14.

JOHN FOWLES

"The Cloud"
  Aubrey, James R. *John Fowles* . . . , 116.
  Salami, Mahmoud. *John Fowles's Fiction* . . . , 145–146.
  Vieth, Lynne S. "The Re-humanization of Art: Pictorial Aesthetics
    in John Fowles's *The Ebony Tower* and *Daniel Martin*," *Mod
    Fiction Stud*, 37 (1991), 224–228.
"The Ebony Tower"
  Aubrey, James R. *John Fowles* . . . , 111.
  Salami, Mahmoud. *John Fowles's Fiction* . . . , 142–145.
  Vieth, Lynne S. "The Re-humanization of Art . . . ," 219–224.
"Eliduc"
  Salami, Mahmoud. *John Fowles's Fiction* . . . , 140–141.
"The Enigma"
  Aubrey, James R. *John Fowles* . . . , 114–115.
"Poor Koko"
  Aubrey, James R. *John Fowles* . . . , 113.
  Salami, Mahmoud. *John Fowles's Fiction* . . . , 154–157.

MARY E. WILKINS FREEMAN

"About Hannah Stone"
  Reichardt, Mary R. *A Web of Relationships* . . . , 120–122.
"Amanda and Love"
  Reichardt, Mary R. *A Web of Relationships* . . . , 116–117.
"Arethusa"
  Reichardt, Mary R. *A Web of Relationships* . . . , 95–96.
"The Buckley Lady"
  Reichardt, Mary R. *A Web of Relationships* . . . , 60–61.
  ———. " 'The Web of Self-Strangulation': Mothers, Daughters and
    the Question of Marriage in the Short Stories of Mary Wilkins
    Freeman," in Mink, JoAnna S., and James D. Ward, Eds. *Joinings
    and Disjoinings* . . . , 111–112.
"The Chance of Araminta"
  Reichardt, Mary R. *A Web of Relationships* . . . , 82–83.
"Emancipation"
  Reichardt, Mary R. *A Web of Relationships* . . . , 72.

"Gentian"
   Gardner, Kate. "The Subversion of Genre in the Short Stories of
   Mary Wilkins Freeman," *New England Q*, 65 (1992), 466–467.
"A Gentle Ghost"
   Reichardt, Mary R. *A Web of Relationships* . . . , 53–54.
   Wynne, Beth. "The 'Faces of Children That Had Never Been': Ghost
   Stories by Mary Wilkins Freeman," in Carpenter, Lynette, and
   Wendy K. Kolmar, Eds. *Haunting the House* . . . , 45–48.
"An Honest Soul"
   Romines, Ann. *The Home Plot* . . . , 97–101.
"The Horn of Plenty"
   Reichardt, Mary R. *A Web of Relationships* . . . , 89.
"A Humble Romance"
   Reichardt, Mary R. *A Web of Relationships* . . . , 79–80.
"Hyacinthus"
   Reichardt, Mary R. *A Web of Relationships* . . . , 67.
   ———. " 'The Web . . . ," 114–115.
"I Am a Rebel"
   Reichardt, Mary R. *A Web of Relationships* . . . , 127–129.
"In Butterfly Time"
   Gardner, Kate. "The Subversion . . . ," 457–458.
"An Independent Thinker"
   Gardner, Kate. "The Subversion . . . ," 456–457.
"Julia—Her Thanksgiving"
   Reichardt, Mary R. *A Web of Relationships* . . . , 109.
"Juliza"
   Reichardt, Mary R. *A Web of Relationships* . . . , 80–82.
"The Liar"
   Reichardt, Mary R. *A Web of Relationships* . . . , 108.
"The Little Maid at the Door"
   Wynne, Beth. "The 'Faces . . . ," 50–53.
"The Long Arm"
   Reichardt, Mary R. *A Web of Relationships* . . . , 109.
"The Lost Ghost"
   Wynne, Beth. "The 'Faces . . . ," 57–60.
"Louisa"
   Gardner, Kate. "The Subversion . . . ," 460–461.
   Reichardt, Mary R. *A Web of Relationships* . . . , 64–66.
   ———. " 'The Web . . . ," 114.
"Lydia Hersey of East Bridgewater"
   Reichardt, Mary R. *A Web of Relationships* . . . , 84, 85–86.
"A Modern Dragon"
   Reichardt, Mary R. *A Web of Relationships* . . . , 68, 69–70.
   ———. " 'The Web . . . ," 116–117.

"Mother-Wings"
    Reichardt, Mary R. *A Web of Relationships* . . . , 67–68.
    ———. " 'The Web . . . ,'' 115.
"A New England Nun"
    Brown, Lynda. "Anderson's Wing Biddlebaum and Freeman's
      Louisa Ellis," *Stud Short Fiction,* 27 (1990), 413–414.
    Cassill, R. V. . . . *Instructor's Handbook*, 72–73.
    Gardner, Kate. "The Subversion . . . ,'' 461–463.
    Reichardt, Mary R. *A Web of Relationships* . . . , 91–93.
    Romines, Ann. *The Home Plot* . . . , 102–106.
"A Patient Waiter"
    Reichardt, Mary R. *A Web of Relationships* . . . , 87–88.
"A Poetess"
    Gardner, Kate. "The Subversion . . . ,'' 447–448, 451–453, 454–456.
    Reichardt, Mary R. *A Web of Relationships* . . . , 144–145.
    Romines, Ann. *The Home Plot* . . . , 112–115.
    Wynne, Beth. "The 'Faces . . . ,'' 49–50.
"The Prism"
    Reichardt, Mary R. *A Web of Relationships* . . . , 94–95.
"The Revolt of Mother"
    Cutter, Martha J. "Frontiers of Language: Engendering Discourse in
      'The Revolt of Mother,' " *Am Lit,* 63 (1991), 279–291.
    Keating, Helane L., and Walter Levy. *Instructor's Manual: Lives*
      Through Literature . . . , 113.
    Orr, Elaine. "Reading Negotiation and Negotiated Reading: A
      Practice with/in 'A White Heron' and 'The Revolt of Mother,' "
      CEA Critic, 53, iii (1991), 49–51, 56–65.
    +Charters, Ann, and William E. Sheidley. *Resources for Teach-*
      ing . . . , 3rd ed., 78–79.
    Reichardt, Mary R. *A Web of Relationships* . . . , 48–53.
"The Secret"
    Reichardt, Mary R. *A Web of Relationships* . . . , 84–86.
"The Selfishness of Amelia Lamkin"
    Cutter, Martha J. "Beyond Stereotypes: Mary Wilkins Freeman's
      Radical Critique of Nineteenth-Century Cults of Femininity,"
      Women's Stud, 21, iv (1992), 383–395.
"Silence"
    Romines, Ann. *The Home Plot* . . . , 116–120.
"Sister Liddy"
    Reichardt, Mary R. *A Web of Relationships* . . . , 113–114.
"A Tardy Thanksgiving"
    Romines, Ann. *The Home Plot* . . . , 92–97.
"A Tragedy of the Trivial"
    Reichardt, Mary R. *A Web of Relationships* . . . , 96–97.
"Up Primrose Hill"
    Reichardt, Mary R. " 'The Web . . . ,'' 113–114.

"A Village Singer"
 Gardner, Kate. "The Subversion . . . ," 447–448, 451–453, 454–456, 459.
 Reichardt, Mary R. *A Web of Relationships* . . . , 145–150.
"The Willow-Ware"
 Romines, Ann. *The Home Plot* . . . , 120–125.
"The Wind in the Rose Bush"
 Wynne, Beth. "The 'Faces . . . ," 55–57.
"The Witch's Daughter"
 Reichardt, Mary R. " 'The Web . . . ," 116.

ALICIA FREILICH

"Colombina descubierta"
 Cunha-Giabbai, Gloria de. "Encubrimiento/Descubrimiento de la historia: 'Colombina descubierta' de Alicia Freilich," *Monographic R*, 8 (1992), 273–279.

LAURA FREIXAS

"My Momma Spoils Me"
 Squier, Susan M. "Fetal Voices: Speaking for the Margins Within," *Tulsa Stud Women's Lit*, 10, i (1991), 23–27.

RICARDO JAIME FREYRE

"En las montañas"
 Scott, Robert. "The Visual Artistry of Ricardo Jaimes Freyre's 'En las montañas,' " *Stud Short Fiction*, 28 (1991), 195–201.

CARLOS FUENTES

"Aura"
 García Núñez, Fernando. "La poética narrativa de Carlos Fuentes," *Bull Hispanique*, 94, i (1992), 264–272.
"The Doll Queen"
 Charters, Ann, and William E. Sheidley. *Resources for Teaching* . . . , 3rd ed., 80–81.
"El prisionero de las lomas"
 García, Audry E. " 'El prisionero de las lomas': Pistas para el desengaño," *Romance Lang Annual*, 3 (1991), 444–448.
"The Two Helens"
 Gonçalves, Gracia R. "The Myth of Helen and Her Two Husbands: Ferreira and Fuentes Mirroring Their Selves," *Monographic R*, 7 (1991), 317–318, 321–323.

Pérez de Mendiola, Marina. "Carlos Fuentes y la representación del 'sistema genérico/sexual,' " *Chasqui,* 20, ii (1991), 103–104.

FÜRUZAN

"The Girl from the Provinces"
Bertram, Carel. "Genderized Space in the Modern Turkish Short Story," *Turkish Stud Assn Bull,* 16 (1992), 29–30.

ERNEST GAINES

"Bloodline"
Gaudet, Marcia. "The Failure of Traditional Religion in Ernest Gaines' Short Stories," *J Short Story Engl,* 18 (Spring, 1992), 84–85.

"Boy in a Double-Breasted Suit"
Gaudet, Marcia. "The Failure . . . ," 82.

"Just Like a Tree"
Gaudet, Marcia. "The Failure . . . ," 85–86.

"A Long Day in November"
Doyle, Mary E. "The Best of *Bloodline,* 'Camcorder' Narration in Two Short Stories by Ernest Gaines," *J Short Story Engl,* 18 (Spring, 1992), 64–69.
Gaudet, Marcia. "The Failure . . . ," 82–83.

"The Sky Is Gray"
Doyle, Mary E. "The Best . . . ," 64–68.
Gaudet, Marcia. "The Failure . . . ," 83–84.

"Three Men"
Gaudet, Marcia. "The Failure . . . ," 84.

GAKAARDA WA WANJAŪ

"Nobody Learns His Lesson Through Another's Mistakes"
Biersteker, Ann. "An Alternative East Afrikan Voice: The Wa-Nduuta Stories of Gakaarda wa Wanjaū," *Research African Lit,* 22, iv (1991), 65–68.

"Wa-Nduuta Gets in Trouble"
Biersteker, Ann. "An Alternative . . . ," 68–70.

"Wa-Nduuta: The Time of 'Power' "
Biersteker, Ann. "An Alternative . . . ," 70–74.

MAVIS GALLANT

"About Geneva"
Siemerling, Winfried. "Perception, Memory, Irony: Mavis Gallant

Greets Proust and Flaubert," *Essays Canadian Writing*, 42 (1990), 144–145.
Smythe, Karen. *Figuring Grief . . .* , 34–35.

"An Alien Flower"
Smythe, Karen. *Figuring Grief . . .* , 102–104.

"An Autobiography"
Smythe, Karen. *Figuring Grief . . .* , 97–100.

"Baum, Gabriel—"
Smythe, Karen. *Figuring Grief . . .* , 87–89.

"Bernadette"
Smythe, Karen. *Figuring Grief . . .* , 39–40.

"Between Zero and One"
Regan, Stephen. " 'The Presence of the Past': Modernism and Postmodernism in Canadian Short Fiction," in Howells, Coral A., and Lynette Hunter, Eds. *Narrative Strategies . . .* , 116, 117–118.

"An Emergency Case"
Smythe, Karen. *Figuring Grief . . .* , 36–37.

"The End of the World"
Smythe, Karen. *Figuring Grief . . .* , 37–38.

"From the Fifteenth District"
Smythe, Karen. *Figuring Grief . . .* , 80.

"Grippes and Poche"
Siemerling, Winfried. "Perception . . . ," 131–132, 152.

"The Ice Wagon Going Down the Street"
Smythe, Karen. *Figuring Grief . . .* , 41–43.

"In Transit"
Smythe, Karen. *Figuring Grief . . .* , 56–57.

"In Youth Is Pleasure"
Regan, Stephen. " 'The Presence . . . ," 116–117.

"Its Image on the Mirror"
Smythe, Karen. *Figuring Grief . . .* , 43–50.

"My Heart Is Broken"
Cassill, R. V. . . . *Instructor's Handbook*, 74.

"The Moabitess"
Smythe, Karen. *Figuring Grief . . .* , 40–41.

"The Moslem Wife"
Smythe, Karen. *Figuring Grief . . .* , 82–85.

"O Lasting Peace"
Smythe, Karen. *Figuring Grief . . .* , 100–102.

"The Other Paris"
Siemerling, Winfried. "Perception . . . ," 140–143.

"Overheard in a Balloon"
Smythe, Karen. *Figuring Grief . . .* , 77–79.

"The Pegnitz Junction"
Smythe, Karen. *Figuring Grief* . . . , 90–97.
"The Remission"
Smythe, Karen. *Figuring Grief* . . . , 85–87.
"Speck's Idea"
Smythe, Karen. *Figuring Grief* . . . , 76–77.
"Varieties of Exile"
Regan, Stephen. " 'The Presence . . . ," 118–119.
"Virus X"
Keefer, Janice K. "Bridges and Chasmus: Multiculturalism and Mavis Gallant's 'Virus X,' " *World Lit Written Engl*, 31, ii (1991), 100–111.
"Wing's Chips"
Smythe, Karen. *Figuring Grief* . . . , 31–34.

JOHN GALSWORTHY

"The Japanese Quince"
Coleman, William G. "The Chatmanese Quince: In Search of Kernal Consensus, A Critical Analysis," *Language Q*, 30, i-ii (1992), 62–76.
Lanier, Doris. "The Blackbird in John Galsworthy's 'The Japanese Quince,' " *Engl Lang Notes*, 30 (1992), 57–62.

FANNY GARCIA

"Teacher"
Lucero, Rosario Cruz. "The Philippine Short Story, 1981–1990: The Voice of the Self-Authenticating Other," *Tenggara*, 26 (1990), 78–79.

GABRIEL GARCÍA MÁRQUEZ

"Artificial Roses"
Keating, Helane L., and Walter Levy. *Instructor's Manual: Lives Through Literature* . . . , 5–6.
Oberhelman, Harley D. . . . *A Study of the Short Fiction,* 30–31.
"Balthazar's Wonderful Afternoon"
Oberhelman, Harley D. . . . *A Study of the Short Fiction,* 24–27.
"Big Mama's Funeral"
Clark, John R. *The Modern Satiric Grotesque* . . . , 100–101.
Oberhelman, Harley D. . . . *A Study of the Short Fiction,* 31–35.
"Blacamán the Good, Vendor of Miracles"
Oberhelman, Harley D. . . . *A Study of the Short Fiction,* 46–48.
"Death Constant Beyond Love"
Oberhelman, Harley D. . . . *A Study of the Short Fiction,* 42–44.

"The Handsomest Drowned Man in the World"
+ Cassill, R. V. . . . *Instructor's Handbook*, 75–76.
Friedman, Mary L. "The Paradigm of the Outsider in the Work of Gabriel García Márquez," in Gascón-Vera, Elena, and Joy Renjilian-Burgy, Eds. *Justina* . . . , 149–150.
Oberhelman, Harley D. . . . *A Study of the Short Fiction*, 40–42.

"The Incredible and Sad Tale of Innocent Eréndira and Her Heartless Grandmother"
Beesley, Frank. "The Battle for Eréndira: Reason vs. Procreative Force in García Márquez's 'La cándida Eréndira,' " *Chasqui*, 20, ii (1991), 20–29.
Oberhelman, Harley D. . . . *A Study of the Short Fiction*, 48–52.

"The Last Voyage of the Ghost Ship"
Oberhelman, Harley D. . . . *A Study of the Short Fiction*, 44–46.

"Montiel's Widow"
Oberhelman, Harley D. . . . *A Study of the Short Fiction*, 27–28.

"The Night of the Curlews"
Carvalho, Susan. "Origins of Social Pessimism in García Márquez: 'The Night of the Curlews,' " *Stud Short Fiction*, 28 (1991), 334–337.

"One Day After Saturday"
Friedman, Mary L. "The Paradigm . . . ," 144–147.
Oberhelman, Harley D. . . . *A Study of the Short Fiction*, 28–30.

"One of These Days"
Oberhelman, Harley D. . . . *A Study of the Short Fiction*, 22–23.

"El rastro de tu sangre sobre la nieve"
Palls, Terry L. "La Alusión y la naturaleza intertextual de 'El rastro de tu sangre sobre la nieve' de Gabriel García Márquez," *Siglo*, 9, i-ii (1991–1992), 135–149.

"The Sea of Lost Time"
Oberhelman, Harley D. . . . *A Study of the Short Fiction*, 39–40.

"There Are No Thieves in This Town"
Oberhelman, Harley D. . . . *A Study of the Short Fiction*, 23–24.

"Tuesday Siesta"
+ Bohner, Charles H. *Instructor's Manual* . . . , 44–45.
Friedman, Mary L. "The Paradigm . . . ," 142–143.
Oberhelman, Harley D. . . . *A Study of the Short Fiction*, 20–22.

"El verano feliz de la señora Forbes"
Neustadt, Bob. "Borges y García Márquez: Paralelismos narrativos," *Confluencia*, 7, i (1991), 82, 83–84, 85, 86.

"A Very Old Man with Enormous Wings"
+ Charters, Ann, and William E. Sheidley. *Resources for Teaching* . . . , 3rd ed., 82–83.
Friedman, Mary L. "The Paradigm . . . ," 142–143.
Oberhelman, Harley D. . . . *A Study of the Short Fiction*, 37–39.

ADELAIDA GARCÍA MORALES

"Bene"
Mazquiarán de Rodríguez, Mercedes. "Gothic Imagery, Dreams, and
Vampirism: The Haunting Narrative of Adelaida García Morales,"
Monographic R, 8 (1992), 167–170.
"El sur"
Mazquiarán de Rodríguez, Mercedes. "Gothic . . . ," 165–167.

ENRIQUE GARCÍA VELLOSO

"La casa de la soltera"
Masiello, Francine. *Between Civilization* . . . , 170–171.

JOHN GARDNER

"The King's Indian"
Winther, Per. *The Art of John Gardner*, 78–82, 94–95, 100–101,
114–118, 136–142.
"Nimram"
Winther, Per. *The Art of John Gardner*, 10–12.
"Redemption"
Winther, Per. *The Art of John Gardner*, 12–16.
"Vlemk, the Box Painter"
Winther, Per. *The Art of John Gardner*, 25–27, 76–77.

HAMLIN GARLAND

"A Branch Road"
Weber, Ronald. *The Midwestern* . . . , 43–44, 45.
"A Day's Pleasure"
Weber, Ronald. *The Midwestern* . . . , 45–46.
"The Return of a Private"
Weber, Ronald. *The Midwestern* . . . , 44–45.
"Under the Lion's Paw"
Weber, Ronald. *The Midwestern* . . . , 41–42.
"Up the Coule"
Weber, Ronald. *The Midwestern* . . . , 42–43.

ELENA GARRO

"El anillo"
Rojas-Trempe, Lady. "La ronda mágica y la palabra del deseo,"
Lenguas, Literaturas, Sociedades, 3 (1990), 138–142.

"El árbol"
   Rojas-Trempe, Lady. "La alteridad indígena y mágica en la narrativa
   de Elena Garro, Manuel Scorza y Gioconda Belli," *Alba de
   América*, 9 (1991), 141–144, 146, 148–149, 152.

"La culpa es de los tlaxcaltecas"
   Fox-Lockert, Lucía. "El discurso femenino en los cuentos de Rosario
   Ferré y de Elena Garro," in Erro-Orthmann, Nora, and Juan Cruz
   Mendizábal, Eds. *La escritora* . . . , 85–87.
   González, José Ramón. "Estrategias discursivas y relato fantástico:
   Sobre 'La culpa es de los tlaxcaltecas' de Elena Garro," *Torre*, 5,
   xx (October-December, 1991), 475–488.

"El día que fuimos perros"
   San Pedro, Teresa. "El acto de nombrar en el cuento de Elena Garro:
   'El día que fuimos perros,' " *Explicación de Textos Literarios*, 19,
   i (1990–1991), 17–26.

"El Duende"
   Duncan, Cynthia. "Narrative Tension and Perpetual Subversion in
   Elena Garro's Short Fiction," *Letras Femeninas*, 15, i-ii (1989),
   13–16.

"La semana de colores"
   Duncan, Cynthia. "Narrative Tension . . . ," 16–19.
   Rojas-Trempe, Lady. "La ronda mágica . . . ," 142–148.

WILLIAM GASS

"The Clairvoyant"
   Wilson, Lucy. "Alternatives to Transcendence in William Gass's
   Short Fiction," *R Contemp Fiction*, 11, iii (1991), 82–83.

"I Wish You Wouldn't"
   Wilson, Lucy. "Alternatives to Transcendence . . . ," 84–86.

"Icicles"
   Wilson, Lucy. "Alternatives to Transcendence . . . ," 79–81.

"In the Heart of the Heart of the Country"
   Maniez, Claire. "The World Within the Words of William H. Gass's
   'In the Heart of the Heart of the Country," *Études Anglaises*, 45, i
   (1992), 27–37.

"Order of Insects"
   Stavans, Ilan. "Kafka, Cortázar, Gass," *R Contemp Fiction*, 11, iii
   (1991), 133–134.
   Wilson, Lucy. "Alternatives to Transcendence . . . ," 81–82.

"The Sugar Crock"
   Schneider, Richard J. "Rejecting the Stone: William Gass and
   Emersonian Transcendence," *R Contemp Fiction*, 11, iii (1991),
   116–119.
   Wilson, Lucy. "Alternatives to Transcendence . . . ," 83–84.

"The Pedersen Kid"
Dettman, Kevin J. H. "''yung and easily freudened': William Gass's
'The Pedersen Kid,' " R Contemp Fiction, 11, iii (1991), 88–101.
Eckford-Prossor, Melanie. "Layered Apparitions: Philosophy and
'The Pedersen Kid,' " R Contemp Fiction, 11, iii (1991), 102–114.

THÉOPHILE GAUTIER

"Arria Marcella"
Crichfield, Grant. "Fantasmagoria and Optics in Théophile Gautier's
'Arria Marcella,' " in Saciuk, Olena H., Ed. The Shape . . . , 85–92.
"Fortunio"
Lacoste, Claudine. "La Femme orientale vue et rêvée par le poète,"
Bull de la Soc Théophile Gautier, 1, xii (1990), 11–16.
"La Morte Amoureuse"
Cummiskey, Gary. The Changing . . . , 69–74.
"Onuphrius"
Cummiskey, Gary. The Changing . . . , 74–78.
"Spirite"
Crichfield, Grant. "Fantasmagoria . . . ," 155–161.
Lefebvre, Anne-Marie. " 'Spirite' à la lumière de l'Orient," Bull de
la Soc Théophile Gautier, 1, xii (1990), 233–250.

JOSEPH GEHA

"Almost Thirty"
Safie, Doris. "Joseph Geha's Toledo Stories," Paintbrush, 18
(Spring, 1991), 81.
"Everything, Everything"
Safie, Doris. "Joseph Geha's . . . ," 81–82.
"Through and Through"
Robb, Kenneth A. "The Fading Narrator in Joseph Geha's 'Through
and Through,' " Notes Contemp Lit, 22, iii (1992), 9–11.

WILLIAM GIBSON

"Burning Chrome"
McGuirk, Carol. "The 'New' Romancers: Science Fiction Innovators
from Gernsback to Gibson" in Slusser, George, and Tom Shippey,
Eds. Fiction 2000 . . . , 113, 114.
Slusser, George. "The Frankenstein Barrier," in Slusser, George,
and Tom Shippey, Eds. Fiction 2000 . . . , 68–69.
"The Gernsback Continuum"
McGuirk, Carol. "The 'New' Romancers . . . ," 111–112.
Shippey, Tom. "Semiotic Ghosts and Ghostliness in the Work of

Bruce Sterling," in Slusser, George, and Tom Shippey, Eds. *Fiction 2000* . . . , 210–211, 212.

Westfahl, Gary. " 'The Gernsback Continuum': William Gibson in the Context of Science Fiction," in Slusser, George, and Tom Shippey, Eds. *Fiction 2000* . . . , 89–90.

ANDRÉ GIDE

"El Hadj"
Pollard, Patrick. *André Gide* . . . , 319–322.

"The Immoralist"
Pollard, Patrick. *André Gide* . . . , 350–365.

ELLEN GILCHRIST

"The Last Diet"
Smith, Virginia. "Proust's Mother, Food and Contemporary Southern Women's Fiction," *Southern Q*, 30, ii-iii (1992), 49.

"Traceless at Dawn"
Smith, Virginia. "Proust's Mother . . . ," 49–50.

"Traveler"
Cassill, R. V. . . . *Instructor's Handbook*, 76–77.

ZENY GILES

"Telling Tales"
Gunew, Sneja. "Authentic Self-Representation and the Temptations of Irony in Recent Australian Migrant (non Anglo-Celtic) Women's Writing," *R Japanese Culture & Soc*, 4 December, 1991, 13.

CHARLOTTE PERKINS GILMAN

"The Girl in the Pink Hat"
Masse, Michelle A. *In the Name of Love* . . . , 267–269, 272–273.

"Through This"
Knight, Denise D. "The Reincarnation of Jane: 'Through This'—Gilman's Companion to 'The Yellow Wallpaper,' " *Women's Stud*, 20, iii-iv (1992), 289–298.

"The Yellow Wallpaper"
Ammons, Elizabeth. *Conflicting Stories* . . . , 34–43.
+Bohner, Charles H. *Instructor's Manual* . . . , 45–46.
Boyles, Mary. "Woman: The Inside Outsider," in Crafton, John M., Ed. *Selected Essays* . . . , 121–123.
Chandler, Marilyn R. *Dwelling in the Text* . . . , 139–147.
+Charters, Ann, and William E. Sheidley. *Resources for Teaching* . . . , 3rd ed., 84–85.

De Koven, Marianne. *Rich and Strange* . . . , 39–47.

Hume, Beverly A. "Gilman's 'Interminable Grotesque': The Narrator of 'The Yellow Wallpaper,' " *Stud Short Fiction*, 28 (1991), 477–484.

Johnston, Georgia. "Exploring Lack and Absence in the Body/Text: Charlotte Perkins Gilman Prewriting Irigaray," *Women's Stud*, 21, i (1992), 75–86.

Long, Charles. "Gilman's 'The Yellow Wallpaper,' " *Explicator,* 50, i (1991), 32–33.

Masse, Michelle A. *In the Name of Love* . . . , 29–39.

Owens, E. Suzanne. "The Ghostly Double Behind the Wallpaper in Charlotte Perkins Gilman's 'The Yellow Wallpaper,' " in Carpenter, Lynette, and Wendy K. Kolmar, Eds. *Haunting the House of Fiction* . . . , 64–79.

Robinson, Fred M. *Comic Moments*, 93–97.

Shumaker, Conrad. "Realism, Reform, and the Audience: Charlotte Perkins Gilman's Unreadable Wallpaper," *Arizona Q*, 47, i (1991), 87–92.

Wardley, Lynn. "Relic, Fetish, Femmage: The Aesthetics of Sentiment in the Work of Stowe," in Samuels, Shirley, Ed. *The Culture of Sentiment* . . . , 218–220.

Wiesenthal, C. S. " 'Unheard-of Contradictions': The Language of Madness in C. P. Gilman's 'The Yellow Wallpaper,' " *Wascana R*, 25, ii (1990), 1–17.

ELLEN GLASGOW

"Dare's Gift"
Carpenter, Lynette. "Visions of Female Community in Ellen Glasgow's Ghost Stories," in Carpenter, Lynette, and Wendy K. Kolmar, Eds. *Haunting the House of Fiction* . . . , 125–126.

"The Past"
Carpenter, Lynette. "Visions . . . ," 126–127, 130–132.

"The Shadowy Third"
Carpenter, Lynette. "Visions . . . ," 120–125, 136–137.

"Whispering Leaves"
Carpenter, Lynette. "Visions . . . ," 132–136.

ELLEN GODFREY

"Common or Garden Murder"
Škvorecký, Josef. "Detective Stories: Some Notes on the *Fingerprint*," in Friedland, M. L., Ed. *Rough Justice* . . . , 243–244.

NIKOLAI GOGOL

"The Diary of a Madman"
Weiskopf, Mikhail. "The Bird Troika and the Chariot of the Soul:

Plato and Gogol," in Fusso, Susanne, and Priscilla Meyer, Eds. *Essays on Gogol* . . . , 132–133.

"A May Night"
  Meyer, Priscilla. "False Pretenders and the Spiritual City: 'A May Night' and 'The Overcoat,' " in Fusso, Susanne, and Priscilla Meyer, Eds. *Essays on Gogol* . . . , 65–72.

"The Nose"
  Bocharov, Sergei. "Around 'The Nose,' " in Fusso, Susanne, and Priscilla Meyer, Eds. *Essays on Gogol* . . . , 19–39.
  Morson, Gary S. "Gogol's Parables of Explanation: Nonsense and Prosaics," in Fusso, Susanne, and Priscilla Meyer, Eds. *Essays on Gogol* . . . , 226–233.
  Terras, Victor. *A History of Russian Literature*, 258–259.

"The Overcoat"
  +Bohner, Charles H. *Instructor's Manual* . . . , 46–47.
  Brombert, Victor. "Meanings and Indeterminacy in Gogol's 'The Overcoat,' " in Toumayan, Alain, Ed. *Literary Generations* . . . , 48–54.
  +Charters, Ann, and William E. Sheidley. *Resources for Teaching* . . . , 3rd ed., 87–88.
  Meyer, Priscilla. "False Pretenders . . . ," 68–74.
  Terras, Victor. *A History of Russian Literature*, 259.

"Old-World Landowners"
  Kornblatt, Judith D. *The Cossack Hero* . . . , 58.

"The Portrait"
  Jackson, Robert L. "Gogol's 'The Portrait': The Simultaneity of Madness, Naturalism, and the Supernatural," in Fusso, Susanne, and Priscilla Meyer, Ed. *Essays on Gogol* . . . , 105–111.
  Waszink, Paul M. "Artist, Writer and Peircean Interpretant: Some Observations on Russian Nineteenth-Century Art and Literature," *Zeitschrift für Slavische Philologie*, 50 (1990), 315–318.

"The Tale of How Ivan Ivanovich Quarreled with Ivan Nikiforovich"
  Kornblatt, Judith D. *The Cossack Hero* . . . , 59.

"Starosvetkie pomeshchiki"
  Kornblatt, Judith D. "Gogol and the Muses of *Mirgorod*," *Slavic R*, 50 (1991), 311–312.

"Taras Bulba"
  Kornblatt, Judith D. "Gogol . . . ," 313–316.

"Viy"
  Kornblatt, Judith D. "Gogol . . . ," 312–313.

WILLIAM GOLDING

"Clonk, Clonk"
  D'Amelio, Nadia. "Equivocation in *The Scorpion God*," in Delbaere, Jeanne, Ed. *William Golding* . . . , 116, 120–121.

"Envoy Extraordinary"
D'Amelio, Nadia. "Equivocation . . . ," 116–117, 121–122.

"The Inheritors"
Adriaens, Mark. "Style in 'The Inheritors,' in Delbaere, Jeanne, Ed. *William Golding* . . . , 45–60.

Delbaere, Jeanne. "Lok-Lik-Log: Structure and Imagery in 'The Inheritors,' " in Delbaere, Jeanne, Ed. *William Golding* . . . , 61–73.

François, Pierre. "The Rule of Oa in 'The Inheritors,' " in Delbaere, Jeanne, Ed. *William Golding* . . . , 74–83.

"The Scorpion God"
D'Amelio, Nadia. "Equivocation . . . ," 116, 117–120.

REBECCA GOLDSTEIN

"The Legacy of Raizel Kaidish"
Klingenstein, Susanne. "Destructive Intimacy: The Shoah between Mother and Daughter in Fictions by Cynthia Ozick, Norma Rosen, and Rebecca Goldstein," *Stud Am Jewish Lit*, 11 (1992), 169–171.

JOSÉ LUIS GONZÁLEZ

"En el fondo del caño hay un negrito"
Sanabria Santaliz, Edgardo. "Testimonio del cuento al cuento," *Cupey*, 6, i-ii (1989), 49–52.

N. V. M. GONZALEZ

"Far Horizons"
Campomanes, Oscar V. "Filipinos in the United States and Their Literature of Exile," in Lim, Shirley G., and Amy Ling, Eds. *Reading the Literatures* . . . , 66–67.

ALLEGRA GOODMAN

"Onionskin"
Pinsker, Sanford. "Satire, Social Realism, and Moral Seriousness: The Case of Allegra Goodman," *Stud Am Jewish Lit*, 11, ii (1992), 192–193.

"Oral History"
Pinsker, Sanford. "Satire . . . ," 184–185, 185–186.

"The Succession"
Pinsker, Sanford. "Satire . . . ," 189–191.

"Total Immersion"
Pinsker, Sanford. "Satire . . . ," 193.

"The Wedding of Henry Markowitz"
   Pinsker, Sanford. "Satire . . . ," 188–189.
"Wish List"
   Pinsker, Sanford. "Satire . . . ," 186–188.

NADINE GORDIMER

"Ah, Woe Is Me"
   Smith, Roland. "Masters and Servants: Nadine Gordimer's *July's People* and the Themes of Her Fiction," in Smith, Roland, Ed. *Critical Essays* . . . , 145–146.
"Blinder"
   Lazar, Karen. "Feminism as 'piffling'? Ambiguities in Some of Nadine Gordimer's Short Stories," *Current Writing* 2, i (1990), 108–109.
"The Bridegroom"
   Driver, Dorothy. "Nadine Gordimer: The Politicisation of Women," in Smith, Roland, Ed. *Critical Essays* . . . , 191–192.
"The Catch"
   Magarey, Kevin. "Cutting the Jewel: Facets of Art in Nadine Gordimer's Short Stories," in Smith, Roland, Ed. *Critical Essays* . . . , 50–51.
"Check Yes or No"
   Magarey, Kevin. "Cutting the Jewel . . . ," 55–56.
"A Chip of Glass Ruby"
   Lazar, Karen. "Feminism . . . ," 110–111.
"A Company of Laughing Faces"
   Wilkinson, Jane. "Feasting to Death: 'Garden Party' Variations," in Bardolph, Jacquelin, Ed. *Short Fiction* . . . , 23–25.
"Friday's Footprint"
   Magarey, Kevin. "Cutting the Jewel . . . ," 62–69.
"Good Climate, Friendly Inhabitants"
   Lazar, Karen. "Feminism . . . ," 106–108.
"Happy Event"
   Lazar, Karen. "Feminism . . . ," 105–106.
"An Intruder"
   Driver, Dorothy. "Nadine Gordimer . . . ," 192–195.
   Lazar, Karen. "Feminism . . . ," 111–113.
"Is There Nowhere Else Where We Can Meet?"
   Smith, Roland. "Masters and Servants . . . ," 143–144.
   Clingman, Stephen. "Deep History," in Smith, Roland, Ed. *Critical Essays* . . . , 210–211.
"The Life of the Imagination"
   Bohner, Charles H. *Instructor's Manual* . . . , 48–49.

"Message in a Bottle"
Magarey, Kevin. "Cutting the Jewel . . . ," 60–61.

"Six Feet of the Country"
Driver, Dorothy. "Nadine Gordimer . . . ," 191.

"The Soft Voice of the Serpent"
Magarey, Kevin. "Cutting the Jewel . . . ," 49–50.

"Some Monday For Sure"
Magarey, Kevin. "Cutting the Jewel . . . ," 47–48.

"Something Out There"
Lazar, Karen R. " 'Something Out There'/Something In There:
Gender and Politics in Gordimer's Novella," *Engl Africa*, 19, i
(1992), 53–65.

"A Style of Her Own"
Magarey, Kevin. "Cutting the Jewel . . . ," 57–59.

"The Termitary"
Lazar, Karen. "Feminism . . . ," 113–114.

"A Third Presence"
Keating, Helane L., and Walter Levy. *Instructor's Manual: Lives
Through Literature . . .* , 35.
Lazar, Karen. "Feminism . . . ," 104–105.

"Town and Country Lovers"
+ Charters, Ann, and William E. Sheidley. *Resources for Teaching . . .* , 3rd ed., 89–91.

"Which New Era Would That Be?"
Driver, Dorothy. "Nadine Gordimer . . . ," 197–198.

CAROLINE GORDON

"Cock-Crow"
Henderson, Kathleen B. "Sketches for an Unfinished Portrait:
Autobiography and Fiction in Caroline Gordon's Last Published
Stories," *J Short Story Engl*, 18 (Spring, 1992), 95–96.

"A Narrow Heart"
Henderson, Kathleen B. "Sketches . . . ," 93–94.

"A Visit to the Grove"
Henderson, Kathleen B. "Sketches . . . ," 99–101.

ANGÉLICA GORODISCHER

"La perfecta cadada"
Eberle-McCarthy, Karen. "Worlds Within Argentine Women," in
Erro-Orthmann, Nora, and Juan Cruz Mendizábal, Eds. *La
escritora . . .* , 237–242.

MAXIM GORKY

"The Cemetery"
  Scherr, Barry. "Impressions of a Transient: The Meandering
  Gor'kij," *Russian, Croatian*, 29 (1991), 463–464.

"The Deceased"
  Scherr, Barry. "Impressions . . . ," 463, 464.

"My Fellow Traveller"
  Barratt, Andrew. "Gorky's 'My Fellow Traveller': Parable and
  Metaphor," in Elsworth, John, Ed. *The Silver Age* . . . , 136–155.

JUANA MANUELA GORRITI

"El lucero del manantial"
  Masiello, Francine. *Between Civilization* . . . , 49.

"El pozo de Yocci"
  Masiello, Francine. *Between Civilization* . . . , 48–49.

"La Quena"
  Masiello, Francine. *Between Civilization* . . . , 50.

WILLIAM GOYEN

"In the Icebound Hothouse"
  Repusseau, Patrice. "Lunar Plexus: On William Goyen's 'In the
  Icebound Hothouse,' " *Mid-American R*, 13, i (1992), 9–38.

"The Road Runner in Woolworth's"
  Wilner, Eleanor. " 'The Road Runner in Woolworth's': An
  Appreciation," *Mid-American R*, 13, i (1992), 55–61.

ROBERT GRAVES

"The Shout"
  Beetz, Kirk H. "Robert Graves's Dilemma of the Storyteller:
  Multiple Narratives in 'The Shout,' " *Univ Mississippi Stud Engl*,
  10 (1992), 86–94.

GRAHAM GREENE

"The Basement Room"
  Kelly, Richard. *Graham Greene*, 151–153.

"A Chance for Mr. Lever"
  Kelly, Richard. *Graham Greene*, 154–155.

"Cheap in August"
  Kelly, Richard. *Graham Greene*, 162–164.

"A Day Saved"
  Colburn, Steven E. "Graham Greene's 'A Day Saved': A Modern
  Tale of Time and Identity," *Stud Short Fiction*, 29 (1992), 377–384.
"The Destructors"
  Kelly, Richard. *Graham Greene*, 145–147.
"Dream of a Strange Land"
  Kelly, Richard. *Graham Greene*, 158–159.
"A Drive in the Country"
  Kelly, Richard. *Graham Greene*, 147–148.
"The End of the Party"
  Kelly, Richard. *Graham Greene*, 150–151.
"The Hint of an Explanation"
  Kelly, Richard. *Graham Greene*, 153–154.
"I Spy"
  Kelly, Richard. *Graham Greene*, 149–150.
"A Little Place Off the Edgeware Road"
  Kelly, Richard. *Graham Greene*, 148–149.
"Two Gentle People"
  Bohner, Charles H. *Instructor's Manual . . .* , 49–50.
"Under the Garden"
  Kelly, Richard. *Graham Greene*, 156–158.

FRANZ GRILLPARZER

"The Poor Player"
  Mullan, Boyd. "Characterization and Narrative Technique in
  Grillparzer's 'Der arme Spielmann' and Storm's *Ein Stiller
  Musikant*," *Germ Life and Letters*, 44 (1991), 187–197.

ANGELINA WELD GRIMKE

"Blackness"
  Hirsch, David A. H. "Speaking Silences in Angelina Weld Grimke's
  'The Closing Door' and 'Blackness,' " *African Am R*, 26 (1992),
  466–472.
"The Closing Door"
  Hirsch, David A. H. "Speaking Silences . . . ," 462–466.
  Tate, Claudia. *Domestic Allegories . . .* , 215–216, 219–222.
"Goldie"
  Tate, Claudia. *Domestic Allegories . . .* , 216, 219–222.
"Jettisoned"
  Tate, Claudia. *Domestic Allegories . . .* , 216–217.

VASILY GROSSMAN

"Four Days"
  Nakhimovsky, Alice S. *Russian-Jewish Literature . . .* , 109–110.

"In the Town of Berdichev"
Nakhimovsky, Alice S. *Russian-Jewish Literature* . . . , 118–120.

BEATRICE GUIDO

"Usurpación"
Pita, Beatrice. "Manipulaciones del discurso femenino: 'Yo y la otra'
en 'Usurpación' de Beatriz Guido y 'Lejana' de Julio Cortázar,"
Crítica, 2, ii (1990), 78, 80–81, 82, 83.

JOE HALDEMAN

"More Than the Sum of His Parts"
Gordon, Joan. "Joe Haldeman: Cyberpunk Before Cyberpunk Was
Cool?" in Morse, Donald E., Marshall B. Tymn, and Csilla Bertha,
Eds. *The Celebration* . . . , 252.

DONALD HALL

"Argument and Persuasion"
Bohner, Charles H. *Instructor's Manual* . . . , 50–51.

ALBERT HALPER

"Scab!"
Hanley, Lawrence F. "Cultural Work and Class Politics: Re-reading
and Remaking *Proletarian Literature in the United States*," *Mod
Fiction Stud*, 38 (1992), 726.

PETER HANDKE

"Der Chinese des Schmerzes"
Barry, Thomas F. "Nazi Signs: Peter Handke's Reception of Austrian
Fascism," in Daviau, Donald G., Ed. *Austrian Writers* . . . ,
307–311.
Mahlendorf, Ursula R. "Confronting the Fascist Past and Coming to
Terms With It: Peter Handke's 'Der Chinese des Schmerzes,' " in
Daviau, Donald G., Ed. *Austrian Writers* . . . , 286–297.
"Die Linkshändige Frau"
Ingalsbe, Lori A. "Woman Beyond the Myth: A Feminist Reading of
Peter Handke's 'Linkshändige Frau,' " *New Germ R*, 7 (1991),
1–14.

BARRY HANNAH

"Behold the Husband in His Perfect Agony"
Seib, Kenneth. " 'Sabers, Gentlemen, Sabers': The J.E.B. Stuart
Stories of Barry Hannah," *Mississippi Q*, 45, i (1991–1992), 48–51.

"Dragged Fighting From His Tomb"
  Seib, Kenneth. " 'Sabers . . . ,'' 44–46.

"Knowing He Was Not My Kind Yet I Followed"
  Seib, Kenneth. " 'Sabers . . . ,'' 46–48.

THOMAS HARDY

"Destiny and a Blue Cloak"
  Dalziel, Pamela. "Introduction," *Thomas Hardy* . . . [by Thomas Hardy], 28.

"The Distracted Preacher"
  King, Kathryn. "Introduction," *Wessex Tales* [by Thomas Hardy], xviii.

"The Doctor's Legend"
  Dalziel, Pamela. "Introduction," 240.

"How I Built Myself a House"
  Dalziel, Pamela. "Introduction," 13–15.

"An Imaginative Woman"
  Pether, Penelope. "Hardy and the Law," *Thomas Hardy J*, 7, i (1991), 36–38.

"An Indiscretion in the Life of an Heiress"
  Dalziel, Pamela. "Introduction," 71–85.

"The Melancholy Hussar of the German Legion"
  Pether, Penelope. "Hardy . . . ," 38–40.

"On the Western Circuit"
  Pether, Penelope. "Hardy . . . ," 30, 31–32, 33–36.

"Our Exploits at West Poley"
  Dalziel, Pamela. "Introduction," 165–166.

"The Spectre and the Real"
  Dalziel, Pamela. "Introduction," 275–280.

"The Thieves Who Couldn't Help Sneezing"
  Dalziel, Pamela. "Introduction," 55–57.

"The Three Strangers"
  King, Kathryn. "Introduction," xviii-xix.

"Tony Kytes, the Arch-Deceiver"
  Bohner, Charles H. *Instructor's Manual* . . . , 51–52.

FRANCES ELLEN WATKINS HARPER

"The Two Offers"
  Scheick, William J. "Strategic Ellipsis in Harper's 'The Two Offers,' " *Southern Lit J*, 23, ii (1991), 14–18.

BRET HARTE

"The Outcasts of Poker Flat"
  Oriard, Michael. *Sporting with the Gods* . . . , 72–73.
"How Santa Claus Came to Simpson Bar"
  Kohl, Harold H. "The Outcast of Literary Flat: Bret Harte as
    Humorist," *Am Lit Realism,* 23, ii (1991), 59–61.

EPELI HAU'OFA

"Blessed Are The Meek"
  Ryan, J. S. "Epeli Hau'ofa's Polynesian Human Comedy," *New Lit
    R*, 20 (1990), 33–34.
"The Glorious Pacific Way"
  Ryan, J. S. "Epeli Hau'ofa's . . . ," 34–35.
"The Second Coming"
  Watts, Edward. "The Only Teller of Big Truths: Epeli Hau'ofe's
    Tales of the Tikongs and Biblical Contexts of Post-Colonialism,"
    Lit & Theology, 6, iv (1992), 376–378.
"The Seventh and Other Days"
  Watts, Edward. "The Only . . . ," 372.
"The Tower of Babel"
  Watts, Edward. "The Only . . . ," 374–376, 378, 379–380.

NATHANIEL HAWTHORNE

"Alice Doane's Appeal"
  Cooper, Allene. "The Discourse of Romance: Truth and Fantasy in
    Hawthorne's Point of View," *Stud Short Fiction*, 28 (1991),
    503–505.
  Millington, Richard H. *Practicing Romance* . . . , 33–40.
  Smith, S. McClure. "Void in the Narrative: The Seduction of the
    Reader in Nathaniel Hawthorne's 'Alice Doane's Appeal,' " *Am
    Transcendental Q*, N.S., 5 (1991), 73–82.
  Swann, Charles. *Nathaniel Hawthorne* . . . , 18–43.
"The Artist of the Beautiful"
  Bethea, Dean W. "Heat, Light, and the Darkening World:
    Hawthorne's 'The Artist of the Beautiful,' " *So Atlantic Q*, 56, iv
    (1991), 23–35.
  Cooper, Allene. "The Discourse . . . ," 501–503.
  Jones, E. Michael. *The Angel and the Machine* . . . , 134–135.
  Person, Leland S. "Hawthorne's Bliss of Paternity: Sophia's
    Absence from 'The Old Manse,' " *Stud Novel*, 23 (1991), 54–57.
  Stern, Milton R. *Contexts for Hawthorne* . . . , 51–54.
  Wentworth, Dean. "Heat, Light, and the Darkening World:
    Hawthorne's 'The Artist of the Beautiful,' " *So Atlantic R,* 56, iv
    (1991), 23–35.

+ Yoder, R. A. "Hawthorne and His Artist," in Frank, Albert J. von, Ed. *Critical Essays* . . . , 173–186.

"The Birthmark"
+ Bohner, Charles H. *Instructor's Manual* . . . , 53–54.
+ Cassill, R. V. . . . *Instructor's Handbook*, 79–80.
Jones, E. Michael. *The Angel and the Machine* . . . , 131–134.
Pfister, Joel. *The Production of Personal Life* . . . , 17–19.
Porte, Joel. *In Response to Egotism* . . . , 144–148.

"Drowne's Wooden Image"
Newberry, Frederick. "Fantasy, Reality, and Audience in Hawthorne's 'Drowne's Wooden Image,' " *Stud Novel*, 23 (1991), 28–45.

"Egotism; or, The Bosom Serpent"
Pfister, Joel. *The Production of Personal Life* . . . , 31–33.

"Edward Randolph's Portrait"
Smith, Geoffrey D. "The Reluctant Democrat and the Amiable Whig: Nathaniel Hawthorne, Edmund Quincy and the Politics of History," *Nathaniel Hawthorne R*, 18, ii (1992), 12.

"Endicott and the Red Cross"
Koreneva, Maya. "The Romantic Poetics of Hawthorne," in Chakovsky, Sergei, and M. Thomas Inge, Eds. *Russian Eyes* . . . , 27–29.

"Ethan Brand"
Eisen, Kurt. "The Tragical History of Ethan Brand," *Essays Lit*, 19, i (1992), 55–60.
Swann, Charles. *Nathaniel Hawthorne* . . . , 54–62.

"Feathertop"
Elbert, Monika M. "Hawthorne's 'Hollow Men: Fabricating Masculinity in 'Feathertop,' " *Am Transcendental Q*, N.S., 5 (1991), 169–182.

"The Hall of Fantasy"
Jones, E. Michael. *The Angel and the Machine* . . . , 129–130.

"The Haunted Mind"
Selzer, Linda F. "Beyond Anxiety and Wishfulfillment: 'The Haunted Mind' as Public Meditation," *Nathaniel Hawthorne R*, 16, ii (1990), 1, 3–6.

"Howe's Masquerade"
Smith, Geoffrey D. "The Reluctant . . . ," 10.

"Lady Eleanore's Mantle"
Boyd, Richard. "Mimetic Desire and the American Revolution: Hawthorne's 'Lady Eleanore's Mantle,' " *Univ Hartford Stud Lit*, 22, ii-iii (1990), 23–43.
Smith, Geoffrey D. "The Reluctant . . . ," 12, 13.

"The Maypole of Merry Mount"
+ Leavis, Q. D. "Hawthorne as Poet," in Frank, Albert J. von, Ed. *Critical Essays* . . . , 96–102.

"The Minister's Black Veil"
 Freedman, William. "The Artist's Symbol and Hawthorne's Veil:
  'The Minister's Black Veil' *Resartus*," *Stud Short Fiction*, 29
  (1992), 353–362.
 Millington, Richard H. *Practicing Romance* . . . , 29–32.
 Porte, Joel. *In Response to Egotism* . . . , 139–144.
 + Stibitz, E. Earle. "Ironic Unity in Hawthorne's 'The Minister's
  Black Veil,' " in Frank, Albert J. von, Ed. *Critical Essays* . . . ,
  157–164.

"Monsieur du Miroir"
 Richards, Sylvie L. F. "Nathaniel Hawthorne's 'Monsieur du Miroir'
  Through Jacques Lacan's Looking Glass," *Nathaniel Hawthorne
  R*, 18, i (1992), 15–20.

"My Kinsman, Major Molineux"
 Charters, Ann, and William E. Sheidley. *Resources for Teach-
  ing* . . . , 3rd ed., 92–93.
 Millington, Richard H. *Practicing Romance* . . . , 40–41.
 Herbert, T. Walter. "Doing Cultural Work: 'My Kinsman, Major
  Molineux' and the Construction of the Self-Made Man," *Stud
  Novel*, 23 (1991), 23–26.

"Old Esther Dudley"
 Smith, Geoffrey D. "The Reluctant . . . ," 12–13.

"Rappaccini's Daughter"
 Baris, Sharon D. "Giovanni's Garden: Hawthorne's Hope for
  America," *Mod Lang Stud*, 12, iv (1982), 75–90.
 Cooper, Allene. "The Discourse . . . ," 475–501.
 Leavy, Barbara F. *To Blight With Plague* . . . , 168–183.
 Jones, E. Michael. *The Angel and the Machine* . . . , 136–137.
 Miller, John. "Fidelism vs. Allegory in 'Rappaccini's Daughter,' "
  Nineteenth-Century Lit, 46 (1991), 223–244.
 Pfister, Joel. *The Production of Personal Life* . . . , 60–64.

"Rappaccini's Son"
 Bailey, Herbert S. "On 'Rappaccini's Son': A Note on a Twice-Told
  Tale," *Nathaniel Hawthorne R*, 17, i (1991), 5–8.

"Roger Malvin's Burial"
 + Crews, Frederick. "The Logic of Compulsion," in Frank, Albert
  J. von, Ed. *Critical Essays* . . . , 123–133.
 Millington, Richard H. *Practicing Romance* . . . , 16–25.

"Sunday at Home"
 Koreneva, Maya. "The Romantic . . . ," 30–31.

"A Virtuoso's Collection"
 Jones, E. Michael. *The Angel and the Machine* . . . , 126–127.

"Wakefield"
 Brand, Dana. *The Spectator and the City* . . . , 113–121.
 O'Keefe, Richard R. "The Gratuitous Act in 'Wakefield': A Note on
  Hawthorne's Modernism," *Nathaniel Hawthorne R*, 17, i (1991),
  17–19.

"The Wives of the Dead"
  Harris, Mark. "The Wives of the Living?: Absence of Dreams in
  Hawthorne's 'The Wives of the Dead,' " *Stud Short Fiction*, 29
  (1992), 323–329.

"Young Goodman Brown"
  + Bohner, Charles H. *Instructor's Manual . . .* , 54–55.
  + Cassill, R. V. *. . . Instructor's Handbook*, 77–78.
  + Charters, Ann, and William E. Sheidley. *Resources for Teach-
  ing . . .* , 3rd ed., 94–95.
  Coldiron, A. E. B. "Laughter as Thematic Marker in 'Young
  Goodman Brown,' " *Nathaniel Hawthorne R*, 17, i (1991), 19.
  Easterly, Joan E. "Lachrymal Imagery in Hawthorne's 'Young
  Goodman Brown,' " *Stud Short Fiction*, 28 (1991), 339–343.
  + Guerin, Wilfred, Earle Labor, Lee Morgan, Jeanne C. Reesman,
  and John R. Willingham, Eds. *A Handbook . . .* , 3rd ed., 52–61,
  88–98, 133–136, 171–173, 226–229.
  Park, Yangkeun. "Application of Discourse Analysis to Literature:
  Reinterpretation of Hawthorne's 'Young Goodman Brown,' " *J
  Engl Lang & Lit*, 37 (1991), 901–919.

SHIRLEY HAZZARD

"The Party"
  Twidale, K. M. "Discontinuous Narrative and Aspects of Love in
  Shirley Hazzard's Short Stories," *J Commonwealth Lit*, 26, i
  (1991), 109–111.

"The Picnic"
  Twidale, K. M. "Discontinuous . . . ,"106, 107–109.

"A Place in the Country"
  Twidale, K. M. "Discontinuous . . . ," 106–107, 111–112, 114.

BESSIE HEAD

"A Collector of Treasure"
  MacKenzie, Craig. "Short Fiction in the Making: The Case of Bessie
  Head," in Bardolph, Jacquelin, Ed. *Short Fiction . . .* , 241–242.
  Rooney, Caroline. "Are We in the Company of Feminists? A Preface
  for Bessie Head and Ama Ata Adoo," in Jump, Harriet D., Ed.
  Diverse Voices . . . , 239–240.

"The Deep River"
  Sample, Maxine. "Landscape and Spatial Metaphor in Bessie Head's
  The Collector of Treasures," *Stud Short Fiction*, 28 (1991),
  313–314.

"Heaven Is Not Closed"
  Balogun, F. Odun. *Tradition and Modernity . . .* , 12.
  MacKenzie, Craig. "Short Fiction . . . ," 239–241.

"Jacob: The Story of a Faith-Healing Priest"
Sample, Maxine. "Landscape . . . ," 314–316.
"Life"
Charters, Ann, and William E. Sheidley. *Resources for Teaching* . . . , 3rd ed., 96–97.
Sample, Maxine. "Landscape . . . ," 317–318.

LAFCADIO HEARN

"Creole Character"
Roskelly, Hephzibah. "Cultural Translator: Lafcadio Hearn," in Kennedy, Richard S., Ed. *Literary New Orleans* . . . , 23–24.
"Ghosteses"
Roskelly, Hephzibah. "Cultural Translator . . . , 21–22.

ANNE HÉBERT

"L'Ange de Dominique"
Dionne, René. " 'L'Ange de Dominique' ou l'Art poétique d'Anne Hébert," *Australian J French Stud*, 28, ii (1991), 196–202.

MARK HELPRIN

"A Vermont Tale"
Bohner, Charles H. *Instructor's Manual* . . . , 55–56.

ERNEST HEMINGWAY

"The Battler"
Tetlow, Wendolyn E. *Hemingway's "In Our* . . . , 65–68.
"Big Two-Hearted River"
Burke, Daniel. *Beyond Interpretation* . . . , 121–143.
Lamb, Robert P. "Fishing for Stories: What 'Big Two-Hearted River' Is Really About," *Mod Fiction Stud,* 37 (1991), 164–180.
Mellow, James R. *Hemingway* . . . , 101–102, 161, 250, 271–273.
Messent, Peter. *Ernest Hemingway*, 7–9, 25, 130–131.
Tetlow, Wendolyn E. *Hemingway's "In Our* . . . , 90–97.
Weber, Ronald. *The Midwestern* . . . , 217–218.
Westbrook, Max. "Text, Ritual, and Memory: Hemingway's 'Big Two-Hearted River,' " *No Dakota Q*, 60, iii (1992), 14–25.
"Cat in the Rain"
Adair, William. "Hemingway's 'Cat in the Rain': George's Winter Death-Bed," *Hemingway R*, 12, i (1992), 73–76.
Barrio Marco, José M. " 'Cat in the Rain': un preludio simbólico-narrativo en la obra de Ernest Hemingway," *Revista Alicantina de Estudios Ingleses*, 3 (November, 1990), 7–15.

Mellow, James R. *Hemingway* . . . , 222, 226, 386.
Tetlow, Wendolyn E. *Hemingway's "In Our* . . . , 78–81.
"Che Ti Dice la Patria?"
Mellow, James R. *Hemingway* . . . , 347.
"A Clean Well-Lighted Place"
Aldridge, John W. *Talents and Technicians* . . . , 49–50.
Griffin, Paul F. "Chances of Being Kind: Rorty, Irony, and Teaching
Modern Literature," *Lit Theory Classroom,* 18, ii (1991), 112–113.
"Cross-Country Snow"
Mellow, James R. *Hemingway* . . . , 221–222, 226.
Tetlow, Wendolyn E. *Hemingway's "In Our* . . . , 84–87.
"The Doctor and the Doctor's Wife"
Hardy, Donald E. "Presupposition and the Coconspirator," *Style,* 26
(1992), 5–6.
Mellow, James R. *Hemingway* . . . , 268–269.
Monteiro, George. "Waifs and Driftwood—A Melvillean Theme in
Hemingway's 'The Doctor and the Doctor's Wife,' " *Stud Short
Fiction,* 27 (1990), 99–100.
Strong, Paul. "The First Nick Adams Stories," *Stud Short Fiction,*
28 (1991), 85–88.
Tetlow, Wendolyn E. *Hemingway's "In Our* . . . , 55–57.
"The End of Something"
Mellow, James R. *Hemingway* . . . , 108–109, 110.
Stampfl, Barry. "Similes as Thematic Clues in Three Hemingway
Short Stories," *Hemingway R,* 10, ii (1991), 34.
Tetlow, Wendolyn E. *Hemingway's "In Our* . . . ," 58–60.
"Fathers and Sons"
Keating, Helane L., and Walter Levy. *Instructor's Manual: Lives
Through Literature* . . . , 9–10.
Mellow, James R. *Hemingway* . . . , 33–34.
Messent, Peter. *Ernest Hemingway,* 49–51, 52.
"Hills Like White Elephants"
Abdoo, Sherlyn. "Hemingway's 'Hills Like White Elephants,' "
Explicator, 49, iv (1991), 238–240.
+ Bohner, Charles H. *Instructor's Manual* . . . , 56–58.
+ Cassill, R. V. . . . *Instructor's Handbook,* 81–82.
Charters, Ann, and William E. Sheidley. *Resources for Teach-
ing* . . . , 3rd ed., 92–93.
Hannum, Howard L. " 'Jig Jig to Dirty Ears': White Elephants to
Let," *Hemingway R,* 11, ii (1991), 46–54.
Hardy, Donald E. "Presupposition . . . ," 6–8.
Mellow, James R. *Hemingway* . . . , 384.
Messent, Peter. *Ernest Hemingway,* 89–92.
O'Brien, Timothy D. "Allusion, Word-Play, and the Central Conflict
in Hemingway's 'Hills Like White Elephants,' " *Hemingway R,*
12, i (1992), 19–25.
Stampfl, Barry. "Similes as Thematic . . . ," 36–37.

"In Another Country"
Mellow, James R. *Hemingway* . . . , 353.

"Indian Camp"
Strong, Paul. "The First Nick Adams Stories," 85–88.
Tetlow, Wendolyn E. *Hemingway's "In Our* . . . , 52–55.
Weber, Ronald. *The Midwestern* . . . , 215–216.

"A Lack of Passion"
Beegel, Susan F. "Ernest Hemingway's 'A Lack of Passion,' " in
Scafella, Frank, Ed. *Hemingway* . . . , 62–79.

"The Last Good Country"
Messent, Peter. *Ernest Hemingway*, 131–133.
Weber, Ronald. *The Midwestern* . . . , 219.

"A Man of the World"
Fleming, Robert. "Dismantling the Code: Hemingway's 'A Man of
the World,' " *Hemingway R*, 11, ii (1992), 6–10.

"The Mercenaries"
Mellow, James R. *Hemingway* . . . , 92–93.

"Mr. and Mrs. Elliot"
Comley, Nancy R., and Robert Scholes. "Tribal Things:
Hemingway's Erotics of Truth," *Novel*, 25 (1992), 272–276.
Tetlow, Wendolyn E. *Hemingway's "In Our* . . . , 76–78.

"The Mother of a Queen"
Mellow, James R. *Hemingway* . . . , 411–413.
Sangwan, S. S., and Satyapal Dahiya. "Money and Morals in
Hemingway's Short Stories," *Panjab Univ Research Bull*, 21, ii
(1990), 69–70.
Stampfl, Barry. "Similes as Thematic . . . ," 34–35.

"My Old Man"
Mellow, James R. *Hemingway* . . . , 205.
Tetlow, Wendolyn E. *Hemingway's "In Our* . . . , 87–89.

"A Natural History of the Dead"
Messent, Peter. *Ernest Hemingway*, 136–137.

"Now I Lay Me"
Mellow, James R. *Hemingway* . . . , 354–355, 357.
Messent, Peter. *Ernest Hemingway*, 22–39, 48–49.

"The Old Man and the Sea"
Brenner, Gerry. . . . *Story of a Common Man*, 28–38, 53–67, 79–96.
Hurley, C. Harold. "Just 'a Boy' or 'Already a Man?': Manolin's
Age in 'The Old Man and the Sea,' " *Hemingway R*, 10, ii (1991),
71–72.
Mellow, James R. *Hemingway* . . . , 579–582.
Morgan, Kathleen, and Luis Losada. "Santiago in 'The Old Man and
the Sea': A Homeric Hero," *Hemingway R*, 12, i (1992), 35–51.
Stolzfus, Ben. " 'The Old Man and the Sea': A Lacanian Reading,"
in Scafella, Frank, Ed. *Hemingway* . . . , 190–199.
+ Wagner, Linda W. "The Poem of Santiago and Manolin," in
Wagner, Linda W., Ed. *Ernest Hemingway* . . . , 275–287.

"On the Quai at Smyrna"
Tetlow, Wendolyn E. *Hemingway's "In Our . . .* , 50–52.

"Out of Season"
Mellow, James R. *Hemingway . . .* , 222–224, 226.
Sangwan, S. S., and Satyapal Dahiya. "Money . . . ," 71.
Tetlow, Wendolyn E. *Hemingway's "In Our . . .* , 81–84.

"The Revolutionist"
Tetlow, Wendolyn E. *Hemingway's "In Our . . .* , 37–39, 76.

"The Sea Change"
Comley, Nancy R., and Robert Scholes. "Tribal . . . ," 276–277.
Mellow, James R. *Hemingway . . .* , 399–400.

"Sepi Jingan"
Mellow, James R. *Hemingway . . .* , 26–27, 29.

"The Short and Happy Life of Francis Macomber"
Baym, Nina. *Feminism and . . .* , 71–80.
Blythe, Hal, and Charlie Sweet. "Wilson: Architect of the Macomber
Conspiracy," *Stud Short Fiction*, 28 (1991), 305–309.
Hardy, Donald E. "Presupposition . . . ," 3–4.
Mellow, James R. *Hemingway . . .* , 442–448.
Messent, Peter. *Ernest Hemingway*, 156–161.
Morgan, Kathleen, and Luis A. Losada. "Tracking the Wounded
Buffalo: Authorial Knowledge and the Shooting of Francis
Macomber," *Hemingway R*, 11, ii (1991), 25–30.

"The Snows of Kilimanjaro"
Mellow, James R. *Hemingway . . .* , 448–454.

"Soldier's Home"
Kennedy, J. Gerald, and Kirk Curnutt. "Out of the Picture: Mrs.
Krebs, Mother Stein and 'Soldier's Home,' " *Hemingway R*, 12, i
(1992), 1–11.
Mellow, James R. *Hemingway . . .* , 122–125, 218–219.
Messent, Peter. *Ernest Hemingway*, 15–16.
Spilka, Mark. *Renewing the Normative . . .* , 233–238.
Tetlow, Wendolyn E. *Hemingway's "In Our . . .* , 71–76.
Ullrich, David W. " 'What's in a Name'—Krebs, Crabs, Kraut: The
Multivalence of 'Krebs' in Hemingway's 'Soldier's Home,' " *Stud
Short Fiction*, 29 (1992), 363–374.

"The Three-Day Blow"
Mellow, James R. *Hemingway . . .* , 109–110.
Tetlow, Wendolyn E. *Hemingway's "In Our . . .* , 61–65.

"The Undefeated"
Howell, John M. "Hemingway and Chaplin: Monkey Business in
'The Undefeated,' " *Stud Short Fiction,* 27 (1990), 89–97.
Messent, Peter. *Ernest Hemingway*, 141–142.
Sangwan, S. S., and Satyapal Dahiya. "Money . . . ," 70–71.

"A Very Short Story"
Mellow, James R. *Hemingway . . .* , 97–99.

Sangwan, S. S., and Satyapal Dahiya. "Money . . . ," 72.
Tetlow, Wendolyn E. *Hemingway's "In Our* . . . , 36–37, 68, 69.
"A Way You'll Never Be"
Messent, Peter. *Ernest Hemingway*, 46–48.
"Wine of Wyoming"
Messent, Peter. *Ernest Hemingway*, 129–130.

AMY HEMPEL

"Daylight Come"
Charters, Ann, and William E. Sheidley. *Resources for Teaching* . . . ,
3rd ed., 99–100.
"In the Cemetery Where Al Jolson Is Buried"
+Cassill, R. V. . . . *Instructor's Handbook*, 83–84.

FELISBERTO HERNÁNDEZ

"El acomodador"
Graziano, Frank. "La lujuria de ver: la proyección fantástica en 'El
acomodador' de Felisberto Hernández," *Revista Iberoamericana*,
58 (1992), 1027–1039.

HERMANN HESSE

"Im Presselschen Gartenhaus"
Schneider, Christian I. *Hermann Hesse*, 49–50.
"Klein und Wagner"
Schneider, Christian I. *Hermann Hesse*, 74–75.
"Klingsors letzter Sommer"
Schneider, Christian I. *Hermann Hesse*, 75–76.
"Knulp"
Schneider, Christian I. *Hermann Hesse*, 50–54.
"Die Morgenlandfahrt"
Schneider, Christian I. *Hermann Hesse*, 93–96.

STEFAN HEYM

"The Queen Against Defoe"
Fisher, R. W. "The State Against Stefan Heym: Fact and Fiction in
Heym's 'The Queen Against Defoe,' " *Germ Life & Letters*, 45
(1992), 94–107.

JACKY HEYNS

"Our Last Fling"
Balogun, F. Odun. *Tradition and Modernity* . . . , 41.

PATRICIA HIGHSMITH

"The Empty Birdhouse"
Boucé, Hélène A. "Mise en scene, analyse et anamnèse: 'The Empty
Birdhouse,' " in Duperray, Max, Ed. *Du fantastique* . . . , 153–160.

E[RNEST] T[HEODOR] A[MADEUS] HOFFMANN

"Der Artushof"
Pix, Gunther. "Der Variationskünstler E. T. A. Hoffmann und seine
Erzählung 'Der Artushof,' " *Mitteilungen der E. T. A. Hoffmann-
Gesellschaft*, 35 (1989), 4–20.
"Counselor Krespel"
Dreike, Beate M. "*Der Serapions-Brüder* und der Pyramidendoktor:
Marginalien zu E. T. A. Hoffmans Kritik an der zeitgenössischen
Therapeutik," *Mitteilungen der E. T. A. Hoffmann-Gesellschaft*,
36 (1990), 16–17.
Jennings, Lee B. "E. T. A. Hoffmann's 'Rat Krespel': The Anatomy
of an Eccentric," in *Lit & Psych*, 59–69.
"The Cousin's Corner Window"
Cook, Roger F. "Reader Response and Authorial Strategies: E. T. A.
Hoffmann's View from 'Des Vetters Eckfenster,' " *Germ Stud
Review*, 12, iii (1989), 421–435.
"Don Juan"
Meier, Albert. "Fremdenloge und Wirtstafel: Zur poetischen
Funktion des Realitätsschocks in E. T. A. Hoffmanns
Fantasiestück 'Don Juan,' " *Zeitschrift für Deutsche Philologie*,
111, iv (1992), 516–531.
"The Golden Pot"
Bohm, Arnd. "Consumers' Paradise: E. T. A. Hoffmann's 'Der
goldne Topf,' " *European Romantic R*, 2, i (1991), 1–22.
"Klein Zacches genannt Zinnober"
Weglöhner, Hans Werner. "Die Gesellschaftlichen und politischen
Aspekte in E. T. A. Hoffmanns Märchen 'Klein Zaches genannt
Zinnober,' " *Der Deutschunterricht*, 44, iii (1992), 22–28.
"The Sandman"
Ginsburg, Ruth. "A Primal Scene of Reading: Freud and Hoffmann,"
Lit & Psych, 38, iii (1992), 24–46.
Herdman, John. *The Double* . . . , 48–54.
Staninger, Christiane. "E. T. A. Hoffmann's 'The Sand Man' and the
Night Side of the Enlightenment," in Timm, Eitel, Ed.
Subversive . . . , 94–104.
"Signor Formica"
Dreike, Beate M. "Der Serapions-Brüder . . ." 21–22.

HUGO VON HOFMANNSTHAL

"Das Märchen der 672. Nacht"
Renner, Ursula. "Pavillons, Glashäuser und Seitenwege—Topos und

Vision des Paradiesgartens bei Saar, Hofmannsthal, und Heinrich Mann," *Recherches Germaniques,* 20 (1990), 130–134, 139–140.
"Lucidor"
Ryan, Judith. *The Vanishing Subject* . . . , 124–125.
"The Story of a Horseman"
Ryan, Judith. *The Vanishing Subject* . . . , 115–116.

JAMES HOGG

"Strange Letters of a Lunatic"
Herdman, John. *The Double* . . . , 85–87.

EDUARDO LADISLAU HOLMBERG

"Horacio Kalibang o los autómatas"
Risco, Antón. "Los autómatas de Holmberg," *Mester*, 19, ii (1990), 63–70.
"Nelly"
Masiello, Francine. *Between Civilization* . . . , 89–92.

GILDA HOLST

"Reunión"
García Serrano, M. Victoria. "Sin Pudor: el cuerpo femenino en la narrativa de Gilda Holst," *Chasqui*, 21, ii (1992), 14–19.

ISABEL HUGGAN

"Getting Out of Garten"
Durix, Carole. "The Violence of Growing up in Isabel Huggan's *The Elizabeth Stories*," in Bardolph, Jacquelin, Ed. *Short Fiction* . . . , 180.
"Jack of Hearts"
Durix, Carole. "The Violence . . . ," 174–175.
"Sawdust"
Durix, Carole. "The Violence . . . ," 176–177.
"Sorrows of the Flesh"
Durix, Carole. "The Violence . . . ," 177–178.

LANGSTON HUGHES

"Father and Son"
Hubbard, Dolan. "Symbolizing America in Langston Hughes's 'Father and Son,' " *Langston Hughes R*, 11, i (1992), 14–20.

WILLIAM HUMPHREY

"Quail for Mr. Forester"
    Grammer, John M. "Where the South Draws Up to a Stop: The
    Fiction of William Humphrey," *Mississippi Q,* 44 (1990–1991), 6–8.

ZORA NEAL HURSTON

"The Gilded Six-Bits"
    Baum, Rosalio M. "The Shape of Hurston's Fiction," in Glassman,
    Steve, and Kathryn L. Seidel, Eds. *Zora in Florida,* 101–104.
    Jones, Evora W. "The Pastoral and the Picaresque in Zora Neale
    Hurston's 'The Gilded Six-Bits,' " *Coll Lang Assoc J,* 35 (1992),
    316–324.

"Spunk"
    +Charters, Ann, and William E. Sheidley. *Resources for
    Teaching* . . . , 3rd ed., 100–101.
    Smith-Wright, Geraldine. "In Spite of the Klan: Ghosts in the Fiction
    of Black Women Writers," in Carpenter, Lynette, and Wendy K.
    Kolmar, Eds. *Haunting the House of Fiction* . . . , 150–151.

"Sweat"
    Baum, Rosalio M. "The Shape . . . ," 98–101.
    Seidel, Kathryn L. "The Artist in the Kitchen: The Economics of
    Creativity in Hurston's 'Sweat,' " in Glassman, Steve, and
    Kathryn L. Seidel, Eds. *Zora in Florida,* 110–120.

HWANG SUN-WON

"Conversation in June about Mothers"
    Charters, Ann, and William E. Sheidley. *Resources for Teaching* . . . ,
    3rd ed., 102–103.

EVAN X. HYDE

"Blooming Black Flowers"
    McLeod, Alan. "The Short Fiction of Belize," in Bardolph,
    Jacquelin, Ed. *Short Fiction* . . . , 99.

"Caroline"
    McLeod, Alan. "The Short Fiction . . . ," 99.

"A Conscience for Christmas"
    McLeod, Alan. "The Short Fiction . . . ," 99–100.

"A Guilty Man"
    McLeod, Alan. "The Short Fiction . . . ," 100.

"How He Went"
    McLeod, Alan. "The Short Fiction . . . ," 98–99.

"June and John John"
McLeod, Alan. "The Short Fiction . . . ," 100.

YUSUF [YOUSSEF] IDRIS

"Al-Shaykh Shaykh"
Mikhail, Mona N. *Studies* . . . , 86–92.

"Banquet from Heaven"
Mikhail, Mona N. *Studies* . . . , 64–69.

"The Big Hand"
Mikhail, Mona N. *Studies* . . . , 36–38.

"The Cheapest Nights"
Mikhail, Mona N. *Studies* . . . , 41–43.

"Daood"
Crofoot, John M. "Rhythms of the Body, Rhythms of the Text: Three Short Stories by Yusuf Idris," *Turkish Stud Assn Bull*, 16 (1992), 35–36.

"Died of Old Age: No Proof of Insanity"
Mikhail, Mona N. *Studies* . . . , 39–41.

"Farahat's Republic"
Mikhail, Mona N. *Studies* . . . , 43–44.

"The Great Operation"
Mikhail, Mona N. *Studies* . . . , 49–52.

"Ground Whispers"
Mikhail, Mona N. *Studies* . . . , 110–117, 118–119.

"Heart of the City"
Mikhail, Mona N. *Studies* . . . , 98–103.

"House of Flesh"
Charters, Ann, and William E. Sheidley. *Resources for Teaching* . . . , 3rd ed., 104–105.
Mikhail, Mona N. *Studies* . . . , 126–130.

"The Journey"
Mikhail, Mona N. *Studies* . . . , 38–39.

"The Language of Pain"
Mikhail, Mona N. *Studies* . . . , 44–48.

"Rings of Smooth Brass: Story in Four Squares"
Mikhail, Mona N. *Studies* . . . , 120–126.

"The Siren"
Mikhail, Mona N. *Studies* . . . , 103–110.

"This Time"
Mikhail, Mona N. *Studies* . . . , 137–140.

WASHINGTON IRVING

"Rip Van Winkle"
  Barbarese, J. T. "Landscape of the American Psyche," *Sewanee R*, 100 (1992), 599–603.
  Benoit, Raymond. "Archetypes and Ecotones: The Tree in Faulkner's 'The Bear' and Irving's 'Rip Van Winkle,' " *Notes Contemp Lit*, 22, i (1992), 4–5.

CHRISTOPHER ISHERWOOD

"Sally Bowles"
  Wade, Stephen. *Christopher Isherwood*, 51–56.

LAURA RIDING JACKSON

"Macedonian Times"
  Christensen, Peter G. "Women as a Spiritual Force in Laura Riding's *Lives of Wives*," *Focus on Robert Graves*, 1, xiii (Winter, 1992), 22–26.
"New Ways in Jerusalem"
  Christensen, Peter G. "Women . . . ," 26–31.
"A Persian Lady and Her Contemporaries"
  Christensen, Peter G. "Women . . . ," 20–22.

SHIRLEY JACKSON

"The Lottery"
  +Bohner, Charles H. *Instructor's Manual . . .* , 58–59.
  +Cassill, R. V. *. . . Instructor's Handbook*, 84–85.
  Cervo, Nathan. "Jackson's 'The Lottery,' " *Explicator*, 50, iii (1992), 183–185.
  +Charters, Ann, and William E. Sheidley. *Resources for Teaching . . .* , 3rd ed., 105–106.

HENRY JAMES

"The Altar of the Dead"
  Kaplan, Fred. *Henry James . . .* , 389–390.
"The Aspern Papers"
  Bell, Millicent. *Meaning in Henry James*, 185–203.
  Kaplan, Fred. *Henry James . . .* , 319–320.
  Porsdam, Helle. "The Search for Redemptive Form: Henry James's Use of First-Person," in Jacobson, Eric, Jorgen E. Nielsen, Bruce C. Ross, and James Stewart, Eds. *Studies in . . .* , 22–29.

Richards, Bernard. "How Many Children Had Julia Bordereau?"
Henry James R, 12 (1991), 120–128.

Rogers, Franklin. *Occidental Ideographs . . . ,* 268–269.

Scales, Jean N. "The Ironic Smile: Pushkin's 'The Queen of Spades'
and James' 'The Aspern Papers,' " *Coll Lang Assoc J,* 34 (1991),
486–490.

"The Author of Beltraffio"

Barry, Peter. "Embarrassments and Predicaments: Patterns of
Interaction in James's Writer-Tales," *Orbis Litterarum,* 46 (1991),
90–94.

Walton, Priscilla L. *The Disruption . . . ,* 67–72.

"Barbara Allan"

Martin, W. R., and Warren U. Ober. "Henry James' 'Longstaff's
Marriage' and 'Barbara Allan,' " *Am Lit Realism,* 23, ii (1992),
84–85.

"The Beast in the Jungle"

Bell, Millicent. *Meaning in Henry James,* 262–274.

Kaplan, Fred. *Henry James . . . ,* 456–458.

Perluck, Herbert. "The Dramatics of the Unspoken and Unspeakable
in James's 'The Beast in the Jungle,' " *Henry James R,* 12 (1991),
230–253.

Sedgwick, Eve K. "The Beast in the Closet: James and the Writing
of Homosexual Panic," in Dynes, Wayne R., and Stephen
Donaldson, Eds. *Homosexual Themes . . . ,* 319–334.

Stampfl, Barry. "Filtering Rimmon-Kenan, Chatman, Black, Freud,
and James: Focalization and the Divided Self in 'The Beast in the
Jungle,' " *Style,* 26 (1992), 388–399.

Steele, Meili. "Narration and the Face of Anxiety in Henry James'
'The Beast in the Jungle,' " in Tymieniecka, Anna T., Ed. *The
Elemental Passions . . . ,* 421–428.

"The Chaperon"

Tintner, Adeline R. *Henry James . . . ,* 3, 70–71, 74–77.

"Crapy Cornelia"

Reeve, N. H. "Matches and Mismatches in Two Late James Stories,"
Cambridge Q, 21 (1992), 322–331.

"Daisy Miller"

Bell, Millicent. *Meaning in Henry James,* 48–65.

Kaplan, Fred. *Henry James . . . ,* 196–197.

Woolf, Judith. *Henry James . . . ,* 32–34.

Wardley, Lynn. "Reassembling Daisy Miller," *Am Lit Culture,* 3, ii
(1991), 237–250.

"The Death of the Lion"

Barry, Peter. "Embarrassments . . . ," 96–98.

"The Figure in the Carpet"

Barry, Peter. "Embarrassments . . . ," 98–102.

Kaplan, Fred. *Henry James . . . ,* 412.

Priestman, Martin. *Detective Fiction . . . ,* 136–140.

Walton, Priscilla L. *The Disruption . . .* , 85–91.
White, Robert. "The Figure in the Carpet of James's Temple of
  Delight," *Henry James R,* 13 (1992), 43–49.
"Fordham Castle"
  Reeve, N. H. "Matches . . . ," 331–339.
"Georgina's Reasons"
  Kaplan, Fred. *Henry James . . .* , 286.
"In the Cage"
  Gabler-Hover, Janet. "The Ethics of Determinism in Henry James's
    'In the Cage,' " *Henry James R,* 13 (1992), 253–275.
  Walton, Priscilla L. *The Disruption . . .* , 91–100.
"An International Episode"
  Kaplan, Fred. *Henry James . . .* , 200–201.
"The Jolly Corner"
  Bell, Millicent. *Meaning in Henry James,* 275–288.
  Burleson, Donald R. "James's 'The Jolly Corner,' " *Explicator,* 49,
    ii (1991), 99–100.
  Cassill, R. V. *. . . Instructor's Handbook*, 87–89.
  Rashkin, Esther. *Family Secrets . . .* , 93–122.
  Reisling, Russell J. " 'Doing Good by Stealth': Alice Staverton and
    Women's Politics in 'The Jolly Corner,' " *Henry James R,* 13, i
    (1992), 50–56.
  Smythe, Karen. "Imaging and Imagining: 'The Jolly Corner' and
    Self-construction," *Dalhousie R,* 70 (1991), 375–385.
"Lady Barberina"
  Kaplan, Fred. *Henry James . . .* , 289–290.
  Wilkinson-Dekhuijzen, J. M. " 'Nothing Is My *Last* Word on
    Anything': Henry James's 'Lady Barberina,' " *Engl Stud,* 73
    (1992), 324–336.
"The Lesson of the Master"
  Kaplan, Fred. *Henry James . . .* , 333.
  Walton, Priscilla L. *The Disruption . . .* , 72–76.
"The Liar"
  Orlich, Ileana A. "Framing 'The Liar,' " *Int'l Fiction R,* 18 (1991),
    91–95.
"A Light Man"
  Kaplan, Fred. *Henry James . . .* , 91–92.
"A London Life"
  Tintner, Adeline R. *Henry James . . .* , 43–55.
"Longstaff's Marriage"
  Martin, W. R., and Warren U. Ober. "Henry James' . . . ," 81–83.
"Madame de Mauves"
  Kaplan, Fred. *Henry James . . .* , 147–148.
"The Madonna of the Future"
  Kaplan, Fred. *Henry James . . .* , 140–141.
  Poole, Adrian. *Henry James,* 12–16.

Shackelford, Lynne P. "The Significance of the Raphael Reference in Henry James's 'The Madonna of the Future,' " *Mod Fiction Stud,* 27 (1991), 101–104.

"Master Eustace"
Kaplan, Fred. *Henry James . . . ,* 130–131.

"Maud-Evelyn"
Gage, Richard. "Henry James's 'Maud-Evelyn': *Ménage à Trois Fantastique,*" in Saciuk, Olena H., Ed. *The Shape . . . ,* 67–73.
Heldreth, Leonard. "The Ghost and the Self: The Supernatural Fiction of Henry James," in Morse, Donald E., Marshall B. Tymn, and Csilla Bertha, Eds. *The Celebration . . . ,* 135–136.

"The Middle Years"
Barry, Peter. "Embarrassments . . . ," 94–95.
Walton, Priscilla L. *The Disruption . . . ,* 81–85.

"The Patagonia"
Tick, Stanley. "Sailing Again on 'The Patagonia,' " *J Am Stud,* 26, i (1992), 84–90.

"The Private Life"
Tintner, Adeline R. *Henry James . . . ,* 79–86.

"The Pupil"
Kaplan, Fred. *Henry James . . . ,* 303–304.
Moon, Michael. "A Small Boy and Others: Sexual Disorientation in Henry James, Kenneth Anger, and David Lynch," in Spillers, Hortense J., Ed. *Comparative American Identities . . . ,* 150–152.

"The Real Thing"
Bazargan, Susan. "Representation and Ideology in 'The Real Thing,' " *Henry James R,* 12 (1991), 133–137.
+ Bohner, Charles H. *Instructor's Manual . . . ,* 59–60.
Henricksen, Bruce, " 'The Real Thing': Criticism and the Ethical Turn," *Papers Lang & Lit,* 27 (1991), 475–487, 490.
Walton, Priscilla L. *The Disruption . . . ,* 76–81.

"The Romance of Certain Old Clothes"
Kaplan, Fred. *Henry James . . . ,* 71, 91.

"The Siege of London"
Kaplan, Fred. *Henry James . . . ,* 289.
Tintner, Adeline R. *Henry James . . . ,* 10–21.

"The Story of a Year"
Kaplan, Fred. *Henry James . . . ,* 69–70.

"A Tragedy of Error"
Kaplan, Fred. *Henry James . . . ,* 64.

"Travelling Companions"
Tanner, Tony. *Venice Desired,* 159–166.

"The Tree of Knowledge"
+ Bohner, Charles H. *Instructor's Manual . . . ,* 60–61.
+ Cassill, R. V. *. . . Instructor's Handbook,* 85–87.

"The Turn of the Screw"
Álvarez Amorós, José A. "Possible-Worlds Semantics, Frame Text, Insert Text, and Unreliable Narration: The Case of 'The Turn of the Screw,' " *Style*, 25, i (1991), 42–70.
Bell, Millicent. *Meaning in Henry James,* 223–242.
De Koven, Marianne. *Rich and Strange* . . . , 47–63.
Dry, Helen A., and Susan Kucinkas. "Ghostly Ambiguity: Presuppositional Constructions in 'The Turn of the Screw,' " *Style*, 25, i (1991), 71–88.
Kaplan, Fred. *Henry James* . . . , 413–414.
Newman, Beth. "Getting Fixed: Feminine Identity and Scopic Crisis in 'The Turn of the Screw,' " *Novel*, 26 (1992), 43–63.
Pearson, John H. "Repetition and Subversion in Henry James's 'The Turn of the Screw,' " *Henry James R*, 13 (1992), 276–291.
Poole, Adrian. *Henry James,* 140–159.
Rodríguez-Luis, Julio. *The Contemporary Praxis* . . . , 8–10.
"The Two Faces"
Dyson, J. Peter. "Romance and the Prima Donna Image in the Fiction of Henry James," *Henry James R,* 12 (1991), 130–131.
"The Velvet Glove"
Dyson, J. Peter. "Romance and the Prima Donna Image . . . ," 131–132.
"Washington Square"
Bell, Ian F. A. *Henry James and the Past* . . . , 17–60.
Bell, Millicent. *Meaning in Henry James,* 65–79.
Woolf, Judith. *Henry James* . . . , 29–32.

CLARA JANÉS

"Tentativa de olvido"
Encinar, Angeles. "Escritoras Españolas actuales: una perspectiva a través del cuento," *Hispanic J*, 13 (1992), 188.

ENRIQUE JARAMILLO LEVI

"El agua"
Bustos Arratia, Myriam. "Notas para un análisis de los cuentos de Jaramillo Levi," in *Puertas y Ventanas* . . . , 154–155, 166–169.
Carrillo, Vielka U. de. "¿En contra de qué camina Enrique Jaramillo Levi en *Ahora que soy él* (13 cuentos en contra)?" in *Puertas y Ventanas* . . . , 193–195.
García, Kay. " 'El agua': Un signo polisémico en la obra literaria de Enrique Jaramillo Levi," *Confluencia*, 5, ii (1990), 151–152.
———. " 'El agua': Un signo polisémico en la obra literaria de Enrique Jaramillo Levi," *Puertas y Ventanas* . . . , 231–233.
Hevia, Alicia M. "Construcción de la atmósfera en algunos cuentos de Enrique Jaramillo Levi," in *Puertas y Ventanas* . . . , 201–203.

Zimmerman, Samuel. "La fluidez del ser en *Ahora que soy él*," in *Puertas y Ventanas* . . . , 154–155.
Zlochev, Clark M. "Metáforas de la creación literaria en tres cuentos de Enrique Jaramillo Levi," in *Puertas y Ventanas* . . . , 81–84.
"Agua de mar"
García, Kay. " 'El agua . . . ," 150–151.
"Ahora que soy él"
Hevia, Alicia M. "Construcción . . . ," 200–201.
Zimmerman, Samuel. "La fluidez . . . ," 153.
"Los anteojos"
Duncan, J. Ann. "Fragmentación, escamoteo y síntesis en la obra cuentística de Enrique Jaramillo Levi," in *Puertas y Ventanas* . . . , 65–67.
Mosier, M. Patricia. "Caja de resonancias: resonancias de dobles," in *Puertas y Ventanas* . . . , 141–142.
"Bautismo ausente"
Cruz, Julia G. "Una variante de lo neofantástico: 'Bautismo ausente' de Enrique Jaramillo Levi," in *Puertas y Ventanas* . . . , 211–226.
"Caja de resonancias"
Mosier, M. Patricia. "Caja de resonancias . . . ," 143.
"El cortejo"
Mosier, M. Patricia. "Caja de resonancias . . . ," 144–145.
"Duplicaciones"
Mosier, M. Patricia. "Caja de resonancias . . . ," 146–147.
"Ellas saben"
Hevia, Alicia M. "Construcción . . . ," 205–207.
Zimmerman, Samuel. "La fluidez . . . ," 157–158.
"Engendro en noche triste"
Mosier, M. Patricia. "Caja de resonancias . . . ," 145.
"La fiesta en el sótano"
Mosier, M. Patricia. "Caja de resonancias . . . ," 146.
"La fota"
Carrillo, Vielka U. de. "¿En contra . . . ," 190–191.
Hevia, Alicia M. "Construcción . . . ," 203–204.
Zimmerman, Samuel. "La fluidez . . . ," 155–156.
"La fuente"
García, Kay. " 'El agua' . . . ," 151.
Zimmerman, Samuel. "La fluidez . . . ," 151–152.
"Germinación"
Mosier, M. Patricia. "Caja de resonancias . . . ," 142–143.
"El ladrón"
Zimmerman, Samuel. "La fluidez . . . ," 152–153.
"El lector"
Duncan, J. Ann. "Fragmentación . . . ," 76–78.

Gómez Parham, Mary. "El erotismo en los cuentos de Enrique Jaramillo Levi," in *Puertas y Ventanas* . . . , 183–184.
"Libro sin tapas"
  Mosier, M. Patricia. "Caja de resonancias . . . ," 145–146.
"Luna de miel"
  Carrillo, Vielka U. de. "¿En contra . . . ," 192–193.
  Zimmerman, Samuel. "La fluidez . . . ," 159–160.
  Zlochev, Clark M. "Metáforas . . . ," 84–86.
"Mamá no demora"
  Hevia, Alicia M. "Construcción . . . ," 204–205.
  Zimmerman, Samuel. "La fluidez . . . ," 156.
"Ofertorio"
  Duncan, J. Ann. "Fragmentación . . . ," 75–76.
"Otra vez lo mismo"
  Zimmerman, Samuel. "La fluidez . . . ," 153–154.
"Las palomas"
  Mosier, M. Patricia. "Caja de resonancias . . . ," 140–141.
"El punto de referencia"
  Bustos Arratia, Myriam. "Notas para . . . ," 164–165.
  Zlochev, Clark M. "Metáforas . . . ," 86–88.
"Se llama Lucía"
  Chase, Cida S. "Fantasía y realidad y algunos aspectos de la técnica en *La voz despalabrada*, de Enrique Jaramillo Levi," in *Puertas y Ventanas* . . . , 119–121.
"El silencio"
  Zimmerman, Samuel. "La fluidez . . . ," 155.
"La sombra"
  Carrillo, Vielka U. de. "¿En contra . . . ," 196–197.
  Zimmerman, Samuel. "La fluidez . . . ," 158–159.
"La sopecha de un ejecutivo"
  Zimmerman, Samuel. "La fluidez . . . ," 156–157.
"Suicidio"
  Chase, Cida S. "Fantasía y . . . ," 111–113.
"La tarde del encuentro"
  Mosier, M. Patricia. "Caja de resonancias . . . ," 147–148.
"Te amo, Silvia"
  Chase, Cida S. "Fantasía y . . . ," 117–119.
"Vergüenza"
  Gómez Parham, Mary. "El erotismo . . . ," 182–183.

SARAH ORNE JEWETT

"Andrew's Fortune"
  Roman, Margaret. *Sarah Orne Jewett* . . . , 177–178.

"Autumn Holiday"
Roman, Margaret. *Sarah Orne Jewett* . . . , 135–137.

"The Best China Saucer"
Roman, Margaret. *Sarah Orne Jewett* . . . , 30–32.

"A Bit of Shore Life"
Roman, Margaret. *Sarah Orne Jewett* . . . , 73–74.

"Beyond the Toll Gate"
Roman, Margaret. *Sarah Orne Jewett* . . . , 26–28.

"A Business Man"
Roman, Margaret. *Sarah Orne Jewett* . . . , 177–179.

"The Courting of Sister Wisby"
Roman, Margaret. *Sarah Orne Jewett* . . . , 180–181.

"The Dulham Ladies"
Roman, Margaret. *Sarah Orne Jewett* . . . , 89, 90.

"A Dunnet Shepherdess"
Roman, Margaret. *Sarah Orne Jewett* . . . , 190–191.
Romines, Ann. *The Home Plot* . . . , 83–85.

"The Failure of David Berry"
Roman, Margaret. *Sarah Orne Jewett* . . . , 69, 171.

"Farmer Finch"
Roman, Margaret. *Sarah Orne Jewett* . . . , 14, 15, 125, 139.

"Fair Day"
Roman, Margaret. *Sarah Orne Jewett* . . . , 125–126.

"The Flight of the Betsey Lane"
Mobley, Marilyn S. *Folk Roots and Mythic Wings* . . . , 58–59.

"The Foreigner"
Mobley, Marilyn S. *Folk Roots and Mythic Wings* . . . , 170–173.
Romines, Ann. *The Home Plot* . . . , 79–83.

"Going to Shrewsberry"
Roman, Margaret. *Sarah Orne Jewett* . . . , 69, 153.

"The Guests of Mrs. Timms"
Roman, Margaret. *Sarah Orne Jewett* . . . , 87–88.

"Half-Done Polly"
Roman, Margaret. *Sarah Orne Jewett* . . . , 28–29.

"The Hiltons' Holiday"
Mobley, Marilyn S. *Folk Roots and Mythic Wings* . . . , 59–61.
Roman, Margaret. *Sarah Orne Jewett* . . . , 127, 168–189.

"In Dark New England Days"
Church, Joseph. "Fathers, Daughters, Slaves: The Haunted Scene of
Writing in Jewett's 'In Dark New England Days,' " *Am
Transcendental Q,* N.S., 5 (1991), 205–224.
Roman, Margaret. *Sarah Orne Jewett* . . . , 70–71, 122–123.

"The King of Folly Island"
Roman, Margaret. *Sarah Orne Jewett* . . . , 11–12, 72–73.

"A Late Supper"
  Roman, Margaret. *Sarah Orne Jewett* . . . , 58.
"A Landless Farmer"
  Roman, Margaret. *Sarah Orne Jewett* . . . , 119–120, 175–176.
"The Landscape Chamber"
  Roman, Margaret. *Sarah Orne Jewett* . . . , 71–72, 73.
"The Luck of the Bogans"
  Roman, Margaret. *Sarah Orne Jewett* . . . , 117–118.
"The Mate of the Daylight"
  Roman, Margaret. *Sarah Orne Jewett* . . . , 105–106.
"Marsh Rosemary"
  Roman, Margaret. *Sarah Orne Jewett* . . . , 106–107.
"Martha's Lady"
  Roman, Margaret. *Sarah Orne Jewett* . . . , 60–61, 94.
."Miss Becky's Pilgrimage"
  Roman, Margaret. *Sarah Orne Jewett* . . . , 189–190.
"Miss Debby's Neighbors"
  Roman, Margaret. *Sarah Orne Jewett* . . . , 121–122.
"Miss Esther's Guest"
  Roman, Margaret. *Sarah Orne Jewett* . . . , 194–195.
"Miss Manning's Minister"
  Roman, Margaret. *Sarah Orne Jewett* . . . , 187–188.
"Miss Sydney's Flowers"
  Roman, Margaret. *Sarah Orne Jewett* . . . , 59.
"Miss Tempy's Watchers"
  Roman, Margaret. *Sarah Orne Jewett* . . . , 61–62.
"Mr. Bruce"
  Roman, Margaret. *Sarah Orne Jewett* . . . , 146–152.
"Nancy's Doll"
  Roman, Margaret. *Sarah Orne Jewett* . . . , 57.
"Neighbor's Landmark"
  Roman, Margaret. *Sarah Orne Jewett* . . . , 68, 123–124.
"The Only Rose"
  Roman, Margaret. *Sarah Orne Jewett* . . . , 107–108.
"An Only Son"
  Roman, Margaret. *Sarah Orne Jewett* . . . , 174–175.
"Peach-Tree Joe"
  Roman, Margaret. *Sarah Orne Jewett* . . . , 173–174.
"The Quest of Mr. Teaby"
  Roman, Margaret. *Sarah Orne Jewett* . . . , 186–187.
"The Queen's Twin"
  Roman, Margaret. *Sarah Orne Jewett* . . . , 124–125.
  Romines, Ann. *The Home Plot* . . . , 77–79.

"Recollections of Dr. William Perry of Exeter"
Roman, Margaret. *Sarah Orne Jewett* . . . , 163–164.

"A Second Spring"
Roman, Margaret. *Sarah Orne Jewett* . . . , 188–189.

"Tom's Husband"
Roman, Margaret. *Sarah Orne Jewett* . . . , 137–139.

"The Town Poor"
Roman, Margaret. *Sarah Orne Jewett* . . . , 60, 126–127, 155.

"The Two Browns"
Roman, Margaret. *Sarah Orne Jewett* . . . , 116–117.

"A Village Shop"
Roman, Margaret. *Sarah Orne Jewett* . . . , 82–83, 84, 96, 104–105.

"A War Debt"
Roman, Margaret. *Sarah Orne Jewett* . . . , 102.

"A White Heron"
+ Bohner, Charles H. *Instructor's Manual* . . . , 61–62.
+ Charters, Ann, and William E. Sheidley. *Resources for Teaching* . . . , 3rd ed., 109–110.
Kelchner, Heidi. "Unstable Narrative Voice in Sarah Orne Jewett's 'A White Heron,' " *Colby Q*, 28 (1992), 85–92.
Moreno, Karen K. " 'A White Heron': Sylvia's Lonely Journey," *Connecticut R*, 13, i (1991), 81–85.
Orr, Elaine. "Reading Negotiation and Negotiated Reading: A Practice with/in 'A White Heron' and 'The Revolt of the Mother,' " *CEA Critic,* 53, iii (1991), 49–56, 60–65.
Mobley, Marilyn S. *Folk Roots and Mythic Wings* . . . , 49–58.
Roman, Margaret. *Sarah Orne Jewett* . . . , 197–205.

"William's Wedding"
Roman, Margaret. *Sarah Orne Jewett* . . . , 190–192.
Romines, Ann. *The Home Plot* . . . , 85–90.

"A Winter Courtship"
Roman, Margaret. *Sarah Orne Jewett* . . . , 183–185.

RUTH PRAWER JHABVALA

"The Man with the Dog"
Keating, Helane L., and Walter Levy. *Instructor's Manual: Lives Through Literature* . . . , 88–89.

JIA PINGWA

"Human Extremities"
Louie, Kam. "The Macho Eunuch: The Politics of Masculinity in Jia Pingwa's Human Extremities," *Mod China*, 17 (1991), 163–185.

JOSÉ JIMÉNEZ LOZANO

"La chaquetilla blanca"
  Sherzer, William M. "José Jiménez Lozano: Tale Telling in Old
    Castile," *Revista Hispánica Moderna*, 45, ii (1992), 310–312.
"Los *Episodios Nacionales*"
  Sherzer, William M. "José Jiménez Lozano . . . ," 314–315.
"Los oficios"
  Sherzer, William M. "José Jiménez Lozano . . . ," 313.

NICK JOAQUIN

"The Summer Solstice"
  Ventura, Sylvia M. "Sexism and the Mythification of Woman: A
    Feminist Reading of Nick Joaquin's 'The Summer Solstice' and
    Alfred Yuson's 'The Hill of Samuel,' " in Kintanar, Thelma B.,
    Ed. *Women Reading* . . . , 148–154.

JAMES JOYCE

"After the Race"
  Benstock, Bernard. "*Dubliners*: Double Binds (the Constraints of
    Childhood and Youth)," in Bosinelli, R. M. Bollettieri, C. Marengo
    Vaglio, and Chr. Van Boheemen, Eds. *The Languages of
    Joyce* . . . , 166–168.
  Fairhall, James. "Big-Power Politics and Colonial Economics: The
    Gordon Bennett Cup and 'After the Race,' " *James Joyce Q*, 28
    (1991), 387–397.
  Head, Dominic. *The Modernist* . . . , 56–58.
  Scholes, Robert. *In Search of James Joyce*, 41.
"Araby"
  Benstock, Bernard. "*Dubliners* . . . ," 156–157.
  + Bohner, Charles H. *Instructor's Manual* . . . , 62–63.
  + Cassill, R. V. . . . *Instructor's Handbook*, 90.
  + Charters, Ann, and William E. Sheidley. *Resources for
    Teaching* . . . , 3rd ed., 111–112.
  Conboy, Sheila C. "Exhibition and Inhibition: The Body Scene in
    Dubliners," *Twentieth Century Lit*, 37 (1991), 408–409.
  Head, Dominic. *The Modernist* . . . , 50–53.
  Wachtel, Albert. *The Cracked Lookingglass* . . . , 32–37.
"The Boarding House"
  Bašic, Sonja. "A Book of Many Uncertainties: Joyce's *Dubliners*,"
    Style, 25 (1991), 363–364.
  Benstock, Bernard. "*Dubliners* . . . ," 169–171.
  Conboy, Sheila C. "Exhibition . . . ," 410–411.
  Scholes, Robert. *In Search of James Joyce*, 43–44.

"Clay"
Ames, Christopher. *The Life of the Party* . . . , 42–44.
Head, Dominic. *The Modernist* . . . , 54, 55–56.
Norris, Margot. *Joyce's Web* . . . , 119–138.
Roughley, Alan. *James Joyce* . . . , 26–27, 150–159.
Scholes, Robert. *In Search of James Joyce*, 102–108.
Wales, Katie. *The Language of James Joyce*, 44–47.

"Counterparts"
Griffin, Paul F. "Chances of Being Kind: Rorty, Irony, Teaching
Modern Literature," *Lit Theory Classroom*, 18, ii (1991), 111–112.
Head, Dominic. *The Modernist* . . . , 46–47, 54, 55–56.
Wachtel, Albert. *The Cracked Lookingglass* . . . , 53–62.
Wales, Katie. *The Language of James Joyce*, 39–40.

"The Dead"
Ames, Christopher. *The Life of the Party* . . . , 45–57.
Avery, Bruce. "Distant Music: Sound and the Dialogics of Satire in
'The Dead,' " *James Joyce Q*, 28 (1991), 473–483.
Bašič, Sonja. "A Book of Many Uncertainties . . . ," 372–373.
+Bohner, Charles H. *Instructor's Manual* . . . , 64–65.
Brown, Richard. *James Joyce*, 17–27.
Burke, Daniel. *Beyond Interpretation* . . . , 27–47.
+Cassill, R. V. . . . *Instructor's Handbook*, 93–96.
+Charters, Ann, and William E. Sheidley. *Resources for
Teaching* . . . , 3rd ed., 113–114.
Conboy, Sheila C. "Exhibition . . . ," 407–408, 412–415.
Corcoran, Marlena G. "Language, Character, and Gender in the
Direct Discourse of *Dubliners*," *Style*, 25 (1991), 446–449.
DiBattista, Maria. *First Love* . . . , 29–31.
Garrett, Roland. "Six Theories in the Bedroom of 'The Dead,' "
Philosophy & Lit, 16 (1992), 115–127.
Haas, Robert. "Music in *Dubliners*" *Colby Q*, 28, i (1992), 29–33.
Ingersoll, Earl G. "The Gender of Travel in 'The Dead,' " *James
Joyce Q*, 30 (1992), 41–50.
Keating, Helane L., and Walter Levy. *Instructor's Manual: Lives
Through Literature* . . . , 115–116.
Leonard, Gary. "Joyce and Lacan: 'The Woman' as a Symbol of
'Maculinity' in 'The Dead,' " *James Joyce Q*, 28 (1991), 451–472.
Loe, Thomas. " 'The Dead' as Novella," *James Joyce Q*, 28 (1991),
485–497.
Norris, Margot. *Joyce's Web* . . . , 97–118.
Owens, Cóilín. "The Mystique of the West in Joyce's 'The Dead,' "
Irish Univ R, 22, i (Spring, 1992), 80–91.
Rice, Thomas J. "Dante . . . Browning. Gabriel . . . Joyce: Allusion
and Structure in 'The Dead,' " *James Joyce Q*, 30 (1992), 29–40.
———. "The Geometry of Meaning in *Dubliners*: A Euclidean
Approach," *Style*, 25 (1991), 399–440.
Riquelme, J. R. "Joyce's 'The Dead': The Dissolution of the Self and
the Police," *Style*, 25 (1991), 488–505.
Scott, Bonnie K. "James Joyce: A Subversive Geography of

Gender," in Hyland, Paul, and Niel Sammells, Eds. *Irish Writing* . . . , 161–164.

Sperber, Michael. "Shame and James Joyce's 'The Dead,' " *Lit & Psych,* 37 (1991), 62–71.

Stanzel, Franz K. "Consonant and Dissonant Closure in 'Death in Venice' and 'The Dead,' " in Fehn, Ann Ingeborg Hoestry, and Maria Tatar, Eds. *Neverending Stories* . . . , 114–123.

Wales, Katie. *The Language of James Joyce,* 47–55.

Walsh, Timothy. "The Cognitive and Mimetic Function of Absence in Art, Music, and Literature," *Mosaic,* 25, ii (1992), 80.

Yin, Xiaoling. "The Paralyzed and the Dead: A Comparative Reading of 'The Dead' and 'In a Tavern,' " *Comp Lit Stud,* 29 (1992), 276–278, 281–288, 292, 294.

"An Encounter"

Benstock, Bernard. "*Dubliners* . . . ," 155–156, 160–161.

Conboy, Sheila C. "Exhibition . . . ," 408.

Wachtel, Albert. *The Cracked Lookingglass* . . . , 30–32.

"Eveline"

Benstock, Bernard. "*Dubliners* . . . ," 161–166.

French, Marilyn. "Silences: Where Joyce's Language Stops," in Bosinelli, R. M. Bollettieri, C. Marengo Vaglio, and Chr. Van Boheeman, Eds. *The Languages of Joyce* . . . , 43.

Head, Dominic. *The Modernist* . . . , 66–73.

Roughley, Alan. *James Joyce* . . . , 31–32, 49–51, 52–56.

Wachtel, Albert. *The Cracked Lookingglass* . . . , 40–43.

Wales, Katie. *The Language of James Joyce,* 40–42.

"Grace"

Bašic, Sonja. "A Book of Many Uncertainties . . . ," 358–360.

Corcoran, Marlena G. "Language, Character, and Gender . . . ," 444–446.

Greco Lobner, Corinna del. "Quincunxial Sherlockholmesing in 'Grace,' " *James Joyce Q,* 28 (1991), 445–450.

Osteen, Mark. "Serving Two Masters: Economics and Figures of Power in Joyce's 'Grace,' " *Twentieth Century Lit,* 37 (1991), 76–92.

"Ivy Day in the Committee Room"

Ames, Christopher. *The Life of the Party* . . . , 44–45.

Brian, Michael. " 'A Very Fine Piece of Writing': An Etymological, Dantean, and Gnostic Reading of Joyce's 'Ivy Day in the Committee Room,' " *Style,* 25 (1991), 466–480.

"A Little Cloud"

+ Cassill, R. V. . . . *Instructor's Handbook,* 91–92.

Head, Dominic. *The Modernist* . . . , 58–66.

Ingersoll, Earl G. "Metaphor and Metonymy in James Joyce's 'A Little Cloud' and Bryan MacMahon's 'Exile's Return,' " *Canadian J Irish Stud,* 16, ii (1990), 28–32.

Mosher, Harold F. "Cliche and Repetition in *Dubliners*: The Example of 'A Little Cloud,' " *Style,* 25 (1991), 378–392.

O'Grady, Thomas B. "Little Chandler's Song of Experience," *James Joyce Q,* 28 (1991), 399–405.
Wachtel, Albert. *The Cracked Lookingglass . . . ,* 43–49.

"A Mother"
Conboy, Sheila C. "Exhibition . . . ," 409–410.
Miller, James E. " 'O, she's a nice lady!': A Rereading of 'A Mother,' " *James Joyce Q,* 28 (1991), 407–426.
Valente, Joseph. "Joyce's Sexual Differnd: A Example from *Dubliners,*" *James Joyce Q,* 28 (1991), 427–443.

"A Painful Case"
Head, Dominic. *The Modernist . . . ,* 73–76.
Wachtel, Albert. *The Cracked Lookingglass . . . ,* 49–52.
Wales, Katie. *The Language of James Joyce,* 42–44.
Williams, Trevor L. "No Cheer for the 'Gratefully Oppressed' in Joyce's *Dubliners,*" *Style,* 25 (1991), 427–430.

"The Sisters"
Ames, Christopher. *The Life of the Party . . . ,* 40–42.
Benstock, Bernard. "*Dubliners . . . ,*" 159–160.
Booker, M. Keith. "History and Language in 'The Sisters,' " *Criticism,* 33 (1991), 217–233.
Bašič, Sonja. "A Book of Many Uncertainties . . . ," 361.
French, Marilyn. "Silences . . . ," 44–45.
Harty, John. "The Doubling of Dublin Messages in 'The Sisters,' " *Notes Mod Irish Lit,* 4 (1992), 42–44.
Head, Dominic. *The Modernist . . . ,* 42.
Roughley, Alan. *James Joyce . . . ,* 26–27, 150–159.
Wachtel, Albert. *The Cracked Lookingglass . . . ,* 23–29.

"Two Gallants"
Benstock, Bernard. "*Dubliners . . . ,*" 168–169.
Head, Dominic. *The Modernist . . . ,* 45, 54, 55–56.
Williams, Trevor L. "No Cheer . . . ," 433–435.

FRANZ KAFKA

"Alexander the Great"
McCort, Dennis. "Kafka's Koans," *Religion & Lit,* 23, i (1991), 57–60.

"Der Aufbruch"
Beckmann, Martin. "Der Prozess der ästhetischen Erfahrung in drei Parabelstücken Franz Kafkas," *Seminar,* 28, iii (1992), 196–199, 206.

"The Burrow"
Ryan, Judith. *The Vanishing Subject . . . ,* 110–111.

"The Cell"
McCort, Dennis. "Kafka's Koans," 53–55.

"The City Coat of Arms"
Alter, Robert. *Necessary Angels . . . ,* 54–56.

"A Country Doctor"
Steinsaltz, David. "Kafka's Geometry," *Seminar*, 28 (1992), 344–345.
Whitlark, James. *Behind the Great Wall* . . . , 65–71.
————. "Kafka's 'A Country Doctor' as Neoromantic Fairy Tale," in Saciuk, Olena H., Ed. *The Shape* . . . , 43–49.

"Description of a Struggle"
Cooper, Gabriele von Natzmer. *Kafka and Language* . . . , 33–36.
Ryan, Judith. *The Vanishing Subject* . . . , 101–102.
Steinsaltz, David. "Kafka's . . . ," 337–338, 343–344.

"An Everyday Occurrence"
Steinsaltz, David. "Kafka's . . . ," 338–339.

"Gibs auf"
Beckmann, Martin. "Der Prozess der äesthetischen Erfahrung . . . ," 191–196, 206.

"The Great Wall of China"
Fickert, Kurt J. "The Emperor's Message: Truth and Fiction in Kafka," *Int'l Fiction R*, 18 (1991), 76–80.
Steinsaltz, David. "Kafka's . . . ," 339.
Whitlark, James. *Behind the Great Wall* . . . , 217–230.

"A Hunger Artist"
+ Bohner, Charles H. *Instructor's Manual* . . . , 65–66.
+ Cassill, R. V. . . . *Instructor's Handbook*, 101–102.
Charters, Ann, and William E. Sheidley. *Resources for Teaching* . . . , 3rd ed., 116–117.
Cervo, Nathan. "Kafka's 'The Hunger Artist,' " *Explicator*, 50, ii (1991), 99–100.
Hoffman, Anne G. *Between Exile and Return* . . . , 49–52.
Medeiros, Paulo. "Cannibalism and Starvation: The Parameters of Eating Disorders in Literature," in Furst, Lilian R., and Peter W. Graham, Eds. *Disorderly Eaters* . . . , 20–21.

"An Imperial Message"
Fickert, Kurt J. "The Emperor's Message: Truth and Fiction in Kafka," *Int'l Fiction R*, 18 (1991), 76–80.
Kluback, William. "Liberation Through Parable in Franz Kafka," *J Evolutionary Psych*, 12 (1991), 110–115.

"In the Gallery"
Boa, Elizabeth. "Kafka's 'Auf der Galerie': A Resistent Reading," *Deutsche Vierteljahrsschrift*, 65 (1991), 486–501.

"In the Penal Colony"
Hoffman, Anne G. *Between Exile and Return* . . . , 23–30.
Jayne, Richard. "Kafka's 'In der Strafkolonie' and the Aporias of Textual Interpretation," *Deutsche Vierteljahrsschrift*, 66 (1992), 94–120.
Kerckhoff, Annette. "Interpreting and Translating Gestures for Power Play in Kafka's 'In the Penal Colony,' " *TTR Traduction, Terminologie, Rédaction*, 2 (1992), 195–222.

"Investigations of a Dog"
  Ryan, Judith. *The Vanishing Subject* . . . , 109–110.
"The Judgement"
  Politi, Jina. " 'Not (Not I),' " *Lit & Theology*, 6, iv (1992), 348–352.
  Ryan, Judith. *The Vanishing Subject* . . . , 102–106.
"Metamorphosis"
  Arie-Gaifman, Hana. "Milena, Odradek, Samsa. Zu tschechischen
    Etymologie einiger Eigennamen bei Kafka," *Germanisch-
    Romanische Monatsschrift*, 41, i (1991), 95–99.
  +Cassill, R. V. . . . *Instructor's Handbook*, 98–100.
  +Charters, Ann, and William E. Sheidley. *Resources for
    Teaching* . . . , 3rd ed., 118–119.
  Hahn, Hannelore. "Comparación de 'Axolotl' de Julio Cortázar y
    'La metamorfosis' de Franz Kafka," *Nuez*, 4, x–xi (1992), 26,
    27, 28.
  Hoffman, Anne G. *Between Exile and Return* . . . , 50–51.
  Murphy, Richard. "Semiotic Excess, Semantic Vacuity and the
    Photograph of the Imaginary: The Interplay of Realism and the
    Fantastic in Kafka's 'Die Verwandlung,' " *Deutsche
    Vierteljahrsschrift*, 65, ii (1991), 311–313, 315–316.
  Rodríguez-Luis, Julio. *The Contemporary Praxis* . . . , 7–8.
  Ryan, Judith. *The Vanishing Subject* . . . , 107–108.
  Stavans, Ilan. "Kafka, Cortázar, Gass," *R Contemp Fiction*, 11, iii
    (1991), 131–132.
"The New Advocate"
  Alter, Robert. *Necessary Angels* . . . , 102–103.
  Steinmetz, Ralph-Henning. "Kafkas neuer Advokat," *Wirkendes
    Wort*, 41, i (1991), 72–76, 78–79.
  Wasserman, Martin. "Kafka's 'The New Attorney': A Therapeutic
    Poem Offering a Jewish Way to Face Death," *Cithara*, 31, i
    (1991), 3–15.
"The Next Village"
  Steinsaltz, David. "Kafka's . . . ," 345.
"Robinson Crusoe"
  McCort, Dennis. "Kafka's Koans," 55–57.
"Sancho Panza"
  McCort, Dennis. "Kafka's Koans," 66–67.
"The Silence of the Sirens"
  Whitlark, James. *Behind the Great Wall* . . . , 58–60.
"The Spring"
  McCort, Dennis. "Kafka's Koans," 64–65.
"Von den Gleichnissen"
  Beckmann, Martin. "Der Prozess der äesthetischen Erfahrung . . . ,"
    200–205, 206.

KARL J. KALFAIAN

"Juno in the Pine Ring"
  Bedrosian, Margaret. "Transplantation," in Bedrosian, Margaret,
  Ed. *The Magic Pine Ring*, 64–68.

JOHANNA KAPLAN

"Sour or Suntanned, It Makes No Difference"
  Gladsky, Thomas S. *Princes, Peasants . . .* , 216–217.

NIKOLAY KARAMZIN

"The Beautiful Princess and the Fortunate Dwarf"
  Hammarberg, Gitta. *From the Idyll . . .* , 207–221.
"The Bird of Paradise"
  Hammarberg, Gitta. *From the Idyll . . .* , 109–112.
"A Blossom on the Grave of My Agathon"
  Hammarberg, Gitta. *From the Idyll . . .* , 168–169.
"Bornholm Island"
  Hammarberg, Gitta. *From the Idyll . . .* , 182–207.
"The Countryside"
  Hammarberg, Gitta. *From the Idyll . . .* , 76–78.
"The Deep Forest"
  Hammarberg, Gitta. *From the Idyll . . .* , 112–121.
"Eugene and Julia"
  Hammarberg, Gitta. *From the Idyll . . .* , 132–138.
"The Flood"
  Hammarberg, Gitta. *From the Idyll . . .* , 61–64.
"Gessner's Death"
  Hammarberg, Gitta. *From the Idyll . . .* , 52–53.
"Liodor"
  Hammarberg, Gitta. *From the Idyll . . .* , 167–181.
"My Confession"
  Hammarberg, Gitta. *From the Idyll . . .* , 240–251.
"Night"
  Hammarberg, Gitta. *From the Idyll . . .* , 87–92.
"Palemon and Daphnis"
  Hammarberg, Gitta. *From the Idyll . . .* , 54–61.
"Poor Liza"
  Hammarberg, Gitta. *From the Idyll . . .* , 138–159.
"A Promenade"
  Hammarberg, Gitta. *From the Idyll . . .* , 65–76.

"Sierra-Morena"
Hammarberg, Gitta. *From the Idyll . . .* , 159–167.

JANET KAUFFMAN

"Patriotic"
Dwyer, June. "Janet Kauffman's 'Patriotic': Woman's Work," *Stud Short Fiction*, 28 (1991), 55–62.

BEL KAUFMAN

"Sunday in the Park"
Nelson, Ronald J. "The Battlefield in Bel Kaufman's 'Sunday in the Park,' " *Engl Lang Notes*, 30, i (1992), 61–68.

GARRISON KEILLOR

"Aprille"
Lee, Judith Y. *Garrison Keillor . . .* , 164–170.
"David and Agnes"
Lee, Judith Y. *Garrison Keillor . . .* , 152–153.
"Don: The True Story of a Young Person"
Lee, Judith Y. *Garrison Keillor . . .* , 137–138.
"Friendly Neighbor"
Lee, Judith Y. *Garrison Keillor . . .* , 176–178.
"Homecoming"
Lee, Judith Y. *Garrison Keillor . . .* , 156–157.
"If Robert Frost Had an Apple"
Lee, Judith Y. *Garrison Keillor . . .* , 140–141.
"Life Is Good"
Lee, Judith Y. *Garrison Keillor . . .* , 158.
"My North Dakota Railroad Days"
Lee, Judith Y. *Garrison Keillor . . .* , 126–128.
"Nana Hami Ba Reba"
Lee, Judith Y. *Garrison Keillor . . .* , 133–134.
"Plainfolks"
Lee, Judith Y. *Garrison Keillor . . .* , 125.
"Post Office"
Lee, Judith Y. *Garrison Keillor . . .* , 151–152.
"The Slim Graves Show"
Lee, Judith Y. *Garrison Keillor . . .* , 122–124.
"The Tip-Top Club"
Lee, Judith Y. *Garrison Keillor . . .* , 130–131.

"What Did We Do Wrong"
Lee, Judith Y. *Garrison Keillor* . . . , 143–146.

GOTTFRIED KELLER

"Kleider machen Leute"
Fickel, Irene. "Die Gestaltung von Widerspruch und Konflikt in
Gottfried Kellers Novelle 'Kleider machen Leute,' " *Arbeiten
Deutschen Philologie,* 18 (1989), 36–45.

"Spiegel, das Kätzchen"
Friedrichsmeyer, Erhard. "Keller's 'Spiegel, das Kätzchen': A
Eudemonist Answer to Goethe's *Faust?*" in Friedrichsmeyer, Sara,
and Barbara Becker-Cantarino, Eds. *The Enlightenment* . . . ,
131–138.

"Tanzlegendchen"
Cattaneo, Gabriella. "König David in Gottfried Kellers
'Tanzlegendchen,' " *Sprachkunst,* 22, i (1991), 73–77.

JAMES PATRICK KELLY

"Rat"
Cox, F. Brett. "We Mean It, Man: Nancy Kress's 'Out of All Them
Bright Stars' and James Patrick Kelly's 'Rat,' " *New York R Sci
Fiction,* 50 (October, 1992), 17.

WILLIAM KENNEDY

"The Secret of Creative Love"
Van Dover, J. K. *Understanding William Kennedy,* 125–128.

JOMO KENYATTA

"The Gentlemen of the Jungle"
Balogun, F. Odun. *Tradition and Modernity* . . . , 48–49.

HAPET KHARIBIAN

"Home in Exile"
Bedrosian, Margaret. "Transplantation," in Bedrosian, Margaret,
Ed. *The Magic Pine Ring,* 58–59.

DANIIL KHARMS [DANIIL IVANOVICH YUVACHEV]

"The Falling"
Kobrinsky, Aleksandr. "Some Features of the Poetics of Kharms's

Prose: The Story Upadanie ('The Falling')," trans. Neil Cornwell, in Cornwell, Neil, Ed. *Daniil Kharms* . . . , 149–155.

LEONARD KIBERA

"The Spider's Web"
  Balogun, F. Odun. *Tradition and Modernity* . . . , 31–32.

BENEDICT KIELY

"A Ball of Malt and Madame Butterfly"
  O'Grady, Thomas B. "Echoes of William Carleton: Benedict Kiely
    and the Irish Oral Tradition," *Stud Short Fiction*, 28 (1991),
    325–326.

GRACE ELIZABETH KING

"Bayou L'Ombre"
  Coleman, Linda S. "At Odds: Race and Gender in Grace King's
    Short Fiction," in Brown, Dorothy H., and Barbara C. Ewell, Eds.
    Louisiana Women . . . , 43–47.
"A Crippled Hope"
  Coleman, Linda S. "At Odds . . . ," 37–40, 42.
"A Little Convent Girl"
  Coleman, Linda S. "At Odds . . . ," 48–49.
"Madrilène"
  Coleman, Linda S. "At Odds . . . ," 49–51.
"Monsieur Motte"
  Bush, Robert. "The Patrician Voice: Grace King," in Kennedy,
    Richard S., Ed. *Literary New Orleans* . . . , 11–12.
  Coleman, Linda S. "At Odds . . . ," 51–54.
"One of Us"
  Coleman, Linda S. "At Odds . . . ," 40–41.

MAXINE HONG KINGSTON

"The Ghost-Mate"
  Shih, Shu-mei. "Exile and Intertextuality in Maxine Hong Kingston's
    China Men," in Whitlark, James, and Wendell Aycock, Eds. *The
    Literature of Emigration* . . . , 69–71.
"The Great Grandfather of the Sandalwood Mountains"
  Shih, Shu-mei. "Exile and Intertextuality . . . ," 71–72.
"On Discovery"
  Shih, Shu-mei. "Exile and Intertextuality . . . ," 66–69.

"On Morality"
 Shih, Shu-mei. "Exile and Intertextuality . . . ," 72–74.

RUDYARD KIPLING

"The Dream of Duncan Parrenness"
 Herdman, John. *The Double* . . . , 143–145.

"The Gardener"
 Morris, Christopher. "What 'Rolled the Stone Away'? 'The
  Gardener' Reconsidered," *Kipling J,* 65 (September, 1991), 37–43.

"Fairy-Kist"
 Coates, John. "The Redemption Theme in *Limits and Renewals*: Two
  Different Paths," *Kipling J,* 65 (December, 1991), 16–21.

"The Gardener"
 Kemp, Sandra. "Kipling's Women," in Ross, Angus, Ed. *Kipling
  86* . . . , 34–36.

"In Ambush"
 Stewart, D. H. "*Stalky* and the Language of Education," *Children's
  Lit*, 20 (1992), 39.

"Kaa's Hunting"
 McMaster, Juliet. "The Trinity Archetype in *The Jungle Books* and
  The Wizard of Oz," *Children's Lit*, 20 (1992), 94–95, 96.

"The King's Ankus"
 McMaster, Juliet. "The Trinity . . . ," 98.

"A Madonna of the Trenches"
 Kemp, Sandra. "Kipling's . . . ," 32–34.

"The Man Who Would Be King"
 +Bohner, Charles H. *Instructor's Manual* . . . , 66–67.
 Cassill, R. V. . . . *Instructor's Handbook*, 103–104.

"The Manner of Men"
 Coates, John. "The Redemption Theme . . . ," 30–33.

"Mary Postgate"
 Bohner, Charles H. *Instructor's Manual* . . . , 68–69.

"The Miracle of Purun Bhagat"
 Karim, Enamul. " 'The Miracle of Purun Bhagat,' " *Kipling J,* 65
  (March, 1991), 25–34.

"Mrs. Bathurst"
 Mason, Philip. "More Thoughts on 'Mrs. Bathurst,' " *Kipling J,* 66
  (March, 1992), 11–20.

"The Moral Reformers"
 Stewart, D. H. "*Stalky* . . . ," 45–46, 47–48.

"Mowgli's Brothers"
 McMaster, Juliet. "The Trinity . . . ," 95.

"Red Dog"
 McMaster, Juliet. "The Trinity . . . ," 98–99.

"Regulus"
  Stewart, D. H. *"Stalky . . . ,"* 41, 45.

"The Ship that Found Herself"
  Hanquart-Turner, Evelyne. "Devoir et liberté: 'The Ship that Found
    Herself' de Kipling," *Cahiers Victoriens et Edouardiens*, 33
    (1991), 33–42.

"Unprofessional"
  Coates, John. "The Redemption Theme . . . ," 13–16.

"The Wish House"
  Kemp, Sandra. "Kipling's . . . ," 30–32.

PERRI KLASS

"Not a Good Girl"
  + Bohner, Charles H. *Instructor's Manual . . .* , 69–70.

HEINRICH VON KLEIST

"The Beggar Woman of Locarno"
  Hilliard, Kevin. " 'Rittergeschichte mit Gespenst': The Narration of
    the Subconscious in Kleist's 'Das Bettelweib von Locarno,' "
    Germ Life & Letters, 44 (1991), 281–290.

"The Engagement in Santo Domingo"
  Burwick, Roswitha. "Issues of Language and Communication:
    Kleist's 'Die Verlobung in St. Domingo,' " *Germ Q*, 65, iii–iv
    (1992), 318–327.
  Fleming, Ray. "Race and the Difference It Makes in Kleist's 'Die
    Verlobung in St. Domingo,' " *Germ Q*, 65, iii–iv (1992), 306–317.
  Werlen, Hans J. "Seduction and Betrayal: Race and Gender in
    Kleist's 'Die Verlobung in St. Domingo,' " *Monatschefte*, 84
    (1992), 459–471.

"The Foundling"
  Wagner, Irmgard. " 'Der Findling': Erratic Signifier in Kleist and
    Geology," *Germ Q*, 64 (1991), 281–295.

"The Marquise of O—"
  Bentzel, Curtis C. "Knowledge in Narrative: The Significance of the
    Swan in Kleist's 'Die Marquise von O . . . ," *Germ Q*, 64
    (1991), 296–303.
  Rhiel, Mary. "The Taming of the Screw: Rohmer's Filming of
    Kleist's 'Die Marquise von O . . . ,' " Ruddick, Nicholas, Ed.
    State . . . , 83–88.
  Dietrick, Linda. "Immaculate Conceptions: 'The Marquise
    von O . . .' and the Swan," *Seminar*, 27 (1991), 316–329.
  Winnett, Susan. "The Marquise's 'O' and the Mad Dash of
    Narrative," in Higgins, Lynn A., and Brenda R. Silver, Eds. *Rape
    and Representation*, 67–86.

"Michael Kohlhass"
Friedl, Gerhard. " 'Unter diesen Umständen . . . ,' Sprache, Struktur und Erzählperspektive in Kleists 'Michael Kohlhaas,' " *Der Deutschunterricht*, 44, iii (1992), 5–19.
Landwehr, Margarete. "The Mysterious Gypsy in Kleist's 'Michael Kohlhass': The Disintegration of Legal and Linguistic Boundaries," *Monatshefte*, 84 (1992), 431–446.
"The Puppet Theater"
Smith, Brittain. "Pas de Deux: Doing the Dialogic Dance in Kleist's Fictitious Conversation 'About the Puppet Theater,' " in Cope, Kevin L., Ed. *Compendious* . . . , 368–381.
"St. Cecilia or the Power of Music"
Gustavson, Susan E. "Kleist, Freud, and Kristeva: 'Die heilige Cäcilie' and the Unspeakable Abyss," *Seminar*, 28 (1992), 112–128.

WOFRAM KOBER

"The Old Man"
Mabee, Barbara. "Astronauts, Angels, and Time Machines: The Fantastic in Recent German Democratic Republic Literature," in Morse, Donald E., Marshall B. Tymn, and Csilla Bertha, Eds. *The Celebration* . . . , 224–226.

ELLIS AYITEY KOMEY

"I Can Face You"
Balogun, F. Odun. *Tradition and Modernity* . . . , 18–19.

HELGA KÖNIGSDORF

"Ungelegener Befund"
Cosentino, Christine. " 'Heute freilich möchte man fragen . . . ,': Zum Thema von Schuld und Verantwortung in Christa Wolfs 'Was bleibt,' Helga Königsdorfs 'Ungelegener Befund,' und Helga Schuberts 'Judas Frauen,' " *Neophil*, 76, i (1992), 114–116.

JERZY KOSINSKY

"Being There"
Griffiths, Gareth. "Being there, being There: Kosinsky and Malouf," in Adam, Ian, and Helen Tiffin, Eds. *Past the Last Post* . . . , 153–165.

NANCY KRESS

"Out of All Them Bright Stars"
Cox, F. Brett. "We Mean It, Man: Nancy Kress's 'Out of All Them

Bright Stars' and James Patrick Kelly's 'Rat,' '' *New York R Sci Fiction*, 50 (October, 1992), 15–17.

MILAN KUNDERA

"The Hitchhiking Game"
+ Charters, Ann, and William E. Sheidley. *Resources for Teaching* . . . , 3rd ed., 122–123.
"Nobody Will Laugh"
Gaughan, Richard T. " 'Man Thinks; God Laughs': Kundera's 'Nobody Will Laugh,' '' *Stud Short Fiction*, 29 (1992), 1–10.

ALEXANDER KUPRIN

"Zhidorka"
Rischin, Ruth. " 'The Most Historical of Peoples': Yushkevich, Kuprin and the Dubnovian Idea," in Luker, Nicholas, Ed. *The Short Story in Russia* . . . , 36–40, 43, 45.

CARMEN LAFORET

"Rosamunda"
Pérez Firmat, Gustavo. "Carmen Laforet: The Dilemma of Artistic Vocation," in Brown, Joan L., Ed. *Women Writers* . . . , 37–38.

RING LARDNER

"Alibi Ike"
Robinson, Douglas. *Ring Lardner* . . . , 128–133.
"A Busher's Letters Home
Robinson, Douglas. *Ring Lardner* . . . , 118–123.
"Dinner"
Robinson, Douglas. *Ring Lardner* . . . , 133–137.
"Haircut"
+ Bohner, Charles H. *Instructor's Manual* . . . , 70–71.
Robinson, Douglas. *Ring Lardner* . . . , 102–103, 175–180, 183–191.
―――. "Ring Lardner's Dual Audience and the Capitalist Double Bind," *Am Lit His*, 4 (1992), 266–268.
"My Roomy"
Robinson, Douglas. *Ring Lardner* . . . , 128–131.
"Who Dealt?"
Gardiner, Ellen. " 'Engendered in Melancholy': Ring Lardner's 'Who Dealt?' '' in Robinson, Douglas, *Ring Lardner* . . . , 237–260.
Robinson, Douglas. *Ring Lardner* . . . , 3–33, 35–39, 45–51.

MONIQUE LARUE

"Babil"
Fisher, Claudine G. "Sensibilités française et québécoise dans *Plages*," *Revue Francophone de Louisiane*, 5, i (Spring, 1990), 67–68.

MARGARET LAURENCE

"The Loons"
Cassill, R. V. . . . *Instructor's Handbook*, 104–105.
Regan, Stephen. " 'The Presence of the Past': Modernism and Postmodernism in Canadian Short Fiction," in Howells, Colin A., and Lynette Hunter, Eds. *Narrative Strategies* . . . , 122–123.

"The Sound of Singing"
Hartveit, Lars. "Form as Ideological Matrix: Margaret Laurence's Art as a Short Story Writer as Illustrated in *A Bird in the House*," Bardolph, Jacquelin, Ed. *Short Fiction* . . . , 167–168.

"To Set Our House in Order"
Regan, Stephen. " 'The Presence . . . ,'" 120–122.

MARY LAVIN

"At Sallygap"
Loeffelholz, Mary. *Experimental Lives* . . . , 144.

"The Green Grave and the Black Hole"
Loeffelholz, Mary. *Experimental Lives* . . . , 144–145.

D. H. LAWRENCE

"The Blind Man"
Cassill, R. V. . . . *Instructor's Handbook*, 106–107.
Engel, Monroe. "Knowing More Than One Imagines; Imagining More Than One Knows," *Agni*, 31–32 (1990), 169–172, 173, 174, 175.

"The Border Line"
Hyde, Virginia. *The Risen Adam* . . . , 53–56.

"The Captain's Doll"
Holbrook, David. *Where D. H. Lawrence* . . . , 100–106.

"The Fox"
Holbrook, David. *Where D. H. Lawrence* . . . , 86–100.
Kalnins, Mara. "Lawrence's Men and Women: Complements and Opposites," in Minogue, Sally, Ed. *Problems* . . . , 166–170.
Osborn, Marijane. "Complexities of Gender and Genre in Lawrence's 'The Fox,' " *Essays Lit*, 19, i (1992), 84–97.

"The Horse Dealer's Daughter"
+ Bohner, Charles H. *Instructor's Manual . . .* , 71–72.
+ Cassill, R. V. . . . *Instructor's Handbook,* 107–109.
Grmelová, Anna. "Thematic and Structural Diversification of D. H. Lawrence's Short Story in the Wake of World War I," *Litteraria Pragensia,* 2, iv (1992), 62–64.

"In Love"
Spilka, Mark. *Renewing the Normative . . .* , 52–54.

"The Ladybird" [originally "The Thimble"]
Worthen, John. *D. H. Lawrence,* 76–78.

"Laetitia"
Worthen, John. *D. H. Lawrence,* 10–11.

"The Man Who Died" [originally "The Escaped Cock"]
Worthen, John. *D. H. Lawrence,* 118–119.

"Monkey Nuts"
Grmelová, Anna. "Thematic . . . ," 67–68.

"Odour of Chrysanthemums"
+ Charters, Ann, and William E. Sheidley. *Resources for Teaching . . .* , 3rd ed., 125–126.
Holbrook, David. *Where D. H. Lawrence . . .* , 78–86.
Schulz, Volker. "D. H. Lawrence's Early Masterpieces of Short Fiction: 'Odour of Chrysanthemums,' " *Stud Short Fiction,* 28 (1991), 363–369.
Worthen, John. *D. H. Lawrence,* 18–20.

"The Princess"
Spilka, Mark. *Renewing the Normative . . .* , 222–225.

"The Prussian Officer" [originally "Honour and Arms"]
Black, Michael. . . . *The Early Philosophical Works,* 55–57.
Worthen, John. *D. H. Lawrence,* 45–46.

"The Rocking-Horse Winner"
+ Bohner, Charles H. *Instructor's Manual . . .* , 73–74.
Burke, Daniel. *Beyond Interpretation . . .* , 49–63.
+ Cassill, R. V. . . . *Instructor's Handbook,* 110–111.
+ Charters, Ann, and William E. Sheidley. *Resources for Teaching . . .* , 3rd ed., 127–128.
Sklenicka, Carol. *D. H. Lawrence and the Child,* 156–159.

"St. Mawr"
Haegert, John. "Lawrence's 'St. Mawr' and the De-Creation of America," *Criticism,* 34, i (1992), 75–98.
Holbrook, David. *Where D. H. Lawrence . . .* , 114–119.

"The Thorn in the Flesh" [originally "Vin Ordinaire"]
Hyde, Virginia. *The Risen Adam . . .* , 50–53.
Worthen, John. *D. H. Lawrence,* 34–41.

"Tickets, Please"
Grmelová, Anna. "Thematic . . . ," 65–67.

"The Virgin and the Gipsy"
DiBattista, Maria. *First Love* . . . , 57–59.
Holbrook, David. *Where D. H. Lawrence* . . . , 106–114.
Yanada, Noriyuki. " 'The Virgin and the Gipsy': Four Realms and Narrative Modes," *Lang & Culture*, 20 (1991), 144–146.

"The Woman Who Rode Away"
Holbrook, David. *Where D. H. Lawrence* . . . , 119–129.
Kinkead-Weekes, Mark. "The Gringo Señora Who Rode Away," *D. H. Lawrence R,* 22 (1990), 251–265.
Mohanty, Sachidananda. " 'The Woman Who Rode Away': Defeat of Feminism?" *Aligarh J Engl Stud*, 14, i (1989), 96–107.
Vichy, Thérèse. "L'ironie dans 'The Woman Who Rode Away,' " *Études Lawrenciennes*, 6 (1991), 69–81.
Worthen, John. *D. H. Lawrence,* 86–89.

HENRY LAWSON

"The Bush Undertaker"
Lee, Christopher. "What Colour Are the Dead? Madness, Race and the National Gaze in Henry Lawson's 'The Bush Undertaker,' " *Kunapipi*, 13, iii (1991), 14–25.

"The Drover's Wife"
Thieme, John. "Drovers' Wives," in Bardolph, Jacquelin, Ed. *Short Fiction* . . . , 69–71.

FERNANDO LEAÑO

"Coward"
Grow, L. M. "Fernando Leaño's 'Coward,' " *Philippine Stud*, 40 (1992), 361–367.

DAVID LEAVITT

"Territory"
+Charters, Ann, and William E. Sheidley. *Resources for Teaching* . . . , 3rd ed., 232–233.
Klarer, Mario. "David Leavitt's 'Territory': René Girard's Homoerotic 'Trigonometry' and Julia Kristeva's 'Semiotic Chora,' " *Stud Short Fiction,* 28 (1991), 63–76.

VERNON LEE [VIOLET PAGET]

"Prince Alberic and the Snake Lady"
Robbins, Ruth. "Vernon Lee: Decadent Woman?" in Stokes, John, Ed. *Fin de Siècle* . . . , 153–158.

JOSEPH SHERIDAN LE FANU

"A Bird of Passage"
    Milbank, Alison. *Daughters of the House* . . . , 164–165.
"Carmilla"
    Girard, Gaid. "Les écrits de Laura: Analyse de 'Carmilla,' de J. S.
        Le Fanu," in Bozzetto, Roger, Max Duperray, and Alain Chareyre-
        Mejan, Eds. *Eros* . . . , 23–33.
    Rance, Nicholas. . . . *Walking the Moral Hospital,* 57–59.
    Stoddard, Helen. " 'The Precautions of Nervous People Are
        Infectious': Sheridan Le Fanu's Symptomatic Gothic," *Mod Lang
        R,* 86, (1991), 27–33, 34.
    Waller, Gregory A. *The Living and the Undead* . . . , 50–55.
    Welch, Robert. *Irish Writers* . . . , 69–70.
"The Familiar"
    Milbank, Alison. *Daughters of the House* . . . , 162–164.
"Green Tea"
    Stoddard, Helen. " 'The Precautions . . . ,'' 20–27, 33–34.
    Milbank, Alison. *Daughters of the House* . . . , 66–69.
"Schalken the Painter"
    Milbank, Alison. *Daughters of the House* . . . , 160–162.

URSULA K. LE GUIN

"The Dragon of Pendor"
    Barrow, Craig, and Diana Barrow. "Le Guin's Earthsea: Voyages in
        Consciousness," *Extrapolation,* 32, i (1991), 28–30.
"The Hawk's Flight"
    Barrow, Craig, and Diana Barrow. "Le Guin's . . . ,'' 30–32.
"The Ones Who Walk Away from Omelas"
    Cassill, R. V. . . . *Instructor's Handbook,* 112–113.
    + Charters, Ann, and William E. Sheidley. *Resources for
        Teaching* . . . , 3rd ed., 132–133.
"The Loosing of the Shadow"
    Barrow, Craig, and Diana Barrow. "Le Guin's . . . ,'' 28.
"The Professor's Houses"
    Bohner, Charles H. *Instructor's Manual* . . . , 74–75.

ELLA LEFFLAND

"The Linden Tree"
    Cassill, R. V. . . . *Instructor's Handbook,* 114–115.

ROSAMOND LEHMANN

"A Dream of Winter"
    Gindin, James. *British Fiction* . . . , 105.

"The Red-Haired Miss Daintreys"
  Gindin, James. *British Fiction* . . . , 90.
"When the Waters Came"
  Gindin, James. *British Fiction* . . . , 105–106.

STANISLAW LEM

"The Mask"
  Parker, Jo Alyson. "Gendering the Robot: Stanislaw Lem's 'The Mask,' " *Sci-Fiction Stud*, 19 (1992), 178–190.

MIKHAIL LERMONTOV

"Bela"
  Scotto, Peter. "Prisoners of the Caucasus: Ideologies of Imperialism in Lermontov's 'Bela,' " *PMLA*, 107 (1992), 246–260.

TILLIE LERNER

"The Iron Throat"
  Hanley, Lawrence F. "Cultural Work and Class Politics: Re-reading and Remaking *Proletarian Literature in the United States*," *Mod Fiction Stud*, 38 (1992), 728.

DORIS LESSING

"One Off the Short List"
  + Bohner, Charles H. *Instructor's Manual* . . . , 75–76.
"Our Friend Judith"
  Carrera, Isabel. "Metalinguistic Features in Short Fiction by Lessing and Atwood: From Sign and Subversion to Symbol and Deconstruction," in Bardolph, Jacquelin, Ed. *Short Fiction* . . . , 159–160.
"A Sunrise on the Veld"
  Bohner, Charles H. *Instructor's Manual* . . . , 76–77.
"Through the Tunnel"
  Keating, Helane L., and Walter Levy. *Instructor's Manual: Lives Through Literature* . . . , 8–9.
"To Room Nineteen"
  Bell, Glenna. "Lessing's 'To Room Nineteen,' " *Explicator*, 50, iii (1992), 180–183.
  Boyles, Mary. "Woman: The Inside Outsider," in Crafton, John M., Ed. *Selected Essays* . . . , 120–121.
  Cassill, R. V. . . . *Instructor's Handbook*, 115–116.
  + Charters, Ann, and William E. Sheidley. *Resources for Teaching* . . . , 3rd ed., 134–135.

MERIDEL LE SUEUR

"Annunciation"
Leoffelholz, Mary. *Experimental Lives* . . . , 201–202.

MATTHEW GREGORY LEWIS

"The Anaconda"
Geary, Robert F. "M. G. Lewis and Later Gothic Fiction: The
Numinous Dissipated," in Ruddick, Nicholas, Ed. *State* . . . ,
77, 79–80.
"Mistrust"
Geary, Robert F. "M. G. Lewis . . . ," 77–79.

SINCLAIR LEWIS

"Jazz"
Wilson, Christopher P. *White Collar Fiction* . . . , 237–238.

WYNDHAM LEWIS

"Brotcotnaz"
Head, Dominic. *The Modernist* . . . , 145–149, 161.
"The Death of the Ankou"
Head, Dominic. *The Modernist* . . . , 149–152, 161.
"Les Saltimbanques"
Schenker, Daniel. *Wyndham Lewis* . . . , 50–55.
"A Soldier of Humour"
Head, Dominic. *The Modernist* . . . , 154–161.
"Sigismund"
Schenker, Daniel. *Wyndham Lewis* . . . , 67–70.

YI LI

"A Date at Age Twenty-Eight"
Wong, Sau-ling C. "Ethnicizing Gender: An Exploration of Sexuality
as Sign in Chinese Immigrant Literature," in Lim, Shirley G., and
Amy Ling, Eds. *Reading the Literatures* . . . , 114–119, 122.

MEYER LIBEN

"Homage to Benny Leonard"
Gladsky, Thomas S. *Princes, Peasants* . . . , 215–216, 217.

CLARICE LISPECTOR

"Amor"
Mathie, Barbara. "Feminism, Language or Existentialism: The
Search for the Self in the Works of Clarice Lispector," in Shaw,
Philip, and Peter Stockwell, Eds. *Subjectivity and Literature* . . . ,
122–123, 124.

"Before the Bridge over the River Niterói"
Mathie, Barbara. "Feminism, Language . . . ," 132–133.

"Beginnings of a Future"
Mathie, Barbara. "Feminism, Language . . . ," 127.

"Better Than to Burn"
Mathie, Barbara. "Feminism, Language . . . ," 130.

"The Body"
Mathie, Barbara. "Feminism, Language . . . ," 130–131.

"The Buffalo"
Miller, Ingrid R. "The Problematics of the Body in Clarice
Lispector's *Family Ties*," *Chasqui,* 20, i (1991), 39.

"But It's Going to Rain"
Mathie, Barbara. "Feminism, Language . . . ," 132.

"The Chicken"
Charters, Ann, and William E. Sheidley. *Resources for Teaching*
. . . , 3rd ed., 136–137.

"The Crime of the Mathematics Professor"
Mathie, Barbara. "Feminism, Language . . . ," 127–128.

"Daydream of a Drunken Housewife" [same as "Daydream of a
Drunken Woman"]
Miller, Ingrid R. "The Problematics . . . ," 37–39.

"Family Ties"
Mathie, Barbara. "Feminism, Language . . . ," 125–126.

"Happy Birthday"
Mathie, Barbara. "Feminism, Language . . . ," 124–125.

"The Hour of a Star"
Peixoto, Marta. "Rape and Textual Violence in Clarice Lispector,"
in Higgins, Lynn A., and Brenda R. Silver, Eds. *Rape and
Representation,* 191–201.

"The Imitation of the Rose"
Mathie, Barbara. "Feminism, Language . . . ," 128.
Miller, Ingrid R. "The Problematics . . . ," 36–37.

"Love"
Mathie, Barbara. "Feminism, Language . . . ," 122–124.

"Miss Algrave"
Mathie, Barbara. "Feminism, Language . . . ," 131–133.

"Mystery in São Cristóvão"
Peixoto, Marta. "Rape and Textual Violence . . . ," 184–185.

"Pig Latin"
  Peixoto, Marta. "Rape and Textual Violence . . . ," 188–190.
"Praça Mauá"
  Mathie, Barbara. "Feminism, Language . . . ," 131.
"Preciousness"
  Peixoto, Marta. "Rape and Textual Violence . . . ," 185–188.
"The Smallest Woman in the World"
  Mathie, Barbara. "Feminism, Language . . . ," 126.
  Miller, Ingrid R. "The Problematics . . . ," 39–41.
  Platt, Kamala. "Race and Gender Representations in Clarice
    Lispector's 'A Menor Mulher do Mundo' and Carolina Maria de
    Jesus' *Quarto de Despejo*," *Afro-Hispanic R*, 11 (1992), 51–57.

MARÍA ROSA LOJO

"La ciudad de la Rosa"
  Liggera, Rubén A. "La recreación de dos mitos fundantes en un
    cuento de María Rosa Lojo," *Explicación de Textos Literarios,* 20,
    i (1991–1992), 47–60.

TABAN LO LIYONG

"Asu the Great"
  Balogun, F. Odun. *Tradition and Modernity* . . . , 155–156.
"Fixions"
  Balogun, F. Odun. *Tradition and Modernity* . . . , 142–143.
"He and Him"
  Balogun, F. Odun. *Tradition and Modernity* . . . , 141.
"Herolette"
  Balogun, F. Odun. *Tradition and Modernity* . . . , 152–153.
"It is Swallowing"
  Balogun, F. Odun. *Tradition and Modernity* . . . , 156.
"The Old Man of Usumbura and His Misery"
  Balogun, F. Odun. *Tradition and Modernity* . . . , 118–120.
"A Prescription for Idleness"
  Balogun, F. Odun. *Tradition and Modernity* . . . , 166–167.
"Project X"
  Balogun, F. Odun. *Tradition and Modernity* . . . , 154.
"Sages and Wages"
  Balogun, F. Odun. *Tradition and Modernity* . . . , 143–145.
"Stare Decisis Deo"
  Balogun, F. Odun. *Tradition and Modernity* . . . , 141–142.
"Tombe Gworong's Own Story"
  Balogun, F. Odun. *Tradition and Modernity* . . . , 117–118, 145–146.

"The Uniformed Man"
  Balogun, F. Odun. *Tradition and Modernity* . . . , 157.

JACK LONDON

"Aloha Oe"
  Tietze, Thomas R., and Gary Riedl. " 'Saints in Slime': The Ironic
    Use of Racism in Jack London's *South Sea Tales*," *Thalia*, 12, i-ii
    (1992), 64.
"The Chinago"
  Tietze, Thomas R., and Gary Riedl. " 'Saints . . . ,'' 63.
"Chun Ah Chun"
  Tietze, Thomas R., and Gary Riedl. " 'Saints . . . ,'' 62.
"The Heathen"
  Tietze, Thomas R., and Gary Riedl. " 'Saints . . . ,'' 60.
"The House of Pride"
  Tietze, Thomas R., and Gary Riedl. " 'Saints . . . ,'' 64.
"A Hyperborean Brew"
  Berkove, Lawrence. "Thomas Stevens: London's Comic Agent of
    Evolutionary Criticism," *Thalia*, 12, i-ii (1992), 20–23.
"Mauki"
  Tietze, Thomas R., and Gary Riedl. " 'Saints . . . ,'' 61.
"Moonface"
  Dauphin, Laurent. " 'Moonface' or the Rhetoric of the Absurb,"
    Thalia, 12, i-ii (1992), 55–58.
"The Pearls of Parlay"
  Tietze, Thomas R., and Gary Riedl. " 'Saints . . . ,'' 64–65.
"A Relic of Pliocene"
  Berkove, Lawrence. "Thomas Stevens . . . ,'' 15–20.
"Samuel"
  Labor, Earle. "The Archetypal Woman as 'Martyr to Truth': Jack
    London's 'Samuel,' " *Am Lit Realism*, 24, ii (1992), 25–30.
"The Seed of McCoy"
  Tietze, Thomas R., and Gary Riedl. " 'Saints . . . ,'' 63.
"The Terrible Solomons"
  Tietze, Thomas R., and Gary Riedl. " 'Saints . . . ,'' 61.
"To Build a Fire"
  + Bohner, Charles H. *Instructor's Manual* . . . , 77–78.
"The Unparalleled Invasion"
  Berkove, Lawrence I. "A Parallax Correction in London's 'The
    Unparalleled Invasion,' " *Am Lit Realism*, 24, ii (1992), 33–39.
"The Water Baby"
  Tietze, Thomas R., and Gary Riedl. " 'Saints . . . ,'' 65.
"The Whale Tooth"
  Tietze, Thomas R., and Gary Riedl. " 'Saints . . . ,'' 63.

"Yah! Yah! Yah!"
Tietze, Thomas R., and Gary Riedl. " 'Saints . . . ," 61.

"The Wife of a King"
Woodward, Servanne. " 'The Wife of a King' from a Bergsonian
Perspective," *Thalia*, 12, i-ii (1992), 47–54.

JOSÉ LÓPEZ PORTILLO Y ROJAS

"Reloj sin dueño"
Parsons, Robert A. " 'Watches Without Owners': Variations on a
Spanish American Satirical Theme," *Confluencia*, 7, i (1991),
55–56, 57, 58, 59, 60, 61.

H[OWARD] P. LOVECRAFT

"The Call of Cthulhu"
Cannon, Peter. "Letters, Diaries, and Manuscripts: The Handwritten
Word in Lovecraft," in Schultz, David E., and S. T. Joshi, Eds. *An
Epicure in the Terrible* . . . , 150–151.
Dziemianowicz, Stefan. "Outsiders and Aliens: The Uses of Isolation
in Lovecraft's Fiction," in Schultz, David E., and S. T. Joshi, Eds.
An Epicure in the Terrible . . . , 174–176.

"The Colour Out of Space"
Blake, Ian. "Lovecraft and the Dark Grail," *Lovecraft Stud*, 26
(Spring, 1992), 16–18.
Burleson, Donald R. "Lovecraft's 'The Colour Out of Space,' "
Explicator, 52, i (1992), 48–50.
———. "Prismatic Heroes: The Colour out of Dunwich," *Lovecraft
Stud*, 25 (Fall, 1991), 13–18.
Dziemianowicz, Stefan. "Outsiders . . . ," 176–178.

"The Diary of the Alonzo Typer"
Cannon, Peter. "Letters, Diaries . . . ," 156–157.

"Dreams in the Witch House"
Dziemianowicz, Stefan. "Outsiders . . . ," 182–183.

"The Dunwich Horror"
Burleson, Donald R. "Prismatic Heroes . . . ," 13–18.
Cannon, Peter. "Letters, Diaries . . . ," 152–153.
Dziemianowicz, Stefan. "Outsiders . . . ," 179–180.

"The Festival"
Dziemianowicz, Stefan. "Outsiders . . . ," 170–171.

"The Haunter of the Dark"
Dziemianowicz, Stefan. "Outsiders . . . ," 185–186.
Mariconda, Steven J. "Lovecraft's Comic Imagery," in Schultz,
David E., and S. T. Joshi, Eds. *An Epicure in the Terrible* . . . ,
196–197.

"Hypnos"
Dziemianowicz, Stefan. "Outsiders . . . ," 164–165.

"The Mount"
Cannon, Peter. "Letters, Diaries . . . ," 153–155.

"The Music of Erich Zann"
Buchanan, Carl. " 'The Music of Erich Zann': A Psychological
Interpretation (or Two)," *Lovecraft Stud*, 27 (Fall, 1992), 10–13.
Burleson, Donald R. "On Lovecraft's Themes: Touching the Glass,"
in Schultz, David E., and S. T. Joshi, Eds. *An Epicure in the
Terrible* . . . , 139–140.
Dziemianowicz, Stefan. "Outsiders . . . ," 169–170.

"The Other Gods"
Setiya, K. "Science and Religion in 'The Other Gods,' " *Lovecraft
Stud*, 26 (Spring, 1992), 14–15.

"The Outsider"
Burleson, Donald R. "On Lovecraft's Themes . . . ," 138–139.
Dziemianowicz, Stefan. "Outsiders . . . ," 165–166.

"Pickman Model"
Setiya, K. "Aesthetics and the Artist in 'Pickman's Model,' "
Lovecraft Stud, 26 (Spring, 1992), 15–16.

"The Shadow Out of Time"
Cannon, Peter. "Letters, Diaries . . . ," 155–156.
Dziemianowicz, Stefan. "Outsiders . . . ," 184–185.
Eckhardt, Jason C. "The Cosmic Yankee," in Schultz, David E., and
S. T. Joshi, Eds. *An Epicure in the Terrible* . . . , 95–97.

"The Shadow over Innsmouth"
Dziemianowicz, Stefan. "Outsiders . . . ," 181–182.

"The Terrible Old Man"
Burleson, Donald R. "On Lovecraft's Themes . . . ," 137.

"The Tomb"
Dziemianowicz, Stefan. "Outsiders . . . ," 161–163.

MALCOLM LOWRY

"Elephant and Colosseum"
Head, Dominic. *The Modernist* . . . , 176–181.
Linguanti, Elsa. " 'Hear us O Lord' and Lowry's Micro/Macro
Text," in Grace, Sherrill, Ed. *Swinging the Maelström* . . . ,
211–215.

"The Forest Path to Spring"
Head, Dominic. *The Modernist* . . . , 168–176, 183.

"Strange Comfort Afforded by the Profession"
Head, Dominic. *The Modernist* . . . , 181–182.

"Through the Panama"
Head, Dominic. *The Modernist* . . . , 182–183.

LU XÜN

"Diary of a Madman"
Tang, Xiaobing. "Lu Xün's 'Diary of a Madman' and a Chinese
Modernism," *PMLA*, 107 (1992), 1222, 1225–1233.

"In a Tavern"
Yin Xiaoling. "The Paralyzed and the Dead: A Comparative Reading
of 'The Dead' and 'In a Tavern,' " *Comp Lit Stud*, 29 (1992), 276,
278–281, 288–295.

LEOPOLDO LUGONES

"Abuela Julieta"
Sáenz de Tejada, Cristina. " 'Abuela Julieta': Un cuento de amor
esotérico," *Chasqui*, 21, i (1992), 92–100.

"An Inexplicable Phenomenon"
Kason, Nancy M. "The Fantastic Stories in *Las Fuerzas Extrañas*
by Leopoldo Lugones," in Saciuk, Olena H., Ed. *The Shape . . .* ,
96–97.

"The Origin of the Deluge"
Kason, Nancy M. "The Fantastic . . . ," 97–98.

"The Toad"
Kason, Nancy M. "The Fantastic . . . ," 94–96.

PAUL LUNDT

"Horn Concerto"
Smith, Rupert. "One-Handed Reading," in Lilly, Mark, Ed. *Lesbian
and Gay . . .* , 168–169.

MARTA LYNCH

"Malas noticias"
Galván, Delia V. "Hacia la vejez en *No te duermas, no me dejes* de
Marta Lynch," *Alba de América*, 10 (1992), 210, 211.

"La vida"
Galvan, Delia V. "Hacia la vejez . . . ," 210, 211.

MARY McCARTHY

"The Man in the Brooks Brothers Shirt"
Castronovo, David. *The American Gentleman . . .* , 137–138.

CARSON McCULLERS

"A Tree, A Rock, A Cloud"
+ Bohner, Charles H. *Instructor's Manual* . . . , 78–79.
"Wunderkind"
Kissel, Susan S. "Carson McCullers's 'Wunderkind': A Case Study
in Female Adolescence," *Kentucky Philol R*, 6 (1991), 17–19.

IAN McEWAN

"Homemade"
Broughton, Lynda. "Portrait of the Subject as a Young Man: The
Construction of Masculinity Ironized in 'Male' Fiction," in Shaw,
Philip, and Peter Stockwell, Eds. *Subjectivity and Literature* . . . ,
135–145.

ARTHUR MACHEN

"The Great God Pan"
Eckersley, Adrian. "A Theme in the Early Work of Arthur Machen:
'Degeneration,' " *Engl Lit Transition*, 35 (1992), 283–284.
"The Inmost Light"
Eckersley, Adrian. "A Theme in . . . ," 284–285.
"The Novel of the Black Seal"
Eckersley, Adrian. "A Theme in . . . ," 282–283.
"The Novel of the White Powder"
Eckersley, Adrian. "A Theme in . . . ," 280–282.

GEORGIA McKINLEY

"The Crime"
Chandler, Marilyn R. *Dwelling in the Text* . . . , 280–282.

ALISTAIR MacLEOD

"The Boat"
Berces, Francis. "Existential Maritimer: Alistair MacLeod's *The
Lost Salt Gift of Blood*," *Stud Canadian Lit*, 16, i (1991), 117–119.
Nickolson, Colin. "The Tuning of Memory: Alistair MacLeod's Short
Fiction," in Howells, Colin A., and Lynette Hunter, Eds. *Narrative
Strategies.* . . , 32–35.
"The Closing Down of Summer"
Nickolson, Colin. "The Tuning . . . ," 35–58.
"The Fall"
Berces, Francis. "Existential . . . ," 119–122.

"The Lost Salt Gift of Blood"
   Berces, Francis. "Existential . . . ," 123–125.
"The Road to Rankin's Point"
   Berces, Francis. "Existential . . . ," 125–126.
"The Vastness of the Dark"
   Berces, Francis. "Existential . . . ," 122–123.

BRYAN MacMAHON

"Exile's Return"
   Ingersoll, Earl G. "Metaphor and Metonymy in James Joyce's 'A
   Little Cloud' and Bryan MacMahon's 'Exile's Return,' " *Canadian
   J Irish Stud*, 16, ii (1990), 32–34.

JAMES ALAN McPHERSON

"Gold Coast"
   Cassill, R. V. . . . *Instructor's Handbook*, 117–118.

R. J. MacSWEEN

"Another Desperate Cry"
   Dudek, Louis. "Blighted Lives: The Prose Fiction of R. J.
   MacSween," *Antigonish R*, 87–88 (1991–1992), 268.
"The Scream"
   Dudek, Louis. "Blighted Lives . . . ," 269–270.
"Weariness"
   Dudek, Louis. "Blighted Lives . . . ," 268–269.

JULIAN MAGTULIS

"Fanatic"
   Lucero, Rosario Cruz. "The Philippine Short Story, 1981–1990: The
   Voice of the Self-Authenticating Other," *Tenggara*, 26 (1990),
   84–85.

NAGUIB MAHFOUZ

"Lover's Lane"
   Mikhail, Mona N. *Studies* . . . , 130–136.
"Spirit of the Curer of Hearts"
   Mikhail, Mona N. *Studies* . . . , 80–86.

"Story Without Beginning or End"
Mikhail, Mona N. *Studies . . .* , 69–76.

"Under the Bus Shelter"
Mikhail, Mona N. *Studies . . .* , 56–59.

NORMAN MAILER

"Advertisements for Myself on the Way Out"
Rollyson, Carl. *The Lives of Norman Mailer . . .* , 121–122.

"A Calculus at Heaven"
Rollyson, Carl. *The Lives of Norman Mailer . . .* , 26–27.

"The Language of Men"
Cassill, R. V. *. . . Instructor's Handbook*, 118–120.

"The Last Night"
Clark, John R. *The Modern Satiric Grotesque . . .* , 146–147.

"The Man Who Studied Yoga"
Rollyson, Carl. *The Lives of Norman Mailer . . .* , 81–84.

"Maybe Next Time"
Rollyson, Carl. *The Lives of Norman Mailer . . .* , 19–20.

BERNARD MALAMUD

"Angel Levine"
Aarons, Victoria. "'In Defense of the Human': Compassion and Redemption in Malamud's Short Fiction," *Stud Am Fiction*, 20, i (1992), 62, 71.
Cassill, R. V. *. . . Instructor's Handbook*, 120–121.

"Idiots First"
Aarons, Victoria. "'In Defense . . . ," 57–59.

"The Jewbird"
Charters, Ann, and William E. Sheidley. *Resources for Teaching . . .* , 3rd ed., 137–138.

"Lady of the Lake"
Gittleman, Sol. "Witnessing the Holocaust in American Literature: A Note to Bonnie Lyons," *Yiddish*, 7, iv (1990), 37–38.

"The Last Mohican"
Keating, Helane L., and Walter Levy. *Instructor's Manual: Lives Through Literature . . .* , 70–71.

"The Letter"
Aarons, Victoria. " 'In Defense . . . ," 66–67.

"The Magic Barrel"
Adler, Brian. "*Akedah* and Community in 'The Magic Barrel,' " *Stud Am Jewish Lit*, 10, ii (1991), 188–196.
+ Bohner, Charles H. *Instructor's Manual . . .* , 79–80.

"The Mourners"
Baris, Sharon D. "Intertextuality and Reader Responsibility: Living
On in Malamud's 'The Mourners,' " *Stud Am Jewish Lit*, 11, i
(1992), 45–61.

"My Son the Murderer"
Aarons, Victoria. " 'In Defense . . . ," 64–65, 67–70.

"The Silver Crown"
Aarons, Victoria. " 'In Defense . . . ," 61–64.

ALBERT MALTZ

"A Man on the Road"
Hanley, Lawrence F. "Cultural Work and Class Politics: Re-reading
and Remaking *Proletarian Literature in the United States*," *Mod
Fiction Stud*, 38 (1992), 726–727.

MŪSṬAFA LŪṬFĪ MANFALŪṬĪ

"The Orphan"
Peled, M. "Did al-Manfalūṭī Really Shed Tears for His Protagonist?"
Arabica, 38, i (1991), 64–72.

HEINRICH MANN

"Das Wunderbare"
Renner, Ursula. "Pavillons, Glashäuser und Seitenwege—Topos und
Vision des Paradiesgartens bei Saar, Hofmannsthal, und Heinrich
Mann," *Recherches Germaniques,* 20 (1990), 134–137, 140.

"Die Rückkehr vom Hades"
Bennett, Timothy A. "Heinrich Mann's 'Die Rückkehr vom Hades':
The Outsider's Delirium," in Crafton, John M., Ed. *Selected
Essays* . . . , 75–86.

THOMAS MANN

"Die Betrogene"
Bryson, Cynthia B. "The Imperative Daily Nap: Or, Aschenbach's
Dream in 'Death in Venice,' " *Stud Short Fiction*, 29 (1992),
181–193.
Runge, Doris. "Die Betrogene," *Thomas Mann Jahrbuch,* 4 (1991),
110, 111–118.

"Death in Venice"
Del Caro, Adrian. "Philosophizing and Poetic License in Mann's
Early Fiction," in Berlin, Jeffrey B., Ed. *Approaches* . . . , 46–48.
Furst, Lilian R. "Reading 'Nasty' Great Books," in Nemoianu,
Virgil, and Robert Royal, Eds. *The Hospitable Canon* . . . , 40–50.

Gillespie, Gerald. "Mann and the Modernist Tradition," in Berlin, Jeffrey B., Ed. *Approaches* . . . , 98–104.

Martin, Robert K. "Gender, Sexuality, and Identity in Mann's Short Fiction," in Berlin, Jeffrey B., Ed. *Approaches* . . . , 63–66.

Smith, Herbert O. "Prologue to the Great War: Encounters with Apollo and Dionysus in 'Death in Venice,' " *Focus on Robert Graves*, 1, xiii (Winter, 1992), 36–42.

Timms, Edward. " 'Death in Venice' as Psychohistory," in Berlin, Jeffrey B., Ed. *Approaches* . . . , 134–139.

Travers, Martin. *Thomas Mann*, 48–59.

"Disorder and Early Sorrow"

+Cassill, R. V. . . . *Instructor's Handbook*, 121–123.

Charters, Ann, and William E. Sheidley. *Resources for Teaching* . . . , 3rd ed., 139–140.

"Enttäuschung"

Burgard, Peter J. "From 'Enttäuschung' to 'Tristan': The Devolution of a Language Crisis in Thomas Mann's Early Work," *Germ Q*, 59 (1986), 433–440, 444–445.

"Das Gesetz"

Lubich, Frederick A. " 'Fascinating Fascism': Thomas Manns 'Das Gesetz' und seine Selbst-de-Montage als Moses-Hitler," *Germ Stud R*, 14 (1991), 554–573.

"The Hungry"

Dedner, Burghard. "Satire Prohibited: Laughter, Satire, and Irony in Thomas Mann's Oeuvre," in Grimm, Reinhold, and Jost Hermand, Eds. *Laughter Unlimited* . . . , 37–38.

"Little Herr Friedemann"

Travers, Martin. *Thomas Mann*, 35–37.

"Luischen"

Weinzierl, Ulrich. "Die 'besorgniserregende Frau': Anmerkungen zu 'Luischen,' Thomas Manns 'peinlichster Novelle,' *Thomas Mann Jahrbuch*, 4 (1991), 13–20.

"Mario and the Magician"

Bridges, George. "Thomas Mann's 'Mario und der Zauberer': 'Aber zum Donnerwetter! Deshalb bringt man doch niemand um!' " *Germ Q*, 64 (1991), 501–517.

Travers, Martin. *Thomas Mann*, 60–73.

"Tonio Kröger"

Del Caro, Adrian. "Philosophizing . . . ," 43–46.

Eddy, Beverley D. "Teaching 'Tonio Kröger' as Literature About Literature," in Berlin, Jeffrey B., Ed. *Approaches* . . . , 121–125.

Gillespie, Gerald. "Mann and the Modernist . . . ," 94–98.

Hoffmeister, Werner. "Humor and Comedy in Mann's Short Fiction," in Berlin, Jeffrey B., Ed. *Approaches* . . . , 73–76.

Martin, Robert K. "Gender, Sexuality . . . ," 57–63.

Neubauer, John. "Identity by Metamorphosis: *A Portrait of the Artist* and 'Tonio Kröger,' " in Fehn, Ann, Ingeborg Hoestery, and Maria Tatar, Eds. *Neverending Stories* . . . , 129–132.

Symington, Rodney. "Tonio Kröger's Conversation with Lisaweta Iwanowna: Difficulties and Solutions," in Berlin, Jeffrey B., Ed. *Approaches* . . . , 126–132.

Travers, Martin. *Thomas Mann*, 43–47.

"Tristan"

Burgard, Peter J. "From 'Enttäuschung' . . . ," 441–443, 444.

Hoffmeister, Werner. "Humor . . . ," 70–72.

Potter, Edith. "Jugendstil in Mann's Early Short Fiction," in Berlin, Jeffrey B., Ed. *Approaches* . . . , 81–84.

Travers, Martin. *Thomas Mann*, 41–43.

"Das Wunderkind"

Parkes-Perret, Ford B. "Thomas Mann's Novella 'Das Wunderkind,' " *Colloquia Germanica*, 25 (1992), 19–25.

KATHERINE MANSFIELD [KATHERINE BEAUCHAMP]

"At the Bay"

Clayton, Cherry. "Olive Schreiner and Katherine Mansfield: Artistic Transformations of the Outcast Figure by Two Colonial Women Writers," in Bardolph, Jacquelin, Ed. *Short Fiction* . . . , 36.

Dupuis, Michel. "Katherine Mansfield and Anton Chekov's Letters," in Bardolph, Jacquelin, Ed. *Short Fiction* . . . , 13–14.

"Bliss"

Cassill, R. V. . . . *Instructor's Handbook*, 123–124.

+ Charters, Ann, and William E. Sheidley. *Resources for Teaching* . . . , 3rd ed., 141–142.

Hanscombe, Gillian. "Katherine Mansfield's Pear Tree," in Hobby, Elaine, and Chris White, Eds. *What Lesbians* . . . , 111–113.

Head, Dominic. *The Modernist* . . . , 24–25, 29–30, 109, 138, 187.

"A Dill Pickle"

+ Bohner, Charles H. *Instructor's Manual* . . . , 80–81.

"The Fly"

Burke, Daniel. *Beyond Interpretation* . . . , 65–77.

Charters, Ann, and William E. Sheidley. *Resources for Teaching* . . . , 3rd ed., 143.

"The Garden Party"

+ Cassill, R. V. . . . *Instructor's Handbook*, 125–126.

Head, Dominic. *The Modernist* . . . , 131–138, 188.

Wilkinson, Jane. "Feasting to Death: 'Garden Party' Variations," in Bardolph, Jacquelin, Ed. *Short Fiction* . . . , 23–29.

"Her First Ball"

Head, Dominic. *The Modernist* . . . , 128–130.

"Honeymoon"

Head, Dominic. *The Modernist* . . . , 123–128.

"Je ne parle français"
  Gurr, Andrew. "Katherine Mansfield's Experiments," in Bardolph,
    Jacquelin, Ed. *Short Fiction* . . . , 44–45.
  Head, Dominic. *The Modernist* . . . , 114–117.
"Millie"
  Head, Dominic. *The Modernist* . . . , 111–113.
"Miss Brill"
  + Bohner, Charles H. *Instructor's Manual* . . . , 81–82.
  Head, Dominic. *The Modernist* . . . , 110–111.
"Ole Underwood"
  Head, Dominic. *The Modernist* . . . , 113–114.
"Pictures"
  Kaplan, Sydney J. *Katherine Mansfield* . . . , 73–75.
"Poison"
  Gurr, Andrew. "Katherine Mansfield's . . . ," 43–44.
"Prelude"
  Clayton, Cherry. "Olive Schreiner . . . ," 36.
  Harmat, Andre-Marie. "The 'sound-sense' of Katherine Mansfield
    Stories," in Bardolph, Jacquelin, Ed. *Short Fiction* . . . , 52–53.
  Head, Dominic. *The Modernist* . . . , 117–122, 130–131.
  Kaplan, Sydney J. *Katherine Mansfield* . . . , 113–117.
  Moran, Patricia. "Unholy Meanings: Maternity, Creativity, and
    Orality in Katherine Mansfield," *Feminist Stud*, 17 (1991), 117–121.
"The Singing Lesson"
  Keating, Helane L., and Walter Levy. *Instructor's Manual: Lives
    Through Literature* . . . , 86–87.
"The Tiredness of Rosabel"
  Leoffelholz, Mary. *Experimental Lives* . . . , 132–133.
"The Voyage"
  Clayton, Cherry. "Olive Schreiner . . . ," 36.
  Tytler, Graeme. "Mansfield's 'The Voyage,' " *Explicator*, 50, i
    (1991), 42–45.

EDUARDA MANSILLA

"El ramito de romero"
  Masiello, Francine. *Between Civilization* . . . , 97–98.

DAMBUDZO MARECHERA

"The Slow Sound of His Feet"
  Riemenschneider, Dieter. "Short Fiction from Zimbabwe," in
    Bardolph, Jacquelin, Ed. *Short Fiction* . . . , 257–258.

JOSEFINA MARPONS

"Satanás"
  Masiello, Francine. *Between Civilization* . . . , 185–186.

HELEN REIMENSNYDER MARTIN

"Mrs. Gladfelter's Revolt"
    Madison, Eunice. "Martin's 'Mrs. Gladfelter's Revolt,' " *Explicator*,
    49, iv (1991), 227–229.

EZEQUIEL MARTÍNEZ ESTRADA

"Marta Riquelme"
    Mizraji, Margarita N. "'Marta Riquelme': Una aproximación al
    problema del objeto en la crítica literaria," *Hispamerica*, 20
    (December, 1991), 141–151.

MARINA MARYORAL

"En los parques, al anochecer"
    Pérez, Janet. "Characteristics of Erotic Brief Fiction by Women in
    Spain," *Monographic R*, 7 (1991), 183–185.

BOBBIE ANN MASON

"Offerings"
    Aldridge, John W. *Talents and Technicians* . . . , 86–87.
    Bucher, Tina. "Changing Roles and Finding Stability: Women in
    Bobbie Ann Mason's *Shiloh and Other Stories*," *Border States*, 8
    (1991), 54.
"The Rookers"
    Bucher, Tina. "Changing Roles . . . ," 52–53.
"Shiloh"
    Bucher, Tina. "Changing Roles . . . ," 50–52.
    Cassill, R. V. . . . *Instructor's Handbook*, 127–128.
    +Charters, Ann, and William E. Sheidley. *Resources for Teach-
    ing* . . . , 3rd ed., 144–145.

OLGA MASTERS

"The Snake and Poor Tom"
    Walker, Shirley. "The Deconstruction of the Bush: Australian
    Women Short Story Writers," in Bardolph, Jacquelin, Ed. *Short
    Fiction* . . . , 80.

RAY MATHEW [with MENA ABDULLAH]

"The Babu from Bengal"
    MacDermott, Doireann. "*The Time of the Peacock*: Indian Rural Life

in Australia,'' in Bardolph, Jacquelin, Ed. *Short Fiction* . . . ,
207–208.

"Because of the Rusilla"
MacDermott, Doireann. *"The Time* . . . ,'' 205–206.

"Grandfather Tiger"
MacDermott, Doireann. *"The Time* . . . ,'' 208.

"High Maharaja"
MacDermott, Doireann. *"The Time* . . . ,'' 206–207.

"The Time of the Peacock"
MacDermott, Doireann. *"The Time* . . . ,'' 204–205.

JAMES MATTHEWS

"The Second Coming"
Balogun, F. Odun. *Tradition and Modernity* . . . , 42–43.

ANA MARÍA MATUTE

"Los niños tontos"
Buard, Marie-France. "Les enfants sots d'Anna María Matute," in
Actes du centre . . . , 29–40.

W. SOMERSET MAUGHAM

"The Outstation"
+ Bohner, Charles H. *Instructor's Manual* . . . , 82–83.

"The Yellow Streak"
Holden, Philip. "W. Somerset Maugham's Yellow Streak," *Stud
Short Fiction*, 29 (1992), 578–581.

GUY DE MAUPASSANT

"Apparition"
Cummiskey, Gary. *The Changing* . . . , 133–138.

"La Chevelure"
Bulver, Kathryn M. "Trope et Fantastique dans 'La Chevelure' de
Maupassant," *Iris*, 4, ii (1991), 21–30.

"Un Coq chante"
Issacharoff, Michael. "Description, Seduction," *Rivista di
Letterature*, 44 (1991), 115–119.

"The False Jewels"
Saint-Amand, Pierre. "Tales of Adornment: Fictions of the
Feminine," *Lit & Psych*, 38, iii (1992), 17–19.

"The Horla"
Cummiskey, Gary. *The Changing* . . . , 121–127.

Herdman, John. *The Double* . . . , 145–148.
Srámek, Jiří. "Un Témoignage ambigu: 'Le Horla' de Guy de
Maupassant," *Études Romanes de Brno*, 21, xii (1991), 43–51.

"The Necklace"
+ Bohner, Charles H. *Instructor's Manual* . . . , 83–84.
+ Cassill, R. V. . . . *Instructor's Handbook*, 128–129.
Charters, Ann, and William E. Sheidley. *Resources for Teach-
ing* . . . , 3rd ed., 147–148.
Saint-Amand, Pierre. "Tales . . . ," 6–14.

"La Peur"
Cummiskey, Gary. *The Changing* . . . , 127–138.

"Two Friends"
Calle-Gruber, Mireille. "Quand le mot d'ordre est: Ne pas trahir:
'Deux amis' de Guy de Maupassant," *Revue des Sciences
Humaines*, 95 (1991), 121–123, 129–146.

HERMAN MELVILLE

"Bartleby the Scrivener"
Bergmann, Hans. " 'Turkey on His Back': 'Bartleby' and New York
Words," *Melville Soc Extracts*, 90 (September, 1992), 16–19.
+ Bohner, Charles H. *Instructor's Manual* . . . , 84–85.
Brennan, Matthew C. "Melville's Bartleby as an Archetypal
Shadow," *J Evolutionary Psych*, 13, iii-iv (1992), 318–321.
+ Cassill, R. V. . . . *Instructor's Handbook*, 129–131.
Demure, Catherine. "La Vibration du monde," *Europe*, 69 (1991),
100–108.
Short, Bryan C. *Cast by Means* . . . , 127–130.

"The Bell Tower"
Hattenhauer, Darryl. "The Scarlet Cipher: Bannadonna's Tower as
Number One," *CEA Critic*, 55, ii (1991), 46–53.
Marovitz, Sanford E. "Melville's Temples," in Sten, Christopher,
Ed. *Savage Eye* . . . , 83–84.
Short, Bryan C. " 'Like bed of asparagus': Melville and
Architecture," in Sten, Christopher, Ed. *Savage Eye* . . . , 108–111.

"Benito Cereno"
Hattenhauer, Darryl. " 'Follow Your Leader': Knowing One's Place
in 'Benito Cereno,' " *Rocky Mountain R*, 45, i-ii (1991), 7–17.
Montfort, Bruno. "La Figure du méridien: Lectures croisées de
quelques épisodes melvilliens," *Delta*, 27 Feb. 1989, 1–13, 16,
17, 18.
Nelson, Dana D. *The Word in Black* . . . , 109–130.
Short, Bryan C. *Cast by Means* . . . , 132–135.
Weiner, Susan. " 'Benito Cereno' and the Failure of Law," *Arizona
Q*, 47, ii (1991), 1–28.

"Billy Budd"
Berthold, Michael C. " 'Billy in the Darbies,' 'Lycidas,' and

Melville's Figures of Captivity," *Am Transcendental Q*, N.S., 6 (1992), 109–119.

Coffler, Gail. "Classical Iconography in the Aesthetics of 'Billy Budd, Sailor,' " in Sten, Christopher, Ed. *Savage Eye . . .* , 265–273.

Desai, R. W. "Truth's 'Ragged Edges': A Phenomenological Inquiry into the Captain Vere-Billy Relationship in Melville's 'Billy Budd, Sailor,' " *Stud Hum*, 19, i (June, 1992), 11–26.

Duncan, Charles S. "Melville's 'Billy Budd, Sailor,' " *Explicator*, 49, ii (1991), 89–91.

Koffler, Judith S. "The Feminine Presence in 'Billy Budd,' " *Cardozo Stud Law & Lit*, 1, i (1989), 1–14.

LaRue, L. H. "Paradox and Interpretation," *Cardozo Stud Law & Lit*, 1, i (1989), 106–108.

Mailloux, Steven. "Judging the Judge: 'Billy Budd' and 'Proof to All Sophistries,' " *Cardozo Stud Law & Lit*, 1, i (1989), 83–88.

Mirzuchi, Susan. "Fiction and the Science of Society," in Elliot, Emory, et al. [4], Eds. *The Columbia History of the American Novel*, 193–195.

Munk, Linda. *The Trivial Sublime . . .* , 40–65.

Quinones, Ricardo J. *The Changes of Cain . . .* , 155–166.

Short, Bryan C. *Cast by Means . . .* , 154–157.

Thomas, Brook. " 'Billy Budd' and the Untold Story of the Law," *Cardozo Stud Law & Lit*, 1, i (1989), 49–81.

Weisberg, Richard. "Accepting the Inside Narrator's Challenge: 'Billy Budd' and the 'Legalistic' Reader," *Cardozo Stud Law & Lit*, 1, i (1989), 27–48.

West, Robin. "The Feminine Silence: A Response to Professor Koffler," *Cardozo Stud Law & Lit*, 1, i (1989), 15–20.

"I and My Chimney"

Berthold, Dennis. "Melville and Dutch Genre Painting," in Sten, Christopher, Ed. *Savage Eye . . .* , 230–232.

Fredericks, Nancy. "Melville and the Woman's Story," *Stud Am Fiction,* 19, i (1991), 46–47.

"The Paradise of Bachelors and the Tartarus of Maids"

Gretchko, John M. J. "The White Mountains, Thomas Cole, and 'Tartarus': The Sublime, the Subliminal, and the Sublimated," in Sten, Christopher, Ed. *Savage Eye . . .* , 127, 138–144.

Young, Phillip. "The Machine in Tartarus: Melville's *Inferno,*" *Am Lit,* 63 (1991), 208–224.

"The Piazza"

Fredericks, Nancy. " . . . Woman's Story," 47–51.

Hattenhauer, Darryl. "Space and Place in Melville's 'The Piazza,' " *Am Stud Scandinavia*, 20, ii (1988), 69–81.

MARÍA CRISTINA MENA

"Vine-Leaf"

Ammons, Elizabeth. *Conflicting Stories . . .* , 146–147.

MIGUEL M. MÉNDEZ [same as MIGUEL MÉNDEZ or M. MIGUEL MÉNDEZ]

"Steelio"
    Lerat, Christian. " 'Steelio' de Miguel Méndez: L'Imposible Espace Vital," in Béranger, Jean, et al. [3], Eds. *Multilinguisme* . . . , 23–33.

PROSPER MÉRIMÉE

"La Venus d'Ille"
    Cummiskey, Gary. *The Changing* . . . , 93–96.
    Szabo, Zoltan. "Aspects de la connaissance dans le récit fantastique: 'La Vénus d'Ille' de Mérimée," in Chandès, Gérard, Ed. *Le Merveilleux* . . . , 218–225.
    Viegnes, Michel. "Le retour des anciens dieux: la rêverie mythologique dans 'La Venus d'Ille' de Mérimée," *Nineteenth-Century French Stud*, 20 (1992), 283–294.
"Tamango"
    Little, Roger. *"Oroonoko* and 'Tamango': A Parallel Episode," *French Stud*, 46 (1992), 26, 28, 29, 30.

JUDITH MERRIL

"Daughters of the Earth"
    Cummins, Elizabeth. "Short Fiction by Judith Merril," *Extrapolation*, 33 (1992), 208–209.
"The Lady Was a Tramp"
    Cummins, Elizabeth. "Short Fiction . . . ," 210–211.
"The Lonely"
    Cummins, Elizabeth. "Short Fiction . . . ," 211–212.
"Survival Ship"
    Cummins, Elizabeth. "Short Fiction . . . ," 207–208.
"That Only a Mother"
    Cummins, Elizabeth. "Short Fiction . . . ," 206–207.
"Whoever You Are"
    Cummins, Elizabeth. "Short Fiction . . . ," 209–210.

CONRAD FERDINAND MEYER

"Angela Borgia"
    Lund, Deborah S. "Of Doubtful Virtue: The Virago in C. F. Meyer's 'Angela Borgia,' " *Seminar*, 28, iii (1992), 208–221.
"Der Heilige"
    Holub, Robert C. *Reflections of Realism* . . . , 155–174.

"Gutav Adolfs Page"
  Gerlach, Henry U. "C. F. Meyers 'Gustavs Adolfs Page': Eine neue
  Lesung," *University of Dayton Review,* 21, ii (1991, Summer),
  134–142.
"The Monk's Wedding"
  Holub, Robert C. *Reflections of Realism . . . ,* 155–156.

LEONARD MICHAELS

"The Murderers"
  Ditsky, John. "A Men's Club: The Fiction of Leonard Michaels,"
  Hollins Critic, 28, v (1991), 5.

MISHIMA YUKIO

"The Locked Room"
  Napier, Susan J. *Escape from the Wasteland . . . ,* 57–63.
"Patriotism"
  + Bohner, Charles H. *Instructor's Manual . . . ,* 85–86.
  + Cassill, R. V. *. . . Instructor's Handbook,* 132.
  Napier, Susan J. *Escape from the Wasteland . . . ,* 88–90.
"The Voices of the Hero Spirit"
  Napier, Susan J. *Escape from the Wasteland . . . ,* 162–163.
"Three Million Yen"
  + Charters, Ann, and William E. Sheidley. *Resources for Teaching
  . . . ,* 3rd ed., 153–154.

ROHINTON MISTRY

"Lend Me Your Light"
  Malak, Amin. "Insider/Outsider's Views on Belonging: The Short
  Stories of Bharati Mukherjee and Rohinton Mistry," in Bardolph,
  Jacquelin, Ed. *Short Fiction . . . ,* 194–195.
"Squatter"
  Malak, Amin. "Insider/Outsider's Views . . . ," 192–194.
  Tapping, Craig. "South Asia Writes North America: Prose Fictions
  and Autobiographies from the Indian Diaspora," in Lim, Shirley
  G., and Amy Ling, Eds. *Reading the Literatures. . . ,* 298–299.

MADELEINE MONETTE

"La Plage"
  Fisher, Claudine G. "Sensibilités française et québécoise dans
  Plages," *Revue Francophone de Louisiane,* 5, i (Spring, 1990),
  68–69.

C[ATHERINE] L[UCILLE] MOORE

"Fruit of Knowledge"
    Gamble, Sarah. " 'Shambleau . . . and Others': the Role of the
    Female in the Fiction of C. L. Moore," in Armitt, Lucie, Ed.
    Where No Man Has Gone Before . . . , 44–46.

"Greater than Gods"
    Gamble, Sarah. " 'Shambleau . . . and Others' . . . ," 47–48.

"Jirel Meets Magic"
    Gamble, Sarah. " 'Shambleau . . . and Others' . . . ," 42–43.

"No Woman Born"
    Gamble, Sarah. " 'Shambleau . . . and Others' . . . ," 46–47.

"Scarlet Dreams"
    Gamble, Sarah. " 'Shambleau . . . and Others' . . . ," 41–42.

"Shambleau"
    Gamble, Sarah. " 'Shambleau . . . and Others' . . . ," 32–33.

"The Trees of Life"
    Gamble, Sarah. " 'Shambleau . . . and Others' . . . ," 33–34, 37–39.

LORRIE MOORE

"Go Like This"
    Aldridge, John W. *Talents and Technicians* . . . , 108–110.
    Hornby, Nick. *Contemporary American Fiction*, 17–18, 20.

"How To Be an Other Woman"
    Aldridge, John W. *Talents and Technicians* . . . , 107–109.

"The Jewish Hunter"
    Hornby, Nick. *Contemporary American Fiction*, 25–27.

"To Fill"
    Hornby, Nick. *Contemporary American Fiction*, 20–21.

"Two Boys"
    Hornby, Nick. *Contemporary American Fiction*, 22–24.

"Vissi D'Arte"
    Hornby, Nick. *Contemporary American Fiction*, 24–25.

FRANK MOORHOUSE

"Drover's Wife"
    Thieme, John. "Drovers' Wives," in Bardolph, Jacquelin, Ed. *Short
    Fiction* . . . , 72–73.

ARTHUR MORRISON

"The Affair of the 'Avalanche Bicycle and Tyre Co.' "
    Priestman, Martin. *Detective Fiction* . . . , 112–114.

"Lizerunt"
    Henkle, Roger. "Morrison, Gissing, and the Stark Reality," *Novel*,
    25 (1992), 302–305.

TONI MORRISON

"Sula"
    Carmean, Karen. *Toni Morrison's World* . . . , 31–44.
    Hoffarth-Zelloe, Monika. "Resolving the Paradox?: An Interlinear
    Reading of Toni Morrison's 'Sula,' " *J Narrative Tech*, 22, ii
    (1992), 114–127.
    Lewis, Desiree. "Myths of Motherhood and Power: The Construction
    of 'Black Woman' in Literature," *Engl Africa*, 19, i (1992), 40–43.

KOSTIANTYN MOSKALETS

"Where Should I Go?"
    Shkandrij, Myroslav. "Polarities in Contemporary Ukrainian
    Literature," *Dalhousie Review*, 72 (1992), 245–246.

BEATRIZ DE MOURA

"Quince de agosto"
    Encinar, Angeles. "Escritoras Españolas actuales: una perspectiva a
    través del cuento," *Hispanic J,* 13 (1992), 185–186.

MOHAMMED MRABET

"Baraka"
    Patteson, Richard F. "Paul Bowles/Mohammed Mrabet: Translation,
    Transcultural Discourse," *J Narrative Technique*, 22 (1992),
    186–187.

BHARATI MUKHERJEE

"A Father"
    Malak, Amin. "Insider/Outsider's Views on Belonging: The Short
    Stories of Bharati Mukherjee and Rohinton Mistry," in Bardolph,
    Jacquelin, Ed. *Short Fiction* . . . , 191.
"Jasmine"
    Charters, Ann, and William E. Sheidley. *Resources for Teach-
    ing* . . . , 3rd ed., 155–156.
    Sant-Wade, Arvindra, and Karen M. Radell. "Refashioning the Self:
    Immigrant Women in Bharati Mukherjee's New World," *Stud Short
    Fiction*, 29 (1992), 14–16.

"The Lady from Lucknow"
    Boxill, Anthony. "Women and Migration in Some Short Stories of
        Bharati Mukherjee and Neil Bissoondath," *Literary Half-Yearly*,
        32, ii (1991), 45–46.
    Malak, Amin. "Insider/Outsider's Views . . . ," 190–191.

"The Tenant"
    Sant-Wade, Arvindra, and Karen M. Radell. "Refashioning the
        Self . . . ," 12–14.

"Visitors"
    Boxill, Anthony. "Women and Migration . . . ," 44–45.

"A Wife's Story"
    Sant-Wade, Arvindra, and Karen M. Radell. "Refashioning the
        Self . . . ," 16–17.

CHARLES MUNGOSHI

"Shadows on the Wall"
    Riemenschneider, Dieter. "Short Fiction from Zimbabwe," in
        Bardolph, Jacquelin, Ed. *Short Fiction* . . . , 255, 256–257.

ALICE MUNRO

"Age of Faith"
    Smythe, Karen E. *Figuring Grief* . . . , 126–127.

"Bardon Bus"
    Redekop, Magdalene. *Mothers and Other Clowns* . . . , 13–14, 32.
    Smythe, Karen E. *Figuring Grief* . . . , 150–151.

"Boys and Girls"
    +Bohner, Charles H. *Instructor's Manual* . . . , 87–88.
    Keating, Helane L., and Walter Levy. *Instructor's Manual: Lives
        Through Literature* . . . , 28–29.

"Connection"
    Redekop, Magdalene. *Mothers and Other Clowns* . . . , 160–164.
    Smythe, Karen E. *Figuring Grief* . . . , 143–145.

"Dance of the Happy Shades"
    Redekop, Magdalene. *Mothers and Other Clowns* . . . , 57–59.

"The Day of the Butterfly"
    Smythe, Karen E. *Figuring Grief* . . . , 118.

"Dulse"
    Osmond, Rosaline. "Arrangements, 'Disarrangement,' and 'Ernest
        Deception,' " in Howells, Colin A., and Lynette Hunter, Eds.
        Narrative Strategies . . . , 87–88.
    Smythe, Karen E. *Figuring Grief* . . . , 147–150.
    Thacker, Robert. "Alice Munro's Willa Cather," *Canadian Lit*, 131
        (1992), 42–57.

"Epilogue: The Photographer"
Smythe, Karen E. *Figuring Grief* . . . , 127–128.

"The Found Boat"
Sellwood, Jane. " 'Certain Vague Hopes of Disaster': A
Psychosemiotic Reading of Alice Munro's 'The Found Boat' as the
Flooding Text," *Stud Canadian Lit*, 17, i (1992), 1–16.

"Friend of My Youth"
Redekop, Magdalene. *Mothers and Other Clowns* . . . , 209–216.
Smythe, Karen E. *Figuring Grief* . . . , 135–137.

"Goodness and Mercy"
Smythe, Karen E. *Figuring Grief* . . . , 137–138.

"Hard Luck Stories"
Mayberry, Katherine J. " 'Every Last Thing . . . Everlasting': Alice
Munro and the Limits of Narrative," *Stud Short Fiction*, 29
(1992), 532–540.
Smythe, Karen E. *Figuring Grief* . . . , 151–152.

"Heirs of the Living Body"
Smythe, Karen E. *Figuring Grief* . . . , 123–124.

"How I Met My Husband"
Redekop, Magdalene. *Mothers and Other Clowns* . . . , 93–97.

"Images"
Redekop, Magdalene. *Mothers and Other Clowns* . . . , 43–49.
Smythe, Karen E. *Figuring Grief* . . . , 113–115.

"Labour Day Dinner"
Osmond, Rosalie. "Arrangements . . . ," 86–87.

"Lichen"
Redekop, Magdalene. *Mothers and Other Clowns* . . . , 182–191.

"Marrakesh"
Redekop, Magdalene. *Mothers and Other Clowns* . . . , 18–19.

"Material"
Redekop, Magdalene. *Mothers and Other Clowns* . . . , 15, 31, 89, 221.
Smythe, Karen E. *Figuring Grief* . . . , 119–120.

"Memorial"
Smythe, Karen E. *Figuring Grief* . . . , 115–116.

"Meneseteung"
Huston, Pam. "A Hopeful Sign: The Making of Metonymic Meaning
in Munro's 'Meneseteung,' " *Kenyon R*, N.S., 14, i (1992), 85–91.
Redekop, Magdalene. *Mothers and Other Clowns* . . . , 216–228.

"The Moon in the Orange Street Skating Rink"
Redekop, Magdalene. *Mothers and Other Clowns* . . . , 192–201.

"The Moons of Jupiter"
Osmond, Rosalie. "Arrangements . . . ," 91–92.
Redekop, Magdalene. *Mothers and Other Clowns* . . . , 167–173.
Smythe, Karen E. *Figuring Grief* . . . , 138–142, 144.

"The Office"
Boyles, Mary. "Woman: The Inside Outsider," in Crafton, John M., Ed. *Selected Essays* . . . , 118–120.
Redekop, Magdalene. *Mothers and Other Clowns* . . . , 49–50.

"Ottawa Valley"
Redekop, Magdalene. *Mothers and Other Clowns* . . . , 103–114.
Smythe, Karen E. *Figuring Grief* . . . , 132–133.

"The Peace of Utrecht"
Osmond, Rosalie. "Arrangements . . . ," 125–126.
Redekop, Magdalene. *Mothers and Other Clowns* . . . , 50–57.
Regan, Stephen. " 'The Presence of the Past': Modernism and Postmodernism in Canadian Short Fiction," in Howells, Coral Ann, and Lynette Hunter, Eds. *Narrative Strategies* . . . , 125–126.
Smythe, Karen E. *Figuring Grief* . . . , 130–132.

"Princess Ida"
Smythe, Karen E. *Figuring Grief* . . . , 124–126.

"The Progress of Love"
Osmond, Rosalie. "Arrangements . . . ," 89–91.
Redekop, Magdalene. *Mothers and Other Clowns* . . . , 174–176, 177, 178–182.
Smythe, Karen E. *Figuring Grief* . . . , 133–135.

"Prue"
Cassill, R. V. . . . *Instructor's Handbook*, 135–136.

"Red Dress—1946"
Regan, Stephen. " 'The Presence . . . ," 124.

"Royal Beatings"
Cassill, R. V. . . . *Instructor's Handbook*, 133–134.

"Simon's Luck"
Noonan, Gerald. "Alice Munro's Short Stories and the Art-That-Distrusts-Art," in Bardolph, Jacquelin, Ed. *Short Fiction* . . . , 141–142.

"Something I've Been Meaning to Tell You"
Osmond, Rosalie. "Arrangements . . . ," 83–84.
Redekop, Magdalene. *Mothers and Other Clowns* . . . , 97–103.
Suarez-Lafuente, María. "Fiction and Reality in Alice Munro's Short Stories," in Bardolph, Jacquelin, Ed. *Short Fiction* . . . , 149–150.

"Spelling"
Redekop, Magdalene. *Mothers and Other Clowns* . . . , 139–142.

"The Stone in the Field"
Redekop, Magdalene. *Mothers and Other Clowns* . . . , 164–167.
Smythe, Karen E. *Figuring Grief* . . . , 142–143, 144.

"Tell Me Yes or No"
Redekop, Magdalene. *Mothers and Other Clowns* . . . , 89–93.
Smythe, Karen E. *Figuring Grief* . . . , 120–121.

"The Time of Death"
Smythe, Karen E. *Figuring Grief* . . . , 116–117.

"Visitors"
Smythe, Karen E. *Figuring Grief* . . . , 146–147.

"Walker Brothers Cowboy"
Charters, Ann, and William E. Sheidley. *Resources for Teaching* . . . , 3rd ed., 157.
Redekop, Magdalene. *Mothers and Other Clowns* . . . , 37–43.
Smythe, Karen E. *Figuring Grief* . . . , 112–113.

"Walking on Water"
Carrington, Ildikó de Papp. "Definitions of a Fool: Alice Munro's 'Walking on Water' and Margaret Atwood's *Two Stories About Emma*: 'The Whirlpool Rapids' and 'Walking on Water,' " *Stud Short Fiction*, 28 (1991), 126, 138, 139–141, 142–143, 146.

"White Dump"
Noonan, Gerald. "Alice Munro's Short Stories . . . ," 144–145.
Redekop, Magdalene. *Mothers and Other Clowns* . . . , 176, 177, 201–208.

"Who Do You Think You Are?"
Lynch, Gerald. "The One and the Many: English Canadian Short Story Cycles," *Canadian Lit*, 130 (Autumn, 1991), 100–102.
Redekop, Magdalene. *Mothers and Other Clowns* . . . , 142–148.

"Winter Wind"
Redekop, Magdalene. *Mothers and Other Clowns* . . . , 104–105.
Smythe, Karen E. *Figuring Grief* . . . , 118–119.

NELLIE MUSIAL

"Auto-Worker's Son"
Gladsky, Thomas S. *Princes, Peasants* . . . , 236.

ROBERT MUSIL

"The Portuguese Lady"
O'Connon, Kathleen. *Robert Musil* . . . , 86–95.

"Tonka"
Jungk, Peter S. "Die Vergessene. Robert Musil und Herma Dietz. Ein Beitrag zur Musil-Forschung," *Neue Rundschau*, 103, ii (1992), 151–152, 154, 156, 158–159.
Mabee, Barbara. "Images of Woman in Musil's 'Tonka': Mystical Encounters and Borderlines between Self and Other," *Michigan Academician*, 24 (1992), 369–381.
O'Connon, Kathleen. *Robert Musil* . . . , 116–130.
Ryan, Judith. *The Vanishing Subject* . . . , 212–214.

MOTHOBI MUTLOATSE

"Mama Ndiyalila"
Worsfold, Brian. "Middle-Class Trappings and Urban Aspirations in

Motobi Mutloatse's 'Mama Ndiyalila,' " in Bardolph, Jacquelin, Ed. *Short Fiction* . . . , 226–230.

VLADIMIR NABOKOV

"The Admiralty Spire"
Connolly, Julian W. *Nabokov's Early Fiction* . . . , 140–143.

"An Affair of Honor"
Connolly, Julian W. *Nabokov's Early Fiction* . . . , 48–53.

"The Circle"
Foster, John B. *Nabokov's Art* . . . , 85–86.

"Cloud, Castle, Lake"
Duperray, Max. "Au-delà du fantastique: La Naissance douloureuse à l'écriture: 'Cloud, Castle, Lake' de Vladimir Nabokov," in Duperray, Max, Ed. *Du fantastique* . . . , 161–165.

"The Defense"
Barabtarlo, Gennady. " 'The Defense' Marginalia," *Nabokovian*, 28 (1992), 57–64.
Connolly, Julian W. *Nabokov's Early Fiction* . . . , 82–100.

"Details of a Sunset"
Connolly, Julian W. *Nabokov's Early Fiction* . . . , 16–20.

"Grace"
Connolly, Julian W. *Nabokov's Early Fiction* . . . , 24–27.

"A Guide to Berlin"
Connolly, Julian W. *Nabokov's Early Fiction* . . . , 27–31.

"The Leonardo"
Connolly, Julian W. *Nabokov's Early Fiction* . . . , 161–166.

"Lips to Lips"
Connolly, Julian W. *Nabokov's Early Fiction* . . . , 136–140.

"Mademoiselle O"
Foster, John B. *Nabokov's Art* . . . , 110–129.

"The Passenger"
Bohner, Charles H. *Instructor's Manual* . . . , 88–89.
Connolly, Julian W. *Nabokov's Early Fiction* . . . , 45–48.

"The Potato Elf"
Connolly, Julian W. *Nabokov's Early Fiction* . . . , 20–24.

"Recruiting"
Connolly, Julian W. *Nabokov's Early Fiction* . . . , 185–190.

"The Return of Chorb"
Connolly, Julian W. *Nabokov's Early Fiction* . . . , 11–16.

"Reunion"
Foster, John B. *Nabokov's Art* . . . , 84–85.

"Signs and Symbols"
+ Cassill, R. V. . . . *Instructor's Handbook*, 136–137.

Martin, Terry J. "Ways of Knowing in Nabokov's 'Signs and Symbols,' " *J Short Story Engl,* 17 (Autumn, 1991), 75–89.

Mignon, Charles W. "A Referential Reading of Nabokov's 'Signs and Symbols,' " *Stud Short Fiction,* 28 (1991), 169–175.

"Spring in Fialta"

Foster, John B. *Nabokov's Art . . . ,* 130–146.

Nicol, Charles. " 'Ghastly Rich Glass': A Double Essay on 'Spring in Fialta,' " *Russian Lit Triquarterly,* 24 (1990), 173–184.

"Terra Incognita"

Connolly, Julian W. *Nabokov's Early Fiction . . . ,* 131–136.

"Terror"

Connolly, Julian W. *Nabokov's Early Fiction . . . ,* 76–82.

"Torpid Smoke"

Connolly, Julian W. *Nabokov's Early Fiction . . . ,* 190–196.

NAGAI KAFŪ

"Falling Leaves"

Ito, Ken K. *Visions of Desire . . . ,* 40–41.

"The Journal of a Recent Returnee"

Ito, Ken K. *Visions of Desire . . . ,* 43–44.

"The Ranch Road"

Ito, Ken K. *Visions of Desire . . . ,* 35–36.

"A Song of Fukugawa"

Ito, Ken K. *Visions of Desire . . . ,* 44–48.

RABBI BRATYLAV NAHMAN

"The Tale of the Menorah" [same as "The Tale of the Menorah of Defects"]

Hoffman, Anne G. *Between Exile and Return . . . ,* 17–19.

SEEPERSAD NAIPAUL

"Dookhni and Mungal"

Firth, Kathleen. "Seepersad Naipaul's Short Fiction: The Reductive World of Trinidad's First Generation East Indians," in Bardolph, Jacquelin, Ed. *Short Fiction . . . ,* 125.

"Gopi"

Firth, Kathleen. "Seepersad Naipaul's . . . ," 125.

"The Wedding Came, But—,"

Firth, Kathleen. "Seepersad Naipaul's . . . ," 124.

V[IDIADHAR] S[URAJPASAD] NAIPAUL

"In A Free State"
  Weiss, Timothy F. *On the Margins* . . . , 172–178.
"One Out of Many"
  Weiss, Timothy F. *On the Margins* . . . , 10, 11, 12, 169–171.
"Tell Me Who To Kill"
  Weiss, Timothy F. *On the Margins* . . . , 171–172.
"B. Wordsworth"
  Charters, Ann, and William E. Sheidley. *Resources for Teaching* . . . , 3rd ed., 158–159.

R. K. NARAYAN

"A Breath of Lucifer"
  Harrex, S. C. "Mode: Comedy, Type: Rakshasa, Author: R. K. Narayan," *Commonwealth R*, 2, i-ii (1990–1991), 137–142.
"Four Rupees"
  Olinder, Britta. "Irony in R. K. Narayan's Short Fiction," in Bardolph, Jacquelin, Ed. *Short Fiction* . . . , 185.
"A Horse and Two Goats"
  Olinder, Britta. "Irony in . . . ," 184–185.
"House Opposite"
  Charters, Ann, and William E. Sheidley. *Resources for Teaching* . . . , 3rd ed., 160.
"The Performing Child"
  Olinder, Britta. "Irony in . . . ," 185–186.
"A Willing Slave"
  Olinder, Britta. "Irony in . . . ," 186.

GLORIA NAYLOR

"Luciella Louise Turner"
  Cassill, R. V. . . . *Instructor's Handbook*, 138.
  Charters, Ann, and William E. Sheidley. *Resources for Teaching* . . . , 3rd ed., 161–162.

NJABULO SIMAKAHLE NDEBELE

"Fools"
  Phillips, K. J. "Ndebele's *Fools*: A Challenge to the Theory of 'Multiple Meaning,' " *Mosaic*, 23, iv (1990), 94–99.
"The Prophetess"
  Rumboll, Frank. "Discharing Liminality: An Approach to Ndebele's *Fools*," *J Lit Stud*, 7, iii-iv (December, 1991), 281–288.

JOHN G. NEIHARDT

"The End of the Dream"
  Fultz, Jay. "Foreword," *"The End of the Dream"* . . . [by John G.
  Neihardt], xviii-xxi.

GÉRARD DE NERVAL [GÉRARD LABRUNIE]

"L'Illusion"
  Brix, Michel. "Nerval et les 'figures de l'illusion,' " *Oeuvres &*
  Critiques, 17, i (1992), 28–29.
"La Main enchantée" [also "La Main de gloire"]
  Cummiskey, Gary. *The Changing* . . . , 87–91.
"Octavie"
  Brix, Michel. "Nerval et . . . ," 29–30.
"Sylvie"
  Brix, Michel. "Nerval et . . . ," 31–32.
  Newmark, Kevin. *Beyond Symbolism* . . . , 34–67.

NGUGI WA THIONG'O [JAMES T. NGUGI]

"A Mercedes Funeral"
  Balogun, F. Odun. *Tradition and Modernity* . . . , 47–48.
"Minutes of Glory"
  Balogun, F. Odun. *Tradition and Modernity* . . . , 16.

CHARLES NODIER

"La Combe de l'homme mort"
  Cummiskey, Gary. *The Changing* . . . , 58–62.
"Inès de Las Sierras"
  Cummiskey, Gary. *The Changing* . . . , 62–67.

MARTA NOS

"Maleza de papel y trapo"
  Lorente-Murphy, Silvia. "Hacia una lectura de *La silla* de Marta
  Nos," *Alba de América*, 9, xvi-xvii (1991), 80, 81–84.

STANLEY NYAMFUKUDZA

"Aftermaths"
  Riemenschneider, Dieter. "Short Fiction from Zimbabwe," in
  Bardolph, Jacquelin, Ed. *Short Fiction* . . . , 258–259.

JOYCE CAROL OATES

"The Going-Away Party"
+ Bohner, Charles H. *Instructor's Manual* . . . , 90–91.

"How I Contemplated the World from the Detroit House of Correction and Began My Life Over Again"
+ Cassill, R. V. . . . *Instructor's Handbook*, 139–141.

"Ich bin ein Berliner"
Saalman, Dieter. "Joyce Carol Oates: 'Speak to me in Berliner,' or Deconstructing the Logocentric Closure in East-West Relations," *Stud Short Fiction*, 27 (1990), 21–34.

"Our Wall"
Saalman, Dieter. "Joyce Carol Oates . . . ," 21–34.

"Raven's Wing"
Wesley, Marilyn C. "On Sport: Magic and Masculinity in Joyce Carol Oates' Fiction," *Lit Interpretation Theory*, 3, i (1991), 66–68.

"Stalking"
Wesley, Marilyn C. "The Transgressive Heroine: Joyce Carol Oates' 'Stalking,' " *Stud Short Fiction*, 27 (1990), 15–20.

"The Translation"
Burleson, Donald R. "Connings: Bradbury/Oats," *Stud Weird Fiction*, 11 (Spring, 1992), 25–26, 27, 28, 29.

"The Virgin in the Rose-Bower; or, The Tragedy of Glen Mawr Manor"
Smiley, Pamela. "Incest, Roman Catholicism and Joyce Carol Oates," *Coll Lit,* 3, i (1991), 41–42.

"Where Are You Going, Where Have You Been?"
+ Bohner, Charles H. *Instructor's Manual* . . . , 91–92.
Piwinsky, David J. "Oates's 'Where Are You Going, Where Have You Been?' " *Explicator,* 49, iii (1991), 195–196.
+ Charters, Ann, and William E. Sheidley. *Resources for Teaching* . . . , 3rd ed., 163–164.

EDNA O'BRIEN

"The Creature"
Bohner, Charles H. *Instructor's Manual* . . . , 92–93.

FITZ-JAMES O'BRIEN

"The Diamond Lens"
Welch, Robert. *Irish Writers* . . . , 71.

TIM O'BRIEN

"The Things They Carried"
Cassill, R. V. . . . *Instructor's Handbook*, 141–142.

Charters, Ann, and William E. Sheidley. *Resources for Teaching . . .*, 3rd ed., 166–167.

"Where Have You Gone, Charming Billy?"
Wilhelm, Albert E. "Ballad Allusions in Tim O'Brien's 'Where Have You Gone, Charming Billy?' " *Stud Short Fiction*, 28 (1991), 218–222.

SILVINA OCAMPO

"La casa de azúcar"
Duncan, Cynthia. "Double or Nothing? The Fantastic Element in Silvina Ocampo's 'La casa de azúcar,' " *Chasqui*, 20, ii (1991), 64–72.
———. "Hacia una interpretación de lo fantástico en el contexto de la literatura hispanoamericana," *Texto Crítico*, 16 (January–December, 1990), 62.

"La continuación"
Ferreira-Pinto, Cristina. "El narrador intimista de Silvina Ocampo: 'La continuación,' " *Revista de Estudios Hispánicos*, 17–18 (1990–1991), 309–315.

"La red"
Rosarossa, Alejandra. "Espacio y acontecimiento en la focalización de 'La red' de Silvina Ocampo," in Domíguez, Mignon, Ed. *Estudios de narratología*, 124–135.

"El vestido de terciopelo"
Duncan, Cynthia. "Hacia una interpretación . . . ," 61–62.

FLANNERY O'CONNOR

"An Afternoon in the Woods"
Wray, Virginia F. " 'An Afternoon in the Woods': Flannery O'Connor's Discovery of Theme," *Flannery O'Connor Bull*, 20 (1991), 50–52.

"The Artificial Nigger"
Burke, Daniel. *Beyond Interpretation . . .*, 145–161.
Orvell, Miles. *Flannery O'Connor . . .*, 152–160.
Saunders, James R. "The Fallacies of Guidance and Light in Flannery O'Connor's 'The Artificial Nigger,' " *J Short Story Engl*, 17 (Autumn, 1991), 103–113.
Shaw, Mary N. " 'The Artificial Nigger': A Dialogic Narrative," *Flannery O'Connor Bull*, 20 (1991), 104–116.

"The Capture"
Orvell, Miles. *Flannery O'Connor . . .*, 70–72.

"A Circle in the Fire"
Babinec, Lisa S. "Cyclical Patterns of Domination and Manipulation in Flannery O'Connor's Mother-Daughter Relationships," *Flannery O'Connor Bull*, 19 (1990), 21–24, 25, 26.

Keating, Helane L., and Walter Levy. *Instructor's Manual: Lives Through Literature* . . . , 51–52.

"The Comforts of Home"
Gentry, Marshall B. "The Hand of the Writer in 'The Comforts of Home,' " *Flannery O'Connor Bull*, 20 (1991), 61–72.
Orvell, Miles. *Flannery O'Connor* . . . , 160–166.
Wyatt, Bryan N. "The Domestic Dynamics of Flannery O'Connor: *Everything That Rises Must Converge*," *Twentieth Century Lit*, 38 (1992), 77–82.

"The Displaced Person"
Orvell, Miles. *Flannery O'Connor* . . . , 141–152.
Munk, Linda. *The Trivial Sublime* . . . , 119–135.
Westarp, Karl-Heinz. "Flannery O'Connor's Displaced Persons," *Dolphin*, 20 (1991), 89–98.

"The Enduring Chill"
Orvell, Miles. *Flannery O'Connor* . . . , 48–49.
Wyatt, Bryan N. "The Domestic . . . ," 76–77.

"Everything That Rises Must Converge"
+ Bohner, Charles H. *Instructor's Manual* . . . , 93–94.
+ Cassill, R. V. . . . *Instructor's Handbook*, 145–146.
Castronovo, David. *The American Gentleman* . . . , 180–181.
+ Charters, Ann, and William E. Sheidley. *Resources for Teaching* . . . , 3rd ed., 168–169.
Orvell, Miles. *Flannery O'Connor* . . . , 6–10.
Wyatt, Bryan N. "The Domestic . . . ," 68–71.

"The Geranium"
Larsen, Val. "Manor House and Tenement: Failed Communities South and North in Flannery O'Connor's 'The Geranium,' " *Flannery O'Connor Bull*, 20 (1992), 88–103.
Orvell, Miles. *Flannery O'Connor* . . . , 180–187.

"Good Country People"
Babinec, Lisa S. "Cyclical Patterns . . . ," 11–18, 25.
Orvell, Miles. *Flannery O'Connor* . . . , 136–141.
Zacharasiewicz, Waldemar. "Unter der unbarmherzigen Sonne der Gnade: Flannery O'Connors 'Good Country People' und 'Revelation,' " in Engler, Bernd, and Franz Link, Eds. *Zwischen Dogma* . . . , 103–108.

"A Good Man Is Hard to Find"
Blythe, Hal, and Charlie Sweet. "Darwin in Dixie: O'Connor's Jungle," *Notes Contemp Lit*, 21, ii (1991), 8–9.
———. "O'Connor's 'A Good Man Is Hard to Find,' " *Explicator*, 50, iii (1992), 185–187.
+ Bohner, Charles H. *Instructor's Manual* . . . , 94–95.
Burns, Margie. "A Good Rose Is Hard to Find: Southern Gothic as Signs of Social Dislocation in Faulkner and O'Connor," in Downing, David B., and Susan Bazargan, Eds. *Image* . . . , 107, 108, 113–121.
+ Cassill, R. V. . . . *Instructor's Handbook*, 142–144.

Charters, Ann, and William E. Sheidley. *Resources for Teaching* . . . , 3rd ed., 170–171.

Clark, Michael. "Flannery O'Connor's 'A Good Man Is Hard to Find': The Moment of Grace," *Engl Lang Notes,* 29, ii (1991), 66–69.

Donahue, Ronald. "O'Connor's Ancient Comedy: Form in 'A Good Man Is Hard to Find,' " *J Short Story Engl,* 16 (Spring, 1991), 29–39.

Hurd, Myles R. "The Misfit as Parricide in Flannery O'Connor's 'A Good Man Is Hard to Find,' " *Note Contemp Lit,* 22, iv (1992), 5–7.

Orvell, Miles. *Flannery O'Connor* . . . , 130–136.

"Greenleaf"

Meek, Kristen. "Flannery O'Connor's 'Greenleaf' and the Holy Hunt of the Unicorn," *Flannery O'Connor Bull,* 19 (1990), 30–37.

Orvell, Miles. *Flannery O'Connor* . . . , 23–27.

Sexton, Mark S. " 'Blessed Insurance': An Examination of Flannery O'Connor's 'Greenleaf,' " *Flannery O'Connor Bull,* 19 (1990), 38–43.

Walker, Sue. "Spelling Out Illness: Lupus as Metaphor in Flannery O'Connor's 'Greenleaf,' " *Chattahoochee R,* 12, i (1991), 54–63.

Wyatt, Bryan N. "The Domestic . . . ," 71–73.

"Judgement Day"

Orvell, Miles. *Flannery O'Connor* . . . , 180–188.

Wyatt, Bryan N. "The Domestic . . . ," 85–87.

"The Lame Shall Enter First"

Orvell, Miles. *Flannery O'Connor* . . . , 160–161, 177–179.

Wyatt, Bryan N. "The Domestic . . . ," 77–78, 81–82.

"A Late Encounter with the Enemy"

Orvell, Miles. *Flannery O'Connor* . . . , 10–12.

"The Life You Save May Be Your Own"

Clasby, Nancy T. " 'The Life You Save May Be Your Own': Flannery O'Connor as a Visionary Artist," *Stud Short Fiction,* 28 (1991), 509–520.

Orvell, Miles. *Flannery O'Connor* . . . , 134–136.

"Parker's Back"

+ Cassill, R. V. . . . *Instructor's Handbook,* 147–149.

Orvell, Miles. *Flannery O'Connor* . . . , 166–172.

Wyatt, Bryan N. "The Domestic . . . ," 84–85.

"Revelation"

Babinec, Lisa S. "Cyclical Patterns . . . ," 18–21.

Blanch, Mae. "Joy and Terror: Figures of Grace in Cather and O'Connor Stories," *Lit & Belief,* 8 (1988), 109–111.

Rath, Sura P. "Ruby Turpin's Redemption: Thomistic Resolution in Flannery O'Connor's 'Revelation,' " *Flannery O'Connor Bull,* 19 (1990), 1–8.

Wyatt, Bryan N. "The Domestic . . . ," 82–84.

Zacharasiewicz, Waldemar. "Unter der . . . ," 109–112.

"Temple of the Holy Ghost"
Orvell, Miles. *Flannery O'Connor* . . . , 46–47.

"A View of the Woods"
Blanch, Mae. "Joy and Terror . . . ," 102–105.
Orvell, Miles. *Flannery O'Connor* . . . , 13–16, 50–51.
Wyatt, Bryan N. "The Domestic . . . ," 73–76.

"Wildcat"
Orvell, Miles. *Flannery O'Connor* . . . , 61–62.

FRANK O'CONNOR

"Darcy in the Land of Youth"
Throne, Marilyn. "Frank O'Connor's Lost Fatherlands: Displaced
Identity," *Colby Q*, 28, i (1992), 54–55.

"Ghosts"
Throne, Marilyn. "Frank O'Connor's Lost . . . ," 58–60.

"Guests of the Nation"
+ Bohner, Charles H. *Instructor's Manual* . . . , 96–97.
+ Cassill, R. V. . . . *Instructor's Handbook*, 150–152.
+ Charters, Ann, and William E. Sheidley. *Resources for Teaching* . . . , 3rd ed., 173–174.

"The Late Henry Conran"
Throne, Marilyn. "Frank O'Connor's Lost . . . ," 55–56.

"Lost Fatherlands"
Throne, Marilyn. "Frank O'Connor's Lost . . . ," 52–53.

"My Oedipus Complex"
+ Bohner, Charles H. *Instructor's Manual* . . . , 97–98.
+ Cassill, R. V. . . . *Instructor's Handbook*, 153–154.

"Uprooted"
Throne, Marilyn. "Frank O'Connor's Lost . . . ," 53–54.

ŌE KENZABURŌ

"The Day He Himself Shall Wipe My Tears Away"
Napier, Susan J. *Escape from the Wasteland* . . . , 167–172.

"Seventeen"
Napier, Susan J. *Escape from the Wasteland* . . . , 154–160.

"The Swimming Man"
Napier, Susan J. *Escape from the Wasteland* . . . , 63–67.

SEAN O'FAOLAIN

"A Broken World"
Sampson, Denis. "The Big House in Sean O'Faolain's Fiction," in
Genet, Jacqueline, Ed. *The Big House* . . . , 184–188.

"Lord and Master"
  Sampson, Denis. "The Big House . . . ," 188–189.
"Midsummer Night Madness"
  Sampson, Denis. "The Big House . . . ," 181–184.

GRACE OGOT

"The Rain Came"
  Balogun, F. Odun. *Tradition and Modernity* . . . , 15.

JOHN O'HARA

"Do You Like It Here?"
  +Bohner, Charles H. *Instructor's Manual* . . . , 98–99.

O. HENRY [WILLIAM SYDNEY PORTER]

"The Trimmed Lamp"
  Wilson, Christopher P. *White Collar Fiction* . . . , 51–53.

BEN OKRI

"Laughter Beneath the Bridge"
  Niven, Alastair. "Achebe and Okri: Contrasts in the Response to
  Civil War," in Bardolph, Jacquelin, Ed. *Short Fiction* . . . ,
  279–282.

TILLIE OLSEN

"Hey Sailor, What Ship?"
  Coiner, Constance. " 'No One's Private Ground': A Bakhtinian
  Reading of Tillie Olsen's *Tell Me a Riddle*," *Feminist Stud*, 18
  (1992), 266–268.
"I Stand Here Ironing"
  +Bohner, Charles H. *Instructor's Manual* . . . , 99.
  +Charters, Ann, and William E. Sheidley. *Resources for Teach-
  ing* . . . , 3rd ed., 175–176.
  Coiner, Constance. " 'No One's . . . ," 260–264.
  Keating, Helane L., and Walter Levy. *Instructor's Manual: Lives
  Through Literature* . . . , 7–8.
"O Yes."
  Coiner, Constance. " 'No One's . . . ," 265–266, 268–273, 278.
"Tell Me a Riddle"
  +Cassill, R. V. . . . *Instructor's Handbook*, 155–156.
  Coiner, Constance. " 'No One's . . . ," 264–265, 274–278, 279.

JUAN CARLOS ONETTI

"La cara de la desgracia"
  Millington, M. I. "Una lectura del deseo: 'La cara de la desgracia'
  de Juan Carlos Onetti," in *Coloquio internacional* . . . , 285–295.

"A Dream Come True"
  Stavans, Ilan. "Onetti, el teatro y la muerte," *Latin Am Theatre R*,
  25, i (1991), 107–113.

"El infierno tan temido"
  Renaud, Maryse. " 'El infierno tan temido' o la difícil aventura del
  exceso," in *Coloquio internacional* . . . , 297–308.
  Prats Sariol, José. "Onetti, el brujo," *Casa de las Américas*, 30
  (January-February, 1990), 113–116.
  Renart, J. Guillermo. "Bases narratológicas para una nueva lectura
  de 'El infierno tan temido' de Onetti," *Revista Iberoamericana*, 58
  (1992), 1133–1151.

"Jacob y el otro"
  Millington, Mark I. "Masculinity and the Fight for Onetti's 'Jacob y
  el otro,' " *Bull Hispanic Stud*, 69 (1992), 357–368.

"As Sad as She"
  Millington, M. I. "Objects and Objections: Onetti's 'Tan triste como
  ella,' " *Neophil,* 75, ii (1991), 207–221.

LOURDES ORTIZ

"Alicia"
  Pérez, Janet. "Characteristics of Erotic Brief Fiction by Women in
  Spain," *Monographic R*, 7 (1991), 185–186.

"Paisajes y figuras"
  Encinar, Angeles. "Escritoras Españolas actuales: una perspectiva a
  través del cuento," *Hispanic J*, 13 (1992), 190.

SIMON ORTIZ

"The Killing of a State Cop"
  Hoilman, Dennis. "The Ethnic Imagination: A Case History,"
  Canadian J Native Stud, 5, ii (1985), 168–169.

GEORGE ORWELL

"Animal Farm"
  Elbarbary, Samir. "Language as Theme in 'Animal Farm,' " *Int'l
  Fiction R*, 19 (1992), 31–38.
  Fergenson, Laraine. "George Orwell's 'Animal Farm': A Twentieth-
  Century Beast Fable," *Bestia*, 2 (1990), 109–118.

Davidson, Peter. "George Orwell: Dates and Origins," *Library*, 13, ii (1991), 143–144.
Meyers, Valerie. *George Orwell*, 101–113.

THOMAS OWEN

"La Boule noire"
Fratta, Anna S. "La 'Réalité magique' dans l'oeuvre de Thomas Owen," *Ragioni Critiche*, 17, lxiii-lxvi (1988), 139–140.
"Lydia à la folie"
Fratta, Anna S. "La 'Réalité . . . ,'" 136–138.

DAVID OWOYELE

"The Will of Allah"
Balogun, F. Odun. *Tradition and Modernity . . .* , 45.

CYNTHIA OZICK

"Bloodshed"
Friedman, Lawrence S. *Understanding Cynthia Ozick*, 101–106.
"The Butterfly and the Traffic Light"
Friedman, Lawrence S. *Understanding Cynthia Ozick*, 59–61.
"The Dock-Witch"
Friedman, Lawrence S. *Understanding Cynthia Ozick*, 67–72.
"The Doctor's Wife"
Friedman, Lawrence S. *Understanding Cynthia Ozick*, 83–87.
"An Education"
Friedman, Lawrence S. *Understanding Cynthia Ozick*, 88–95.
"Envy; or, Yiddish in America"
Friedman, Lawrence S. *Understanding Cynthia Ozick*, 75–81.
"From a Refugee's Notebook"
Friedman, Lawrence S. *Understanding Cynthia Ozick*, 142–144.
"Levitation"
Friedman, Lawrence S. *Understanding Cynthia Ozick*, 122–126.
"A Mercenary"
Friedman, Lawrence S. *Understanding Cynthia Ozick*, 94–101.
"The Pagan Rabbi"
Friedman, Lawrence S. *Understanding Cynthia Ozick*, 61–68.
Rosenberg, Ruth. "The Ghost Story as Aggada: Cynthia Ozick's 'The Pagan Rabbi' and Sheindel's Scar," in Carpenter, Lynette, and Wendy K. Kolmar, Eds. *Haunting the House of Fiction . . .* , 215–228.
"Puttermesser and Xanthippe"
Friedman, Lawrence S. *Understanding Cynthia Ozick*, 132–139.

"Puttermesser: Her Work History, Her Ancestry, Her Afterlife"
Friedman, Lawrence S. *Understanding Cynthia Ozick,* 127–132.

"Rosa"
Meyers, Judith. "Double Otherness: Woman as Holocaust Survivor in Cynthia Ozick's 'Rosa,' " in Crafton, John M., Ed. *Selected Essays* . . . , 142–151.
Klingenstein, Susanne. "Destructive Intimacy: The Shoah between Mother and Daughter in Fictions by Cynthia Ozick, Norma Rosen, and Rebecca Goldstein," *Stud Am Jewish Lit,* 11, ii (1992), 162–165.

"The Sewing Harem"
Friedman, Lawrence S. *Understanding Cynthia Ozick,* 143–144.

"The Shawl"
Charters, Ann, and William E. Sheidley. *Resources for Teaching* . . . , 3rd ed., 177–178.
Klingenstein, Susanne. "Destructive . . . ," 165–167.
Mathé, Sylvie. "Voix de l'émotion, voix de l'indicible: 'The Shawl' de Cynthia Ozick," in *Voix et langages* . . . , 11–41.

"Shots"
Friedman, Lawrence S. *Understanding Cynthia Ozick,* 138–142.

"The Suitcase"
Borchers, Hans. "Of Suitcases and Other Burdens: The Ambiguities of Cynthia Ozick's Image of Germany," *Centennial R,* 35, iii (1991), 606–613.
Friedman, Lawrence S. *Understanding Cynthia Ozick,* 81–83.

"Usurpation (Other People's Stories)"
Friedman, Lawrence S. *Understanding Cynthia Ozick,* 106–113.

"Virility"
Friedman, Lawrence S. *Understanding Cynthia Ozick,* 72–75.

JOSÉ EMILIO PACHECO

"Civilización y barbarie"
James, Herlinda R. " 'Civilización y barbarie': Un cuento de José Emilio Pacheco," *Dactylus,* 11 (1991), 65–68.

"Tenga para que se entretenga"
Duncan, Cynthia K. "Detecting the Fantastic in José Emilio Pacheco's 'Tenga para que se entretenga,' " *Inti,* 32–33 (Fall, 1990-Spring, 1991), 41–52.

GRACE PALEY

"The Contest"
Cronin, Gloria L. "Melodramas of Beset Womanhood: Resistance, Subversion, and Survival in the Fiction of Grace Paley," *Stud Am Jewish Lit,* 11, ii (1992), 141–142.

"A Conversation with My Father"
+ Bohner, Charles H. *Instructor's Manual* . . . , 100–101.
+ Charters, Ann, and William E. Sheidley. *Resources for Teaching* . . . , 3rd ed., 179–180.
Klinkowitz, Jerome. *Structuring the Void* . . . , 131–132.

"Faith in a Tree"
Baba, Minako. "Faith Darwin as Writer-Heroine: A Study of Grace Paley's Short Stories," *Stud Am Jewish Lit*, 7, i (1988), 45–46.

"Faith in the Afternoon"
Baba, Minako. "Faith Darwin . . . ," 43–44.

"Friends"
Baba, Minako. "Faith Darwin . . . ," 48–50, 51.

"Goodbye and Good Luck"
Cronin, Gloria L. "Melodramas . . . ," 142.

"Listening"
Baba, Minako. "Faith Darwin . . . ," 51–52.
Cronin, Gloria L. "Melodramas . . . ," 145.

"The Little Girl"
Klinkowitz, Jerome. *Structuring the Void* . . . , 129–131.

"The Long Distance Runner"
Baba, Minako. "Faith Darwin . . . ," 46–47.
Klinkowitz, Jerome. *Structuring the Void* . . . , 132–134.

"The Pale Pink Roast"
Cronin, Gloria L. "Melodramas . . . ," 141.

"Politics"
Robinson, Fred M. *Comic Moments*, 88–92.

"Ruthy and Edie"
Baba, Minako. "Faith Darwin . . . ," 50–51.

"Samuel"
Klinkowitz, Jerome. *Structuring the Void* . . . , 126–128.

"A Subject of Childhood"
Baba, Minako. "Faith Darwin . . . ," 42–43.
Greiner, Hoke. "Two Short Sad Stories from a Long and Happy Life," *Stud Short Fiction*, 29 (1992), 583–586.

"The Story Hearer"
Cronin, Gloria L. "Melodramas . . . ," 144–145.

"The Used Boy Raisers"
Baba, Minako. "Faith Darwin . . . ," 41–42.
+ Cassill, R. V. . . . *Instructor's Handbook*, 157.
Cronin, Gloria L. "Melodramas . . . ," 143.
Greiner, Hoke. "Two Short Sad . . . ," 583–586.

"A Woman Young and Old"
Cronin, Gloria L. "Melodramas . . . ," 141.

JÓHANNES PÁLSSOM

"Álfur of Borg"
  Wolf, Kirsten. "Heroic Past—Heroic Present: Western Icelandic
  Literature," *Scandinavian Stud,* 63 (1991), 437–438.

BREECE D'J PANCAKE

"A Room Forever"
  Edwards, Grace T. "Place and Space in Breece D'J Pancake's 'A
  Room Forever,' " in Lanier, Parks, Ed. *The Poetics . . .* , 141–148.

EMILIA PARDO BAZÁN

"Afra"
  Ashworth, Peter P. "Of Spinning Wheels and Witches: Pardo Bazán's
  'Afra' and *La bruja,*" *Letras Femeninas,* 18, i-ii (1992), 108–118.

"En travía"
  Chico Rico, Francisco. "Sobre el artículo español y su
  comportamiento en el ámbito textual: A propósito de un cuento de
  E. Pardo Bazán," *Analecta Malacitana,* 9, i (1986), 113–125,
  132–135.

BATISTAI PARWADA

"A Story of War"
  Riemenschneider, Dieter. "Short Fiction from Zimbabwe," in
  Bardolph, Jacquelin, Ed. *Short Fiction . . .* , 259–260.

BORIS PASTERNAK

"Aerial Ways"
  Rudova, Larissa. "On Pasternak's 'Aerial Ways,' " *Canadian-
  American Slavic Stud,* 24, i (1990), 33–37, 38–46.

FRANCINE PELLETIER

"The Migrant"
  Vonarburg, Elisabeth. "The Reproduction of the Body in Space," in
  Ruddick, Nicholas, Ed. *State . . .* , 63, 66.

ROSA MARÍA PEREDA

"Poor Tired Tim"
  Encinar, Angeles. "Escritoras Españolas actuales: una perspectiva a
  través del cuento," *Hispanic J,* 13 (1992), 184–185.

BENITO PÉREZ GALDÓS

"La novela en el tranvía"
Rogers, Douglass M. " 'La novela en el tranvía' and the Poetics of
Movement in Galdosian Narrative," *Anales Galdosianos*, 21
(1986), 115–126.

CRISTINA PERI ROSSI

"La influencia de Edgar A. Poe en la poesía de Raimundo Arias"
Schmidt, Cynthia A. "A Satiric Perspective on the Experience of
Exile in the Short Fiction of Cristina Peri Rossi," *Americas R*, 18,
iii–iv (1990), 218, 222–226.

"La tarde del dinosaurio"
Schmidt, Cynthia A. "A Satiric . . . ," 218, 219–222.

NORA PERRY

"Clotilde and the Contraband"
Diffley, Kathleen. *Where My Heart* . . . , 132–133.

MARTA PESSARRODONA

"La búsqueda de Elizabeth"
Encinar, Angeles. "Escritoras Españolas actuales: una perspectiva a
través del cuento," *Hispanic J*, 13 (1992), 189–190.
Schaefer, Claudia. "A Simple Question of Symmetry: Women
Writing in Post-Franco Spain," in Erro-Orthmann, Nora, and Juan
Cruz Mendizábal, Eds. *La escritora* . . . , 282–283, 284.

LJUDMILA PETRUŠEVSKAJA

"The New Robinsons"
Clowes, Edith W. "Ideology and Utopia in Recent Soviet
Literature," *Russian R*, 51, iii (1992), 387–393.

ANN LANE PETRY

"The Bones of Louella Brown"
Smith-Wright, Geraldine. "In Spite of the Klan: Ghosts in the Fiction
of Black Women Writers," in Carpenter, Lynette, and Wendy K.
Kolmar, Eds. *Haunting the House of Fiction* . . . , 147–150.

"Has Anybody Seen Miss Dora Dean?"
Smith-Wright, Geraldine. "In Spite of the Klan . . . ," 150, 151–153.

CARYL PHILLIPS

"The Cargo Rap"
Sarvan, Charles P., and Hasan Marhama. "The Fictional Works of
Caryl Phillips: An Introduction," *World Lit Today*, 65 (1991),
38–39.

"Heartland"
Sarvan, Charles P., and Hasan Marhama. "The Fictional
Works . . . ," 37–38.

"Higher Ground"
Sarvan, Charles P., and Hasan Marhama. "The Fictional
Works . . . ," 39.

JAYNE ANNE PHILLIPS

"Bluegill"
Squier, Susan M. "Fetal Voices: Speaking for the Margins Within,"
Tulsa Stud Women's Lit, 10, i (1991), 20–23.

"Blue Moon"
Hornby, Nick. *Contemporary American Fiction*, 123–124.

"El Paso"
Hornby, Nick. *Contemporary American Fiction*, 120–121.

"Home"
Hornby, Nick. *Contemporary American Fiction*, 117–119.

"Fast Lanes"
Hornby, Nick. *Contemporary American Fiction*, 121–122.

"Souvenir"
+Cassill, R. V. . . . *Instructor's Handbook*, 157–159.

LUISE PICHLER

"The Widow's Son"
Peterson, Brent O. *Popular Narratives* . . . , 197–198.

RICARDO PIGLIA

"Homage to Roberto Arlt"
McCracken, Ellen. "Metaplagiarism and the Critic's Role as
Detective: Ricardo Piglia's Reinvention of Roberto Arlt," *PMLA*,
106 (1991), 1071–1083.

"Luba"
McCracken, Ellen. "Metaplagiarism . . . ," 1071–1083.

VIRGILIO PIÑERA

"Cómo viví y morí"
López Ramírez, Tomás. "Virgilio Piñera: Las ceremonias de la
negación," *Cupey*, 1, ii (1984), 88–89.

"La condecoración"
López Ramírez, Tomás. "Virgilio Piñera . . . ," 87–88.

"Pequeñas maniobras"
Balderston, Daniel. "Estética de la deformación en Gombrowicz y Piñera," *Explicación de Textos Literarios*, 19, ii (1990–1991), 4–6.

"El viaje"
López Ramírez, Tomás. "Virgilio Piñera . . . ," 86–87.

LUIGI PIRANDELLO

"Ciàula scopre la Luna"
Jepson, Lisa. "Filling Space: The Trauma of Birth in Pirandello's Existential Novelle," *Italica*, 69 (1991), 424–427.

"The Trap"
Jepson, Lisa. "Filling Spaces . . . ," 420–421.

"Happiness"
Radcliff-Umstead, Douglas. "Luigi Pirandello as Writer of Short Fiction and Novels," in DiGaetani, John L., Ed. *A Companion* . . . , 348–349.

"The Journey"
Radcliff-Umstead, Douglas. "Luigi Pirandello . . . ," 346–348.

"War"
+ Bohner, Charles H. *Instructor's Manual* . . . , 101–102.
Cassill, R. V. . . . *Instructor's Handbook*, 159–160.

SYLVIA PLATH

"Johnny Panic and the Bible of Dreams"
Hayman, Ronald. *The Death and Life* . . . , 122–123.
Rose, Jacqueline. *The Haunting* . . . , 56–57.

"The Shadow"
Rose, Jacqueline. *The Haunting* . . . , 199, 202.

"Superman and Paula Brown's New Snowsuit"
Rose, Jacqueline. *The Haunting* . . . , 199.

"The Wishing Box"
Rose, Jacqueline. *The Haunting* . . . , 179–181.

ANDREI PLATONOV

"Soul"
Bodin, Per-Arne. "The Promised Land—Desired and Lost: An Analysis of Andrej Platonov's Short Story 'Džan,' " *Scando-Slavica*, 13 (1991), 5–24.

EDGAR ALLAN POE

"Berenice"

Burduck, Michael L. *Grim Phantasms* . . . , 59–63.

Cappello, Mary. " 'Berenice' and Poe's *Marginalia*: Adversaria of Memory," *New Orleans R*, 17, iv (Winter, 1990), 54–65.

Meyers, Jeffrey. *Edgar Allan Poe* . . . , 77–79.

Priestman, Martin. *Detective Fiction* . . . , 40–42.

Ravvin, Norman. "An Irruption of the Archaic: Poe and the Grotesque," *Mosaic*, 25, iv (1992), 9.

"The Black Cat"

Amper, Susan. "Untold Story: The Lying Narrator in 'The Black Cat,' " *Stud Short Fiction*, 29 (1992), 475–485.

Badenhausen, Richard. "Fear and Trembling in Literature of the Fantastic: Edgar Allan Poe's 'The Black Cat,' " *Stud Short Fiction*, 29 (1992), 487–498.

Burduck, Michael L. *Grim Phantasms* . . . , 96–99.

Cleman, John. "Irresistible Impulses: Edgar Allan Poe and the Insanity Defense," *Am Lit*, 63 (1991), 623–640.

Herdman, John. *The Double* . . . , 93–94.

Priestman, Martin. *Detective Fiction* . . . , 39–40.

Ravvin, Norman. "An Irruption of the Archaic: Poe and the Grotesque," *Mosaic*, 25, iv (1992), 11.

"The Cask of Amontillado"

Benton, Richard P. "Poe's 'The Cask' and the 'White Webwork Which Gleams,' " *Stud Short Fiction*, 28 (1991), 183–194.

+Bohner, Charles H. *Instructor's Manual* . . . , 102.

Burduck, Michael L. *Grim Phantasms* . . . , 111–114.

+Charters, Ann, and William E. Sheidley. *Resources for Teaching* . . . , 3rd ed., 181–182.

Meyers, Jeffrey. *Edgar Allan Poe* . . . , 158, 201–202.

"A Descent into the Maelström"

Burduck, Michael L. *Grim Phantasms* . . . , 78–83.

Meyers, Jeffrey. *Edgar Allan Poe* . . . , 125.

Ware, Tracy. " 'A Descent into the Maelström': The Status of Scientific Rhetoric in a Perverse Romance," *Stud Short Fiction*, 29 (1992), 77–84.

"The Devil in the Belfry"

Bachinger, Katrina E. "The Aesthetics of (Not) Keeping in Step Reading the Consumer Mobocracy of Poe's 'The Devil in the Belfry' against Peacock," *Modern Lang Q*, 51 (1990), 513–533.

"The Domain of Arnheim"

Leavy, Barbara F. *To Blight With Plague* . . . , 75–79.

"Eleonora"

Burduck, Michael L. *Grim Phantasms* . . . , 83–86.

Meyers, Jeffrey. *Edgar Allan Poe* . . . , 129–130.

"The Facts in the Case of M. Valdemar"

Burduck, Michael L. *Grim Phantasms* . . . , 107–111.

Meyers, Jeffrey. *Edgar Allan Poe* . . . , 178–180.

"The Fall of the House of Usher"
  Barbarese, J. T. "Landscapes of the American Psyche," *Sewanee R*,
    100 (1992), 603–609.
  +Bohner, Charles H. *Instructor's Manual . . .* , 103.
  Burduck, Michael L. *Grim Phantasms . . .* , 70–75.
  +Cassill, R. V. *. . . Instructor's Handbook*, 161.
  Chandler, Marilyn R. *Dwelling in the Text . . .* , 47–62.
  Elbert, Monika M. " 'The Man of the Crowd' and The Man Outside
    the Crowd: Poe's Narrator and the Democratic Reader," *Mod
    Lang Stud*, 21, iv (1991), 19–20, 21–24, 25.
  Gray, Richard. "Edgar Allan Poe and the Problem of Regionalism,"
    in Lerda, Valeria G., and Tjebbe Westendorp, Eds. *The United
    States South . . .* , 84–90.
  Grillou, Jean-Louis. " 'The Fall of the House of Usher': Un
    cryptogramme alchimique?" in Duperray, Max, Ed. *Du
    fantastique . . .* , 111–126.
  Hoeveler, Diane L. "The Hidden God and the Abjected Woman in
    'The Fall of the House of Usher,' " *Stud Short Fiction*, 29 (1992),
    385–394.
  Hutchinson, Stuart. *The American Scene . . .* , 26–28.
  La Cassagnère, Christian. "Désastre obscur: angoisse et écriture
    dans 'The Fall of the House of Usher,' d'Edgar Allan Poe," in La
    Cassagnère, Christian, Ed. *Visages . . .* , 303–324.
  Meyers, Jeffrey. *Edgar Allan Poe . . .* , 110–113, 158.
  Priestman, Martin. *Detective Fiction . . .* , 37–42.
  Rashkin, Esther. *Family Secrets . . .* , 123–155.
  Richard, Claude. "Edgar A. Poe et l'esthétique du double," in La
    Cassagnère, Christian, Ed. *Visages . . .* , 277–286.
  Rovit, Earl. "Melville and the Discovery of America," *Sewanee R*,
    100 (1992), 587–589.

"The Gold Bug"
  Mathews, James W. "Legrand's Golden Vision: Meaning in 'The
    Gold Bug,' " *CEA Critic,* 53, iii (1991), 23–29.
  Meyers, Jeffrey. *Edgar Allan Poe . . .* , 135–137.
  Ravvin, Norman. "An Irruption of the Archaic: Poe and the
    Grotesque," *Mosaic*, 25, iv (1992), 9.

"Hop-Frog"
  Bachinger, Katrina. "Together (or Not Together) against Tyranny:
    Poe, Byron, and Napoleon Upside Down in 'Hop-Frog,' " *Texas
    Stud Lit & Lang,* 33 (1991), 373–402.
  Burduck, Michael L. *Grim Phantasms . . .* , 114–118.

"The Imp of the Perverse"
  Cleman, John. "Irresistible Impulses . . . ," 623–640.

"King Pest"
  Leavy, Barbara F. *To Blight With Plague . . .* , 79–81.

"Ligeia"
  Burduck, Michael L. *Grim Phantasms . . .* , 66–70.
  Herdman, John. *The Double . . .* , 89–90.

McEntree, Grace. "Remembering Ligeia," *Stud Am Fiction*, 20, i (1992), 75–83.

Meyers, Jeffrey. *Edgar Allan Poe* . . . , 103–105.

Shi, Yaohua. "The Enigmatic Ligeia/'Ligeia,' " *Stud Short Fiction*, 28 (1991), 485–496.

"The Man of the Crowd"

Brand, Dana. *The Spectator and the City* . . . , 10–11.

Elbert, Monika M. " 'The Man . . . ," 20–21, 25–26.

Meyers, Jeffrey. *Edgar Allan Poe* . . . , 115–118.

Nankov, Nikita. "Edgar Allan Poe as an American Romantic," *Occasional Papers*, 41 (July, 1990), 2–6.

Priestman, Martin. *Detective Fiction* . . . , 41–42.

Rignall, John. *Realistic Fiction* . . . , 14–18.

Whalen, Terence. "Edgar Allan Poe and the Horrid Laws of Political Economy," *Am Q*, 44 (1992), 386–387.

"The Masque of the Red Death"

Burduck, Michael L. *Grim Phantasms* . . . , 86–90.

Leavy, Barbara F. *To Blight With Plague* . . . , 68–70.

Meyers, Jeffrey. *Edgar Allan Poe* . . . , 133–134, 302–304.

"Metzengerstein"

Burduck, Michael L. *Grim Phantasms* . . . , 43–46.

Meyers, Jeffrey. *Edgar Allan Poe* . . . , 64.

"Morella"

Burduck, Michael L. *Grim Phantasms* . . . , 63–66.

Meyers, Jeffrey. *Edgar Allan Poe* . . . , 79.

"MS. Found in a Bottle"

Burduck, Michael L. *Grim Phantasms* . . . , 46–49.

Meyers, Jeffrey. *Edgar Allan Poe* . . . , 66–67.

"The Murders in the Rue Morgue"

Brand, Dana. *The Spectator and the City* . . . , 95–99.

Irwin, John T. "A Clew to a Clue: Locked Rooms and Labyrinths in Poe and Borges," *Raritan* 10, iv (1991), 43–45, 50–57.

———. "Reading Poe's Mind: Politics, Mathematics and the Association of Ideas in 'The Murders in the Rue Morgue,' " *Am Lit Hist*, 4 (1992), 187–206.

Leer, David V. "Detecting Truth . . . ," 65, 66, 68, 69–71, 73, 74–75, 79.

Meyers, Jeffrey. *Edgar Allan Poe* . . . , 10, 123–125, 155.

Priestman, Martin. *Detective Fiction* . . . , 42–54.

Vines, Lois D. *Valery and Poe* . . . , 79–90.

Whalen, Terence. "Edgar Allan Poe . . . ," 400–402.

"The Mystery of Marie Roget"

Brand, Dana. *The Spectator and the City* . . . , 99–103.

Meyers, Jeffrey. *Edgar Allan Poe* . . . , 134–135.

Priestman, Martin. *Detective Fiction* . . . , 51–53.

"The Narrative of Arthur Gordon Pym"

Gitelman, Lisa. "Arthur Gordon Pym and the Novel Narrative of Edgar Allan Poe," *Nineteenth-Century Lit*, 47 (1992), 349–361.

Greenfield, Bruce. *Narrating Discovery* . . . , 165–182.

Hammond, Alexander. "Consumption, Exchange, and the Literary Marketplace: From the Folio Club Tales to *Pym*," in Kopley, Richard, Ed. *Poe's "Pym"* . . . , 159–160, 163–166.

Hutchinson, Stuart. *The American Scene* . . . , 21–25.

Irwin, John T. "The Quincuncial Network in Poe's *Pym*" in Kopley, Richard, Ed. *Poe's "Pym"* . . . , 175–187.

Kennedy, J. Gerald. "Decomposing the Textual Body," in Kopley, Richard, Ed. *Poe's "Pym"* . . . , 167–174.

Lenz, William E. "Poe's 'Arthur Gordon Pym' and the Narrative Techniques of Antarctic Gothic," *CEA Critic,* 53, iii (1991), 30–38.

Meyers, Jeffrey. *Edgar Allan Poe* . . . , 95–110.

"The Pit and the Pendulum"

Burduck, Michael L. *Grim Phantasms* . . . , 90–93.

Gauer, Denis. " 'The Pit and the Pendulum': Inconscient et intertextualité," *Revue Française d'Études Américaines*, 15 (July, 1990), 119–136.

Malloy, Jeanne. "Apolcalyptic Imagery and the Fragmentation of the Psyche: 'The Pit and the Pendulum,' " *Nineteenth-Century Lit,* 46, i (1991), 82–95.

"The Premature Burial"

Burduck, Michael L. *Grim Phantasms* . . . , 100–103.

"The Purloined Letter"

+Bohner, Charles H. *Instructor's Manual* . . . , 104.

Cassill, R. V. . . . *Instructor's Handbook*, 162–163.

Irwin, John T. "A Clew to a Clue . . . ," 42, 46–50.

Leer, David V. "Detecting Truth . . . ," 65, 66, 68, 69–71, 73, 74–75,79.

Major, René. "La parabole de la lettre volée: de la direction de la curé et de son récit," *Études Freudiennes*, 30 (October, 1987), 97–130; rpt. "The Parable of the Purloined Letter: The Direction of the Curé and Its Telling," trans. John Forrester, *Stanford Lit R,* 8, i-ii (Spring-Fall, 1991), 67–102.

Meyers, Jeffrey. *Edgar Allan Poe* . . . , 155–156.

Priestman, Martin. *Detective Fiction* . . . , 53–57.

Schweizer, Harold. "Nothing and Narrative 'Twitching' in 'The Purloined Letter,' " *Lit & Psych,* 37, iv (1991), 63–69.

Whalen, Terence. "Edgar Allan Poe . . . ," 405, 406–408.

"Shadow—A Parable"

Burduck, Michael L. *Grim Phantasms* . . . , 53–56.

Leavy, Barbara F. *To Blight With Plague* . . . , 71–72.

"Silence—A Fable"

Burduck, Michael L. *Grim Phantasms* . . . , 56–59.

"The System of Doctor Tarr and Professor Fether"

Burduck, Michael L. *Grim Phantasms* . . . , 103–107.

"A Tale of the Ragged Mountains"

Herdman, John. *The Double* . . . , 91–92.

Meyers, Jeffrey. *Edgar Allan Poe* . . . , 153–154.

"The Tell-Tale Heart"
  Benfey, Christopher. "Poe and the Unreadable . . . ," 30–35, 37, 38, 39, 40–41.
  Burduck, Michael L. *Grim Phantasms* . . . , 93–95.
  Cleman, John. "Irresistible Impulses . . . ," 623–640.
  Gauer, Denis. " 'The Tell-Tale Heart' de Poe: Angoisse et stratégie littéraire," *Revue Française d'Études Americaines*, 14 (November, 1989), 395–406.
  Meyers, Jeffrey. *Edgar Allan Poe* . . . , 137–138.
  Zimmerman, Brett. " 'Moral Insanity' or Paranoid Schizophrenia: Poe's 'The Tell-Tale Heart,' " *Mosaic*, 25, ii (1992), 39–48.
"The Thousand-and-Second Tale of Scheherazade"
  Denuccio, Jerome D. "Fact, Fiction, Fatality: Poe's 'The Thousand-and-Second Tale of Scheherazade," *Stud Short Fiction*, 27 (1990), 365–370.
"The Unparalleled Adventure of One Hans Pfaall"
  Meyers, Jeffrey. *Edgar Allan Poe* . . . , 79–81.
"William Wilson"
  Burduck, Michael L. *Grim Phantasms* . . . , 75–78.
  Herdman, John. *The Double* . . . , 94–98.
  Keating, Helane L., and Walter Levy. *Instructor's Manual: Lives Through Literature* . . . , 47–48.

JOHN WILLIAM POLIDORI

"The Vampyre"
  Barbour, Judith. "Dr. John William Polidori, Author of 'The Vampyre,' " in Coleman, Deirdre, and Peter Otto, Eds. *Imagining Romanticism* . . . , 85–110.
  MacDonald, David L. *Poor Polidori* . . . , 97–98, 192–203, 221–222.

KERIMA POLOTAN

"The Sounds of Sunday"
  Evasco, Marjorie. "The Writer and Her Roots," in Kintanar, Thelma B., Ed. *Women Reading* . . . , 16–17.
"The Virgin"
  Evasco, Marjorie. "The Writer . . . ," 15–16.

YEVGENY POPOV

"The Fence"
  Kustanovich, Konstantin. "The Naturalistic Tendency in Contemporary Soviet Fiction: Thematics, Poetics, Functions," in Graham, Sheelagh D., Ed. *New Directions* . . . , 82–83.
"The Green Tract"
  Kustanovich, Konstantin. "The Naturalistic . . . ," 84–85.

KATHERINE ANNE PORTER

"The Dove of Chapacalo"
Walsh, Thomas F. *Katherine Anne Porter . . .* , 49–56.

"Flowering Judas"
+ Bohner, Charles H. *Instructor's Manual . . .* , 105.
Cassill, R. V. *. . . Instructor's Handbook,* 166–167.
Christensen, Peter G. "Katherine Anne Porter's 'Flowering Judas'
and D. H. Lawrence's *The Plumed Serpent*: Contrasting Visions of
Women in the Mexican Revolution," *So Atlantic R,* 56, i (1991),
35–46.
Lavers, Norman. " 'Flowering Judas' and the Failure of *Amour
Courtois*," *Stud Short Fiction,* 28 (1991), 77–82.
Levy, Helen F. *Fiction of the Home Place . . .* , 136–137.
Loeffelholz, Mary. *Experimental Lives . . .* , 135–136.
Titus, Mary E. "The 'Booby Trap' of Love: Artist and Sadist in
Katherine Anne Porter's Mexico Fiction," *J Mod Lit,* 16 (1990),
619–621.
Walsh, Thomas F. *Katherine Anne Porter . . .* , 122–134.

"The Grave"
+ Bohner, Charles H. *Instructor's Manual . . .* , 106–107.
Levy, Helen F. *Fiction of the Home Place . . .* , 72, 157–158.
Yaeger, Patricia. "The Poetics of Birth," in Stanton, Domna C., Ed.
Discourses of Sexuality . . . , 270–279.

"Hacienda"
Levy, Helen F. *Fiction of the Home Place . . .* , 139–140, 141.
Walsh, Thomas F. *Katherine Anne Porter . . .* , 155–163.

"Holiday"
Hinze, Diana. "Texas and Berlin: Images of Germany in Katherine
Anne Porter's Prose," *Southern Lit J,* 24, i (1991), 78–82.
Skaggs, Merrill. "The Louisianas of Katherine Anne Porter's Mind,"
in Brown, Dorothy H., and Barbara C. Ewell, Eds. *Louisiana
Women . . .* , 163–167.
Walsh, Thomas F. *Katherine Anne Porter . . .* , 101–104.

"The Jilting of Granny Weatherall"
Hoefel, Roseanne L. "The Jilting of (Hetero) Sexist Criticism:
Porter's Ellen Weatherall and Hapsy," *Stud Short Fiction,* 28
(1991), 9–20.
Levy, Helen F. *Fiction of the Home Place . . .* , 137–139.

"Leaning Tower"
Hinze, Diana. "Texas and . . . ," 82–87.

"The Lovely Legend"
Titus, Mary E. "The 'Booby . . . ," 626, 627–629.

"Magic"
Llewellyn, Kurtis L. "Structure and Theme in Katherine Anne
Porter's 'Magic,' " *Mod Fiction Stud,* 37 (1991), 104–106.
Lytle, Andrew. "Mirror, Mirror on the Wall," *Mod Age,* 33 (1991),
367–369.

"María Concepción"
    Burke, Daniel. *Beyond Interpretation* . . . , 79–102.
    Levy, Helen F. *Fiction of the Home Place* . . . , 135–136.
    Walsh, Thomas F. *Katherine Anne Porter* . . . , 74–83.

"The Martyr"
    Titus, Mary E. "The 'Booby . . . ," 626–627.

"Old Mortality"
    Levy, Helen F. *Fiction of the Home Place* . . . , 141–147, 152.
    Skaggs, Merrill. "The Louisianas . . . ," 157–163.

"The Old Order"
    Davis, Thadios M. "Race and Region," in Elliot, Emory, et al.[4],
        Eds. *The Columbia History of the American Novel*, 425–426.

"Pale Horse, Pale Rider"
    Leavy, Barbara F. *To Blight With Plague* . . . , 139–155.
    Levy, Helen F. *Fiction of the Home Place* . . . , 147–152.
    Loeffelholz, Mary. *Experimental Lives* . . . , 136–137.
    Walsh, Thomas F. *Katherine Anne Porter* . . . , 183–193.

"That Tree"
    Walsh, Thomas F. *Katherine Anne Porter* . . . , 169–173.

"Theft"
    Cassill, R. V. . . . *Instructor's Handbook*, 164–165.
    Charters, Ann, and William E. Sheidley. *Resources for Teaching* . . . , 3rd ed., 184–185.

"Virgin Violeta"
    Titus, Mary E. "The 'Booby . . . ," 623–626.
    Walsh, Thomas F. *Katherine Anne Porter* . . . , 96–100.

J. F. POWERS

"The Valiant Woman"
    + Bohner, Charles H. *Instructor's Manual* . . . , 107–108.
    + Cassill, R. V. . . . *Instructor's Handbook*, 168.

KOOS PRINSLOO

"Young Man's Cupboard"
    Coetzee, Ampie. "The Ideological Burden of Afrikaans," in
        Nethersole, Reingard, Ed. *Emerging Literatures*, 63–70.

V[ICTOR] S[AWDON] PRITCHETT

"The Accompanist"
    Stinson, John J. *V. S. Pritchett* . . . , 64–66.

"Blind Love"
    Hughes, Douglas A. "[V. S. Pritchett]," in Stinson, John J. *V. S. Pritchett* . . . , 113–115.
    Stinson, John J. *V. S. Pritchett* . . . , 49–51.

"The Cage Birds"
    Stinson, John J. *V. S. Pritchett* . . . , 52–53.

"The Camberwell Beauty"
    Stinson, John J. *V. S. Pritchett* . . . , 55–57.

"A Careless Widow"
    Stinson, John J. *V. S. Pritchett* . . . , 67–68.

"A Change of Policy"
    Stinson, John J. *V. S. Pritchett* . . . , 70–71.

"The Chestnut Tree"
    Stinson, John J. *V. S. Pritchett* . . . , 24.

"Cocky Olly"
    Stinson, John J. *V. S. Pritchett* . . . , 69–70.

"The Diver"
    Bohner, Charles H. *Instructor's Manual* . . . , 108–109.
    Hughes, Douglas A. "[V. S. Pritchett]," . . . , 109–110.
    Stinson, John J. *V. S. Pritchett* . . . , 59–61.

"The Fall"
    Stinson, John J. *V. S. Pritchett* . . . , 45–46.

"The Fig Tree"
    Stinson, John J. *V. S. Pritchett* . . . , 66.

"Handsome Is as Handsome Does"
    Stinson, John J. *V. S. Pritchett* . . . , 8–11.

"The Image Trade"
    Stinson, John J. *V. S. Pritchett* . . . , 71–72.

"It May Never Happen"
    Stinson, John J. *V. S. Pritchett* . . . , 21–24.

"The Ladder"
    Stinson, John J. *V. S. Pritchett* . . . , 38–39.

"Lady from Guatemala"
    Stinson, John J. *V. S. Pritchett* . . . , 61–62.

"The Landlord"
    Stinson, John J. *V. S. Pritchett* . . . , 37–38.

"Many Are Disappointed"
    Stinson, John J. *V. S. Pritchett* . . . , 28–29.

"The Marvellous Girl"
    Stinson, John J. *V. S. Pritchett* . . . , 57–59.

"The Nest Builder"
    Stinson, John J. *V. S. Pritchett* . . . , 51–52.

"The Night Worker"
    Stinson, John J. *V. S. Pritchett* . . . , 25–26.

"The Oedipus Complex"
Stinson, John J. *V. S. Pritchett* . . . , 26–27.

"On the Edge of the Cliff"
Hughes, Douglas A. "[V. S. Pritchett]," . . . , 117–118.
Stinson, John J. *V. S. Pritchett* . . . , 63–64.

"Pocock Passes"
Stinson, John J. *V. S. Pritchett* . . . , 27–28.

"The Sailor"
Stinson, John J. *V. S. Pritchett* . . . , 29–34.

"The Saint"
Stinson, John J. *V. S. Pritchett* . . . , 34–36.

"The Satisfactory"
Stinson, John J. *V. S. Pritchett* . . . , 37.

"The Scapegoat"
Stinson, John J. *V. S. Pritchett* . . . , 14–15.

"The Skeleton"
Hughes, Douglas A. "[V. S. Pritchett]," . . . , 115–117.
Stinson, John J. *V. S. Pritchett* . . . , 53–54.

"The Spree"
Hughes, Douglas A. "[V. S. Pritchett]," . . . , 118–119.
Stinson, John J. *V. S. Pritchett* . . . , 61.

"A Trip to the Seaside"
Hughes, Douglas A. "[V. S. Pritchett]," . . . , 119–121.

"The Upright Man"
Stinson, John J. *V. S. Pritchett* . . . , 12–14.

"The Wedding"
Hughes, Douglas A. "[V. S. Pritchett]," . . . , 112–113.
Stinson, John J. *V. S. Pritchett* . . . , 66–67.

"The Wheelbarrow"
Hughes, Douglas A. "[V. S. Pritchett]," . . . , 110–112.
Stinson, John J. *V. S. Pritchett* . . . , 43–45.

"When My Girl Comes Home"
Stinson, John J. *V. S. Pritchett* . . . , 40–43.

"You Make Your Own Life"
Stinson, John J. *V. S. Pritchett* . . . , 11–12.

MARCEL PROUST

"The Death of Baldassare Silvande"
Kingcaid, Renée. *Neurosis and Narrative* . . . , 43–52.

"The End of the Journey"
Kingcaid, Renée. *Neurosis and Narrative* . . . , 65–74.

"Melancholy Summer of Madame de Breyves"
Kingcaid, Renée. *Neurosis and Narrative* . . . , 52–59.

"A Young Girl's Confession"
   Kingcaid, Renée. *Neurosis and Narrative* . . . , 56–65.

SOLEDAD PUÉRTOLA

"A través de las ondas"
   Encinar, Angeles. "Escritoras Españolas actuales: una perspectiva a
   través del cuento," *Hispanic J,* 13 (1992), 187–188.

"La indiferencia de Eva"
   Tsuchiya, Akiko. "Language, Desire, and Feminine Riddle in
   Soledad Puértola's 'La indiferencia de Eva,' " *Revista Estudios
   Hispánicos,* 35, i (1991), 69–79.

MARÍA LUISA PUGA

"Ramiro"
   Rodríguez-Hernández, Raúl. "María Luisa Puga: Aspectos de una
   nueva sensibilidad de narrar," in Erro-Orthmann, Nora, and Juan
   Cruz Mendizábal, Eds. *La escritora* . . . , 155–158.

ALEXANDER PUSHKIN

"The Queen of Spades"
   Doherty, Justin. "Fictional Paradigms in Pushkin's 'Pikovaya
   dama,' " *Essays Poetics,* 17, i (1992), 49–66.
   Scales, Jean N. "The Ironic Smile: Pushkin's 'The Queen of Spades'
   and James' 'The Aspern Papers,' " *Coll Lang Assoc J,* 34 (1991),
   486–490.
   Shrayer, Maxim D. "Rethinking Romantic Irony: Puškin, Byron,
   Schlegel and 'The Queen of Spades,' " *Slavic & East European J,*
   36 (1992), 397–414.

"The Shot"
   + Bohner, Charles H. *Instructor's Manual* . . . , 110–111.

BARBARA PYM

"Across a Crowded Room"
   Wyatt-Brown, Anne M. *Barbara Pym* . . . , 140–142.

"Back to St. Petersburg"
   Weld, Annette. *Barbara Pym* . . . , 156–158.

"The Christmas Visit"
   Wyatt-Brown, Anne M. *Barbara Pym* . . . , 139–140.

"The Day Music Came"
   Weld, Annette. *Barbara Pym* . . . , 35–37.

"English Ladies"
   Weld, Annette. *Barbara Pym* . . . , 153–156.

"A Few Days Before Winter"
    Weld, Annette. *Barbara Pym* . . . , 38–39.
"The Funeral"
    Weld, Annette. *Barbara Pym* . . . , 37–38.
"The German Baron"
    Weld, Annette. *Barbara Pym* . . . , 159–160.
"Goodbye, Balkan Capital"
    Weld, Annette. *Barbara Pym* . . . , 41–45.
"The Painted Heart"
    Weld, Annette. *Barbara Pym* . . . , 158–159.
"Unpast Alps"
    Weld, Annette. *Barbara Pym* . . . , 34–35.
"The White Elephant"
    Weld, Annette. *Barbara Pym* . . . , 39–41.

THOMAS PYNCHON

"Entropy"
    Smetak, Jacqueline R. "Thomas Pynchon's Short Stories and Jung's
    Concept of the Anima," *J Evolutionary Psych*, 11, i-ii (1990),
    186–189.
"Lowlands"
    Smetak, Jacqueline R. "Thomas Pynchon's . . . ," 181–186.
"Mortality and Mercy in Vienna"
    Keesey, Douglas. "The Politics of Doubling in 'Mortality and Mercy
    in Vienna,' " *Pynchon Notes*, 24–25 (Spring-Fall, 1989), 5–19.
    Smetak, Jacqueline R. "Thomas Pynchon's . . . ," 186.
"The Secret Integration"
    Smetak, Jacqueline R. "Thomas Pynchon's . . . ," 190–192.
"The Small Rain"
    Smetak, Jacqueline R. "Thomas Pynchon's . . . ," 180–181.

RAQUEL DE QUEIROZ

"Metonymy, or the Husband's Revenge"
    Keating, Helane L., and Walter Levy. *Instructor's Manual: Lives
    Through Literature* . . . , 112.

HORACIO QUIROGA

"A la deriva"
    Paoli, Roberto. "El perfecto cuentista: comentario a tres textos de
    Horacio Quiroga," *Revista Iberoamericana*, 58 (1992), 953–959.

"The Dead Man"
Llurba, Ana María. "Un discurso doblemente transpuesto," in
Domíguez, Mignon, Ed. *Estudios de narratología*, 65–80.
Paoli, Roberto. "El perfecto cuentista . . . ," 959–968.
"El desierto"
Cluff, Russell M. "La omisión conspicua en Juan Rulfo y Salvador
Elizondo," *Palabra y Hombre*, 78 (April-June, 1991), 275.
"El perro rabioso"
Rosemberg, Fernando. "Un innovador relato de Horacio Quiroga,"
Estudios de Literatura Argentina, 7, ii (1982), 157–167.
"The Son"
Paoli, Roberto. "El perfecto cuentista . . . ," 968–974.

WILHELM RAABE

"Die schwarze Galeere"
Marhoff, Lydia. "Wilhelm Raabes 'Die scwarze Galeere' als Perseus
und Andromeda-Allegorie," *Jahrbuch der Raabe-Gesellschaft*,
[n.v.] (1992), 48–50.
"Zum wilden Mann"
Schmidt, Michael. "Nichts als Vettern? Anspielungsstructuren in
Wilhelm Raabes Erzählung 'Zum wilden Mann,' " *Jahrbuch der
Raabe-Gesellschaft*, [n.v.] (1992), 111–138.

RACHILDE

"The Frog Killer"
Kingcaid, Renée. *Neurosis and Narrative* . . . , 140–144.

JULIAN RALPH

"Dutch Kitty's White Slippers"
Hapke, Laura. "The American Working Girl and the New York
Tenement Tale of the 1890s," *J Am Culture*, 15, ii (1992), 46–47.

JAYAPRAGA REDDY

"Friends"
Van Niekerk, Annemarie. "Aspects of Race, Class and Gender in
Jayapraga Reddy's *On the Fringe of Dreamtime and Other
Stories*," *Unisa Engl Stud*, 30, ii (1992), 37–38.
"The Spirit of Two Worlds"
Van Niekerk, Annemarie. "Aspects . . . ," 38–39.
"The Stolen Hours"
Van Niekerk, Annemarie. "Aspects . . . ," 36–37.

"A Time to Yield"
Van Niekerk, Annemarie. "Aspects . . . ," 39–40.

HENRI DE RÉGNIER

"La Mort de Monsieur de Nouâtre et de Madame de Ferlinde"
Cummiskey, Gary. *The Changing* . . . , 142–146.

MIKE RESNICK

"Kirinyaga"
Van Gelder, Gordon. "Let's Go Look at the Natives: Conflicts of
Culture in Mike Resnick's 'Kirinyaga,' " *New York R Sci Fiction*,
9 May 1989, 11–14.
Tilton, Lois. "Strangling the Baby: Cultural Relativism in Mike
Resnick's 'Kirinyaga,' " *New York R Sci Fiction*, 9 May 1989,
11–12.

JOSÉ REVUELTAS

"El lenguage de nadie"
Duncan, Cynthia. "Language as a Barrier to Communication
Between the Classes in Rosario Castellanos's 'La tregua' and José
Revueltas's 'El lenguaje de nadie,' " *Hispania*, 74 (1991), 871–874.

ALFONSO REYES

"Silueta del indio Jesús"
Robb, James W. "Alfonso Reyes y el indio Jesús (Una autobiografía
poética)," *Revista Hispánica Moderna*, 54, i (June, 1991), 138–143.

GREMER CHAN REYES

"A Trail Toward the Sun"
Lucero, Rosario Cruz. "The Philippine Short Story, 1981–1990: The
Voice of the Self-Authenticating Other," *Tenggara*, 26 (1990), 81.

JUN CRUZ REYES

"Sharing"
Lucero, Rosario Cruz. "The Philippine Short Story, 1981–1990: The
Voice of the Self-Authenticating Other," *Tenggara*, 26 (1990), 80.

JEAN RHYS [ELLA GWENDOLEN REES WILLIAMS]

"The Day They Burned the Books"
    Howells, Coral A. *Jean Rhys*, 139–141.

"Goodbye Marcus, Goodbye Rose"
    Howells, Coral A. *Jean Rhys*, 135–138.
    James, Louis. "The Other Side of the Mirror: The Short Stories of
        Jean Rhys and Olive Senior," in Bardolph, Jacquelin, Ed. *Short
        Fiction . . .* , 90–91.

"I Spy a Stranger"
    Howells, Coral A. *Jean Rhys,* 144–146.
    Wilson, Lucy. "European or Caribbean: Jean Rhys and the Language
        of Exile," in Bevan, David, Ed. *Literature and Exile*, 82–84.

"Illusion"
    Fido, Elaine S. "The Politics of Colours and the Politics of Writing in
        the Fiction of Jean Rhys," *Jean Rhys R*, 4, ii (1991), 3–12.

"The Imperial Road"
    O'Connor, Teresa F. "Jean Rhys, Paul Theroux, and the Imperial
        Road," *Twentieth Century Lit*, 38 (1992), 404–414.

"La Grosse Fifi"
    Howells, Coral A. *Jean Rhys,* 38–39.

"Let Them Call It Jazz"
    Howells, Coral A. *Jean Rhys,* 126–129.
    James, Louis. "The Other Side . . . ," 93.

"Pioneers, Oh Pioneers"
    James, Louis. "The Other Side . . . ," 92.

"The Sound of the River"
    Howells, Coral A. *Jean Rhys,* 126–132.

"Temps Perdi"
    Howells, Coral A. *Jean Rhys,* 141–144.
    Wilson, Lucy. "European or . . . ," 81–82, 84–86.

"Tigers Are Better Looking"
    Howells, Coral A. *Jean Rhys,* 129–132.

"Vienna"
    Howells, Coral A. *Jean Rhys,* 40–42.
    Wilson, Lucy. "European or . . . ," 80–82.

JULIO RAMÓN RIBEYRO

"La insignia"
    Rodero, Jesús. "Juego e ironía en dos relatos de Julio Ramón
        Ribeyro," *Cincinnati Romance R*, 10 (1991), 179–184.

"Sobre los modos de ganar la guerra"
    Rodero, Jesús. "Juego . . . ," 184–189.

JULIO RICCI

"El apartamento"
Ulla, Noemí. "Tradición y transgresión en los cuentos de Julio
Ricci," *Revista Iberoamericana*, 58 (1992), 1075.
"Pivoski"
Ulla, Noemí. "Tradición . . . ," 1073–1074.

JACK RICHARDSON

"In the Final Years of Grace"
Callens, John. "Of Novices and Scapegoats: Jack Richardson's 'In
the Final Years of Grace,' " *Texas Stud Lit & Lang*, 34 (1992),
41–86.

CARMEN RIERA

"El reportaje"
Encinar, Angeles. "Escritoras Españolas actuales: una perspectiva a
través del cuento," *Hispanic J*, 13 (1992), 186–187.

ALIFA RIFAAT

"Bahiyya's Eyes"
Salti, Ramzi M. "Feminism and Religion in Alifa Rifaat's Short
Stories," *Int'l Fiction R,* 18 (1991), 110–112.

TOMÁS RIVERA

" . . . And the Earth Did Not Part"
Olivares, Julián. "Introduction," *Tomás Rivera: The Complete Works*
[by Tomás Rivera], 16–20.
"Eva and Daniel"
Olivares, Julián. "Introduction," 30–31.
"The Harvest"
Olivares, Julián. "Introduction," 32–33.
"Inside the Window"
Olivares, Julián. "Introduction," 35.
"It Is Painful"
Olivares, Julián. "Introduction," 18.
"Looking for Borges"
Olivares, Julián. "Introduction," 35–36.
"The Lost Year"
Olivares, Julián. "Introduction," 16–17.

"Pete Fonseca"
  Olivares, Julián. "Introduction," 29–30.
"The Salamanders"
  Olivares, Julián. "Introduction," 31–32.
"When We Arrive"
  Olivares, Julián. "Introduction," 20–21.
"Zoo Island"
  Olivares, Julián. "Introduction," 33–34.

AUGUSTO ROA BASTOS

"Moriencia"
  Luna Sellés, Carmen. "El nivel discursivo en el relato 'Moriencia' de
  Augusto Roa Bastos," *Iris*, [n.v.] (1992), 111–122.

MARY ROBISON

"Coach"
  Cassill, R. V. . . . *Instructor's Handbook*, 169.
"The Dictionary in the Laundry Chute"
  Aldridge, John W. *Talents and Technicians* . . . , 91–92.
"Sisters"
  Keating, Helane L., and Walter Levy. *Instructor's Manual: Lives
  Through Literature* . . . , 33–34.

MIREYA ROBLES

"La ciudad flotante"
  Collman, Lilliam O. "El patrón de renacimiento en *Frigorífico del
  este* de Mireya Robles," in Erro-Orthmann, Nora, and Juan Cruz
  Mendizábal, Eds. *La escritora* . . . , 56–59.
"En la otra mitad del tiempo"
  Collman, Lilliam O. "El patrón . . . ," 52–54.
"Frigorífico del este"
  Collman, Lilliam O. "El patrón . . . ," 50–52.
"El vampiro que da sangre"
  Collman, Lilliam O. "El patrón . . . ," 54–56.

MONTSERRAT ROIG

"Before the Civil War"
  Encinar, Angeles. "Escritoras Españolas actuales: una perspectiva a
  través del cuento," *Hispanic J*, 13 (1992), 190–191.

ANA ROSSETTI

"La sortija y el sortilegio"
Pérez, Janet. "Characteristics of Erotic Brief Fiction by Women in
Spain," *Monographic R*, 7 (1991), 186–188.

PHILIP ROTH

"The Conversion of the Jews"
+ Bohner, Charles H. *Instructor's Manual* . . . , 111–112.
+ Cassill, R. V. . . . *Instructor's Handbook*, 170–171.
"Eli the Fanatic"
Gittleman, Sol. "Witnessing the Holocaust in American Literature:
A Note to Bonnie Lyons," *Yiddish*, 7, iv (1990), 36–37.
Simon, Elliott M. "Philip Roth's 'Eli the Fanatic': The Color of
Blackness," *Yiddish*, 7, iv (1990), 39–48.

INA ROUSSEAU

"Do You Remember Helena Lem?"
Sorapure, Madeleine. "Reading Ina Rousseau's 'Do You Remember
Helena Lem?' " *Stud Short Fiction*, 28 (1991), 453–458.

GABRIELLE ROY

"Où iras-tu Sam Lee Wong?"
Dansereau, Estelle. "Convergence/éclatement: L'Immigrant au
risque de la perte de soi dans la nouvelle 'Où iras-tu Sam Lee
Wong?' de Gabrielle Roy," *Canadian Lit*, 127 (1990), 94–109.

JUAN RULFO

"Acuérdate"
García-Nieto Onrubia, M. Luisa, and Carmen González Dávila. "*El
llano en llamas* o el largo camino hacia la desesperanza," *Castilla*,
6–7 (1983–1984), 55–56.
"Al amanecer"
Reinhardt-Childers, Ilva. "Sensuality, Brutality, and Violence in Two
of Rulfo's Stories: An Analytical Study," *Hispanic J*, 12, i (1991),
69–70.
"La cuesta de las comadres"
García-Nieto Onrubia, M. Luisa, and Carmen González Dávila. "*El
llano* . . . ," 54.
"El día del derrumbe"
Fares, Gustavo. "La filosofía del mito: Rodolfo Kusch y Juan Rulfo,"
J Interdisciplinary Lit Stud, 3, ii (1992), 191–192.

García-Nieto Onrubia, M. Luisa, and Carmen González Dávila. "*El llano* . . . ," 63–64.

"¡Diles que no me maten!"
García-Nieto Onrubia, M. Luisa, and Carmen González Dávila. "*El llano* . . . ," 54–55.

"En la madrugada"
Cluff, Russell M. "La omisión conspicua en Juan Rulfo y Salvador Elizondo," *Palabra y Hombre*, 78 (April-June, 1991), 276–277.
García-Nieto Onrubia, M. Luisa, and Carmen González Dávila. "*El llano* . . . ," 67–68.
Ostrov, Andrea. " 'En la madrugada' de Juan Rulfo: Una indagación sobre las causas," *Literatura Mexicana*, 2, ii (1991), 427–437.

"Es que somos muy pobres"
Campbell, Ysla. "La ideología en 'Es que somos muy pobres' de Juan Rulfo," *Palabra y Hombre*, 78 (April-June, 1991), 280–286.

"El hombre"
García-Nieto Onrubia, M. Luisa, and Carmen González Dávila. "*El llano* . . . ," 56–58.

"El llano en llamas"
Reinhardt-Childers, Ilva. "Sensuality . . . ," 70–72.

"Luvina"
Fares, Gustavo. "La filosofía . . . ," 183–190.
García-Nieto Onrubia, M. Luisa, and Carmen González Dávila. "*El llano* . . . ," 58–62.
Llarena, Alicia. "La actitud narrativa y la imagen creándose a sí misma ('Luvina' de Juan Rulfo)," *Revista Filología,* 10 (1991), 244–248.
Ríos de Torres, Rosario E. "*El llano en llamas* o donde la soledad laberíntica soberana reina," *Cupey*, 1, ii (1984), 110–111.

"Macario"
García-Nieto Onrubia, M. Luisa, and Carmen González Dávila. "*El llano* . . . ," 69–70.
Gnutzmann, Rita. "Teoría y práctica acerca del lector implícito," *Revista de literatura*, 53 (1991), 5–17.

"No oyes ladrar los perros"
García-Nieto Onrubia, M. Luisa, and Carmen González Dávila. "*El llano* . . . ," 53–54.

"Nos han dado la tierra"
García-Nieto Onrubia, M. Luisa, and Carmen González Dávila. "*El llano* . . . ," 62–63.

"Talpa"
García-Nieto Onrubia, M. Luisa, and Carmen González Dávila. "*El llano* . . . ," 64–67.

FERDINAND VON SAAR

"Schloss Kostenitz"
Renner, Ursula. "Pavillons, Glashäuser und Seitenwege—Topos und

Vision des Paradiesgartens bei Saar, Hofmannsthal, und Heinrich
Mann," *Recherches Germaniques,* 20 (1990), 124–129, 137–138.

JUAN JOSÉ SAER

"La mayor"
Solotorevsky, Myrna. " 'La mayor' de Juan José Saer y el efecto
modelizador del *nouveau roman*," *Neophil*, 75, iii (1991), 399–407.

ASENSIO SAEZ GARCÍA

"Boda civil"
Thacker, Verónica D. "Tradición y soledad en los cuentos de Asensio
Saez," *Murgetana*, 78 (1989), 32–33.

"La carta"
Thacker, Verónica D. "Tradición . . . ," 35–36.

"Novelista"
Thacker, Verónica D. "Tradición . . . ," 31–32.

"Señorita fotógrafo"
Thacker, Verónica D. "Tradición . . . ," 33–34.

"Tarde de marzo con viento"
Thacker, Verónica D. "Tradición . . . ," 34–35.

PATSY SAIKA

"The Unwilling Bride"
Sumida, Stephen H. "Sense of Place, History, and the Concept of
the 'Local' in Hawaii's Asian/Pacific American Literatures," in
Lim, Shirley G., and Amy Ling, Eds. *Reading the
Literatures* . . . , 227–228.

PEDRO SALINAS

"Cita de los tres"
Feal, Carlos. "Lo real, lo imaginario y lo simbólico en *Víspera del
gozo* de Pedro Salinas," *Mod Lang Notes*, 106 (1991), 320–324.

"Delirios del chopo y el ciprés"
Feal, Carlos. "Lo real . . . ," 324–325.

"Entrada en Sevilla"
Feal, Carlos. "Lo real . . . ," 318–320.

"Mundo cerrado"
Feal, Carlos. "Lo real . . . ," 315–317.

"Volverla a ver"
Feal, Carlos. "Lo real . . . ," 326–328.

GEORGE SAND

"La Fille d'Albano"
Powell, David A. *George Sand*, 27–28.

"La Marquise"
Nassardier-Kennedy, Françoise. "L'Espace du féminin dans 'La
Marquise,' " *George Sand Stud*, 10, i-ii (1990–1991), 28–33.
Powell, David A. *George Sand*, 30.

"Mattea"
Powell, David A. *George Sand*, 48, 75–76.

"Melchior"
Powell, David A. *George Sand*, 30.

"Metella"
Powell, David A. *George Sand*, 34.

"Mouny-Robin"
Glasgow, Janis. " 'Mouny-Robin,' nouvelle fantastique de George
Sand (1841)," *George Sand Stud*, 10, i-ii (1990–1991), 3–10.

"Pauline"
Powell, David A. *George Sand*, 30.

"Queen Coax"
Penrod, Lynn K. "Aurore Inscribing Aurore: A Reading of 'La Reine
Coax,' " in Datlof, Natalie, Jean Fuchs, and David A. Powell, Eds.
The World of George Sand, 75–83.

LILIA QUINDOZA SANTIAGO

"The Last Story of Huli"
Lucero, Rosario Cruz. "The Philippine Short Story, 1981–1990: The
Voice of the Self-Authenticating Other," *Tenggara*, 26 (1990), 87.

BIENVENIDO N. SANTOS

"The Day the Dancers Came"
Campomanes, Oscar V. "Filipinos in the United States and Their
Literature of Exile," in Lim, Shirley G., and Amy Ling, Ed.
Reading the Literatures . . . , 60–63.

JEAN-PAUL SARTRE

"Dépaysement"
Thibault, Bruno. " 'Dépaysement': une nouvelle 'manquée' de Jean-
Paul Sartre," *French Forum*, 16, i (1991), 81–90.

"The Wall"
Keating, Helane L., and Walter Levy. *Instructor's Manual: Lives
Through Literature . . .* , 50–51.
Siebers, Tobin. *Morals and Stories*, 122–127.

JOHN SAYLES

"I-80 Nebraska, M. 490—M. 205"
+ Bohner, Charles H. *Instructor's Manual* . . . , 112.

GALINA ALEKSANDROVNA ŠČERBAKOVA

"The Wall"
Polowy, Teresa. "Embattled Silence: The Alcoholic Marriage in
Galina Ščerbakova's 'The Wall,' " *Slavic and East European J*, 36
(1992), 452–462.

ARTHUR SCHNITZLER

"Dream Novella"
Ryan, Judith. *The Vanishing Subject* . . . , 131–132.
"Lieutenant Gustl"
Ryan, Judith. *The Vanishing Subject* . . . , 132–133.
"Miss Else"
Ryan, Judith. *The Vanishing Subject* . . . , 133–135.
"The Wise Man's Wife"
Ryan, Judith. *The Vanishing Subject* . . . , 130–131.

OLIVE SCHREINER

"Prelude"
Clayton, Cherry. "Olive Schreiner and Katherine Mansfield: Artistic
Transformations of the Outcast Figure by Two Colonial Women
Writers," in Bardolph, Jacquelin, Ed. *Short Fiction* . . . , 35–36.

MARCEL SCHWOB

"La Cité dormante"
Cummiskey, Gary. *The Changing* . . . , 138–142.
"La machine à parler"
Schuerewegen, Franc. " 'La machine à parler': A partir d'un conte
de Marcel Schwob," *L'Esprit Createur*, 32, iv (1992), 31–39.
"The Veiled Man"
Black, Joel. *The Aesthetics of Murder* . . . , 96–97, 104–106.
"Mr. Burke and Mr. Hare, Assassins"
Black, Joel. *The Aesthetics of Murder* . . . , 83–88.

EVELYN SCOTT

"Kalicz"
Gladsky, Thomas S. *Princes, Peasants* . . . , 85–87.

CATHARINE SEDGWICK

"Cacoethes Scribendi"
  Fick, Thomas. "Catharine Sedgwick's 'Cacoethes Scribendi':
  Romance in Real Life," *Stud Short Fiction*, 27 (1990), 567–576.

ANNA SEGHERS

"Auf dem Wege zur amerikanischen Botschaft"
  Rapisarda, Cettina. "Women and Peace in Literature and Politics:
  The Example of Anna Seghers," in Williams, Rhys W., Stephen
  Parker, and Colin Riordan, Eds. *German Writers* . . . , 171–172.

"Das Duell"
  Bergstedt, Alfred, and Kerstin Morling. "Das Duell: Zu Anna
  Seghers' Erzählung 'Das Duell' (1965) und Heiner Müllers
  'Wolokolamsker Chaussee—Teil III: Das Duell' (1986),"
  Wissenschaftliche Zeitschrift, 34, v (1990), 694–698, 699.

"Der gerechte Richter"
  Klotz, Christian. " 'Der gerechte Richter' von Anna Seghers: Kritik
  eines Unkritablen" *Literatur für Leser*, 4 (1990), 202–212.

"Die Rückkehr"
  Kane, Martin. "Roles for the Writer: East German Literature and the
  Creation of National Consciousness, 1945–1952," *Mod Lang R*, 87
  (1992), 363.

"Marie geht in die Versammlung"
  Rapisarda, Cettina. "Women . . . ," 172.

"Tales of the Extraterrestrials"
  Mabee, Barbara. "Astronauts, Angels, and Time Machines: The
  Fantastic in Recent German Democratic Republic Literature," in
  Morse, Donald E., Marshall B. Tymn, and Csilla Bertha, Eds. *The
  Celebration* . . . , 228–229.

"Three Women from Haiti"
  Rützou Petersen, Vibeke. "Revolution or Colonization: Anna
  Seghers's 'Drei Frauen aus Haiti,' " *Germ Q*, 65 (1992), 398–404.

JORGE DE SENA

"Caim"
  Fagundes, Francisco C. *In the Beginning* . . . , 85–111.

"A Janela da Esquina"
  Fagundes, Francisco C. "Love on Death's Edge: Jorge de Sena's 'A
  Janela da Esquina,' " *Portuguese Stud*, 7 (1991), 151–169.

"Mar de Pedras"
  Fagundes, Francisco Cota. "Jorge de Sena's 'Mar de Pedras': Fictive
  Biography as Self-expression," *Bull Hispanic Stud*, 68 (1991),
  395–404.

"Paradiso perdido"
Fagundes, Francisco C. *In the Beginning* . . . , 65–84.

OLIVE SENIOR

"Ballad"
James, Louis. "The Other Side of the Mirror: The Short Stories of Jean Rhys and Olive Senior," in Bardolph, Jacquelin, Ed. *Short Fiction* . . . , 93.

"The Boy Who Loved Ice Cream"
James, Louis. "The Other Side . . . ," 92–93.

"Confirmation Day"
James, Louis. "The Other Side . . . ," 91.

"Do Angels Wear Brassieres?"
James, Louis. "The Other Side . . . ," 91–92.

"Real Old Time T'ing"
Pollard, Velma. "Mothertongue Voices in the Writings of Olive Senior and Laura Goodison," in Nasta, Susheila, Ed. *Motherlands* . . . , 240–243.

"Summer Lightning"
Louvel, Liliane. " 'Summer Lightning': A Reading of Olive Senior's Short Story," *Commonwealth Essays & Stud*, 13, ii (1991), 42–48.

DANIEL SERNINE

"Only a Lifetime"
Vonarburg, Elisabeth. "The Reproduction of the Body in Space," in Ruddick, Nicholas, Ed. *State* . . . , 61, 63–65, 70.

VARLAM SHALAMOV

"A Day Off"
Toker, Leona. "A Tale Untold: Varlam Shalamov's 'A Day Off,' " *Stud Short Fiction,* 28 (1991), 1–8.

IRWIN SHAW

"The Eighty-Yard Run"
Reynolds, Fred. "Irwin Shaw's 'The Eighty-Yard Run,' " *Explicator,* 49, ii (1991), 121–123.

VASILY MAKAROVICH SHUKSHIN

"Broken Down"
Morgan, Lyndall. "The Subversive Sub-Text: Allegorical Elements

in the Short Stories of Vasily Shukshin," *Australian Slavonic*, 5, i (1991), 72–73.

"Cut Down"
Morgan, Lyndall. "The Subversive . . . ," 68, 73.

"Muzhik Deryabin"
Morgan, Lyndall. "The Subversive . . . ," 74–75.

"The Shameless Ones"
Morgan, Lyndall. "The Subversive . . . ," 73–74.

"The Strong Man"
Morgan, Lyndall. "The Subversive . . . ," 65, 66–67.

LESLIE MARMON SILKO

"Tony's Story"
Hoilman, Dennis. "The Ethnic Imagination: A Case History," *Canadian J Native Stud*, 5, ii (1985), 169–172.

"Yellow Woman"
Charters, Ann, and William E. Sheidley. *Resources for Teaching . . .* , 3rd ed., 186.

JESSIE GEORGINA SIME

"An Irregular Union"
Campbell, Sandra. " 'Gently Scan': Theme and Technique in J. G. Sime's 'Sister Woman' (1919)," *Canadian Lit*, 133 (1992), 46.

WILLIAM GILMORE SIMMS

"Caloya"
Guilds, John C. *Simms: A Literary Life*, 102–103, 179.

"The Giant's Coffin"
Guilds, John C. *Simms: A Literary Life*, 178.

"Grayling"
Guilds, John C. *Simms: A Literary Life*, 12–13, 176.

"Oakatibbe"
Guilds, John C. *Simms: A Literary Life*, 29, 179.

"Sergeant Barnacle"
Guilds, John C. *Simms: A Literary Life*, 179.

"Those Old Lunes"
Guilds, John C. *Simms: A Literary Life*, 179.

"The Two Camps"
Guilds, John C. *Simms: A Literary Life*, 177.

ISAAC BASHEVIS SINGER

"Song of Love"
Steinberg, Peter. *Journey to Oblivion* . . . , 76–78.

"Gimpel the Fool"
+ Bohner, Charles H. *Instructor's Manual* . . . , 113–114.
Cassill, R. V. . . . *Instructor's Handbook*, 171–172.
Charters, Ann, and William E. Sheidley. *Resources for Teaching* . . . , 3rd ed., 187–188.

"Tanhum"
Boland, Margaret M. "Isaac Bashevis Singer's 'Tanhum': An Exegetical Approach," *Tamkang Journal*, 28 (May, 1990), 203–215.

"Yentl the Yeshiva Boy"
Levine, Hershel. "The Sisterhood of Hedda and Yentl," *J Evolutionary Psych*, 12, i-ii (1991), 105–109.

LEE SMITH

"All the Days of Our Lives"
Smith, Virginia. "Proust's Mother, Food and Contemporary Southern Women's Fiction," *Southern Q,* 30, ii-iii (1992), 50–51.

"Cakewalk"
Smith, Virginia. "Proust's Mother . . . ," 51–52.

"Dead Phil Donahue"
Smith, Virginia. "Proust's Mother . . . ," 51.

PAULINE SMITH

"The Schoolmaster"
Hopper, Myrtle. "The Renunciation of Voice and the Language of Silence: Pauline Smith's 'The Schoolmaster,' " *Engl Stud Africa,* 34, i (1991), 21–26.

FËDOR SOLOGUB [FËDOR KUZ'MICH TETERNIKOV]

"In the Crowd"
Löve, Katharina H. "The Structure of Space in F. Sologub's 'V Tolpe,' " *Russian L,* 30 (1991), 109–133.

SUSAN SONTAG

"The Way We Live Now"
Charters, Ann, and William E. Sheidley. *Resources for Teaching* . . . , 3rd ed., 188–189.

GARY SOTO

"Being Mean"
   Torres, Hector A. "Genre-shifting, Political Discourse, and the
      Dialectics of Narrative Syntax in Gary Soto's *Living up the
      Street*," *Crítica: J Critical Essays*, 2, i (1988), 40–48.
"A Good Day"
   Torres, Hector A. "Genre-shifting . . . ," 48, 49, 53.
"Short Takes"
   Torres, Hector A. "Genre-shifting . . . ," 48–53.

WOLE SOYINKA

"Madame Etienne's Establishment"
   Gibbs, James. "An Examination of Three of the Short Stories of
      Wole Soyinka," in Bardolph, Jacquelin, Ed. *Short Fiction . . . ,*
      264–265.
"Mr. Pinkerton's First Morning"
   Gibbs, James. "An Examination . . . ," 267–268.
"A Tale of Two Cities"
   Gibbs, James. "An Examination . . . ," 265–267.

SEVGI SOYSAL

"The Junk Peddlar"
   Bertram, Carel. "Genderized Space in the Modern Turkish Short
      Story," *Turkish Stud Assn Bull*, 16 (1992), 30.

ELIZABETH SPENCER

"The Cousins"
   Prenshaw, Peggy W. "The Persisting South in the Fiction of Elizabeth
      Spencer," *J Short Story Engl*, 18 (Spring, 1992), 39–41.

JEAN STAFFORD

"In the Zoo"
   +Cassill, R. V. . . . *Instructor's Handbook*, 172–174.

CHRISTINA STEAD

"The Puzzleheaded Girl"
   Gardiner, Judith K. " 'Caught but not caught': Psychology and
      Politics in Christina Stead's 'The Puzzleheaded Girl,' " *World Lit
      Written Engl*, 32, i (1992), 26–41.

WALLACE STEGNER

"Chip Off the Old Block"
Leavy, Barbara F. *To Blight With Plague* . . . , 128–139.

"The City of the Living"
Zahlan, Ann R. "Cities of the Living: Disease and the Traveler in *Collected Stories* by Wallace Stegner," *Stud Short Fiction*, 29 (1992), 512–515.

GERTRUDE STEIN

"Melanctha"
De Koven, Marianne. *Rich and Strange* . . . , 71–74, 78–84.

JOHN STEINBECK

"Breakfast"
Meyer, Michael J. " 'Symbols for the Wordlessness': Steinbeck's Silent Message in 'Breakfast,' " in Hayashi, Tetsumaro, Ed. *Steinbeck's Short Stories* . . . , 32–37.
Schmidt, Gary D. "Steinbeck's 'Breakfast': A Reconsideration," *Western Am Lit*, 26 (1992), 303–311.

"The Chrysanthemums"
+Bohner, Charles H. *Instructor's Manual* . . . , 114–115.
+Cassill, R. V. . . . *Instructor's Handbook*, 174–175.
+Charters, Ann, and William E. Sheidley. *Resources for Teaching* . . . , 3rd ed., 190–192.
Shillinglaw, Susan. " 'The Chrysanthemums': Steinbeck's *Pygmalion*," in Hayashi, Tetsumaro, Ed. *Steinbeck's Short Stories* . . . , 1–9.

"Flight"
Benton, Robert M. "A Search for Meaning in 'Flight,' " in Hayashi, Tetsumaro, Ed. *Steinbeck's Short Stories* . . . , 18–25.

"The Harness"
Owens, Louis. " 'Bottom and Upland': The Balanced Man in Steinbeck's 'The Harness,' " in Hayashi, Tetsumaro, Ed. *Steinbeck's Short Stories* . . . , 44–48.

"Johnny Bear"
Mandia, Patricia M. "Chaos, Evil, and the Dredger Subplot in Steinbeck's 'Johnny Bear,' " in Hayashi, Tetsumaro, Ed. *Steinbeck's Short Stories* . . . , 54–62.

"The Murder"
Mandia, Patricia M. "Sexism and Racism, or Irony? Steinbeck's 'The Murder,' " in Hayashi, Tetsumaro, Ed. *Steinbeck's Short Stories* . . . , 62–69.

"The Raid"
Meyer, Michael J. " 'The Illusion of Eden': Efficacious Commitment

and Sacrifice in 'The Raid,' " in Hayashi, Tetsumaro, Ed. *Steinbeck's Short Stories . . .* , 38–43.

"The Red Pony"
Sakai, Yasuhiro. "Steinbeck's 'The Red Pony': A Study from the Viewpoint of Developmental Psychology," *Chu-Shikoku Stud Am Lit*, No. 28 (June, 1992), 32–41.

"The Snake"
Benton, Robert M. " 'The Snake' and Its Anomalous Nature," in Hayashi, Tetsumaro, Ed. *Steinbeck's Short Stories . . .* , 26–31.

"St. Katy the Virgin"
Tammaro, Thomas M. " 'Saint Katy the Virgin': The Key to Steinbeck's Secret Heart," in Hayashi, Tetsumaro, Ed. *Steinbeck's Short Stories . . .* , 70–78.

"The Vigilante"
Owens, Louis. " 'The Little Bit of a Story': Steinbeck's 'The Vigilante,' " in Hayashi, Tetsumaro, Ed. *Steinbeck's Short Stories . . .* , 49–53.

"The White Quail"
Meyer, Michael J. "Pure and Corrupt: Agency and Communion in the Edenic Garden of 'The White Quail,' " in Hayashi, Tetsumaro, Ed. *Steinbeck's Short Stories . . .* , 10–17.

KARLHEINZ and ANGELA STEINMÜLLER

"The Laplasque Demon"
Mabee, Barbara. "Astronauts, Angels, and Time Machines: The Fantastic in Recent German Democratic Republic Literature," in Morse, Donald E., Marshall B. Tymn, and Csilla Bertha, Eds. *The Celebration . . .* , 232.

BRUCE STERLING

"Dinner in Audoghast"
Shippey, Tom. "Semiotic Ghosts and Ghostliness in the Work of Bruce Sterling," in Slusser, George, and Tom Shippey, Eds. *Fiction 2000 . . .* , 211–212.

"Green Days in Brunei"
Shippey, Tom. "Semiotic Ghosts . . . ," 212–214.

"Telliamed"
Shippey, Tom. "Semiotic Ghosts . . . ," 208–209, 210, 211.

ROBERT LOUIS STEVENSON

"Markheim"
Herdman, John. *The Double . . .* , 129–131.

"The Strange Case of Dr. Jekyll and Mr. Hyde"
Herdman, John. *The Double* . . . , 131–137.
Tropp, Martin. " 'Dr. Jekyll and Mr. Hyde,' Schopenhauer and the
Power of Will," *Midwest Q,* 32 (1991), 141–155.

"Thrawn Jacket"
McCracken-Flesher, Caroline. "Thinking Naturally/Writing
Colonially? Scott, Stevenson, and England," *Novel,* 24 (1991),
313–317.

ADALBERT STIFTER

"Brigitta"
Howe, Patricia. "Ugly Heroines in Stifter's 'Brigitta,' Fontane's
Schach von Wutherow, and Saar's *Sappho,*" *Germ Life & Letters,*
N.S., 44 (1991), 428–432.

JAMES STILL

"I Love My Rooster"
Runyon, Randolph P. "Looking the Story in the Eye: James Still's
'Rooster,' " *Southern Lit J,* 23, ii (1991), 55–64.

"The Nest"
Willoughby, Ron. "The Nest: Images of Lost Intimacy," in Lanier,
Parks, Ed. *The Poetics* . . . , 95–101.

CHARLES WARREN STODDARD

"Hearts of Oak"
Austen, Roger. *Genteel Pagan* . . . , 10–12.

"The Schism of St. Aidenn"
Austen, Roger. *Genteel Pagan* . . . , 100–101.

ELIZABETH DREW BARSTOW STODDARD

"The Chimneys"
Zagarell, Sandra. "Introduction to 'The Chimneys,' " *Legacy,* 7, ii
(Fall, 1990), 27–28.

ROBERT STONE

"Helping"
Cassill, R. V. . . . *Instructor's Handbook,* 176–177.

THEODOR STORM

"Angelica"
Jackson, David A. *Theodor Storm* . . . , 83.

"Aquis Submersus"
Holub, Robert C. *Reflections of Realism* . . . , 132–151.
Jackson, David A. *Theodor Storm* . . . , 204, 205.
Pizer, John. "Guilt, Memory, and the Motif of the Double in Storm's 'Aquis submersus' and 'Ein Doppelgänger,' " *Germ Q*, 65 (1992), 179–183, 188.

"Beim Vetter Christian"
Jackson, David A. *Theodor Storm* . . . , 192–193.

"Bötjer Basch"
Jackson, David A. *Theodor Storm* . . . , 238–241.

"Carsten Curator"
Jackson, David A. *Theodor Storm* . . . , 208.

"Ein Doppelgänger"
Cozic, Alain. "Theodor Storm, 'Ein Doppelgänger': Un Cas limite de 'réalisme subjectif,' " *Littératures*, 24 (Spring, 1991), 83–95.
Jackson, David A. *Theodor Storm* . . . , 242–246.
Pizer, John. "Guilt, Memory . . . ," 184–189.

"Drüben am Markt"
Jackson, David A. *Theodor Storm* . . . , 99–100.

"Ein grünes Blatt"
Jackson, David A. *Theodor Storm* . . . , 61.

"Eine Halligfahrt"
Jackson, David A. *Theodor Storm* . . . , 185–187.

"Hans und Heinz Kirch"
Jackson, David A. *Theodor Storm* . . . , 210–211.

"Der Herr Etatsrat"
Jackson, David A. *Theodor Storm* . . . , 208–210.

"Immensee"
Jackson, David A. *Theodor Storm* . . . , 62–69.
Wünsch, Marianne. "Experimente Storms an den Grenzen des Realismus: neue Realitäten in 'Schweigen' und 'Ein Bekenntnis,' " *Schriften der Theodor-Storm-Gesellschaft*, 41 (1992), 14–15.

"Im Schloss"
Jackson, David A. *Theodor Storm* . . . , 107–144.

"Im Sonnenschein"
Jackson, David A. *Theodor Storm* . . . , 83.

"Im St. Jürgen"
Jackson, David A. *Theodor Storm* . . . , 153–156.

"Marthe und ihre Uhr"
Jackson, David A. *Theodor Storm* . . . , 48–50.

"Pole Poppenspäler"
Jackson, David A. *Theodor Storm* . . . , 65, 194–195.

"The Rider of the White Horse"
Holub, Robert C. *Reflections of Realism* . . . , 154–155.

"Der Schimmelreiter"
Jackson, David A. *Theodor Storm* . . . , 246–257.

"Schweigen"
Wünsch, Marianne. "Experimente Storms . . . ," 15–18, 21–22.

"Späte Rosen"
Jackson, David A. *Theodor Storm* . . . , 99–100.

"Veronica"
Jackson, David A. *Theodor Storm* . . . , 104–106, 120.

"Viola tricolor"
Downing, Eric. "Repetition and Realism: The 'Ligeia' Impulse in
Theodor Storm's 'Viola tricolor,' " *Deutsche Vierteljahrsschrift*,
65 (1991), 265–303.
Jackson, David A. *Theodor Storm* . . . , 193–194.

"Von jenseit des Meeres"
Jackson, David A. *Theodor Storm* . . . , 134–137.

"Waldwinkel"
Jackson, David A. *Theodor Storm* . . . , 195–197.

GERTRUDE STORY

"No More Song"
Lenoski, Daniel S. "Reaching for a Larger Stage: The Fiction of
Gertrude Story," *Prairie Fire*, 11, iii (1990), 65–66, 67.

"Swan Again"
Lenoski, Daniel S. "Reaching . . . ," 65.

JESSE STUART

"Dawn of Remembered Spring"
Miller, Danny L. "Jesse Stuart's 'Dawn of Remembered Spring,' "
Border States, 8 (1991), 20–25.

WILLIAM STYRON

"The Long March"
Coale, Samuel. *William Styron Revisited*, 50–60.

RUTH SUCKOW

"A Rural Community"
Weber, Ronald. *The Midwestern* . . . , 180.

JAMES W. SULLIVAN

"Minnie Kelsey's Wedding"
Hapke, Laura. "The American Working Girl and the New York
Tenement Tale of the 1890s," *J Am Culture*, 15, ii (1992), 45–46.

LEON SUMELIAN

"The Sombrero"
Bedrosian, Margaret. "Transplantation," in Bedrosian, Margaret,
Ed. *The Magic Pine Ring*, 78–79.

GRAHAM SWIFT

"Cliffedge"
Louvel, Liliane. " 'Cliffedge' de Graham Swift: L'Ambiguïté comme
stratégie narrative," *Caliban*, 29 (1992), 109–120.

AMY TAN

"Two Kinds"
Charters, Ann, and William E. Sheidley. *Resources for Teaching . . .* , 3rd ed., 193–194.

TANIZAKI JUN'ICHIRŌ

"Children"
Ito, Ken K. *Visions of Desire . . .* , 57–63.

"Longing for Mother"
Ito, Ken K. *Visions of Desire . . .* , 24–25.

"The Tale of Shunkin" [same as "A Portrait of Shunkin"]
Ito, Ken K. *Visions of Desire . . .* , 168–184.

"The Tattooer"
Ito, Ken K. *Visions of Desire . . .* , 55–57.

PETER TAYLOR

"Dean of Men"
Castronovo, David. *The American Gentlemen . . .* , 175–176.

"The Instruction of a Mistress"
Kuehl, Linda K. "Peter Taylor's 'The Instruction of a Mistress': The
Voice As Executioner," *Stud Short Fiction*, 29 (1992), 331–339.

"A Long Fourth"
Metress, Chris. "Peter Taylor's Tennessee Dubliners: Paralysis and

Silence in *A Long Fourth and Other Stories*," *J Short Story Engl*,
18 (Spring, 1992), 111–113.

"Miss Leonora When Last Seen"
Cassill, R. V. . . . *Instructor's Handbook*, 178–179.

"The Scoutmaster"
Metress, Chris. "Peter Taylor's Tennessee . . . ," 109–111.

"Venus, Cupid, Folly, and Time"
Castronovo, David. *The American Gentleman* . . . , 174–175.

CAN THEMBA

"Mob Passion"
Chapman, Michael. "Can Themba, Story-Teller and Journalist of the
1950s: The Text in Context," in Bardolph, Jacquelin, Ed. *Short
Fiction* . . . , 218–219.

AUDREY THOMAS

"Kill Day on the Government Wharf"
Regan, Stephen. " 'The Presence of the Past': Modernism and
Postmodernism in Canadian Short Fiction," in Howells, Colin A.,
and Lynette Hunter, Eds. *Narrative Strategies in Canadian
Literature* . . . , 128–129.

JAMES THOMPSON

"Arnold's Revenge"
McCauley, Michael J. *Jim Thompson* . . . , 51–54.

"Time Without End"
McCauley, Michael J. *Jim Thompson* . . . , 61–63.

THORSTEIN TH. THORSTEINSSON

"In the Days of Yore"
Wolf, Kirsten. "Heroic Past—Heroic Present: Western Icelandic
Literature," *Scandinavian Stud*, 63 (1991), 441–442.

JAMES THURBER

"The Catbird Seat"
+ Bohner, Charles H. *Instructor's Manual* . . . , 115–116.

"The Secret Life of Walter Mitty"
Cassill, R. V. . . . *Instructor's Handbook*, 179–180.

+Charters, Ann, and William E. Sheidley. *Resources for Teaching*
. . . , 3rd ed., 194–195.

JOHANN LUDWIG TIECK

"Der fünfzehnte November"
  Klett, Dwight A. " 'Eine schwere Heimsuchung': Nature as an
  Avenging Force in Ludwig Tieck's 'Der fünfzehnte November,' "
  West Virginia Univ Philol Papers, 37 (1991), 32–38.

KATHERINE DAVIS CHAPMAN TILLMAN

"Beryl Weston's Ambition"
  Tate, Claudia. "Introduction," *The Works of Katherine Davis
  Chapman Tillman,* ed. Claudia Tate, 23–28.
"Clancy Street"
  Tate, Claudia. "Introduction," 28–31.
"The Preacher at Hill Station"
  Tate, Claudia. "Introduction," 32–33.

LYNNE TILLMAN

"The Museum of Hyphenated Americans"
  Young, Elizabeth. "Silence, Exile, and Cunning: The Writing of
  Lynne Tillman," in Young, Elizabeth, and Graham Caveney.
  Shopping in Space . . . , 206–207.

J[OHN] R[ONALD] R[EUEL] TOLKIEN

"Beren and Luthien the Elf-maiden"
  Duriez, Colin. *The J. R. R. Tolkien Handbook* . . . , 42–51.
"Farmer Giles of Ham"
  Dunsire, Brin. "Of Ham, and What Became of It," *Amon Hen*, 98
  (July, 1989), 17–18.
  Rosebury, Brian. *Tolkien: A Critical Assessment*, 114–115, 140.
"Leaf by Niggle"
  Duriez, Colin. *The J. R. R. Tolkien Handbook* . . . , 148–150.
  Rosebury, Brian. *Tolkien: A Critical Assessment*, 115–117, 140.
"Of Tuor and his Coming to Gondolin"
  Rosebury, Brian. *Tolkien: A Critical Assessment*, 100.

TATYANA TOLSTAYA

"The Most Beloved"
  Goscilo, Helena. "Tolstaian Times: Traversals and Transfers," in
  Graham, Sheelagh D., Ed. *New Directions* . . . , 43–45.

"On the Golden Porch"
Goscilo, Helena. "Tolstaian Times . . . ," 46–48.

"Sweet Shura"
Goscilo, Helena. "Tolstaian Times . . . ," 54–55.

"Okkervil River"
Goscilo, Helena. "Tolstaian Times . . . ," 48–50.

"Sleepwalker in a Fog"
Goscilo, Helena. "Tolstaian Times . . . ," 55–57.

LEO TOLSTOY

"After the Ball"
Siebers, Tobin. *Morals and Stories*, 164–165.

"The Death of Ivan Ilych"
+ Bohner, Charles H. *Instructor's Manual . . .* , 116–117.
Cassill, R. V. . . . *Instructor's Handbook*, 181–182.
+ Charters, Ann, and William E. Sheidley. *Resources for Teaching . . .* , 3rd ed., 196–197.
Siebers, Tobin. *Morals and Stories*, 161–163, 165–166.

"The Kreutzer Sonata"
Knapp, Liza. "Tolstoy on Musical Mimesis: Platonic Aesthetics and Erotics in 'The Kreutzer Sonata,' " *Tolstoy Studies J*, 4 (1991), 25–42.

"The Raid"
White, Duffield. "An Evolutionary Study of Tolstoy's First Story, 'The Raid,' " *Tolstoy Stud J*, 4 (1991), 43–72.

SU TONG

"Breaking Away in a Coaster"
Duke, Michael S. "Walking Toward the World: A Turning Point in Contemporary Chinese Fiction," *World Lit Today*, 65 (1991), 393.

"Nineteen Thirty-Four Escape"
Duke, Michael S. "Walking Toward the World . . . ," 392.

"A Profusion of Wives and Concubines"
Duke, Michael S. "Walking Toward the World . . . ," 392–393.

"A Strange Visitor"
Duke, Michael S. "Walking Toward the World . . . ," 393–394.

MIGUEL TORGA

"Mariana"
Lisboa, Maria Manuel. "Madwomen, Whores and Torga: Desecrating the Canon?" *Portuguese Stud*, 7 (1991), 175–183.

GONZALO TORRENTE BALLESTER

"Gerineldo"
Pérez, Janet. "Fascist Models and Literary Subversion: Two
Fictional Modes," *South Central R*, 6, ii (1989), 84–85; rpt. Golsan,
Richard J., Ed. *Fascism, Aesthetics . . .* , 140–141.

SUSANA TORRES MOLINA

"Impressions of a Mother-to-Be"
Foster, David W. *Gay and Lesbian Themes . . .* , 133–136.

MICHEL TOURNIER

"Amandine"
Easterlin, Nancy L. "Initiation and Counter-Initiation: Progress
Toward Adulthood in the Stories of Michel Tournier," *Stud Short
Fiction*, 28 (1991), 154–158.

"Le Coq de Bruyère"
Stivale, Charles J. " 'Le Coq de Bruyère' de Tournier: Ecritures/
lectures multiples," in Brau, Jean-Louis, and Gérard Lavergne,
Eds. *La Focalisation*, 291–301.

"Gilles et Jeanne"
Levy, Karen D. "Tournier's Ultimate Perversion: The Historical
Manipulation of 'Gilles et Jeanne,' " *Papers Lang & Lit*, 28, i
(1992), 72–88.

"Prikli"
Easterlin, Nancy L. "Initiation . . . ," 162–167.

"Tom Thumb Runs Away"
Easterlin, Nancy L. "Initiation . . . ," 158–162.

TRÂN DIÊU HĂNG

"Darkness, Strange Land"
Tran, Qui-Phiet. "From Isolation to Integration: Vietnamese
Americans in Tran Dieu Hang's Fiction," in Lim, Shirley G., and
Amy Ling, Eds. *Reading the Literatures . . .* , 275–276.

"The Dream of Grass"
Tran, Qui-Phiet. "From Isolation . . . ," 280–281, 282, 283.

"There Will Come New Days"
Tran, Qui-Phiet. "From Isolation . . . ," 279–280, 280–281, 282, 283.

"The Trip to Dai Tu Village"
Tran, Qui-Phiet. "From Isolation . . . ," 279–280.

"The Young Cousin"
Tran, Qui-Phiet. "From Isolation . . . ," 280–281, 283.

MARTA TRABA

"La identificación"
    García Serrano, M. Victoria. "Incompatibilidades: Existencialismo y
    feminismo en 'La identificación' de Marta Traba," *Inti*, 34–35
    (1991–1992), 131–140.

BRUNO TRAVEN [RET MARUT?]

"The Night Visitor"
    Payne, Kenneth. " 'The Night Visitor': B. Traven's Tale of the
    Mexican Bush Reconsidered," *So Central R*, 8, i (1991), 46–58.

"When the Priest Is Not at Home"
    Payne, Kenneth. "Superstition and the Miraculous in B. Traven's
    Short Story of Mexico, 'When the Priest Is Not at Home,' " *New
    Mexico Hum R*, 34 (1991), 50–59.

WILLIAM TREVOR [TREVOR COX]

"A Meeting in Middle Age"
    Doherty, Francis. "William Trevor's 'A Meeting in Middle Age' and
    Romantic Irony," *J Short Story Engl*, 16 (Spring, 1991), 19–28.

YURY TRIFONOV

"Another Life"
    Kolesnikoff, Nina. *Yury Trifonov* . . . , 13, 53, 54, 55, 56, 69–73.

"At the End of the Season"
    Kolesnikoff, Nina. *Yury Trifonov* . . . , 23, 29–30.

"Cats or Rabbits"
    Kolesnikoff, Nina. *Yury Trifonov* . . . , 107, 108, 110.

"The Conqueror of the Swedes"
    Kolesnikoff, Nina. *Yury Trifonov* . . . , 30.

"Death in Sicily"
    Kolesnikoff, Nina. *Yury Trifonov* . . . , 107, 108, 110, 111.

"Eternal Themes"
    Kolesnikoff, Nina. *Yury Trifonov* . . . , 107, 108, 110, 111, 112, 113.

"The Exchange"
    Kolesnikoff, Nina. *Yury Trifonov* . . . , 13, 53, 54, 55, 56–59.

"The Eyeglasses"
    Kolesnikoff, Nina. *Yury Trifonov* . . . , 25–26, 27.

"Far Away in the Mountains"
    Kolesnikoff, Nina. *Yury Trifonov* . . . , 31.

"The Gray Sky, Masts, and a Chestnut Horse"
    Kolesnikoff, Nina. *Yury Trifonov* . . . , 109, 110.

"The House of Embankment"
Kolesnikoff, Nina. *Yury Trifonov* . . . , 15, 79–87.

"In an Autumn of Mushrooms"
Kolesnikoff, Nina. *Yury Trifonov* . . . , 12–13, 46, 48, 49–51.

"The Loneliness of Klych Durda"
Kolesnikoff, Nina. *Yury Trifonov* . . . , 24, 27, 31.

"The Long Goodbye"
Kolesnikoff, Nina. *Yury Trifonov* . . . , 13, 53, 55, 56, 64–68.

"The Overturned House"
Kolesnikoff, Nina. *Yury Trifonov* . . . , 110, 111, 113.

"The Poppies"
Kolesnikoff, Nina. *Yury Trifonov* . . . , 25, 26.

"The Stimulus"
Kolesnikoff, Nina. *Yury Trifonov* . . . , 30–31.

"A Summer Midday"
Kolesnikoff, Nina. *Yury Trifonov* . . . , 12–13, 46–47, 48, 49.

"Taking Stock"
Kolesnikoff, Nina. *Yury Trifonov* . . . , 13, 53, 54, 55, 56, 59–64.

"The Translucent Autumn Sun"
Kolesnikoff, Nina. *Yury Trifonov* . . . , 29.

"Vera and Aoyka"
Kolesnikoff, Nina. *Yury Trifonov* . . . , 12–13, 46, 48–49.

"Visiting Marc Chagall"
Kolesnikoff, Nina. *Yury Trifonov* . . . , 109–111.

LIONEL TRILLING

"Of This Time, Of That Place"
Stedman, Barbara. "Names and Namers in 'Of This Time, Of That
Place,' " *Stud Short Fiction*, 28 (1991), 96–99.

ELSA TRIOLET

"Les Amants d'Avignon"
Atack, Margaret. "Narratives of Disruption 1940–1944," *French
Cultural Stud*, 1, iii (October, 1990), 238–240.

"Yvette"
Atack, Margaret. "Narratives . . . ," 240–244.

IVAN SERGEEVICH TURGENEV

"Andrei Kolosov"
Allen, Elizabeth C. *Beyond Realism* . . . , 158–162.

"Asya"
   Allen, Elizabeth C. *Beyond Realism* . . . , 61, 92, 108, 112–113, 120,
      150–151, 157.
   Seeley, Frank F. *Turgenev* . . . , 153–155.
"Bezhin Meadow"
   Seeley, Frank F. *Turgenev* . . . , 111–113.
"The Brigadier-General"
   Seeley, Frank F. *Turgenev* . . . , 272–274.
"The Correspondence"
   Allen, Elizabeth C. *Beyond Realism* . . . , 61, 103, 157, 185–188,
      197–200.
"A Desperate Character"
   Seeley, Frank F. *Turgenev* . . . , 320–323.
"The Diary of a Superfluous Man"
   Seeley, Frank F. *Turgenev* . . . , 127–131.
"The District Doctor"
   Masing-Delic, Irene. "Philosophy, Myth, and Art in Turgenev's
      Notes of a Hunter," *Russian R*, 50 (1991), 441–443.
   Seeley, Frank F. *Turgenev* . . . , 104–105.
"The Dog"
   Seeley, Frank F. *Turgenev* . . . , 258–262.
"The Dream"
   Seeley, Frank F. *Turgenev* . . . , 262–266.
"The Duellist" [same as "The Swashbuckler"]
   Seeley, Frank F. *Turgenev* . . . , 91–94.
"Enough"
   Allen, Elizabeth C. *Beyond Realism* . . . , 172–175.
"Father Aleksei's Story"
   Seeley, Frank F. *Turgenev* . . . , 266–269.
"Faust"
   Allen, Elizabeth C. *Beyond Realism* . . . , 128–129.
   Seeley, Frank F. *Turgenev* . . . , 148–153.
"First Love"
   Allen, Elizabeth C. *Beyond Realism* . . . , 162–167, 180–181, 207–210.
   DiBattista, Maria. *First Love* . . . , 27–29.
   Seeley, Frank F. *Turgenev* . . . , 155–160.
"Hamlet from Shchigry District"
   Masing-Delic, Irene. "Philosophy . . . ," 437–441.
"The Jew"
   Seeley, Frank F. *Turgenev* . . . , 94–95.
"Journey into the Woodland"
   Seeley, Frank F. *Turgenev* . . . , 132–136.
"Khor and Kalinych"
   Allen, Elizabeth C. *Beyond Realism* . . . , 74–75, 144–145.
   Masing-Delic, Irene. "Philosophy . . . ," 447.

"A King Lear of the Steppes"
  Seeley, Frank F. *Turgenev* . . . , 287–293.

"Klara Milich"
  Seeley, Frank F. *Turgenev* . . . , 325–328.
  Waddington, Patrick. "Two Authors of Strange Stories: Bulwer-
    Lytton and Turgenev," *New Zealand Slavonic J*, [n.v.] (1992),
    50–51.

"Knock . . . Knock . . . Knock!"
  Seeley, Frank F. *Turgenev* . . . , 277–280.
  Waddington, Patrick. "Two Authors . . . ," 47–48.

"Living Relics"
  Allen, Elizabeth C. *Beyond Realism* . . . , 54, 56, 80, 191–193.
  Frost, Edgar L. "Hidden Traits: The Subtle Imagery of 'Living
    Relics,' " *Slavic & East European J*, 36, i (1992), 36–54.

"My Neighbor Radilov"
  Allen, Elizabeth C. *Beyond Realism* . . . , 56, 82, 146, 237–238.

"Petrushko"
  Seeley, Frank F. *Turgenev* . . . , 96–98.

"Punin and Baburin"
  Seeley, Frank F. *Turgenev* . . . , 301–303.

"A Quiet Place"
  Allen, Elizabeth C. *Beyond Realism* . . . , 77, 82–84, 108, 120.

"The Singer"
  Allen, Elizabeth C. *Beyond Realism* . . . , 58, 76, 148–149.

"The Song of Triumphant Love"
  Allen, Elizabeth C. *Beyond Realism* . . . , 49, 140–141.
  Waddington, Patrick. "Two Authors . . . ," 48–51.

"A Strange Story"
  Allen, Elizabeth C. *Beyond Realism* . . . , 81, 129–130.
  Waddington, Patrick. "Two Authors . . . ," 45–47.

"Spring Torrents"
  Seeley, Frank F. *Turgenev* . . . , 294–301.

"Three Meetings"
  Seeley, Frank F. *Turgenev* . . . , 99–100.

"Three Portraits"
  Seeley, Frank F. *Turgenev* . . . , 89–91.

"The Tryst"
  + Bohner, Charles H. *Instructor's Manual* . . . , 117–118.

"An Unhappy Girl"
  Allen, Elizabeth C. *Beyond Realism* . . . , 46, 77, 81, 83, 84, 101,
    113–115, 125, 138, 157, 215–216.
  Seeley, Frank F. *Turgenev* . . . , 283–287.

"Visions: A Fantasy"
  Waddington, Patrick. "Two Authors . . . ," 42–44.

"Yakov Pasynkov"
  Seeley, Frank F. *Turgenev* . . . , 146–148.

ESTHER TUSQUETS

"La niña lunática"
  Pérez, Janet. "Characteristics of Erotic Brief Fiction by Women in
  Spain," *Monographic R*, 7 (1991), 188–191.
"Las sutiles leyes de la simetría"
  Encinar, Angeles. "Escritoras Españolas actuales: una perspectiva a
  través del cuento," *Hispanic J*, 13 (1992), 188–189.
  Schaefer, Claudia. "A Simple Question of Symmetry: Women
  Writing in Post-Franco Spain," in Erro-Orthmann, Nora, and Juan
  Cruz Mendizábal, Eds. *La escritora* . . . , 282, 283–284.

AMOS TUTUOLA

"The Palm-Wine Drinkard's First Journey"
  Charters, Ann, and William E. Sheidley. *Resources for Teaching* . . . ,
  3rd ed., 198–199.
"Segi and the Boa-Constrictor"
  Lindfors, Bernth. "Tutuola's Latest Stories," in Bardolph, Jacquelin,
  Ed. *Short Fiction* . . . , 275–276.

MARK TWAIN [SAMUEL L. CLEMENS]

"The Celebrated Jumping Frog of Calaveras County"
  + Bohner, Charles H. *Instructor's Manual* . . . , 27–28.
  Cassill, R. V. . . . *Instructor's Handbook*, 34–35.
"The Man That Corrupted Hadleyburg"
  Briden, Earl F. "Twainian Pedagogy and the No-Account Lessons of
  'Hadleyburg,' " *Stud Short Fiction*, 28 (1991), 125–134.
  Church, Joseph. "Twain's 'The Man That Corrupted Hadleyburg,' "
  Explicator, 49, ii (1991), 94–97.
  Mandia, Patrick M. *Comedic Pathos* . . . , 68–82.
"The Mysterious Stranger"
  Jackson, Fleda B. "Reconciliation and Optimism in Twain's
  'Mysterious Stranger' Manuscripts," *Coll Lang Assoc J*, 35
  (1991), 57–71.
  Mandia, Patrick M. *Comedic Pathos* . . . , 102–120.
"The £1 Million Banknote"
  Hoffman, Andrew J. "The Unspendable Fortune: From Mark Twain's
  'The £1 Million Banknote' to *Trading Places*," *Connecticut R*, 13,
  ii (1991), 55–57, 58, 59, 60.

MIGUEL DE UNAMUNO

"Aunt Tula"
Sinclair, Alison. "The Envy of Motherhood: Destructive Urges in
Unamuno," in Condé, L. P., and S. M. Hart, Eds. *Feminist
Readings* . . . , 49–58.

"Abel Sánchez"
Quinones, Ricardo J. *The Changes of Cain* . . . , 173–181.
Jurkevich, Gayana. *The Elusive Self* . . . , 108–133.

"Nada menos que todo un hombre"
Jurkevich, Gayana. *The Elusive Self* . . . , 94–102.
Moon, Harold K. "Unamunian Doubles: From Conflict to
Reconciliation," *Hispano*, 105, iii (1992), 6–7.

"San Manuel Bueno, mártir"
Jurkevich, Gayana. *The Elusive Self* . . . , 134–152.

"Two Mothers"
Moon, Harold K. "Unamunian Doubles . . . ," 5–6.

JOHN UPDIKE

"A & P"
+ Bohner, Charles H. *Instructor's Manual* . . . , 118–119.
+ Cassill, R. V. . . . *Instructor's Handbook*, 183–184.
Charters, Ann, and William E. Sheidley. *Resources for Teaching* . . . ,
3rd ed., 200.

"Flight"
+ Charters, Ann, and William E. Sheidley. *Resources for
Teaching* . . . , 3rd ed., 201–202.

"Giving Blood"
Kleiman, Ed. "John Updike's 'Giving Blood': An Experiment in
Genre," *Stud Short Fiction*, 29 (1992), 153–160.

"Made in Heaven"
Bohner, Charles H. *Instructor's Manual* . . . , 119–120.

"The Music School"
+ Bohner, Charles H. *Instructor's Manual* . . . , 120–121.

"Wife-Wooing"
Keating, Helane L., and Walter Levy. *Instructor's Manual: Lives
Through Literature* . . . , 110.

ARTURO USLAR PIETRI

"Simeón Calamaris"
Smith, Esther. " 'Simeón Calamaris': una búsqueda de la identidad,"
in Domíguez, Mignon, Ed. *Estudios de narratología*, 149–165.

LUISA VALENZUELA

"At Night I Am Your Horse" [or "I'm Your Horse in the Night"]
   Charters, Ann, and William E. Sheidley. *Resources for Teaching* . . . ,
   3rd ed., 203–204.
   Tyler, Joseph. "Repression and Violence in Selected Contemporary
   Argentine Stories," *Discurso*, 9, ii (1992), 95–96.
   ———. "Tales of Repression and 'Desaparecidos' in Valenzuela and
   Cortázar," *Romance Lang Annual*, 3 (1991), 605.
   Gold, Janet. "Feminine Space and the Discourse of Silence: Yolanda
   Oreamuno, Elena Poniatowska, and Luisa Valenzuela," in Valis,
   Noël, and Carol Maier, Eds. *In the Feminine Mode* . . . , 198–199.

"Ceremonias de rechazo"
   Morello-Frosch, Marta. "Discurso erótico y escritura femenina," in
   Coloquio internacional . . . , 27–28.

"Change of Guard"
   Hicks, D. Emily. *Border Writing* . . . , 11–22.
   Muñoz, Willy O. "Del falogocentrismo a la escritura ginocéntrica:
   'Cambio de armas' de Luisa Valenzuela," *Antípodas*, 3 (July,
   1991), 125–134.
   Morello-Frosch, Marta. "Discurso erótico . . . , 24–27.

"Fourth Version"
   Castillo, Debra A. *Talking Back* . . . , 110–113.
   García-Moreno, Laura. "Other Weapons, Other Words: Literary and
   Political Reconsiderations in Luisa Valenzuela's *Other Weapons*,"
   Latin Am Lit R, 19 (July-December, 1991), 10.

"Los mejor calzados"
   Tyler, Joseph. "Repression . . . ," 93–94.
   ———. "Tales . . . ," 604–605.

"Other Weapons"
   Castillo, Debra A. *Talking Back* . . . , 107–132.
   García-Moreno, Laura. "Other Weapons . . . ," 12–15, 19.

JUAN VALERA

"El bermejino prehistórico"
   Duarte Berrocal, María I. "Juan Valera, narrador de lo maravilloso,"
   Analecta Malacitana, 9, ii (1986), 379, 381–382, 384, 387, 388, 392.

"La buena fama"
   Duarte Berrocal, María I. "Juan Valera . . . ," 382–383, 385–386,
   389, 390–391, 392.

RIMA DE VALLBONA

"Cosecha de pecadores"
   Rosas, Yolanda. "Hacia una identidad en *Cosecha de Pecadores* de
   Rima de Vallbona," *Americas R*, 19, iii–iv (1991), 141–142.

"Desde aquí"
Rosas, Yolanda. "Hacia una identidad . . . ," 137–138.
"El hondón de las sorpresas"
Rosas, Yolanda. "Hacia una identidad . . . ," 136–137.
"Infame retorno"
Rosas, Yolanda. "Hacia una identidad . . . ," 138–139.
"El muro"
Rosas, Yolanda. "Hacia una identidad . . . ," 139–140.
"Tierra de sécano"
Rosas, Yolanda. "Hacia una identidad . . . ," 140–141.

RAMÓN DEL VALLE-INCLÁN

"Beatriz"
Ramos, Rosa A. "Valle-Inclán's 'Beatriz': A Tale of the Symbolist Fantastic," *Discurso*, 9, ii (1992), 75–86.
"Condesa de Cela"
Güntert, Georges. "De *Femeninas* a *Las sonatas*: Evolución del arte narrativo de Valle-Inclán," *Revista de Literatura*, 54 (1992), 258–259.
"Juan Quinto"
Miller, Martha L. "The Feminization and Emasculation of Galicia in Valle-Inclán's *Jardín umbrío*," *Romance Q*, 39 (1992), 89–91.
"Mi bisabuelo"
Miller, Martha L. "The Feminization . . . ," 91–92.
"Rosarito"
Güntert, Georges. "De *Femeninas* . . . ," 260–261.
Predmore, Michael. "The Murder of Rosarito: An Inquiry Into Its Mystery," *Crítica*, 2 (1990), 258–268.
"Rosita"
Nickel, Catherine. "Representation and Gender in Valle-Inclán's 'Rosita,' " *Revista de Estudios Hispánicos*, 25, iii (1991), 35–55.
"Sonata de otoño"
Güntert, Georges. "De *Femeninas* . . . ," 261–263.
"Sonata de primavera"
Güntert, Georges. "De *Femeninas* . . . ," 264–265.

ANA LYDIA VEGA

"Caso omisa"
Boling, Becky. "The Reproduction of Ideology in Lydia Vega's 'Pasión de historia' and 'Caso omisa,' " *Letras Femeninas*, 17, ii (1991), 95–97.

"Letra para salsa y dos sones por encargo"
Carney, Carmen V. "El amor como discurso político en Ana Lydia
Vega y Rosario Ferré," *Letras Femeninas*, 17, ii (1991), 83.
"Pasión de historia"
Boling, Becky. "The Reproduction of Ideology . . . ," 89–95.
"Pollito-chicken"
Carney, Carmen V. "El amor . . . ," 82, 85.

VERCORS [JEAN BRULLER]

"The Silence of the Seas"
Brown, James W. "Literary Introduction," in *"The Silence of the
Seas": A Novel of French Resistance* . . . , [by Jean Bruller
(Vercors)], 30–40.
"Le Songe"
Atack, Margaret. "Narratives of Disruption 1940–1944," *French
Cultural Stud*, 1, iii (October, 1990), 244–245.

LAWRENCE VERNON

"As Sacrosanct as Motherhood"
McLeod, Alan. "The Short Fiction of Belize," in Bardolph,
Jacquelin, Ed. *Short Fiction* . . . , 96.
"A Present for His Mother"
McLeod, Alan. "The Short Fiction . . . ," 96.
"The Third Wish"
McCleod, Alan. "The Short Fiction . . . ," 96.

SABINE VERREAULT [ELISABETH VONARBURG]

"Eon"
Vonarburg, Elisabeth. "The Reproduction of the Body in Space," in
Ruddick, Nicholas, Ed. *State* . . . , 61, 63, 65–67.

[COUNT] VILLIERS DE L'ISE-ADAM [JEAN MARIE MATTHIAS PHILIPPE AUGUSTE]

"L'Intersigne"
Cummiskey, Gary. *The Changing* . . . , 109–114.
Mellerski, Nancy C. "Structures of Exchange in Villiers de l'Isle-
Adam's 'L'Intersigne,' " in Saciuk, Olena H., Ed. *The
Shape* . . . , 135–142.
Rashkin, Ester. *Family Secrets* . . . , 64–80.
"Véra"
Cummiskey, Gary. *The Changing* . . . , 114–120.

HELENA MARIA VIRAMONTES

"Caribou Café"
Castillo, Debra A. *Talking Back* . . . , 76–95.

WILHELM HEINRICH WACKENRODER

"Herzensergigßungen eines kunstliebenden Klosterbruders"
Yee, Kevin F. "Joseph Berlinger: The Frair's Alter Ego in
Wackenroder's and Tieck's 'Kerzensergießungen eines
kunstliebenden Klosterbruders,' " *Germ Notes*, 23 (1992), 69–72.

ALICE WALKER

"Advancing Luna and Ida B. Wells"
McKay, Nellie Y. "Alice Walker's 'Advancing Luna and Ida B. Wells:
A Struggle Toward Sisterhood,' " in Higgins, Lynn A., and Brenda
R. Silver, Eds. *Rape and Representation*, 248–260.

"The Child Who Favored Daughter"
Bauer, Margaret D. "Alice Walker: Another Southern Writer
Criticizing Codes Not Put to 'Everyday Use,' " *Stud Short Fiction*,
29 (1992), 143–146.

"The Diary of an African Nun"
Bauer, Margaret D. "Alice Walker . . . ," 146–148.

"Entertaining God"
Bauer, Margaret D. "Alice Walker . . . ," 149–150.

"Everyday Use"
Bauer, Margaret D. "Alice Walker . . . ," 150–151.
+Cassill, R. V. . . . *Instructor's Handbook*, 185–186.
Freedman, Diane. *An Alchemy of Genres* . . . , 129–133.
Keating, Helane L., and Walter Levy. *Instructor's Manual: Lives
Through Literature* . . . , 4–5.

"Roselily"
Bohner, Charles H. *Instructor's Manual* . . . , 121–122.
+Charters, Ann, and William E. Sheidley. *Resources for
Teaching* . . . , 3rd ed., 204–205.

"To Hell with Dying"
+Bohner, Charles H. *Instructor's Manual* . . . , 122–123.

"The Welcome Table"
Bauer, Margaret D. "Alice Walker . . . ," 148–149.

MARTIN WALSER

"A Runaway Horse"
Schote, Joaquim. "Martin Walsers Novelle 'Ein fliehendes Pferd,' "
Orbis Litterarum, 46 (1992), 52–63.

ROBERT WALSER

"The Walk"
    Lopate, Phillip. " 'The Walk' as a Species of Walk Literature," *R Contemp Fiction*, 12, i (1992), 87–94.

RODOLFO WALSH

"Variaciones en rojo"
    Cohen Imach, Victoria. "Las máscaras o el pintor de paredes: Asunción de la periferia en 'Variaciones en rojo' de Rodolfo Walsh," *Hispamerica*, 20 (1991), 3–15.

JOHN WALTER

"Encounter with a Renegade"
    McLeod, Alan. "The Short Fiction of Belize," in Bardolph, Jacquelin, Ed. *Short Fiction* . . . , 96–97.
"The Reincarnated Innkeeper"
    McLeod, Alan. "The Short Fiction . . . ," 96.

ROBERT PENN WARREN

"Blackberry Winter"
    Bohner, Charles H. *Instructor's Manual* . . . , 123–124.
    Dietrich, Bryan. "Christ or Antichrist: Understanding Eight Words in 'Blackberry Winter,' " *Stud Short Fiction*, 29 (1992), 215–220.
"A Christmas Gift"
    Clark, William C. *The American Vision* . . . , 63–66.
"Her Own People"
    Clark, William C. *The American Vision* . . . , 66–67.
"The Patented Gate and the Mean Hamburger"
    Bohner, Charles H. *Instructor's Manual* . . . , 124–125.

SHEILA WATSON

"Antigone"
    Legge, Valerie. "Sheila Watson's 'Antigone': Anguished Rituals and Public Disturbances," *Stud Canadian Lit*, 17, ii (1992), 28–46.

EVELYN WAUGH

"Work Suspended"
    Beaty, Frederick. L. *The Ironic World of* . . . , 131–144.

W. D. WEATHERHILL

"The Man Who Loved Leavittown"
  Chandler, Marilyn R. *Dwelling in the Text* . . . , 282–286.

JEROME WEIDMAN

"I Thought about This Girl"
  Gladsky, Thomas S. *Princes, Peasants* . . . , 214–215.
"My Father Sits in the Dark"
  Gladsky, Thomas S. *Princes, Peasants* . . . , 213–214.

SYLVIE WEIL

"Marceline"
  Fisher, Claudine G. "Sensibilités française et québécoise dans
  Plages," *Revue Francophone de Louisiane*, 5, i (Spring, 1990),
  69–70.

HELEN WEINZWEIG

"What Happened to Ravel's *Bolero*?"
  MacGillivray, S. R., and Noreen Ivancic. " 'What Happened to
  Ravel's *Bolero*?': Weinzweig's Serialism," *Engl Stud Canada*, 17,
  ii (1991), 225–234.

FAY WELDON

"Weekend"
  Charters, Ann, and William E. Sheidley. *Resources for Teaching* . . . ,
  3rd ed., 207–208.

H. G. WELLS

"Aepyornis Island"
  Hammond, J. R. *H. G. Wells* . . . , 60–63.
"Answer to Prayer"
  Hammond, J. R. *H. G. Wells* . . . , 139–141.
"The Apple"
  Hammond, J. R. *H. G. Wells* . . . , 134–136.
"A Catastrophe"
  Hammond, J. R. *H. G. Wells* . . . , 52–55.
"The Cone"
  Hammond, J. R. *H. G. Wells* . . . , 82–86.

"The Country of the Blind"
Hammond, J. R. *H. G. Wells* . . . , 121–125.

"The Door in the Wall"
Hammond, J. R. *H. G. Wells* . . . , 125–131.

"A Dream of Armageddon"
Hammond, J. R. *H. G. Wells* . . . , 141–148.

"The Flowering of the Strange Orchid"
Hammond, J. R. *H. G. Wells* . . . , 76–79.

"Miss Winchelsea's Heart"
Hammond, J. R. *H. G. Wells* . . . , 55–57.

"Mr. Skelmersdale in Fairyland"
Hammond, J. R. *H. G. Wells* . . . , 116–121.

"The Plattner Story"
Hammond, J. R. *H. G. Wells* . . . , 93–96.

"The Presence by Fire"
Hammond, J. R. *H. G. Wells* . . . , 107–108.

"The Purple Pileus"
Hammond, J. R. *H. G. Wells* . . . , 48–52.

"The Red Room"
Hammond, J. R. *H. G. Wells* . . . , 79–82.

"The Remarkable Case of Davidson's Eyes"
Hammond, J. R. *H. G. Wells* . . . , 90–93.

"The Sea Raiders"
Hammond, J. R. *H. G. Wells* . . . , 63–66.

"A Slip under the Microscope"
Hammond, J. R. *H. G. Wells* . . . , 104–106.

"The Stolen Body"
Hammond, J. R. *H. G. Wells* . . . , 100–102.

"The Story of the Last Trump"
Hammond, J. R. *H. G. Wells* . . . , 136–139.

"The Story of the Late Mr. Elvesham"
Hammond, J. R. *H. G. Wells* . . . , 96–100.

"Through a Window"
Hammond, J. R. *H. G. Wells* . . . , 44–48.

"The Time Machine"
Showalter, Elaine. "The Apocalyptic Fables of H. G. Wells," in
Stokes, John. *Fin de Siècle* . . . , 73–77.

"Under the Knife"
Hammond, J. R. *H. G. Wells* . . . , 70–74.

"The Valley of Spiders"
Hammond, J. R. *H. G. Wells* . . . , 110–113.

"Waydes' Essence"
Hammond, J. R. *H. G. Wells* . . . , 109–110.

"The Wild Asses of the Devil"
  Hammond, J. R. *H. G. Wells* . . . , 86–88.

EUDORA WELTY

"At the Landing"
  Kreyling, Michael. "The Natchez Trace in Eudora Welty's Fiction,"
    Southern Q, 29, iv (1991), 166–169.
  Roberts, Diane. "The Rapist Bridegroom: Sexual Violence in the
    Fiction of Eudora Welty," in Jump, Harriet D., Ed. *Diverse
    Voices* . . . , 194–197.
  Romines, Ann. *The Home Plot* . . . , 207–210.
  Schmidt, Peter. *The Heart of the Story* . . . , 127–130.
"The Burning"
  Romines, Ann. *The Home Plot* . . . , 248–253.
"Circe"
  Keating, Helane L., and Walter Levy. *Instructor's Manual: Lives
    Through Literature* . . . , 90.
  Romines, Ann. *The Home Plot* . . . , 3–4, 256–257.
  Schmidt, Peter. *The Heart of the Story* . . . , 188–192.
"Clytie"
  Schmidt, Peter. *The Heart of the Story* . . . , 27–32.
"Curtain of Green"
  Schmidt, Peter. *The Heart of the Story* . . . , 23–27.
"Death of a Traveling Salesman"
  Hoberman, Michael. "Demythologizing Myth Criticism: Folklife and
    Modernity in Eudora Welty's 'Death of a Traveling Salesman,' "
    Southern Q, 30, i (1991), 24–34.
  Romines, Ann. *The Home Plot* . . . , 194–200, 202.
"First Love"
  Kreyling, Michael. "The Natchez Trace . . . ," 164–166.
"Flowers for Marjorie"
  Romines, Ann. *The Home Plot* . . . , 201–202.
  Schmidt, Peter. *The Heart of the Story* . . . , 53–56.
"June Recital"
  Donaldson, Susan V. "Recovering Otherness in *The Golden Apples*,"
    Am Lit, 63 (1991), 493–494, 496, 498–501.
  Harrison, Suzan. " 'The Other Way to Live': Gender and Selfhood
    in *Delta Autumn* and *The Golden Apples*," *Mississippi Q*, 44
    (1990–1991), 63–64.
  Schmidt, Peter. *The Heart of the Story* . . . , 86–108.
"Kin"
  Prenshaw, Peggy W. "Southern Ladies and the Southern Literary
    Renaissance," in Manning, Carol S., Ed. *The Female
    Tradition* . . . , 84–86.
  Romines, Ann. *The Home Plot* . . . , 253–256.

"Lily Daw"
    Schmidt, Peter. *The Heart of the Story* . . . , 11–16.
"Livvie"
    Romines, Ann. *The Home Plot* . . . , 204–207.
"Moon Lake"
    Donaldson, Susan V. "Recovering Otherness . . . ," 502.
    Roberts, Diane. "The Rapist Bridegroom . . . ," 208–210.
    Romines, Ann. *The Home Plot* . . . , 239–240.
    Schmidt, Peter. *The Heart of the Story* . . . , 162–172.
"Music from Spain"
    Donaldson, Susan V. "Recovering Otherness . . . ," 502–503.
    Schmidt, Peter. *The Heart of the Story* . . . , 58–79.
"Old Mr. Marblehall"
    Schmidt, Peter. *The Heart of the Story* . . . , 19–23.
"Petrified Man"
    + Bohner, Charles H. *Instructor's Manual* . . . , 126–127.
    Schmidt, Peter. *The Heart of the Story* . . . , 76–86.
"A Piece of News"
    Schmidt, Peter. *The Heart of the Story* . . . , 31–40.
"Powerhouse"
    + Cassill, R. V. . . . *Instructor's Handbook*, 186–187.
    Schmidt, Peter. *The Heart of the Story* . . . , 39–48.
    Burke, Daniel. *Beyond Interpretation* . . . , 163–169.
"Sir Rabbit"
    Donaldson, Susan V. "Recovering Otherness . . . ," 501–502.
    Roberts, Diane. "The Rapist Bridegroom . . . ," 204–206.
"A Still Moment"
    Gibley, Kevin C. " 'Half-Concealed and Half-Sought for': Eudora
        Welty's 'A Still Moment' as Aesthetic Allegory," *J Short Story
        Engl*, 18 (Spring, 1992), 43–51.
"A Visit of Charity"
    Schmidt, Peter. *The Heart of the Story* . . . , 16–24.
"The Wanderers"
    Donaldson, Susan V. "Recovering Otherness . . . ," 504–506.
    Roberts, Diane. "The Rapist Bridegroom . . . ," 210–221.
    Romines, Ann. *The Home Plot* . . . , 240–245.
    Schmidt, Peter. *The Heart of the Story* . . . , 172–189.
"Where Is the Voice Coming From?"
    Gretlund, Jan N. "A Neighborhood Voice: Eudora Welty's Sense of
        Place," *Dolphin*, 20 (Spring, 1991), 99–107.
"The Whistle"
    Yaeger, Patricia. "Edible Labor," *Southern Q*, 30 (1992), 157–158.
"The Whole World Knows"
    Donald, Susan V. "Recovering Otherness . . . ," 494–495.
    Roberts, Diane. "The Rapist Bridegroom . . . ," 203–208.
    Schmidt, Peter. *The Heart of the Story* . . . , 58–79.

"Why I Live at the P.O."
Schmidt, Peter. *The Heart of the Story* . . . , 112–120.
Whitaker, Elaine E. "Welty's 'Why I Live at the P.O.,' " *Explicator*,
50, ii (1992), 115–117.

"The Wide Net"
Schmidt, Peter. *The Heart of the Story* . . . , 135–144.
Yaeger, Patricia. "The Poetics of Birth," in Stanton, Domna C., Ed.
Discourses of Sexuality . . . , 281–284.

"The Winds"
Schmidt, Peter. *The Heart of the Story* . . . , 144–155.

"*Women*!! Make Turban in Own Home!"
Schmidt, Peter. *The Heart of the Story* . . . , 109–112.

"A Worn Path"
+ Bohner, Charles H. *Instructor's Manual* . . . , 127.
+ Cassill, R. V. . . . *Instructor's Handbook*, 188.
+ Charters, Ann, and William E. Sheidley. *Resources for
Teaching* . . . , 3rd ed., 210.
Orr, Elaine. " 'Unsettling Every Definition of Otherness': Another
Reading of Eudora Welty's 'A Worn Path,' " *So Atlantic R*, 57, ii
(1992), 57–72.
Schmidt, Peter. *The Heart of the Story* . . . , 37–40.

ALBERT WENDT

"The Balloonfish and the Armadillo"
O'Rourke, Valerie. "A Tribute to the *fa'a Samoa*: Albert Wendt's
Birth and Death of the Miracle Man," *World Lit Today*, 66 (1992),
51–52.

"Birthdays"
O'Rourke, Valerie. "A Tribute . . . ," 52.

"Crocodile"
O'Rourke, Valerie. "A Tribute . . . ," 53.

"Elena's Son"
O'Rourke, Valerie. "A Tribute . . . ," 52.

"Hamlet"
O'Rourke, Valerie. "A Tribute . . . ," 53–54.

"Justice"
O'Rourke, Valerie. "A Tribute . . . ," 52.

"Talent"
O'Rourke, Valerie. "A Tribute . . . ," 52–53.

GLENWAY WESCOTT

"Good-Bye Wisconsin"
Weber, Ronald. *The Midwestern* . . . , 203–205.

NATHANAEL WEST

"The Dream Life of Balso Snell"
 Merrill, Catherine. "West's 'The Dream Life of Balso Snell,' "
  Explicator, 50, iii (1992), 170–172.
"Miss Lonelyhearts"
 Fuchs, Miriam. "Nathanael West's 'Miss Lonelyhearts': *The Waste
  Land* Rescripted," *Stud Short Fiction*, 29 (1992), 43–55.
 Hattenhauer, Darryl. "West's 'Miss Lonelyhearts,' " *Explicator*, 49
  (1991), 120–121.

PAUL WEST

"Those Pearls His Eyes"
 Mooney, William. " 'Those Pearls His Eyes': Paul West's Blind
  Monologuists and Deaf Auditors," *R Contemp Fiction*, 11, i
  (1991), 267–270.

REBECCA WEST

"At Valladolid"
 Hammond, J. R. *H. G. Wells and Rebecca West*, 71–72.

EDITH WHARTON

"After Holbein"
 White, Barbara A. *Edith Wharton* . . . , 93–96.
"All Souls"
 Lewis, R. W. B. "Introduction," *The Selected Short Stories of Edith
  Wharton*, ed. R. W. B. Lewis, xvii–xviii.
 White, Barbara A. *Edith Wharton* . . . , 96–97, 101–103, 105–106.
 Zilversmit, Annette. " 'All Souls': Wharton's Last Haunted House
  and Future Directions for Criticism," in Bendixen, Alfred, and
  Annette Zilversmit, Eds. *Edith Wharton* . . . , 315–329.
"The Angel at the Grave"
 Raphael, Lev. *Edith Wharton's Prisoners* . . . , 201.
 White, Barbara A. *Edith Wharton* . . . , 52–56.
 Widdicombe, Toby. "Wharton's 'The Angel at the Grave' and the
  Glories of Transcendentalism: Deciduous or Evergreen?" *Am
  Transcendental Q*, N.S., 6 (1992), 47–57.
"April Showers"
 Raphael, Lev. *Edith Wharton's Prisoners* . . . , 193–194.
 White, Barbara A. *Edith Wharton* . . . , 31–32, 34.
"Atrophy"
 White, Barbara A. *Edith Wharton* . . . , 100.

"Autre Temps"
 Raphael, Lev. *Edith Wharton's Prisoners* . . . , 45–46.
 White, Barbara A. *Edith Wharton* . . . , 74–75.

"Beatrice Palmato"
 Joslin, Katherine. *Edith Wharton*, 111–112.

"Bewitched"
 White, Barbara A. *Edith Wharton* . . . , 104.

"The Bolted Door"
 Raphael, Lev. *Edith Wharton's Prisoners* . . . , 191–192.
 White, Barbara A. *Edith Wharton* . . . , 73–74.

"A Bottle of Perrier"
 Singley, Carol J. "Gothic Borrowings and Innovations in Edith
  Wharton's 'A Bottle of Perrier,' " in Bendixen, Alfred, and
  Annette Zilversmit, Eds. *Edith Wharton* . . . , 271–290.

"Coming Home"
 White, Barbara A. *Edith Wharton* . . . , 85–86.

"Confession"
 Raphael, Lev. *Edith Wharton's Prisoners* . . . , 107–110.

"Copy"
 Raphael, Lev. *Edith Wharton's Prisoners* . . . , 212–213.
 White, Barbara A. *Edith Wharton* . . . , 38.

"The Day of the Funeral"
 White, Barbara A. *Edith Wharton* . . . , 84–85.

"The Dilettante"
 White, Barbara A. *Edith Wharton* . . . , 59–60.

"Disintegration"
 Raphael, Lev. *Edith Wharton's Prisoners* . . . , 42.

"Ethan Frome"
 Raphael, Lev. *Edith Wharton's Prisoners* . . . , 284–289.

"Expiation"
 Raphael, Lev. *Edith Wharton's Prisoners* . . . , 213–214.

"The Eyes"
 Lewis, R. W. B. "Introduction," xx–xxi.
 Raphael, Lev. *Edith Wharton's Prisoners* . . . , 205–206.
 White, Barbara A. *Edith Wharton* . . . , 64–67, 73.

"Friends"
 White, Barbara A. *Edith Wharton* . . . , 30–31.

"Full Circle"
 Raphael, Lev. *Edith Wharton's Prisoners* . . . , 209–212.

"Her Son"
 Raphael, Lev. *Edith Wharton's Prisoners* . . . , 103–107.

"The Hermit and the Wild Woman"
 White, Barbara A. *Edith Wharton* . . . , 71–72.

"The House of the Dead Hand"
 Carpenter, Lynette. "Deadly Letters, Sexual Politics, and the

Dilemma of the Woman Writer: Edith Wharton's 'The House of the Dead Hand,' " *Am Lit Realism*, 24, ii (1992), 55–69.

Erlich, Gloria. *The Sexual Education . . .* , 41–42.

White, Barbara A. *Edith Wharton . . .* , 39–40, 41.

"In Trust"

Raphael, Lev. *Edith Wharton's Prisoners . . .* , 203–204.

"Joy in the House"

Raphael, Lev. *Edith Wharton's Prisoners . . .* , 198–199.

"Kerfol"

White, Barbara A. *Edith Wharton . . .* , 69–70.

"The Lady's Maid's Bell"

Fedorko, Kathy A. "Edith Wharton's Haunted Fiction: 'The Lady's Maid's Bell,' and *The House of Mirth*," in Carpenter, Lynette, and Wendy K. Kolmar, Eds. *Haunting the House of Fiction . . .* , 83–92.

White, Barbara A. *Edith Wharton . . .* , 68–69.

"The Lamb of Psyche"

Fracasso, Evelyn E. "The Evolution of Theme and Technique in Selected Tales of Edith Wharton," *J Short Story Engl*, 16 (Spring, 1991), 43–46.

"The Last Asset"

White, Barbara A. *Edith Wharton . . .* , 77–78.

"The Legend"

Raphael, Lev. *Edith Wharton's Prisoners . . .* , 192–193.

"The Letter"

Fracasso, Evelyn E. "The Evolution Theme . . . ," 46–49.

"The Letters"

White, Barbara A. *Edith Wharton . . .* , 78–79.

"The Long Run"

Raphael, Lev. *Edith Wharton's Prisoners . . .* , 197–198.

White, Barbara A. *Edith Wharton . . .* , 70–71.

"Miss Mary Pask"

Thomas, Jennice G. "Spook or Spinster? Edith Wharton's 'Miss Mary Pask,' " in Carpenter, Lynette, and Wendy K. Kolmar, Eds. *Haunting the House of Fiction . . .* , 108–116.

"The Mission of Jane"

Lewis, R. W. B. "Introduction," xii.

"Mrs. Manstey's View"

White, Barbara A. *Edith Wharton . . .* , 29–30.

"The Muse's Tragedy"

Cassill, R. V. *. . . Instructor's Handbook*, 189–190.

Nettels, Elsa. "Texts Within Texts: The Power of Letters in Edith Wharton's Fiction," in Prier, Raymond A., Ed. *Countercurrents . . .* , 194–200.

Raphael, Lev. *Edith Wharton's Prisoners . . .* , 247–248.

Witzig, M. Denise. " 'The Muse's Tragedy' and the Muse's Text:

Language and Desire in Wharton,'' in Bendixen, Alfred, Annette Zilversmit, Eds. *Edith Wharton . . .* , 261–270.

"The Old Maid"
Castronovo, David. *The American Gentleman . . .* , 62–64.

"The Other Two"
Bohner, Charles H. *Instructor's Manual . . .* , 128–129.
White, Barbara A. *Edith Wharton . . .* , 12–18, 57, 58, 81.

"The Pelican"
Lewis, R. W. B. "Introduction," xiii.
White, Barbara A. *Edith Wharton . . .* , 31–32, 34, 35–36, 61–62.

"Pomegranate Seed"
Singley, Carol J., and Susan E. Sweeney. "Forbidden Reading and Ghostly Writing: Anxious Power in Wharton's 'Pomegranate Seed,' " *Women's Stud*, 20, ii (1991), 177–203.

"The Portrait"
Raphael, Lev. *Edith Wharton's Prisoners . . .* , 207–208.
White, Barbara A. *Edith Wharton . . .* , 38–39, 50.

"The Potboiler"
Raphael, Lev. *Edith Wharton's Prisoners . . .* , 208.

"The Pretext"
Raphael, Lev. *Edith Wharton's Prisoners . . .* , 123–126.
White, Barbara A. *Edith Wharton . . .* , 18–24.

"The Quicksand"
Raphael, Lev. *Edith Wharton's Prisoners . . .* , 201–203.
White, Barbara A. *Edith Wharton . . .* , 76–77.

"The Recovery"
Raphael, Lev. *Edith Wharton's Prisoners . . .* , 194–197.

"The Refugees"
Raphael, Lev. *Edith Wharton's Prisoners . . .* , 165–169.

"The Rembrandt"
White, Barbara A. *Edith Wharton . . .* , 62.

"Roman Fever"
+ Bohner, Charles H. *Instructor's Manual . . .* , 129–131.
+ Charters, Ann, and William E. Sheidley. *Resources for Teaching . . .* , 3rd ed., 212–213.
Keating, Helane L., and Walter Levy. *Instructor's Manual: Lives Through Literature . . .* , 46–47.
White, Barbara A. *Edith Wharton . . .* , 7–12.

"The Seed of the Faith"
White, Barbara A. *Edith Wharton . . .* , 91–92.

"Souls Belated"
Raphael, Lev. *Edith Wharton's Prisoners . . .* , 219–220.
White, Barbara A. *Edith Wharton . . .* , 58–59.

"Summer"
Blackall, Jean F. "Charity at the Window: Narrative Technique in

Edith Wharton's 'Summer,' " in Bendixen, Alfred, Annette
Zilversmit, Eds. *Edith Wharton . . .* , 115–126.
"The Temperate Zone"
Raphael, Lev. *Edith Wharton's Prisoners . . .* , 215–216.
"That Good May Come"
Raphael, Lev. *Edith Wharton's Prisoners . . .* , 206–207.
"The Touchstone"
Erlich, Gloria. *The Sexual Education . . .* , 77–79, 82–83, 84–85.
"The Verdict"
Raphael, Lev. *Edith Wharton's Prisoners . . .* , 197.
"Writing a War Story"
Raphael, Lev. *Edith Wharton's Prisoners . . .* , 162–165.
White, Barbara A. *Edith Wharton . . .* , 86–87.
"The Young Gentleman"
White, Barbara A. *Edith Wharton . . .* , 89–91.

RUDY WIEBE

"An Indication of Burning"
Howells, Robin. "Esch-sca(r)-toloty: Rudy Wiebe's 'An Indication
of Burning,' " *J Commonwealth Lit*, 27, i (1992), 87–95.
"Where Is the Voice Coming From?"
Regan, Stephen. " 'The Presence of the Past': Modernism and
Postmodernism in Canadian Short Fiction," in Howells, Colin A.,
and Lynette Hunter, Eds. *Narrative Strategies in Canadian
Literatures . . .* , 129–131.

ERNST WIECHERT

"Geschichte Eines Knaben"
Deighton, Alan. "Ernst Wiechert's 'Novelle' *'Geschichte Eines
Knaben'* and the Reception of Wolfram von Eschenbach's
Parzival," *Forum Mod Lang Stud*, 28, i (1992), 43–45, 46–54.

OSCAR WILDE

"The Portrait of Mr. W. H."
Priestman, Martin. *Detective Fiction . . .* , 142–143.

MICHAEL WILDING

"Knock, Knock"
Vauthier, Simone. "Reading the Signs of Michael Wilding's 'Knock,
Knock,' " *Australian Lit Stud*, 15, ii (1991), 128–139.

CHARLES WILLIAMS

"Et in Sempiternum Pereant"
Beach, Charles F. " 'A Place Where One Lives Without Learning':
Intellectual Pilgrimage in Charles Williams's 'Et in Sempiternum
Pereant,' " *Stud Short Fiction*, 28 (1991), 459–466.
Kenny, Stuart. "The Now of Salvation: Thoughts on Charles
Williams' 'Et in Sempiternum Pereant,' " *Mythlore*, 17, iv (1991),
43–44.

JOY WILLIAMS

"The Little Winter"
Hornby, Nick. *Contemporary American Fiction*, 127, 128–129.
"The Lover"
Hornby, Nick. *Contemporary American Fiction*, 125–126.
"Rot"
Hornby, Nick. *Contemporary American Fiction*, 129–131.
"The Skater"
Hornby, Nick. *Contemporary American Fiction*, 127–128.
"The Wedding"
Hornby, Nick. *Contemporary American Fiction*, 124–125.

WILLIAM CARLOS WILLIAMS

"Comedy Entombed: 1930"
Callan, Ron. *William Carlos Williams* . . . , 100.

"The Great American Novel"
Jarraway, David R. "The Novelty of Revolution/The Revolution of
Novelty: Williams' First Fiction," *William Carlos Williams R*, 18,
i (1992), 21–33.

"Jean Beicke"
Callan, Ron. *William Carlos Williams* . . . , 85, 86.

"Old Doc Rivers"
Monteiro, George. "Doc Rivers, Rogue Physician," *William Carlos
Williams R*, 17, ii (1991), 52–58.

"The Use of Force"
+ Bohner, Charles H. *Instructor's Manual* . . . , 131–132.
Cassill, R. V. . . . *Instructor's Handbook*, 191.

HERBERT WILNER

"A Gift Every Morning"
Gladsky, Thomas S. *Princes, Peasants* . . . , 217–218.

RICHARD WOLCOTT

"Hopeful Tackett—His Mark"
Diffley, Kathleen. *Where My Heart* . . . , 128–130, 131.
"A Night in the Wilderness"
Diffley, Kathleen. *Where My Heart* . . . , 128–130, 131.
"The Wounded Soldier and the Old Colored Woman"
Diffley, Kathleen. *Where My Heart* . . . , 128–130, 131.

CHRISTA WOLF

"Juninachmittag"
Graves, Peter. "Christa Wolf's *Sommerstück*: An Intensified June
Afternoon," *Mod Lang R*, 87 (1992), 393–395, 403, 404.
"Sommerstück"
Finney, Gail. "The Christa Wolf Controversy: Wolf's 'Sommerstück'
as Chekovian Commentary," *Germ R*, 67 (1992), 107–110.
"Störfall"
Bohm, Arndt. "Christa Wolf's 'Stoerfall' and Chingiz Aitmov's 'I
dol'sche veka dlitsia den': Technology and History," *Germano-
Slavica*, 6 (1992), 332.
Eysel, Karin. "History, Fiction, Gender: The Politics of Narrative
Intervention in Christa Wolf's 'Störfall,' " *Monatshefte*, 84 (1992),
284–298.
Saalman, Dieter. "Elective Affinities: Christa Wolf's 'Störfall' and
Joseph Conrad's 'Heart of Darkness,' " *Comp Lit Stud*, 29 (1992),
238–258.
"Unter den Linden"
Hardy, Beverley. "Romanticism and Realism: Christa Wolf's 'Unter
den Linden': The Appropriation of a Hoffmannesque Reality," in
Gaskill, Howard, Karin McPherson, and Andrew Barker, Eds.
Neue Ansichten . . . , 73–84.
"Was bleibt"
Cosentino, Christine. "Christa Wolfs 'Was bleibt': was bleibt von,
was wird aus der DDR-Literatur," *Germ Notes*, 22, i–ii (1991),
12–14.
————. " 'Heute freilich möchte man fragen . . . ,': Zum Thema von
Schuld und Verantwortung in Christa Wolfs 'Was bleibt,' Helga
Königsdorfs 'Ungelegener Befund,' und Helga Schuberts 'Judas
Frauen,' " *Neophil*, 76, i (1992), 112–114.
Hörnigk, Therese. "Von 'Mutter Wolfen' zur 'bösen' Wolf. Oder: Die
fremdgesteuerte Metamorphose einer Schriftstellerin im Jahr der
deutschen Einheit," *GDR Bull*, 17, i (Spring, 1991), 5.
Jackman, Graham. " 'Wann, Wenn Nicht Jetzt?' Conceptions of
Time and History in Christa Wolf's 'Was bleibt' and *Nachden Uber
Christa T.*," *Germ Life & Letters*, N.S., 45 (1992), 358–375.
Juers, Evelyn. "Who's Afraid of Christa Wolf?" *Cambridge Q*, 21
(1992), 213–221.

Lehnert, Herbert. "Fictionalität und Autobiographische Motive: Zu Christa Wolfs Erzählung 'Was bleibt,' *Weimarer Beiträge*, 37, iii (1991), 423–444.

Zehl-Romero, Christiane. "Was bleibt," *GDR Bull*, 17, i (1991, Spring), 1–3.

THOMAS WOLFE

"The Lost Boy"
  Phillipson, John S. " 'The Lost Boy': 'Caught Upon This Point of Time,' " *Thomas Wolfe R*, 15, i (1991), 79–82.

TOBIAS WOLFF

"The Barracks Thief"
  Hornby, Nick. *Contemporary American Fiction*, 141–144.

"An Episode in the Life of Professor Brooke"
  Hornby, Nick. *Contemporary American Fiction*, 134–135, 137.

"Face to Face"
  Hornby, Nick. *Contemporary American Fiction*, 138–139.

"Hunters in the Snow"
  Charters, Ann, and William E. Sheidley. *Resources for Teaching . . .*, 3rd ed., 214–215.

"In the Garden of the North American Martyrs"
  +Cassill, R. V. . . . *Instructor's Handbook*, 192–193.

"The Rich Brother"
  Keating, Helane L., and Walter Levy. *Instructor's Manual: Lives Through Literature . . .*, 29–30.

"Smokers"
  Bohner, Charles H. *Instructor's Manual . . .*, 132–133.

VIRGINIA WOOLF

"The Evening Party"
  Head, Dominic. *The Modernist . . .*, 90–99.

"Kew Gardens"
  +Cassill, R. V. . . . *Instructor's Handbook*, 193–194.
  Charters, Ann, and William E. Sheidley. *Resources for Teaching . . .*, 3rd ed., 215–216.
  Head, Dominic. *The Modernist . . .*, 99–103.
  McVicker, Jeanette. "Vast Nests of Chinese Boxes, or Getting from Q to R: Critiquing Empire in 'Kew Gardens' " in Hussey, Mark, and Vara Neverow-Turk, Eds. *Virginia Woolf . . .*, 41.

"The Lady in the Looking Glass"
  Head, Dominic. *The Modernist . . .*, 80, 86–89.

"The Legacy"
Keating, Helane L., and Walter Levy. *Instructor's Manual: Lives Through Literature* . . . , 114.

"The Mark on the Wall"
Head, Dominic. *The Modernist* . . . , 106–108.
Narey, Wayne. "Virginia Woolf's 'The Mark on the Wall': An Einsteinian View of Art," *Stud Short Fiction*, 29 (1992), 35–42.

"Monday or Tuesday"
Head, Dominic. *The Modernist* . . . , 103–105.

"The Shooting Party"
Head, Dominic. *The Modernist* . . . , 89.

"An Unwritten Novel"
Head, Dominic. *The Modernist* . . . , 80, 84–86.

RICHARD WRIGHT

"Long Black Song"
Hurd, Myles R. "Between Blackness and Bitonality: Wright's 'Long Black Song,' " *Coll Lang Assoc J*, 35 (1991), 42–56.

"The Man Who Was Almost a Man"
+ Bohner, Charles H. *Instructor's Manual* . . . , 133–134.
+ Cassill, R. V. . . . *Instructor's Handbook*, 194–195.
+ Charters, Ann, and William E. Sheidley. *Resources for Teaching* . . . , 3rd ed., 217.

WILLIAM WRIGHT [DAN DE QUILLE]

"A Christmas Story"
Berkove, Lawrence I. "De Quille Sells a Christmas Story," *Palimpsest*, 69, iv (1988), 188–190.

"Pahnenit, Prince of the Land of Lakes"
Berkove, Lawrence I. "Introduction to 'Pahnenit, Prince of the Land of Lakes,' " *Nevada Historical Soc Q*, 31, ii (1988), 79–86.

RUDOLPH WURLITZER

"The Boiler Room"
Seed, David. *Rudolph Wurlitzer* . . . , 30–32.

BAI XIANYONG [KENNETH PAI]

"Excursion to Fire Island"
Wong, Sau-Ling C. "Ethnicizing Gender: An Exploration of Sexuality as Seen in Chinese Immigrant Literature," in Lim,

Shirley G., and Amy Ling, Eds. *Reading the Literature . . . ,*
121–123.

HISAYE YAMAMOTO

"Seventeen Syllables"
Cheung, King-Kok. "Double-Telling: Intertextual Silence in Hisaye
Yamamoto's Fiction," *Am Lit Hist*, 3 (1991), 280–286.
Yogi, Stan. "Rebels and Heroines: Subversive Narratives in the
Stories of Wakako Yamauchi and Hisaye Yamamoto" in Lim,
Shirley G., and Amy Ling, Eds. *Reading the Literatures . . . ,*
142–146.

"Yoneko's Earthquake"
Cheung, King-Kok. "Double-Telling . . . ," 286–288.
Yogi, Stan. "Rebels and Heroines . . . ," 139–142.

WAKAKO YAMAUCHI

"And the Soul Shall Dance"
Yogi, Stan. "Rebels and Heroines: Subversive Narratives in the
Stories of Wakako Yamauchi and Hisaye Yamamoto," in Lim,
Shirley G., and Amy Ling, Eds. *Reading the Literatures . . . ,*
132–136.

"Songs My Mother Taught Me"
Yogi, Stan. "Rebels and Heroines . . . ," 136–139.

JACK B. YEATS

"Ah Well"
McGuinness, Nora A. *The Literary Universe . . . ,* 138–150.

ABRAHAM B. YEHOSHUA

"Flood Tide"
Morahg, Gilead. "A Symbolic Psyche: The Structure of Meaning in
A. B. Yehoshua's 'Flood Tide,' " *Hebrew Stud*, 29 (1988), 81–100.

MARGUERITE YOURCENAR

"The End of Marko Kraliévitch"
Howard, Joan E. *From Violence to Vision . . . ,* 108–111.

"The First Night"
Restori, Enrica. " 'Le Premier Soir' ou l'immobilité en marche," in
Biondi, Carminella, and Corrado Rossi, Eds. *Voyage . . . ,* 221–231.

"How Wang Fo Was Saved"
    Howard, Joan E. *From Violence to Vision* . . . , 80–82.
"The Last Love of Prince Genji"
    Howard, Joan E. *From Violence to Vision* . . . , 91–92.
"The Man Who Loved the Nereids"
    Howard, Joan E. *From Violence to Vision* . . . , 92–98.
"Milk of Death"
    Howard, Joan E. *From Violence to Vision* . . . , 87–91.
"Our Lady of the Swallows"
    Howard, Joan E. *From Violence to Vision* . . . , 98–103.
"The Sadness of Cornelius Berg"
    Howard, Joan E. *From Violence to Vision* . . . , 111–115.

SEMËN YUSHKEVICH

"Kabatchik Geiman"
    Rischin, Ruth. " 'The Most Historical of Peoples': Yushkevich,
        Kuprin and the Dubnovian Idea," in Luker, Nicholas, Ed. *The
        Short Story in Russia* . . . , 28–36, 43, 44–45.

ALFRED A. YUSON

"The Hill of Samuel"
    Ventura, Sylvia M. "Sexism and the Mythification of Woman: A
        Feminist Reading of Nick Joaquin's 'The Summer Solstice' and
        Alfred Yuson's 'The Hill of Samuel,' " in Kintanar, Thelma B.,
        Ed. *Women Reading* . . . , 154–160.
"A Voice in the Hills"
    Lucero, Rosario Cruz. "The Philippine Short Story, 1981–1990: The
        Voice of the Self-Authenticating Other," *Tenggara*, 26 (1990),
        81–82.

ERACLIO ZEPEDA

"Benzulul"
    Marcos, Juan Manuel. "El arte compilatorio de Eraclio Zepeda,"
        Palabra y Hombre, 78 (April–June, 1991), 269.
"De la marimba al son"
    Marcos, Juan Manuel. "El arte . . . ," 272.
"Don Chico que vuela"
    Marcos, Juan Manuel. "El arte . . . ," 271.
"Gente Bella"
    Marcos, Juan Manuel. "El arte . . . ," 270–271.
"No se asombre, sargento"
    Marcos, Juan Manuel. "El arte . . . ," 270.

"Los pálpitos del coronel"
Marcos, Juan Manuel. "El arte . . . ," 271–272.

"Los trabajos de la ballena"
Marcos, Juan Manuel. "El arte . . . ," 270.

"Quien dice verdad"
Marcos, Juan Manuel. "El arte . . . ," 269–270.

ZHANG JIE

"Love Must Not Be Forgotten"
Knapp, Betty. "The New Era for Women Writers in China," *World Lit Today*, 65 (1991), 435–436.

ZHANG KANGKANG

"White Poppies"
Knapp, Betty. "The New Era for Women Writers in China," *World Lit Today*, 65 (1991), 437–438.

WILHELM ZIETHE

"The Locksmith from Philadelphia"
Peterson, Brent O. *Popular Narratives* . . . , 192–197.

ÉMILE ÉDOURARD CHARLES ANTOINE ZOLA

"La vierge au cirage"
Johnson, Roger. "Looking and Screening in Zola's *Vierge au cirage*," *Stud Short Fiction*, 29 (1992), 19–25.

PU ZONG

"My Shell"
Knapp, Betty. "The New Era for Women Writers in China," *World Lit Today*, 65 (1991), 438–439.

JUAN EDUARDO ZÚÑIGA

"Nubes de polvo y humo"
Percival, Anthony. "El cuento de la Guerra Civil Española: Del neo-realismo al 'posmodernismo' (*Valor y miedo* de Arturo Barea y *Largo noviembre de Madrid* de Juan Eduardo Zúñiga)," in Boland, Roy, and Alun Kenwood, Eds. *War and Revolution* . . . , 145–146.

"Presagios de noche"
Percival, Anthony. "El cuento de la Guerra . . . ," 147–148.

"Puertas abiertas, puertas cerradas"
Carmona, Elena Reina, and Erica C. García. "Open Reading of a
Closed Text: Zúñiga's 'Puertas abiertas, puertas cerradas,' " in
Tobin, Yishai, Ed. *From Sign* . . . , 235–251.

UNICA ZÜRN

"Dunkler Frühling"
Weinhold, Ulrike. "Leere und Wucherung. Bemerkungen zur
weiblichen Phantasie in literarischen Zeugnissen des späten 19. und
des beginnenden 20. Jahrhunderts," *Neophil*, 76, i (1992), 96–100.

A Checklist of Books Used

Actes du Centre de recherches: Sémiologie de l'amour dans les civilisations méditerra-néennes. Paris: Les Belles Lettres, 1985.

Adam, Ian, and Helen Tiffin, Eds. *Past the Last Post: Theorizing Post Colonialism and Post-Modernism.* Alberta: Univ. of Calgary Press, 1990.

Alcott, Louisa May. *Moods,* ed. Sarah Elberg. New Brunswick: Rutgers Univ. Press, 1991.

Aldridge, John W. *Talents and Technicians: Literary Chic and the New Assembly-Line Fiction.* New York: Scribner's, 1992.

Allen, Elizabeth C. *Turgenev's Poetics of Secular Salvation.* Stanford: Stanford Univ. Press, 1992.

Alter, Robert. *Necessary Angels: Tradition and Modernity in Kafka, Benjamin, and Scholem.* Cambridge: Harvard Univ. Press, 1991.

Ambrosini, Richard. *Conrad's Fiction as Critical Discourse.* Cambridge: Cambridge Univ. Press, 1991.

Ames, Christopher. *The Life of the Party: Festive Vision in Modern Fiction.* Athens: Univ. of Georgia Press, 1991.

Ammons, Elizabeth. *Conflicting Stories: American Women Writers at the Turn into the Twentieth Century.* New York: Oxford Univ. Press, 1991.

Arac, Jonathan, and Harriet Ritvo, Eds. *Macropolitics of Nineteenth-Century Litera-ture: Nationalism, Exoticism, Imperialism.* Philadelphia: Univ. of Pennsylvania Press, 1991.

Armitt, Lucie, Ed. *Where No Man Has Gone Before: Women and Science Fiction.* London: Routledge, 1991.

Aubrey, James R. *John Fowles: A Reference Companion.* Westport: Greenwood, 1991.

Austen, Roger. *Genteel Pagan: The Double Life of Charles Warren Stoddard.* Amherst: Univ. of Massachusetts Press, 1991.

Azuela, Mariano. *The Underdogs.* Trans. Frederick H. Fornoff. Pittsburgh: Univ. of Pittsburgh Press, 1992.

Bach, Gerhard, Ed. *Saul Bellow at Seventy-Five: A Collection of Critical Essays.* Tübingen: Narr, 1991.

Balogun, F. Odun. *Tradition and Modernity in the African Short Story: An Introduc-tion to a Literature in Search of Critics.* Westport: Greenwood, 1991.

Bardolph, Jacquelin, Ed. *Short Fiction in the New Literatures in English.* Nice: Fac. des Lettres & Sciences Humaines, 1989.

Baudelaire, Charles. *The Prose Poems and "La Fanfarlo,"* ed. Rosemary Lloyd. Oxford: Oxford Univ. Press, 1991.

Baym, Nina. *Feminism and American Literary History: Essays.* New Brunswick: Rutgers Univ. Press, 1992.

Beaty, Frederick L. *The Ironic World of Evelyn Waugh: A Study of Eight Novels.* Dekalb: Northern Illinois Univ. Press, 1992.

Bedrosian, Margaret, Ed. *The Magic Pine Ring.* Detroit: Wayne State Univ. Press, 1992.

Bell, Elizabeth S. *Kay Boyle: A Study of the Short Fiction.* New York: Twayne, 1992.

Bell, Ian F. *Henry James and the Past: Readings into Time.* New York: St. Martin's Press, 1991.

Bell, Millicent. *Meaning in Henry James*. Cambridge: Harvard Univ. Press, 1991.

Bendixen, Alfred, and Annette Zilversmit, Eds. *Edith Wharton: New Critical Essays*. New York: Garland, 1992.

Benfey, Christopher. *The Double Life of Stephen Crane*. New York: Alfred A. Knopf, 1992.

Bennett, Carl D. *Joseph Conrad*. New York: Continuum, 1991.

Béranger, Jean, Ed. *L'Ici et l'ailleurs: Multilinguisme et multiculturalisme en Amérique du Nord*. Bordeaux: Presses Universitaires de Bordeaux, 1991.

————, Jean Cazemajou, Jean-Michel Lacroix, and Pierre Spriet, Eds. *Multilinguisme et multiculturalisme en Amérique du Nord: Espace seuils limites*. Talence Cedex: Presses Universitaires de Bordeaux, 1990.

Berlin, Jeffrey B., Ed. *Approaches to Teaching Thomas Mann's "Death in Venice" and Other Short Fiction*. New York: Modern Lang. Assn., 1992.

Bernstein, Michael A. *Bitter Carnival: "Ressentiment" and the Abject Hero*. Princeton: Princeton Univ. Press, 1992.

Bevan, David, Ed. *Literature and Exile*. Amsterdam: Rodopi, 1990.

Biondi, Carminella, and Corrado Rossi, Eds. *Voyage et connaissance dans l'oeuvre de Marguerite Yourcenar*. Pisa: Goliardica, 1988.

Black, Joel. *The Aesthetics of Murder: A Study in Romantic Literature and Contemporary Culture*. Baltimore: Johns Hopkins Univ. Press, 1991.

Black, Michael. *D. H. Lawrence: The Early Philosophical Works*. Cambridge: Cambridge Univ. Press, 1992.

Blackshire-Belay, Carol A., Ed. *Language and Literature in the African American Imagination*. Westport: Greenwood, 1992.

Bohner, Charles H. *Instructor's Manual [for] Short Fiction: Classic and Contemporary, Second Edition*. Inglewood Cliffs: Prentice-Hall, 1990.

Boland, Roy, and Alun Kenwood, Eds. *War and Revolution in Hispanic Literature*. Melbourne: Voz Hispánica, 1990.

Boren, Lynda S., and Sara D. Davis, Eds. *Kate Chopin Reconsidered: Beyond the Bayou*. Baton Rouge: Louisiana State Univ. Press, 1992.

Bosinelli, R. M. Bollettieri, C. Marengo Vaglio, and Chr. Van Boheemen, Eds. *The Languages of Joyce: Selected Papers from the 11th International James Joyce Symposium, Venice, 12–18 June 1988*. Philadelphia: John Benjamins, 1992.

Bozzetto, Roger, Max Duperray, and Alain Chareyre-Majan, Eds. *Eros, Science & Fiction, Fantastique*. Aix-en-Provence: Univ. of Provence, 1991.

Brady, Kristin. *George Eliot*. New York: St. Martin's Press, 1992.

Brand, Dana. *The Spectator and the City in Nineteenth-Century American Literature*. Cambridge: Cambridge Univ. Press, 1991.

Brau, Jean-Louis, and Gérard Lavergne, Eds. *La Focalisation*. Nice: Pubs. de la Fac. des Lettres & Sciences Humaines de Nice, 1992.

Brenner, Gerry. *"The Old Man and the Sea": Story of a Common Man*. Boston: Twayne, 1991.

Broe, Mary L., Ed. *Silence and Power: A Reevaluation of Djuna Barnes*. Carbondale: Southern Illinois Univ. Press, 1991.

Brown, Dorothy H., and Barbara C. Ewell. *Louisiana Women Writers: New Essays and a Comprehensive Bibliography*. Baton Rouge: Louisiana State Univ. Press, 1992.

Brown, Joan L., Ed. *Women Writers of Contemporary Spain: Essays in the Homeland*. Cranbury, N. Y.: Associated Univ. Presses [for Univ. of Delaware Press], 1991.

Brown, Richard. *James Joyce*. New York: St. Martin's Press, 1992.

Bruller, Jean [Vercors]. *"The Silence of the Seas": A Novel of French Resistance during World War II by "Vercors,"* eds. James W. Brown and Lawrence D. Stokes. Oxford: Berg, 1991.

Burduck, Michael L. *Grim Phantasms: Fear in Poe's Short Fiction*. New York: Garland, 1992.

Burke, Daniel. *Beyond Interpretation: Studies in the Modern Short Story*. Troy, N.Y.: Whitston, 1991.

Calderón, Héctor, and José D. Saldívar, Eds. *Criticism in the Borderlands: Studies in Chicano Literature, Culture, and Ideology*. Durham: Duke Univ. Press, 1991.

Callan, Ron. *William Carlos Williams and Transcendentalism*. New York: St. Martin's Press, 1992.

Carey, Phyllis, and Ed Jewinski, Eds. *RE: Joyce 'n Beckett*. New York: Fordam Univ. Press, 1992.

Carlin, Deborah. *Cather, Canon, and the Politics of Reading*. Amherst: Univ. of Massachusetts Press, 1992.

Carpenter, Lynette, and Wendy K. Kolmar, Eds. *Haunting the House of Fiction: Feminine Perspectives on Ghost Stories by American Women*. Knoxville: Univ. of Tennessee Press, 1991.

Cassill, R. V. *The Norton Anthology of Short Fiction, Fourth Edition*. New York: Norton, 1990.

Castillo, Debra A. *Talking Back: Toward a Latin American Feminist Literary Criticism*. Ithaca: Cornell Univ. Press, 1992.

Castillo-Feliú, Guillermo I., Ed. *The Creative Process in the Works of José Donoso*. Rock Hill, S. C.: Winthrop College, 1982.

Castronovo, David. *The American Gentleman: Social Prestige and the Modern Literary Mind*. New York: Continuum, 1991.

Chakovsky, Sergei, and M. Thomas Inge, Eds. *Russian Eyes on American Literature*. Jackson: Univ. Press of Mississippi, 1992.

Chamberlain, Bobby J. *Jorge Amado*. Boston: Twayne, 1990.

Chandès, Gérard, Ed. *Le Merveilleux et la magic dans la littérature*. Amsterdam: Rodopi, 1992.

Chandler, Marilyn R. *Dwelling in the Text: Houses in American Literature*. Berkeley: Univ. of California Press, 1991.

Charters, Ann, and William E. Sheidley. *Resources for Teaching 'The Story and its Writer: An Introduction to Short Fiction, Third Edition*. New York: St. Martin's Press, 1991.

Clark, John R. *The Modern Satiric Grotesque and Its Traditions*. Lexington: Univ. of Kentucky Press, 1991.

Clark, Suzanne. *Sentimental Modernism: Women Writers and the Revolution of the Word*. Bloomington: Indiana Univ. Press, 1991.

Clark, William C. *The American Vision of Robert Penn Warren*. Lexington: Univ. of Kentucky Press, 1991.

Coale, Samuel. *William Styron Revisited*. Boston: Twayne, 1991.

Cochran, Robert. *Samuel Beckett: A Study of the Short Fiction*. New York: Twayne, 1992.

Coleman, Deirdre, and Peter Otto, Eds. *Imagining Romanticism: Essays on English and Australian Romanticisms*. West Cornwall, Ct.: Locust Hill Press, 1992.

Coloquio internacional: Escritura y sexualidad en la literatura hispanoamericana. Madrid: Centre de Recherches Latino-Americaines, 1990.

Condé, L. P., and S. M. Hart, Eds. *Feminist Readings on Spanish and Latin-American Literature*. Lewiston, N. Y.: Mellen, 1991.

Connolly, Julian W. *Nabokov's Early Fiction: Patterns of Self and Other*. Cambridge: Cambridge Univ. Press, 1992.

Conrad, Joseph. *The Complete Short Fiction of Joseph Conrad: The Tales*, III. Hopewell, N. J.: Ecco Press, 1992.

Conrad, Robert C. *Understanding Heinrich Böll*. Columbia: Univ. of South Carolina Press, 1992.

Cook, Sylvia J. *Erskine Caldwell and the Fiction of Poverty*. Baton Rouge: Louisiana State Univ. Press, 1991.

Cooper, Barbara T., and Mary Donaldson-Evans, Eds. *Modernity and Revolution in*

Late Nineteenth-Century France. Cranbury, N. J.: Assoc. Univ. Presses [for Univ. of Delaware Press], 1992.

Cooper, Gabriele von Natzmer. *Kafka and Language in the Stream of Thought and Life.* Riverside, Calif.: Ariadne, 1991.

Cope, Kevin L., Ed. *Compendious Conversations: The Method of Dialogue in the Early Enlightenment.* Frankfurt: Peter Lang, 1992.

Cornwell, Neil, Ed. *Daniil Kharms and the Poetics of the Absurd: Essays and Materials.* New York: St. Martin's Press, 1991.

Crafton, John M., Ed. *Selected Essays from the International Conference on the Outsider.* Carrollton: West Georgia College, 1990.

Cuevas García, Cristóbal, Ed. *Miguel Delibes: El escritor, la obra, y el lector.* Barcelona: Anthropos, 1992.

Cummiskey, Gary. *The Changing Face of Horror: A Study of the Nineteenth-Century French Fantastic Short Story.* New York: Peter Lang, 1992.

Dannenberg, Lutz, and Friedrich Vollhardt together with Hartmut Böhme and Jörge Schönert. *Vom Umgang mit Literatur und Literaturgeschichte. Positionen und Perspektiven nach der 'Theoriedebatte.'* Stuttgart: J. B. Metzlersche Verlagsbuchhandlung, 1992.

Datlof, Natalie, Jeanne Fuchs, and David A. Powell, Eds. *The World of George Sand.* Westport: Greenwood, 1991.

Daviau, Donald G. *Austrian Writers and the Anschluss: Understanding the Past—Overcoming the Past.* Riverside, Calif.: Ariadne Press, 1991.

De Koven, Marianne. *Rich and Strange: Gender, History, Modernism.* Princeton: Princeton Univ. Press, 1991.

Delbaere, Jeanne, Ed. *William Golding, The Sound of Silence: A Belgian Tribute on His Eightieth Birthday.* Liège: Liège Language and Literature, 1991.

DiBattista, Marie. *The First Love: The Affections of Modern Fiction.* Chicago: Univ. of Chicago Press, 1991.

Diffley, Kathleen. *Where My Heart Is Turning Ever: Civil War Stories and Constitutional Reform.* Athens: Univ. of Georgia Press, 1992.

DiGaetani, John L., Ed. *A Companion to Pirandello Studies.* Westport: Greenwood, 1991.

Domínguez, Mignon, Ed. *Estudios de narratología.* Buenos Aires: Editorial Biblos, 1991.

Downing, David B., and Susan Bazargan, Eds. *Image and Ideology in Modern/Postmodern Discourse.* Albany: State Univ. of New York Press, 1991.

Duperray, Max, Ed. *De fantastique en littérature: Figures et figurations: Eléments pour une poétique du fantastique sur quelques exemples anglo-saxons.* Aix-en-Provence: Univ. de Provence, 1990.

Duriez, Colin. *The J. R. R. Tolkien Handbook: A Comprehensive Guide to His Life, Writings, and World of Middle Earth.* Grand Rapids: Baker Book House, 1992.

Dynes, Wayne R., and Stephen Donaldson, Eds. *Homosexual Themes in Literary Studies.* New York: Garland, 1992.

Elliot, Emory, Cathy N. Davidson, Patrick O' Donnell, Valerie Smith, and Christopher P. Wilson, Eds. *The Columbia History of the American Novel.* New York: Columbia Univ. Press, 1991.

Elsworth, John, Ed. *The Silver Age in Russian Literature: Selected Papers from the Fourth World Congress for Soviet and East European Studies.* London: Macmillan Press, 1992; Am. ed. New York: St. Martin's Press, 1992.

Engler, Bernd, and Franz Link, Eds. *Zwischen Dogma und säkularer Welt.* Paderborn: Schöningh, 1991.

Erdinast-Vulcan, Daphne. *Joseph Conrad and the Modern Temper.* Oxford: Clarendon Press, 1991.

Erlich, Gloria. *The Sexual Education of Edith Wharton.* Los Angeles: Univ. of California Press, 1992.

Erro-Orthmann, Nora, and Juan Cruz Mendizábal, Eds. *La escritora hispánica.* Miami: Universal, 1990.

Fagundes, Francisco C. *In the Beginning There Was Jorge de Sena's GENESIS: The Birth of a Writer.* Santa Barbara: Jorge de Sena Center for Portuguese Studies, 1991.

Fehn, Ann, Ingeborg Hoestry, and Maria Tatar, Eds. *Neverending Stories: Toward a Critical Narratology.* Princeton: Princeton Univ. Press, 1992.

Ferguson, James. *Faulkner's Short Fiction.* Knoxville: Univ. of Tennessee Press, 1991.

Fontana, Biancamaria. *Benjamin Constant and the Post-Revolutionary Mind.* New Haven: Yale Univ. Press, 1991.

Foster, David W. *Gay and Lesbian Themes in Latin American Writing.* Austin: Univ. of Texas Press, 1991.

Fowler, Doreen, and Ann J. Abadie. *Faulkner and Popular Culture: Faulkner and Yoknapatawpha.* Jackson: Univ. Press of Mississippi, 1990.

Fowler, Douglas. *Understanding E. L. Doctorow.* Columbia: Univ. of South Carolina Press, 1992.

Frank, Albert J. von, Ed. *Critical Essays on Hawthorne's Short Stories.* Boston: G. K. Hall, 1991.

Freedman, Diana. *An Alchemy of Genres: Cross Genre Writing by American Feminist Poet-Critics.* Charlottesville: Univ. Press of Virginia, 1992.

Friedland, M. L., Ed. *Rough Justice: Essays on Crime in Literature.* Toronto: Univ. of Toronto Press, 1991.

Friedman, Lawrence S. *Understanding Cynthia Ozick.* Columbia: Univ. of South Carolina Press, 1991.

Friedrichsmeyer, Sara, and Barbara Becker-Cantarino, Eds. *The Enlightenment and Its Legacy: Studies in German Literature in Honor of Helga Slessarev.* Bonn: Bouvier Verlag, 1991.

Furst, Lilian R., and Peter W. Graham, Eds. *Disorderly Eaters: Texts in Self-Empowerment.* University Park: Pennsylvania State Univ. Press, 1992.

Fusso, Susanne, and Priscilla Meyer, Eds. *Essays on Gogol: Logos and the Russian Word.* Evanston, Ill.: Northwestern Univ. Press, 1992.

Gascón-Vera, Elena, and Joy Renjilian-Burgy, Eds. *Justina: Homenaje a Justina Ruiz de Conde en su ochenta cumpleaños.* Erie, P.A.: ALDEEU, 1992.

Gaskill, Howard, Karin McPherson, and Andrew Barker, Eds. *Neue Ansichten: The Reception of Romanticism in the Literature of the GDR.* Amsterdam: Rodopi, 1990.

Gass, William H. *Fiction and the Figures of Life.* Boston: Nonpareil Books, 1971.

Genet, Jacqueline, Ed. *The Big House in Ireland.* Dingle, Ireland: Brandon, 1991; Am. ed. Savage, Md.: Barnes & Noble, 1991.

Giddings, Robert, Ed. *Literature and Imperialism.* New York: St. Martin's Press, 1991.

Gindin, James. *British Fiction in the 1930s: The Dispiriting Decade.* New York: St. Martin's Press, 1992.

Gladsky, Thomas S. *Princes, Peasants, and Other Polish Selves: Ethnicity in American Literature.* Amherst: Univ. of Massachusetts Press, 1992.

Glassman, Steve, and Kathryn L. Seidel, Eds. *Zora in Florida.* Orlando: Univ. of Central Florida Press, 1991.

Goldman, L. H., Gloria L. Cronin, and Ada Aharoni, Eds., *Saul Bellow: A Mosaic.* New York: Lang, 1992.

Golsan, Richard J., Ed. *Fascism, Aesthetics, and Culture.* Hanover, N. H.: Univ. Press of New England, 1992.

González, Eduardo. *The Monstered Self: Narratives of Death and Performance in Latin American Fiction.* Durham: Duke Univ. Press, 1992.

Grace, Sherrill, Ed. *Swinging the Maelström: New Perspectives on Malcolm Lowry.* New York: Scribner's, 1992.

Graham, Sheelagh D., Ed. *New Directions in Soviet Literature: Selected Papers from the Fourth World Congress for Soviet and East European Studies, Harrogate, 1990.* New York: St. Martin's Press, 1992.

Greenfield, Bruce. *Narrating Discovery: The Romantic Explorer in American Literature, 1790–1885.* New York: Columbia Univ. Press, 1992.

Grimm, Reihhold, and Jost Hermand, Eds. *Laughter Unlimited: Essays on Humor, Satire, and the Comic.* Madison: Univ. of Wisconsin Press, 1991.

Guerin, Wilfred L., Earle Labor, Lee Morgan, Jeanne C. Reesman, and John R. Willingham. *A Handbook of Critical Approaches to Literature.* New York: Harper & Row, 1966; 2nd ed. New York: Harper & Row, 1979; 3rd ed. New York: Oxford Univ. Press, 1992.

Guilds, John C. *Simms: A Literary Life.* Fayetteville: Univ. of Arkansas Press, 1992.

Hammarberg, Gitta. *From the Idyll to the Novel: Karamzin's Sentimentalist Prose.* Cambridge: Cambridge Univ. Press, 1991.

Hammond, J. R. *H. G. Wells and Rebecca West.* New York: St. Martin's Press, 1991.

———. *H. G. Wells and the Short Story.* New York: St. Martin's Press, 1992.

Hampson, Robert. *Joseph Conrad: Betrayal and Identity.* New York: St. Martin's Press, 1992.

Hardy, Thomas. *Thomas Hardy: The Excluded and Collaborative Stories*, ed. Pamela Dalziel. Oxford: Clarendon Press, 1992.

———. *Wessex Tales*, ed. Kathryn King. Oxford: Oxford Univ. Press, 1991.

Harrington, John P. *The Irish Beckett.* Syracuse: Syracuse Univ. Press, 1991.

Harris, Sharon M. *Rebecca Harding Davis and American Realism.* Philadelphia: Univ. of Pennsylvania Press, 1991.

Hayashi, Tetsumaro, Ed. *Steinbeck's Short Stories in "The Long Valley": Essays in Criticism.* Muncie, Ind.: Steinbeck Research Institute, Ball State Univ., 1991.

Hayles, N. Katherine, Ed. *Chaos and Order: Complex Dynamics in Literature and Science.* Chicago: Univ. of Chicago Press, 1991.

Hayman, Ronald. *The Death and Life of Sylvia Plath.* New York: Birch Lane, 1991.

Head, Dominic. *The Modernist Short Story: A Study in Theory and Practice.* Cambridge: Cambridge Univ. Press, 1992.

Henricksen, Bruce. *Nomadic Voices: Conrad and the Subject of Narrative.* Urbana: Univ. of Illinois Press, 1992.

Herdman, John. *The Double in Nineteenth-Century Fiction: The Shadow Self.* New York: St. Martin's Press, 1991.

Hicks, D. Emily. *Border Writing: The Multidimensional Text.* Minneapolis: Univ. of Minnesota Press, 1991.

Higgins, Lynn A., and Brenda R. Silver, Eds. *Rape and Representation.* New York: Columbia Univ. Press, 1991.

Hobby, Elaine, and Chris White, Eds. *What Lesbians Do in Books.* London: The Women's Press, 1991.

Hoffman, Anne G. *Between Exile and Return: S. Y. Agnon and the Drama of Writing.* Albany: State Univ. of New York Press, 1991.

Holbrook, David. *Where D. H. Lawrence Was Wrong about Women.* Cranbury, N. J.: Associated Univ. Presses [for Bucknell Univ. Press], 1992.

Holub, Robert C. *Reflections of Realism: Paradox, Norm, and Ideology in Nineteenth-Century German Prose.* Detroit: Wayne State Univ. Press, 1991.

Hornby, Nick. *Contemporary American Fiction.* New York: St. Martin's Press, 1992.

Howard, Joan E. *From Violence to Vision: Sacrifice in the Works of Marguerite Yourcenar.* Carbondale: Southern Illinois Univ. Press, 1992.

Howells, Coral A., and Lynette Hunter, Eds. *Narrative Strategies in Canadian Literature: Feminism and Postcolonialism.* Philadelphia: Open Univ. Press, 1991.

Howells, Coral A. *Jean Rhys.* New York: St. Martin's Press, 1991.

Hume, Kathryn. *Calvino's Fictions: Cogito and Cosmos.* Oxford: Oxford Univ. Press, 1992.

Hussey, Mark, and Vara Neverow-Turk, Eds. *Virginia Woolf Miscellanies: Proceedings of the First Annual Conference on Virginia Woolf.* New York: Pace Univ. Press, 1992.

Hutchinson, Stuart. *The American Scene: Essays on Nineteenth-Century American Literature.* New York: St. Martin's Press, 1991.

Hyde, Virginia. *The Risen Adam: D. H. Lawrence's Revisionist Typology.* University Park: Pennsylvania State Univ. Press, 1992.

Hyland, Paul, and Neil Sammells, Eds. *Irish Writing: Exile and Subversion.* London: Macmillan, 1991; Am. ed. New York: St. Martin's Press, 1991.

Hyland, Peter. *Saul Bellow.* New York: St. Martin's Press, 1992.

Ingham, Patricia. *Dickens, Women and Language.* Toronto: Univ. of Toronto Press, 1992.

Ito, Ken K. *Visions of Desire: Tanazaki's Fictional Worlds.* Stanford: Stanford Univ. Press, 1991.

Jackson, David A. *Theodor Storm: The Life and Works of a Democratic Humanitarian.* New York: Berg, 1992.

Jacobsen, Eric, Jorgen E. Nielsen, Bruce C. Ross, and James Stewart, Eds. *Studies in Modern Fiction: Presented to Bent Nordhjem on his 70th Birthday, 31 May 1990.* Copenhagen: Publication of the Department of English, 1990.

Jones, E. Michael. *The Angel and the Machine: The Rational Psychology of Nathaniel Hawthorne.* Peru, Ill.: Sherwood Sugden, 1991.

Joslin, Katherine. *Edith Wharton.* New York: St. Martin's Press, 1991.

Jump, Harriet D., Ed. *Diverse Voices: Essays on Twentieth-Century Women Writers.* New York: St. Martin's Press, 1991.

Jurkevich, Gayana. *The Elusive Self: Archetypal Approaches to the Novels of Miguel de Unamuno.* Columbia: Univ. of Missouri Press, 1991.

Kaplan, Fred. *Henry James: The Imagination of Genius, A Biography.* New York: William Morrow, 1992.

Kaplan, Sydney J. *Katherine Mansfield and the Origins of Modernist Fiction.* Ithaca: Cornell Univ. Press, 1991.

Keating, Helane L., and Walter Levy. *Instructor's Manual, Lives Through Literature: A Thematic Anthology.* New York: Macmillan, 1991.

Kelly, Richard. *Graham Greene.* New York: Frederich Unger, 1984.

Kennedy, Richard S., Ed. *Literary New Orleans: Essays and Meditations.* Baton Rouge: Louisiana State Univ. Press, 1992.

Kennedy, Thomas E. *Robert Coover: A Study of the Short Fiction.* New York: Twayne, 1992.

King, Adele, Ed. *Camus's "L'Etranger": Fifty Years On.* New York: St. Martin's Press, 1992.

King, Sarah. *The Magical and the Monstrous.* New York: Garland, 1992.

Kingcaid, Renée. *Neurosis and Narrative: The Decadent Short Fiction of Proust, Lorrain, and Rachilde.* Carbondale: Southern Illinois Univ. Press, 1992.

Kintanar, Thelma B., Ed. *Women Reading . . . Feminist Perspectives on Philippine Literary Texts.* Quezon City: Univ. of the Philippines Press, 1992.

Klinkowitz, Jerome. *Structuring the Void: The Struggle for Subject in Contemporary American Fiction.* Durham: Duke Univ. Press, 1992.

Knapp, Bettina L. *Exile and the Writer: Exoteric and Esoteric Experiences—A Jungian Approach.* University Park: Pennsylvania State Univ. Press, 1991.

Kolesnikoff, Nina. *Yury Trifonov: A Critical Study.* Ann Arbor: Ardis, 1992.

Kopley, Richard, Ed. *Poe's "Pym": Critical Explorations.* Durham: Duke Univ. Press, 1992.

Kornblatt, Judith D. *The Cossack Hero in Russian Literature.* Madison: Univ. of Wisconsin Press, 1992.

Kowaleski-Wallace, Elizabeth. *Their Fathers' Daughters: Hannah More, Maria Edgeworth, and Patriarchal Complicity.* New York: Oxford Univ. Press, 1991.

Kraeger, Linda, and Joe Barnhard. *Dostoevsky on Evil and Atonement: The Ontology of Personalism in His Major Fiction.* Lewiston, N. Y.: Edwin Mellen, 1992.

Kramer, Victor A. *Agee and Actuality: Artistic Vision in His Work.* Troy, N. Y.: Whitston, 1991.

Kuehl, John. *F. Scott Fitzgerald: A Study of the Short Fiction.* Boston: Twayne, 1991.

Kushigian, Julia A. *Orientalism in the Hispanic Literary Tradition.* Albuquerque: Univ. of New Mexico Press, 1991.

La Cassagnère, Christian, Ed. *Visages de l'angoisse.* Clermont-Ferrand: Publications de la Faculté des Lettres de Clermont, 1989.

Lanier, Parks, Ed. *The Poetics of Appalachian Space.* Knoxville: Univ. of Tennessee Press, 1991.

Leavy, Barbara F. *To Blight With Plague: Studies in a Literary Theme.* New York: New York Univ. Press, 1992.

Lecker, Robert, Ed. *Canadian Canons: Essays in Literary Value.* Toronto: Univ. of Toronto Press, 1991.

Lee, Judith Y. *Garrison Keillor: A Voice of America.* Jackson: Univ. Press of Mississippi, 1991.

Leondopoulos, Jordan. *Still the Moving World: Intolerance, Modernism and "Heart of Darkness."* New York: Lang, 1991.

Lerda, Valeria, G., and Tjebbe Westendorp, Eds. *The United States South: Regionalism and Identity.* Rome: Bulzoni, 1991.

Levy, Helen F. *Fiction of the Home Place: Jewett, Cather, Glasgow, Porter, Welty, and Naylor.* Jackson: Univ. Press of Mississippi, 1992.

Lilly, Mark, Ed. *Lesbian and Gay Writing: An Anthology of Critical Essays.* Philadelphia: Temple Univ. Press, 1990.

Lim, Shirley G., and Amy Ling, Eds. *Reading the Literatures of Asian America.* Philadelphia: Temple Univ. Press, 1992.

Literature and Psychology. Lisbon: Instituto Superior de Psicologia Aplicada, 1991.

Loeffelholz, Mary. *Experimental Lives: Women and Literature, 1990–1945.* New York: Twayne, 1992.

Luker, Nicholas, Ed. *The Short Story in Russia, 1900–1917.* Nottingham: Astra Press, 1991.

McBride, Joseph. *Albert Camus: Philosopher and Litterateur.* New York: St. Martin's Press, 1992.

McCauley, Michael J. *Jim Thompson: Sleep with the Devil.* New York: Warner, 1991.

MacDonald, David L. *Poor Polidori: A Critical Biography of the Author of "The Vampyre."* Toronto: Univ. of Toronto Press, 1991.

McGuinness, Nora A. *The Literary Universe of Jack B. Yeats.* Washington: Catholic Univ. of America Press, 1992.

McSweeny, Kerry. *George Eliot: A Literary Life.* New York: St. Martin's Press, 1991.

Maltby, Paul. *Dissident Postmodernists: Barthelme, Coover, Pynchon.* Philadelphia: Univ. of Pennsylvania Press, 1991.

Mandia, Patrick M. *Comedic Pathos: Black Humor in Twain's Fiction.* Jefferson, N. C.: McFarland, 1991.

Mangum, Bryant. *A Fortune Yet: Money in the Art of F. Scott Fitzgerald's Short Stories.* New York: Garland, 1991.

Masiello, Francine. *Between Civilization and Barbarism: Women, Nation, and Literary Culture in Modern Argentina.* Lincoln: Univ. of Nebraska Press, 1992.

Masse, Michelle A. *In the Name of Love: Women, Masochism, and the Gothic.* Ithaca: Cornell Univ. Press, 1992.

Mellow, James R. *Hemingway: A Life Without Consequences.* Boston: Houghton Mifflin, 1992.

Merrell, Floyd. *Unthinking Thinking: Jorge Luis Borges, Mathematics, and the New Physics.* West Lafayette: Purdue Univ. Press, 1991.

Messent, Peter. *Ernest Hemingway*. New York: St. Martin's Press, 1992.

Meyers, Jeffrey. *Edgar Allan Poe: His Life and Legacy*. New York: Scribner's, 1992.

Meyers, Valerie. *George Orwell*. New York: St. Martin's Press, 1991.

Mikhail, Mona N. *Studies in the Short Fiction of Mahfouz and Idris*. New York: New York Univ. Press, 1992.

Milbank, Alison. *Daughters of the House: Modes of the Gothic in Victorian Fiction*. New York: St. Martin's Press, 1992.

Miller, J. Hillis. *Adriadne's Thread: Story Lines*. New Haven: Yale Univ. Press, 1992.

Miller, Ruth. *Saul Bellow: A Biography of the Imagination*. New York: St. Martin's Press, 1991.

Millington, Richard H. *Practicing Romance: Narrative Form and Cultural Engagement in Hawthorne's Fiction*. Princeton: Princeton Univ. Press, 1992.

Mink, JoAnna S., and James D. Ward, Eds. *Joinings and Disjoinings: The Significance of Marital Status in Literature*. Bowling Green: Bowling Green State Univ. Popular Press, 1991.

Minogue, Sally, Ed. *Problems for Feminist Criticism*. London: Routledge, 1990.

Mobley, Marilyn S. *Folk Roots and Mythic Wings in Sarah Orne Jewett and Toni Morrison*. Baton Rouge: Louisiana State Univ. Press, 1991.

Moore, Gene M., Ed. *Conrad's Cities: Essays for Hans van Marle*. Amsterdam: Rodopi, 1992.

Morris, Christopher D. *Models of Misinterpretation: On the Fiction of E. L. Doctorow*. Jackson: Univ. Press of Mississippi, 1991.

Morse, Donald E., Marshall B. Tymn, and Csilla Bertha, Eds. *The Celebration of the Fantastic: Selected Papers from the Tenth Anniversary International Conference on the Fantastic in the Arts*. Westport: Greenwood, 1992.

Munk, Linda. *The Trivial Sublime: Theology and American Politics*. New York: St. Martin's Press, 1992.

Nakhimovsky, Alice S. *Russian-Jewish Literature and Identity*. Baltimore: Johns Hopkins Univ. Press, 1992.

Napier, Susan J. *Escape from the Wasteland: Romanticism and Realism in the Fiction of Mishima Yukio and Ōe Kenzaburō*. Cambridge: Harvard Univ. Press, 1991.

Nashta, Susheila, Ed. *Motherlands: Black Women's Writings from Africa, the Caribbean and South Asia*. New Brunswick: Rutgers Univ. Press, 1991.

Neihardt, John G. *"The End of the Dream" and Other Stories*, ed. Hildra Neithardt Petri, with Foreword by Jay Fultz. Lincoln: Univ. of Nebraska Press, 1991.

Nelson, Dana D. *The Word in Black and White: Reading "Race" in American Literature, 1638–1967*. New York: Oxford Univ. Press, 1992.

Nemoianu, Virgil, and Robert Royal, Eds. *The Hospitable Canon: Essays on Literary Play, Scholarly Choice, and Popular Pressures*. Philadelphia: John Benjamins, 1991.

Nethersole, Reingard. Ed. *Emerging Literatures*. Bern: Peter Lang, 1990.

Newmark, Kevin. *Beyond Symbolism: Textual History and the Future of Reading*. Ithaca: Cornell Univ. Press, 1991.

Newton, K. M., Ed. *George Eliot*. London: Longman, 1991.

Norris, Margot. *Joyce's Web: The Social Unraveling of Modernism*. Austin: Univ. of Texas Press, 1992.

Oberhelman, Harley D. *Gabriel García Márquez: A Study of the Short Fiction*. Boston: Twayne, 1991.

O'Connor, Kathleen. *Robert Musil and the Tradition of the German Novelle*. Riverside, Calif.: Adrian, 1992.

Oriard, Michael. *Sporting with the Gods: The Rhetoric of Play in American Culture*. Cambridge: Cambridge Univ. Press, 1991.

Orvell, Miles. *Flannery O'Connor: An Introduction*. Jackson: Univ. Press of Mississippi, 1991.

Papinchak, Robert A. *Sherwood Anderson: A Study of the Short Fiction.* New York: Twayne, 1992.

Peterson, Brent O. *Popular Narratives and Ethnic Identity: Literature and Community in "Die Abendschule."* Ithaca: Cornell Univ. Press, 1991.

Pfister, Joel. *The Production of Personal Life: Class, Gender, and the Psychological in Hawthorne's Fiction.* Stanford: Stanford Univ. Press, 1991.

Phillips, Robert L. *Shelby Foote, Novelist and Historian.* Jackson: Univ. Press of Mississippi, 1992.

Pollard, Patrick. *André Gide: Homosexual Moralist.* New Haven: Yale Univ. Press. 1991.

Poole, Adrian. *Henry James.* New York: St. Martin's Press, 1991.

Porte, Joel. *In Response to Egotism: Studies in American Romantic Writing.* Cambridge: Cambridge Univ. Press, 1991.

Powell, David A. *George Sand.* Boston: Twayne, 1990.

Prier, Raymond A., Ed. *Countercurrents: On the Primacy of Texts in Literary Criticism.* Albany: State Univ. of New York Press, 1992.

Priestman, Martin. *Detective Fiction and Literature: The Figure on the Carpet.* New York: St. Martin's Press, 1991.

Puertas y ventanas: acercamientos a la obra literaria de Enrique Jaramillo Levi. San José, Costa Rica: EDUCA, 1990.

Quinones, Ricardo J. *The Changes of Cain: Violence and the Lost Brother in Cain and Abel Literature.* Princeton: Princeton Univ. Press, 1991.

Rabinovitz, Rubin. *Innovation in Samuel Beckett's Fiction.* Urbana: Univ. of Illinois Press, 1992.

Rance, Nicholas. *Wilkie Collins and the Other Sensational Novelists: Walking the Moral Hospital.* Cranbury, N. J.: Associated Univ. Presses [for Fairleigh Dickinson Univ. Press], 1991.

Raper, Julius R. *Narcissus from Rubble: Competing Models of Character in Contemporary British and American Fiction.* Baton Rouge: Louisiana State Univ. Press, 1992.

Raphael, Lev. *Edith Wharton's Prisoners of Shame: A New Perspective on Her Fiction.* Ann Arbor: UMI Research Press, 1991.

Rashkin, Esther. *Family Secrets and the Psychoanalysis of Narrative.* Princeton: Princeton Univ. Press, 1992.

Redekop, Magdalene. *Mothers and Other Clowns: The Stories of Alice Munro.* London: Routledge, 1992.

Reesman, Jeanne C. *American Designs: The Late Novels of James and Faulkner.* Philadelphia: Univ. of Pennsylvania Press, 1991.

Reichardt, Mary R. *A Web of Relationships: Women in the Short Stories of Mary Wilkins Freeman.* Jackson: Univ. Press of Mississippi, 1992.

Rignall, John. *Realist Fiction and the Strolling Spectator.* London: Routledge, 1992.

Rivera, Tomás. *Tomás Rivera: The Complete Works,* ed. Julián Olivares. Houston: Arte Público Press, 1991.

Robinson, Douglas. *Ring Lardner and the Other.* Oxford: Oxford Univ. Press, 1992.

Robinson, Fred M. *Comic Moments.* Athens: Univ. of Georgia Press, 1992.

Rodríguez-Luis, Julio. *The Contemporary Praxis of the Fantastic: Borges and Cortázar.* New York: Garland, 1991.

Roe, Barbara L. *Donald Barthelme: A Study of the Short Story.* New York: Twayne, 1992.

Rogers, Franklin R. *Occidental Ideographs: Image, Sequence, and Literary History.* Cranbury, N. J.: Associated Univ. Presses [for Bucknell Univ. Press], 1991.

Rollyson, Carl. *The Lives of Norman Mailer: A Biography.* New York: Paragon House, 1991.

Roman, Margaret. *Sarah Orne Jewett: Reconstructing Gender.* Tuscaloosa: Univ. of Alabama Press, 1992.

Romines, Ann. *The Home Plot: Women, Writing & Domestic Ritual*. Amherst: Univ. of Massachusetts Press, 1992.

Rose, Jacqueline. *The Haunting of Sylvia Plath*. Cambridge: Harvard Univ. Press, 1992.

Rosebury, Brian. *Tolkien: A Critical Assessment*. New York: St. Martin's Press, 1992.

Ross, Angus, Ed. *Kipling 86: Papers Read at the University of Sussex in May 1986 as Part of the Commemoration of the Fiftieth Anniversary of Rudyard Kipling's Death*. [Brighton]: Univ. of Sussex Library, 1987.

Roughley, Alan. *James Joyce and Critical Theory: An Introduction*. Univ. of Michigan Press, 1991.

Ruddick, Nicholas, Ed. *State of the Fantastic: Studies in the Theory and Practice of Fantastic Literature and Film*. Westport: Greenwood, 1991.

Runyon, Randolph P. *Reading Raymond Carver*. Syracuse: Syracuse Univ. Press, 1992.

Ryan, Judith. *The Vanishing Subject: Early Psychology and Literary Modernism*. Chicago: Univ. of Chicago Press, 1991.

Saciuk, Olena H., Ed. *The Shape of the Fantastic*. New York: Greenwood, 1990.

Salami, Mahmoud. *John Fowles's Fiction and the Poetics of Postmodernism*. Cranbury, N. J.: Assoc. Univ. Presses [for Fairleigh Dickinson Univ. Press], 1992.

Salwak, Dale, Ed. *Kingsley Amis in Life and Letters*. New York: St. Martin's Press, 1991.

Samuels, Shirley. *The Culture of Sentiment: Race, Gender, and Sentimentality in Nineteenth-Century America*. New York: Oxford Univ. Press, 1992.

Scafella, Frank, Ed. *Hemingway: Essays of Reassessment*. New York: Oxford Univ. Press, 1991.

Schenker, Daniel. *Wyndham Lewis: Religion and Modernism*. Tuscaloosa: Univ. of Alabama Press, 1992.

Schmidt, Peter. *The Heart of the Story: Eudora Welty's Short Fiction*. Jackson: Univ. Press of Mississippi, 1991.

Schneider, Christian I. *Hermann Hesse*. Munich: C. H. Beck'sche Verlagsbuchhandlung, 1991.

Scholes, Robert. *In Search of James Joyce*. Urbana: Univ. of Illinois Press, 1992.

Schultz, David E., and S. T. Joshi, Eds. *An Epicure in the Terrible: A Centennial Anthology in the Honor of H. P. Lovecraft*. Cranbury, N. J.: Assoc. Univ. Presses [for Fairleigh Dickinson Univ. Press], 1991.

Seed, David. *Rudolph Wurlitzer, American Novelist and Screenwriter*. Lewiston, N. Y.: Mellen, 1991.

Seeley, Frank F. *Turgenev: A Reading of His Fiction*. Cambridge: Cambridge Univ. Press, 1991.

Shaw, Phillip, and Peter Stockwell, Eds. *Subjectivity and Literature from Romantics to the Present Day*. London: Pinter, 1991.

Short, Bryan C. *Cast by Means of Figures: Herman Melville's Rhetorical Development*. Amherst: Univ. of Massachusetts Press, 1992.

Siebers, Tobin. *Morals and Stories*. New York: Columbia Univ. Press, 1992.

Sklenicka, Carol. *D. H. Lawrence and the Child*. Columbia: Univ. of Missouri Press, 1991.

Slusser, George, and Tom Shippey, Eds. *Fiction 2000: Cyberpunk and the Future of Narrative*. Athens: Univ. of Georgia Press, 1992.

Smith, Joseph H., Ed. *The World of Samuel Beckett*. Baltimore: Johns Hopkins Univ. Press, 1991.

Smith, Roland. *Critical Essays on Nadine Gordimer*. Boston: G. K. Hall, 1990.

Smythe, Karen E. *Figuring Grief: Gallant, Munro, and the Poetics of Elegy*. Montreal: McGill-Queen's Univ. Press, 1992.

Spilka, Mark. *Renewing the Normative D. H. Lawrence: A Personal Progress*. Columbia: Univ. of Missouri Press, 1992.

Spillers, Hortense J., Ed. *Comparative American Identities: Race, Sex, and Nationality in the Modern Text*. London: Routledge, 1991.

Stanton, Domna C., Ed. *Discourses of Sexuality: From Aristotle to AIDS*. Ann Arbor: Univ. of Michigan Press, 1992.

Steinberg, Peter. *Journey to Oblivion: The End of the East European Yiddish and German Worlds in the Mirror of Literature*. Toronto: Univ. of Toronto Press, 1991.

Sten, Christopher. *Savage Eye: Melville and the Visual Arts*. Kent: Kent State Univ. Press, 1991.

Stern, Milton R. *Contexts for Hawthorne: "The Marble Faun" and the Politics of Openness and Closure in American Literature*. Urbana: Univ. of Illinois Press, 1991.

Stinson, John J. *Anthony Burgess Revisited*. Boston: Twayne, 1991.

————. *V. S. Pritchett: A Study of the Short Fiction*. New York: Twayne, 1992.

Stokes, John, Ed. *Fin de Siècle/Fin du Globe: Fears and Fantasies of the Late Nineteenth Century*. New York: St. Martin's Press, 1992.

Swann, Charles. *Nathaniel Hawthorne: Tradition and Revolution*. Cambridge: Cambridge Univ. Press, 1991.

Tambling, Jeremy. *Narrative and Ideology*. Buckingham: Open Univ. Press, 1991.

Tanner, Tony. *Venice Desired*. Cambridge: Harvard Univ. Press, 1992.

Tate, Claudia. *Domestic Allegories of Political Desire: The Black Heroine's Text at the Turn of the Century*. Oxford: Oxford Univ. Press, 1992.

Terras, Victor. *A History of Russian Literature*. New Haven: Yale Univ. Press, 1991.

Tetlow, Wendolyn E. *Hemingway's "In Our Time."* Cranbury, N. J.: Assoc. Univ. Presses [for Bucknell Univ. Press], 1992.

Tillman, Katherine Davis Chapman. *The Works of Katherine Davis Chapman Tillman*, ed. Claudia Tate. New York: Oxford Univ. Press, 1991.

Timm, Eitel, Ed. *Subversive Sublimities: Undercurrents of the German Enlightenment*. Columbia, S. C.: Camden House, 1992.

Tobin, Uishai, Ed. *From Sign to Text: A Semiotic View of Communication*. Amsterdam: Benjamins, 1989.

Toumayan, Alain, Ed. *Literary Generations: A Festschrift in Honor of Edward D. Sullivan by His Friends, Colleagues, and Former Students*. Lexington, KY: French Forum, 1992.

Travers, Martin. *Thomas Mann*. New York: St. Martin's Press, 1992.

Trimmer, Joseph, and Tilly Warnock, Eds. *Understanding Others: Cultural and Cross-Cultural Studies and the Teaching of Literature*. Urbana, Ill: NCTE, 1992.

Tudeau-Clayton, Margaret, and Martin Warner, Eds. *Addressing Frank Kermode: Essays in Criticism and Interpretation*. Urbana: Univ. of Illinois Press, 1991.

Tyler, Joseph, Ed. *Borges' Craft of Fiction: Selected Essays on His Writing*. Carrollton, Ga.: International Circle of Borges Scholars, 1992.

Tymieniecka, Anna T., Ed. *The Elemental Passions of the Soul: Poetics of the Elements in the Human Condition*. Dordrecht: Kluwer, 1990.

Valis, Noël, and Carol Maier, Eds. *In the Feminine Mode: Essays on Hispanic Women Writers*. Lewisburg: Bucknell Univ. Press, 1990.

Van Dover, J. K. *Understanding William Kennedy*. Columbia: Univ. of South Carolina Press, 1991.

Vines, Lois D. *Valery and Poe: A Literary Legacy*. New York: New York Univ. Press, 1992.

Voix et Langages aux États-Unis, I. Provence: Univ. de Provence, 1992.

Wachtel, Albert. *The Cracked Lookingglass: James Joyce and the Nightmare of History*. Cranbury, N. J.: Assoc. Univ. Presses [for Susquehanna Univ. Press], 1992.

Wade, Stephen. *Christopher Isherwood*. New York: St. Martin's Press, 1991.

Wagner, Linda W. *Ernest Hemingway: Six Decades of Criticism*. East Lansing: Michigan State Univ. Press, 1987.

Wales, Katie. *The Language of James Joyce*. New York: St. Martin's Press, 1992.

Waller, Gregory A. *The Living and the Undead: From Stoker's "Dracula" to Romero's "Dawn of the Dead."* Urbana: Univ. of Illinois Press, 1986.

Walsh, Thomas F. *Katherine Anne Porter and Mexico*. Austin: Univ. of Texas Press, 1992.

Walton, Priscilla L. *The Disruption of the Feminine in Henry James*. Toronto: Toronto Univ. Press, 1992.

Wasserman, Loretta. *Willa Cather: A Study of Short Fiction*. Boston: Twayne, 1991.

Weber, Ronald. *The Midwestern Ascendancy in American Writing*. Bloomington: Indiana Univ. Press, 1992.

Weiss, Timothy F. *On the Margins: The Art of Exile in V. S. Naipaul*. Amherst: Univ. of Massachusetts Press, 1992.

Welch, Robert. *Irish Writers and Religion*. Savage, Md.: Barnes & Noble, 1992.

Weld, Annette. *Barbara Pym and the Novel of Manners*. New York: St. Martin's Press, 1992.

Wharton, Edith. *The Selected Short Stories of Edith Wharton,* ed. R. W. B. Lewis. New York: Scribner's, 1991.

White, Barbara A. *Edith Wharton: A Study of the Short Fiction*. New York: Twayne, 1991.

Whitebrook, Maureen, Ed. *Reading Political Stories*. Lanham, Md.: Rowman & Littlefield, 1992.

Whitlark, James. *Behind the Great Wall: A Post-Jungian Approach to Kafkaesque Literature*. Cranbury, N. J.: Assoc. Univ. Presses [for Fairleigh Dickinson Univ. Press], 1991.

———, and Wendell Aycock, Eds. *The Literature of Emigration and Exile*. Lubbock: Texas Tech Univ. Press, 1992.

Williams, Rhys W., Stephen Parker, and Colin Riordan, Eds. *German Writers and the Cold War*. Manchester: Manchester Univ. Press, 1992.

Wilson, Christopher P. *White Collar Fiction: Class and Social Representation in American Literature, 1885–1925*. Athens: Univ. of Georgia Press, 1992.

Winther, Per. *The Art of John Gardner*. Albany: State Univ. of New York Press, 1992.

Woolf, Judith. *Henry James: The Major Novels*. Cambridge: Cambridge Univ. Press, 1991.

Worthen, John. *D. H. Lawrence*. London: Arnold, 1991.

Wyatt-Brown, Anne M. *Barbara Pym: A Critical Biography*. Columbia: Univ. of Missouri Press, 1992.

Young, Elizabeth, and Graham Caveney. *Shopping in Space: Essays on America's Blank Generation Fiction*. New York: Atlantic Monthly Press, 1992.

A Checklist of Journals Used

African Am R	*African American Review*
Afro-Hispanic R	*Afro-Hispanic Review*
Arbeiten Deutschen Philologie	*Arbeiten zur Deutschen Philologie*
	Agni
	Alba de América
Aligarh J Engl Stud	*The Aligarh Journal of English Studies*
Americas R	*The Americas Review: A Review of Hispanic Literature and Art of the USA*
Am Lit	*American Literature: A Journal of Literary History, Criticism, and Bibliography*
Am Lit Hist	*American Literary History*
Am Lit Realism	*American Literary Realism, 1870–1910*
Am Stud Scandinavia	*American Studies in Scandinavia*
Am Transcendental Q	*American Transcendental Quarterly: A Journal of New England Writers*
	Amon Hen
	Anales Galdosianos
Analecta Malacitana	*Analecta Malacitana: Revista de la Sección de Filología de la Facultad de Filosofía y Letras*
Anthropos R	*Anthropos: Revista de documentación científica de la cultura*
Antípodas	*Antípodas: Journal of Hispanic Studies of the University of Auckland and La Trobe University*
Arabica	*Arabica: Revue d'Études Arabes*
Archiv	*Archiv für das Studium der Nueren Sprachen und Literaturen*
Arizona Q	*Arizona Quarterly*

275

Australian Lit Stud	*Australian Literary Studies*
Australian J French Stud	*Australian Journal of French Studies*
Australian Slavonic	*Australian Slavonic & East European Studies*
Baker Street J	*The Baker Street Journal: An Irregular Quarterly of Sherlockiana*
Bestia	*Bestia: Yearbook of the Beast Fable Society*
Border States	*Border States: Journal of the Kentucky-Tennessee American Studies Association*
Bull de la Soc Théophile Gautier	*Bulletin de la Société Théophile Gautier*
Bull Hispanic Stud	*Bulletin of Hispanic Studies*
	Caliban
Cambridge Q	*The Cambridge Quarterly*
Canadian-American Slavic Stud	*Canadian-American Slavic Studies*
Canadian J Irish Stud	*Canadian Journal of Irish Studies*
Canadian J Native Stud	*Canadian Journal of Native Studies*
Canadian Lit	*Canadian Literature*
	Casa de las Americas
Canadian R Am Stud	*Canadian Review of American Studies*
Cardozo Stud Law & Lit	*Cardozo Studies in Law and Literature*
Castilla	*Castilla: Boletín del Departamento de Literatura Española*
CEA Critic	*College English Association Critic*
CEAMAG	*CEAMAGazine: A Journal of the College English Association, Middle Atlantic Group*
Centennial R	*Centennial Review*
Chasqui	*Chasqui: Revista de Literatura Latinoamericana*
Chattahoochee R	*Chattahoochee Review*
Chesterton R	*The Chesterton Review: The Journal of the Chesterton Society*

Chicago R	*Chicago Review*
Children's Lit	*Children's Literature: Annual of the Modern Language Association Division on Children's Literature and the Children's Literature Association*
Chu-Shikoku Stud Am Lit	*Chu-Shikoku Studies in American Literature*
Cincinnati Romance R	*Cincinnati Romance Review*
Círculo	*Círculo: Revista de Cultura*
Cithara	*Cithara: Essays in the Judeo-Christian Tradition*
Clues	*Clues: A Journal of Detection*
Coll Lang Assoc J	*College Language Association Journal*
Coll Lit	*College Literature*
Colloquia Germanica	*Colloquia Germanica, Internationale Zeitschrift für Germanische Sprach- und Literaturwissenschaft*
Commonwealth Essays & Stud	*Commonwealth Essays and Studies*
Commonwealth R	*The Commonwealth Review*
Confluencia	*Confluencia: Revista Hispánica de Cultura y Literatura*
Connecticut R	*Connecticut Review*
The Conradian	*The Conradian: Journal of the Joseph Conrad Society [U.K.]*
Conradiana	*Conradiana: A Journal of Joseph Conrad*
Crítica	*Crítica: A Journal of Critical Essays*
Criticism	*Criticism: A Quarterly for Literature and Arts*
	Cuadernos Americanos
Cuadernos Hispanoamericanos	*Cuadernos Hispanoamericanos: Revista Mensual de Cultura Hispánica*
Cupey	*Cupey: Revista de la Universidad Metropolitana*
	Current Writing
D. H. Lawrence R	*The D. H. Lawrence Review*

Dalhousie French Stud	*Dalhousie French Studies*
Dalhousie R	*Dalhousie Review*
Delta	*Delta: Revue du Centre d'Études et de Recherche sur les Écrivains du Sud aux États-Unis*
Deutsche Vierteljahrsschrift	*Deutche Vierteljahrsschrift für Literaturwissenschaft und Geistesgeschichte*
Discurso	*Discurso literario: Revista de Estudios Iberoamericanos*
Discurso Literario	*Discurso Literario: Revista de Temas Hispánicos*
Dolphin	*The Dolphin: Publications of the English Department, University of Aarhus*
Durham Univ J	*Durham University Journal*
Dutch Crossing	*Dutch Crossing: A Journal of Low Countries Studies*
Encyclia	*Encyclia: The Journal of the Utah Academy of Sciences, Arts, and Letters*
Engl Africa	*English in Africa*
English	*English: The Journal of the English Association* (London, England)
Engl Lang Notes	English Language Notes
Engl Lit Transition	English Literature in Transition
Engl Stud	English Studies: A Journal of English Language and Literature
Eng Stud Africa	English Studies in Africa: A Journal of the Humanities
Engl Stud Canada	English Studies in Canada
	L'Epoque Conradienne
Escritura	*Escritura: Revista de Teoría y Crítica Literaria*
	L'Esprit Créateur
Essays Canadian Writing	*Essays on Canadian Writing*
Essays French Lit	*Essays in French Literature*
Essays Lit	*Essays in Literature* (Western Illinois)

Essays Poetics	Essays in Poetics
	Estudios Filológicos
	Estudios de Literatura Argentina
	Ethics
Études Anglaises	*Études Anglaises: Grande-Bretagne, États-Unis*
	Études Lawrenciennes
	Études Romanes de Brno
Europe	*Europe: Revue Littéraire Mensuelle*
European Romantic R	*European Romantic Review*
	Explicación de Textos Literarios
	Explicator
	Extrapolation
Faulkner J	*Faulkner Journal*
	Feminaria
Feminist Stud	*Feminist Studies*
Flannery O'Connor Bull	*Flannery O'Connor Bulletin*
Focus on Robert Graves	*Focus on Robert Graves and His Contemporaries*
Forum Mod Lang Stud	*Forum for Modern Language Studies*
Francographies	*Francographies: Bulletin de la Société des Professeurs Français et Francophones d'Amérique*
French Cultural Stud	*French Cultural Studies*
	French Forum
French R	*French Review*
French Stud	*French Studies: A Quarterly Review*
GDR Bull	*GDR Bulletin*
George Eliot-George Henry Lewes Stud	*George Eliot-George Henry Lewes Studies* [Formerly *The George Eliot-George Henry Lewes Newsletter*]
George Sand Stud	*George Sand Studies*
Germ Life & Letters	*German Life and Letters*

Germ Notes	*Germanic Notes*
Germ Q	*German Quarterly*
Germ Stud R	*German Studies Review*
Germ R	*German Review*
Germanisch-Romanische Monatsschrift	*Germanisch-Romanische Monatsschrift,* Neue Fogle
Great Plains Q	*Great Plains Quarterly*
Hebrew Stud	*Hebrew Studies: A Journal Devoted to Hebrew Language and Literature*
Hemingway R	*Hemingway Review*
Henry James R	*Henry James Review*
Hispamerica	*Hispamerica: Revista de Literatura*
Hispania	*Hispania: A Journal Devoted to the Interests of the Teaching of Spanish and Portuguese*
Hispanic J	*Hispanic Journal*
Hispanic R	*Hispanic Review*
Hispano	*Hispanófila*
	Hollins Critic
L'Information Littéraire	*L'Information Littéraire: Revue Parraisant Cinq Fois par An*
Inti	*Inti: Revista de Literatura Hispánica*
Int'l Fiction R	*International Fiction Review*
Iowa R	*The Iowa Review*
	Iris
Irish Univ R	*Irish University Review: A Journal of Irish Studies*
	Italica
James Joyce Q	*James Joyce Quarterly*
	Jahrbuch der Raabe-Gesellschaft
J Am Culture	*Journal of American Culture*
J Am Stud	*Journal of American Studies*

J Commonwealth Lit	*Journal of Commonwealth Literature*
J Engl Lang & Lit	*The Journal of English Language and Literature*
J Evolutionary Psych	*Journal of Evolutionary Psychology*
J Interdisciplinary Lit Stud	*Journal of Interdisciplinary Literary Studies/ Cuadernos Interdisciplinarios de Estudios Literarios*
J Lit Stud	*Journal of Literary Studies/Tydskrif Vir Literaturwetenskap*
J Mod Lit	*Journal of Modern Literature*
J Short Story Engl	*Journal of Short Story in English*
J South Pacific Assn Commonwealth Lit Lang Stud	*Journal of the South Pacific Association for Commonwealth Literature and Language Studies*
Jean Rhys R	*Jean Rhys Review*
Kansas Q	*Kansas Quarterly*
Kentucky Philol R	*Kentucky Philological Review*
Kipling J	*The Kipling Journal*
	Kunapipi
Lang & Culture	*Language and Culture (Kokkaido University)*
Lang & Style	*Language and Style: An International Journal*
Lang Q	*The University of Southern Florida Language Quarterly*
Langston Hughes R	*The Langston Hughes Review*
Latin Am Lit R	*Latin American Literary Review*
Latin Am Theatre R	*Latin American Theatre Review*
Legacy	*Legacy: A Journal of Nineteenth-Century American Women Writers*
	Lenguas, Literaturas, Sociedades
	Letras Femeninas
Lettres Romanes	*Les Lettres Romanes*
Library	*The Library: The Transactions of the Bibliographical Society*
	Literatura Mexicana

Lit & Belief	*Literature and Belief*
Lit & Psych	*Literature and Psychology*
	Literary Half-Yearly
Lit Interpretation Theory	*Lit: Literature Interpretation Theory*
Lit & Theology	*Literature and Theology: An Interdisciplinary Journal of Theory and Criticism*
Lit Theory Classroom	*Literary Theory in the Classroom*
Literator	*Literator: Tydskrif vir Besondere en Vergelykende Taal-en Literatuurstudie/Journal of Literary Criticism, Comparative Linguistics and Literary Studies*
	Literatur für Leser
Litteraria Pragensia	*Litteraria Pragensia: Studies in Literature and Culture* [Supersedes *Philologica Pragensia*]
Littératures	*Littératures* (Toulouse, France)
Louisiana Literature	*Louisiana Literature: A Review of Literature and Humanities*
Lovecraft Stud	*Lovecraft Studies*
	Mester
	Metaphoric and Symbolic Activity
Midamerica	*Midamerica: The Yearbook of the Society for the Study of Midwestern Literature*
Midwest Q	*Midwest Quarterly: A Journal of Contemporary Thought*
	Midwestern Miscellany
	Mississippi Folklore Register
Mississippi Q	*Mississippi Quarterly: The Journal of Southern Culture*
Mitteilungen der E. T. A. Hoffmann	*Mitteilungen der E. T. A. Hoffmann-Gesellschaft-Bamberg*
Mod China	*Modern China*
Mod Fiction Stud	*Modern Fiction Studies*

Mod Lang Notes	*MLN: Modern Language Notes*
Mod Lang Q	*Modern Language Quarterly*
Mod Lang R	*Modern Language Review*
Moderne Sprachen	*Moderne Sprachen: Zeitschrift des Verbandes der Österreichischen Neuphilologen*
Mod Lang Stud	*Modern Language Studies*
Monatshefte	*Monatshefte: Für Deutschen Unterricht, Deutsche Sprache und Literatur*
Monographic R	*Monographic Review/Revista Monográfia*
Mosaic	*Mosaic: A Journal for the Comparative Study of Literature and Ideas for the Interdisciplinary Study of Literature*
Mountain Interstate Foreign Lang Conference R	*Mountain Interstate Foreign Language Conference Review*
	Murgetana
Mundi/Crítica/Literatura	*Mundi: Filosofía/Crítica/Literatura, Buenos Aires*
Mystery Fancier	*The Mystery Fancier*
Nabokovian	*The Nabokovian* [formerly *Vladimir Nabokov Research Newsletter*]
Nathaniel Hawthorne R	*Nathaniel Hawthorne Review*
Neophil	*Neophilologus*
	Neue Rundschau
Nevada Historical Soc Q	*Nevada Historical Society Quarterly*
New England Q	*The New England Quarterly: A Historical Review of New England Life and Letters*
New Lit Hist	*New Literary History*
New Lit R	*New Literatures Review*
New Orleans R	*New Orleans Review*
New Mexico Hum R	*New Mexico Humanities Review*
New York R Sci Fiction	*The New York Review of Science Fiction*
New Zealand J French Stud	*New Zealand Journal of French Studies*

New Zealand Slavonic J	*New Zealand Slavonic Journal*
Nineteenth-Century Lit	*Nineteenth-Century Literature* [formerly *Nineteenth-Century Fiction*]
No Dakota Q	*North Dakota Quarterly*
Notes Contemp Lit	*Notes on Contemporary Literature*
Notes Mod Irish Lit	*Notes on Modern Irish Literature*
Novel	*Novel: A Forum on Fiction*
Nuez	*La Nuez: Revista de Arte y Literatura*
Old Northwest	*The Old Northwest: A Journal of Regional Life and Letters*
Orbis Litterarum	*Orbis Litterarum: International Review of Literary Studies*
Oeuvres & Critiques	*Oeuvres & Critiques: Revue Internationale d'Étude de la Réception Critique d'Étude des Oeuvres Littéraires de Langue Française*
	Palimpsest
Platte Valley R	*Platte Valley Review*
Plural	*Plural: Revista Cultural de Excelsior*
PMLA	*PMLA: Publications of the Modern Language Association of America*
Paintbrush	*Paintbrush: A Journal of Poetry, Translations, and Letters*
Palabra y Hombre	*La Palabra y el Hombre: Revista de la Universidad Veracruzana*
Panjab Univ Research Bull	*Panjab University Research Bulletin (Arts)*
Papers Lang & Lit	*Papers on Language and Literature: A Journal for Scholars and Critics of Language and Literature*
Philippine Stud	*Philippine Studies* (Manila)
Philosophy & Lit	*Philosophy and Literature*
Portuguese Stud	*Portuguese Studies*
Prairie Fire	*Prairie Fire: A Magazine of Canadian Writing*
	Pynchon Notes

Quaderni d'Italianistica	*Quaderni d'Italianistica: The Official Journal of the Canadian Society for Italian Studies*
Quimera	*Quimera: Revista de Literatura*
	Ragioni Critiche
Raritan	*Raritan: A Quarterly Review*
	Recherches Germaniques
R Contemp Fiction	*Review of Contemporary Fiction*
R Japanese Culture & Soc	*Review of Japanese Culture and Society*
R Lettre Modernes	*La Revue des Lettres Modernes: Histoire des Idées des Littératures*
Religion & Lit	*Religion and Literature*
	Representations
Research African Lit	*Research in African Literature*
	Revista Alicantina de Estudios Ingleses
Revista Canadiense	*Revista Canadiense de Estudios Hispánicos*
	Revista Canaria de Estudios Ingleses
	Revista Chilena Literatura
	Revista de Estudios Hispánicos (Poughkeepsie)
	Revista Hispánica Moderna
	Revista Iberoamericana
Revista Interamericana	*Revista Interamericana de Bibliografía/Inter-American Review of Bibliography*
	Revista de Literatura
Revista Filología	*Revista de Filología de la Universidad de La Laguna*
	Revue de Sciences Humaines
Revue Française	*Revue Française d'Études Américaines*
	Revue Francophone de Louisiane
Rivista di Letterature	*Rivista di Letterature Moderne e Comparate*
Romance Stud	*Romance Studies* (Swansea Wales)

Romanic R	*Romanic Review*
Rocky Mountain R	*Rocky Mountain Review of Language and Literature*
Russian, Croatian	*Russian, Croatian and Serbian, Czech and Slovak, Polish Literature*
Russian Lit	*Russian Literature*
Russian Lit Triquarterly	*Russian Literature Triquarterly*
Saul Bellow J	*Saul Bellow Journal* [formerly *Saul Bellow Newsletter*]
Scandinavian Stud	*Scandinavian Studies*
Scando-Slavica	*Scando-Slavica* (Copenhagen, Denmark)
	Schriften der Theodor-Storm-Gesellschaft
Sci-Fiction Stud	*Science-Fiction Studies*
Scottish Slavonic R	*Scottish Slavonic Review: An International Journal Promoting East-West Contacts*
Seminar	*Seminar: A Journal of Germanic Studies*
Shikoku Stud Am Lit	*Shikoku Studies in American Literature*
Siglo	*Siglo XX/20th Century*
Slavic & East European J	*Slavic and East European Journal*
Slavic R	*Slavic Review: American Quarterly of Soviet and East European Studies*
	Sociocriticism
Sprachkunst	*Sprachkunst: Beiträge zur Literaturwissenschaft*
So Atlantic Q	*South Atlantic Quarterly*
So Atlantic R	*South Atlantic Review*
So Central R	*South Central Review*
Southern Lit J	*Southern Literary Journal*
Southern Q	*The Southern Quarterly: A Journal of Arts in the South*
Stanford Lit R	*Stanford Literature Review*
Stephen Crane Stud	*Stephen Crane Studies*

Stud Am Fiction	*Studies in American Fiction*
Stud Am Jewish Lit	*Studies in American Jewish Literature*
Stud Canadian Lit	*Studies in Canadian Literature*
Stud Engl Lang & Lit	*Studies in English Language and Literature* (Kyushu University)
Stud Hum	*Studies in the Humanities*
Stud Novel	*Studies in the Novel*
Stud Short Fiction	*Studies in Short Fiction*
Stud Twentieth-Century Lit	*Studies in Twentieth-Century Literature*
Stud Weird Fiction	*Studies in Weird Fiction*
	Style
SubStance	*SubStance: A Review of Theory and Literary Criticism*
Symposium	*Symposium: A Quarterly Journal of Modern Literatures*
Tamkang R	*Tamkang Review*
	Tenggara
Texas Stud Lit & Lang	*Texas Studies in Literature and Language: A Journal of the Humanities*
	Texto Crítico
Thomas Hardy J	*The Thomas Hardy Journal*
	Thomas Mann Jahrbuch
Thomas Wolfe R	*The Thomas Wolfe Review*
Tolstoy Stud J	*Tolstoy Studies Journal*
Torre	*La Torre: Revista de la Universidad de Puerto Rico*
TTR: Traduction, Terminologie, Rédaction	*TTR: Traduction, Terminologie, Rédaction: Études Sur le Texte et Ses Transformations*
	Travaux de Littérature
Tulsa Stud Women's Lit	*Tulsa Studies in Women's Literature*
Twentieth Century Lit	*Twentieth Century Literature: A Scholarly and Critical Journal*

Unisa Engl Stud	*Unisa English Studies: Journal of the Department of English*
Univ Dayton R	*University of Dayton Review*
Univ Hartford Stud Lit	*University of Hartford Studies in Literature: A Journal of Interdisciplinary Criticism*
Univ Mississippi Stud Engl	*University of Mississippi Studies in English*
Virginia Q R	*Virginia Quarterly Review: A National Journal of Literature and Discussion*
Wascana R	*Wascana Review*
Weimarer Beiträge	*Weimarer Beiträge: Zeitschrift für Literaturwissenschaft, Äesthetik und Kulturwissenschaften*
West Georgia Coll R	*West Georgia College Review*
West Virginia Univ Philol Papers	*West Virginia University Philological Papers*
Western Am Lit	*Western American Literature*
	Willa Cather Pioneer Memorial Newsletter
William Carlos Williams R	*William Carlos Williams Review*
Wirkendes Wort	*Wirkendes Wort: Deutsche Sprache in Forschung und Lehre*
	Wissenschaftliche Zeitschrift der Ernst Moritz Arndt-Universität Greifswald
Women's Studies	*Women's Studies: An Interdisciplinary Journal*
World Lit Today	*World Literature Today: A Literary Quarterly of the University of Oklahoma*
World Lit Written Engl	*World Literature Written in English*
	Yiddish
	Zeitschrift für Deutsche Philologie
	Zeitschrift für Slavische Philologie

Index of Short Story Writers

Abad, Mercedes 1
Abdullah, Mena 1
Abernathy, Richard 1
Achebe, Chinua 1
Adams, Alice 2
Agee, James 2
Agnon, Shmuel Yosef 2
Agulto, Tomas F. 3
Aichinger, Ilse 3
Aidoo, Ama Ata 3
Alcott, Louisa May 3
Aleichem, Sholem 4
Alfon, Estrella 4
Algren, Nelson 4
Allen, Woody 4
Allende, Isabel 4
Amado, Jorge 4
Amis, Kingsley 5
Amis, Martin 5
Andersen, Hans Christian 5
Anderson, Jessica 5
Anderson, Sherwood 6
Andreev, Leonid 7
Anonymous 7
Apple, Max 7
Arenas, Reinaldo 7
Arévalo Martínez, Rafael 8
Arredondo, Inés 8
Arreola, Juan José 8
Arguedas, José María 8
Artsybashev, Mikhail 9
Asturias, Miguel Angel 9
Atwood, Margaret 9
Auchincloss, Louis 10
Austin, William 10
Ayala, Francisco 10
Azuela, Mariano 10

Babel, Isaac 11
Bail, Murray 11
Baldwin, James 11
Ballem, John 12
Balzac, Honoré de 12
Bambara, Toni Cade 13
Banks, Russell 13
Barba, Harry 13

Barbey d'Aurevilly, Jules-Amédée 13
Barea, Arturo 14
Bareiro Saquier, Rubén 14
Barnes, Djuna 14
Barth, John 15
Barthelme, Donald 15
Barthelme, Frederick 18
Baudelaire, Charles 18
Baynton, Barbara 18
Beattie, Ann 18
Beckett, Samuel 19
Bécquer, Gustavo Adolfo 20
Beerbohm, Max 21
Bellow, Saul 21
Benedetti, Mario 22
Bestard Vásquez, Joaquín 22
Bianco, José 22
Bierce, Ambrose 22
Bioy Casares, Adolfo 23
Bishop, Elizabeth 23
Bissoondath, Neil 23
Bjarnason, Jóhann Magnús 24
Blanchot, Maurice 24
Blei, Norbert 24
Bødker, Cecil 24
Böll, Heinrich 24
Bombal, María Luisa 25
Borges, Jorge Luis 25
Borowski, Tadeusz 29
Bowen, Elizabeth 29
Bowles, Paul 29
Boyle, Kay 30
Bradbury, Ray 32
Bradley, Leo 32
Braun, Johanna and Günter 32
Brentano, Clemens 32
Brillantes, Gregorio 32
Brown, Larry 33
Brulotte, Gaétan 33
Brumana, Herminia 33
Bryce Echenique, Alfredo 33
Bukoski, Anthony 34
Bulosan, Carlos 34
Bulwer-Lytton, Edward George 34
Burgess, Anthony 35
Byatt, Antonia 35

Cable, George Washington   35
Cabrera, Lydia   35
Caldwell, Erskine   35
Callaghan, Morley   36
Calvino, Italo   36
Calviño, Julio Iglesias   37
Camus, Albert   37
Cantwell, Robert   39
Cardoso Pires, José   39
Carey, Peter   39
Carleton, William   40
Carter, Angela   40
Carver, Ada Jack   40
Carver, Raymond   40
Cassill, R. V.   44
Castellanos, Rosario   44
Cather, Willa   45
Cela, Camilo José   47
Chacel, Rosa   47
Chamisso, Adelbert von   48
Chandler, Raymond   48
Chateaubriand, François-René de   48
Chatrian, Alexandre   48
Cheever, John   48
Chekhov, Anton   49
Chesnutt, Charles W.   50
Chesterton, Gilbert Keith   51
Child, Lydia Maria   52
Chin, Frank   52
Chollet, Louise E.   52
Chopin, Kate   52
Cisneros, Sandra   53
Clarín   53
Clarke, Arthur C.   54
Clarke, Austin   54
Cobb, Jack Fletcher   54
Colette, Sidonie-Gabrielle   54
Collins, Wilkie   54
Conrad, Joseph   54
Conroy, Jack   58
Constant, Benjamin   58
Constante, Susana   58
Cooper, J. California   58
Coover, Robert   58
Cordero-Fernando, Gilda   60
Cortázar, Julio   61
Couperus, Louis Marie Anne   63
Crane, Stephen   64
Curvers, Alexis   65

Dabit, Eugène   65
Dahl, Roald   65
Dall, Caroline Wells Healey   65
Darío, Rubén   66
Daudet, Alphonse   66

Dávila, Amparo   66
Davis, Rebecca Harding   66
De La Houssaye, Sidonie   67
Delibes, Miguel   67
Denser, Marcia   67
Díaz-Mas, Paloma   68
Díaz Rodríguez, Jesús   68
Dickens, Charles   68
Dinesen, Isak   68
Dixon, Stephen   69
Djebar, Assia   69
Doctorow, E. L.   69
Donoso, José   70
Dorian, Edward O.   71
Dostoevsky, Fyodor   71
Doyle, Arthur Conan   71
Drake, Robert   73
Dray, Nazli   73
Dubus, Andre   73
Dumont, Fernand   73
Dunbar-Nelson, Alice   74
Duncan, Sara Jeannette   74
Duras, Marguerite   74
Dybek, Stuart   74

Edgeworth, Maria   75
Edwards, Jorge   75
Eichendorff, Joseph von   75
Eliot, George   75
Elizondo, Salvador   76
Elizondo, Sergio   76
Elliott, George   76
Ellison, Harlan   77
Ellison, Ralph   77
Elsschot, Willem   77
Erckmann, Emile   77
Erdrich, Louise   77
Espina-Moore, Lina   77
Espínola, Francisco   78

Fagundes Telles, Lygia   78
Farmer, Philip José   78
Faulkner, William   78
Ferber, Edna   81
Fernández Cubas, Cristina   81
Fernández Santos, Jesús   82
Ferré, Rosario   82
Findley, Timothy   82
Fitzgerald, F. Scott   82
Flaubert, Gustave   87
Fontane, Theodeor   87
Foote, Shelby   87
Ford, Aida Rivera   88
Ford, Richard   88
Foreshaw, Thelma   88

Forster, E. M.   88
Fowles, John   89
Freeman, Mary E. Wilkins   89
Freilich, Alicia   92
Freixas, Laura   92
Freyre, Ricardo Jaime   92
Fuentes, Carlos   92
Füruzan   93

Gaines, Ernest   93
Gakaarda Wa Wanjaū   93
Gallant, Mavis   93
Galsworthy, John   95
Garcia, Fanny   95
García Márquez, Gabriel   95
García Morales, Adelaida   97
García Velloso, Enrique   97
Gardner, John   97
Garland, Hamlin   97
Garro, Elena   97
Gass, William   98
Gautier, Théophile   99
Geha, Joseph   99
Gibson, William   99
Gide, André   100
Gilchrist, Ellen   100
Giles, Zeny   100
Gilman, Charlotte Perkins   100
Glasgow, Ellen   101
Godfrey, Ellen   101
Gogol, Nikolai   101
Golding, William   102
Goldstein, Rebecca   103
González, José Luis   103
Gonzalez, N. V. M.   103
Goodman, Allegra   103
Gordimer, Nadine   104
Gordon, Caroline   105
Gorodischer, Angélica   105
Gorky, Maxim   106
Gorriti, Juana Manuela   106
Goyen, William   106
Graves, Robert   106
Greene, Graham   106
Grillparzer, Franz   107
Grimke, Angelina Weld   107
Grossman, Vasily   107
Guido, Beatriz   108

Haldeman, Joe   108
Hall, Donald   108
Halper, Albert   108
Handke, Peter   108
Hannah, Barry   108
Hardy, Thomas   109

Harper, Frances Ellen Watkins   109
Harte, Bret   110
Hau'ofa, Epeli   110
Hawthorne, Nathaniel   110
Hazzard, Shirley   113
Head, Bessie   113
Hearn, Lafcadio   114
Hébert, Anne   114
Helprin, Mark   114
Hemingway, Ernest   114
Hempel, Amy   118
Hernández, Felisberto   118
Hesse, Hermann   118
Heym, Stefan   118
Heyns, Jacky   118
Highsmith, Patricia   119
Hoffmann, E[rnest] T[heodor] A[madeus]   119
Hoffmansthal, Hugo von   119
Hogg, James   120
Holmberg, Eduardo Ladislau   120
Holst, Gilda   120
Huggan, Isabel   120
Hughes, Langston   120
Humphrey, William   121
Hurston, Zora Neal   121
Hwang Sun-won   121
Hyde, Evan X.   121

Idris, Yusuf   122
Irving, Washington   123
Isherwood, Christopher   123

Jackson, Laura Riding   123
Jackson, Shirley   123
James, Henry   123
Janés, Clara   127
Jaramillo Levi, Enrique   127
Jewett, Sarah Orne   129
Jhabvala, Ruth Prawer   132
Jia Pingwa   132
Jiménez Lozano, José   133
Joaquin, Nick   133
Joyce, James   133

Kafka, Franz   136
Kalfaian, Karl J.   139
Kaplan, Johanna   139
Karamzin, Nikolay   139
Kauffman, Janet   140
Kaufman, Bel   140
Keillor, Garrison   140
Keller, Gottfried   141
Kelly, James Patrick   141
Kennedy, William   141

Kenyatta, Jomo   141
Kharibian, Hapet   141
Kharms, Daniil   141
Kibera, Leonard   142
Kiely, Benedict   142
King, Grace Elizabeth   142
Kingston, Maxine Hong   142
Kipling, Rudyard   143
Klass, Perri   144
Kleist, Heinrich von   144
Kober, Wofram   145
Komey, Ellis Ayitey   145
Königsdorf, Helga   145
Kosinsky, Jerzy   145
Kress, Nancy   145
Kundera, Milan   146
Kuprin, Aleksandr   146

Laforet, Carmen   146
Lardner, Ring   146
Larue, Monique   147
Laurence, Margaret   147
Lavin, Mary   147
Lawrence, D. H.   147
Lawson, Henry   149
Leaño, Fernando   149
Leavitt, David   149
Lee, Vernon   149
Le Fanu, Joseph Sheridan   150
Le Guin, Ursula K.   150
Leffland, Ella   150
Lehmann, Rosamond   150
Lem, Stanislaw   151
Lermontov, Mikhail   151
Lerner, Tillie   151
Lessing, Doris   151
Le Sueur, Meridel   152
Lewis, Matthew Gregory   152
Lewis, Sinclair   152
Lewis, Wyndham   152
Li, Yi   152
Liben, Meyer   152
Lispector, Clarice   153
Lojo, María Rosa   154
Lo Liyong, Taban   154
London, Jack   155
López Portillo y Rojas, José   156
Lovecraft, H[oward] P.   156
Lowry, Malcolm   157
Lu Xün   158
Lugones, Leopoldo   158
Lundt, Paul   158
Lynch, Marta   158

McCarthy, Mary   158
McCullers, Carson   159

McEwan, Ian   159
Machen, Arthur   159
McKinley, Georgia   159
MacLeod, Alistair   159
MacMahon, Bryan   160
McPherson, James Alan   160
MacSween, R. J.   160
Magtulis, Julian   160
Mahfouz, Naguib   160
Mailer, Norman   161
Malamud, Bernard   161
Maltz, Albert   162
Manfalūṭī, Mūṣṭafa Lūṭfī   162
Mann, Heinrich   162
Mann, Thomas   162
Mansfield, Katherine   164
Mansilla, Eduarda   165
Marechera, Dambudzo   165
Marpons, Josefina   165
Martin, Helen Reimensnyder   166
Martínez Estrada, Ezequiel   166
Maryoral, Marina   166
Mason, Bobbie Ann   166
Masters, Olga   166
Mathew, Ray   166
Matthews, James   167
Matute, Ana María   167
Maugham, W. Somerset   167
Maupassant, Guy de   167
Melville, Herman   168
Mena, María Cristina   169
Méndez, Miguel M.   170
Mérimée, Prosper   170
Merril, Judith   170
Meyer, Conrad Ferdinand   170
Michaels, Leonard   171
Mishima, Yukio   171
Mistry, Rohinton   171
Monette, Madeleine   171
Moore, C[atherine] L[ucille]   172
Moore, Lorrie   172
Moorhouse, Frank   172
Morrison, Arthur   172
Morrison, Toni   173
Moskalets, Kostiantyn   173
Moura, Beatriz de   173
Mrabet, Mohammed   173
Mukherjee, Bharati   173
Mungoshi, Charles   174
Munro, Alice   174
Musial, Nellie   177
Musil, Robert   177
Mutloatse, Mothobi   177

Nabokov, Vladimir   178
Nagai, Kafū   179

Nahan, Rabbi Bratylav 179
Naipaul, Seepersad 179
Naipaul, V[idiadhar] S[urajpasad] 180
Narayan, R. K. 180
Naylor, Gloria 180
Ndebele, Njabulos Simakahle 180
Neihardt, John G. 181
Nerval, Gérard de 181
Ngugi Wa Thiong'o 181
Nodier, Charles 181
Nos, Marta 181
Nyamfukudza, Stanley 181

Oates, Joyce Carol 182
O'Brien, Edna 182
O'Brien, Fitz-James 182
O'Brien, Tim 182
Ocampo, Silvina 183
O'Connor, Flannery 183
O'Connor, Frank 186
Ōe, Kenzaburō 186
O'Faolain, Sean 186
Ogot, Grace 187
O'Hara, John 187
O. Henry 187
Okri, Ben 187
Olsen, Tillie 187
Onetti, Juan Carlos 188
Ortiz, Lourdes 188
Ortiz, Simon 188
Orwell, George 188
Owen, Thomas 189
Owoyele, David 189
Ozick, Cynthia 189

Pacheco, José Emilio 190
Paley, Grace 190
Pálssom, Jóhannes 192
Pancake, Breece D'J 192
Pardo Bazán, Emilia 192
Parwada, Batistai 192
Pasternak, Boris 192
Pelletier, Francine 192
Pereda, Rosa María 192
Pérez Galdós, Benito 193
Peri Rossi, Cristina 193
Perry, Nora 193
Pessarrodona, Marta 193
Petruevskaja, Ljudmila 193
Petry, Ann Lane 193
Phillips, Caryl 194
Phillips, Jayne Anne 194
Pichler, Luise 194
Piglia, Ricardo 194
Piñera, Virgilio 194

Pirandello, Luigi 195
Plath, Sylvia 195
Platonov, Andrei 195
Poe, Edgar Allan 196
Polidori, John William 200
Polotan, Kerima 200
Popov, Yevgeny 200
Porter, Katherine Anne 201
Powers, J. F. 202
Prinsloo, Koos 202
Pritchett, V. S. 202
Proust, Marcel 204
Puértola, Soledad 205
Puga, María Luisa 205
Pushkin, Alexander 205
Pym, Barbara 205
Pynchon, Thomas 206

Queiroz, Raquel de 206
Quiroga, Horacio 206

Raabe, Wilhelm 207
Rachilde 207
Ralph, Julian 207
Reddy, Jayapraga 207
Régnier, Henri de 208
Resnick, Mike 208
Revueltas, José 208
Reyes, Alfonso 208
Reyes, Gremer Chan 208
Reyes, Jun Cruz 208
Rhys, Jean 209
Ribeyro, Julio Ramón 209
Ricci, Julio 210
Richardson, Jack 210
Riera, Carmen 210
Rifaat, Alifa 210
Rivera, Tomás 210
Roa Bastos, Augusto 211
Robison, Mary 211
Robles, Mireya 211
Roig, Montserrat 211
Rossetti, Ana 212
Roth, Philip 212
Rousseau, Ina 212
Roy, Gabrielle 212
Rulfo, Juan 212

Saar, Ferdinand von 213
Saer, Juan José 214
Saez García, Asensio 214
Saika, Patsy 214
Salinas, Pedro 214
Sand, George 215
Santiago, Lilia Quindoza 215

Santos, Bienvenido   215
Sartre, Jean-Paul   215
Sayles, John   216
Ščerbakova, Galina
   Aleksandrovna   216
Schnitzler, Arthur   216
Schreiner, Olive   216
Schwob, Marcel   216
Scott, Evelyn   216
Sedgwick, Catharine   217
Seghers, Anna   217
Sena, Jorge de   217
Senior, Olive   218
Sernine, Daniel   218
Shalamov, Varlam   218
Shaw, Irwin   218
Shukshin, Vasily Makarovich   218
Silko, Leslie Marmon   219
Sime, Jessie Georgina   219
Simms, William Gilmore   219
Singer, Isaac Bashevis   220
Smith, Lee   220
Smith, Pauline   220
Sologub, Fëdor   220
Sontag, Susan   220
Soto, Gary   221
Soyinka, Wole   221
Soysal, Sevgi   221
Spencer, Elizabeth   221
Stafford, Jean   221
Stead, Christina   221
Stegner, Wallace   222
Stein, Gertrude   222
Steinbeck, John   222
Steinmüller, Karlheinz and Angela   223
Sterling, Bruce   223
Stevenson, Robert Louis   223
Stifter, Adalbert   224
Still, James   224
Stoddard, Charles Warren   224
Stoddard, Elizabeth Drew Barstow   224
Stone, Robert   224
Storm, Theodor   225
Story, Gertrude   226
Stuart, Jesse   226
Styron, William   226
Suckow, Ruth   226
Sullivan, James W.   227
Sumelian, Leon   227
Swift, Graham   227

Tan, Amy   227
Tanizaki Jun'ichirō   227
Taylor, Peter   227
Themba, Can   228

Thomas, Audrey   228
Thompson, James   228
Thorsteinsson, Thorstein Th.   228
Thurber, James   228
Tieck, Johann Ludwig   229
Tillman, Katherine Davis
   Chapman   229
Tillman, Lynne   229
Tolkien, J. R. R.   229
Tolstaya, Tatyana   229
Tolstoy, Leo   230
Tong, Su   230
Torga, Miguel   230
Torrente Ballester, Gonzalo   231
Torres Molina, Susana   231
Tournier, Michel   231
Trân Diêu Hång   231
Traba, Marta   232
Traven, Bruno   232
Trevor, William   232
Trifonov, Yury   232
Trilling, Lionel   233
Triolet, Elsa   233
Turgenev, Ivan Sergeevich   233
Tusquets, Esther   236
Tutuola, Amos   236
Twain, Mark   236

Unamuno, Miguel de   237
Updike, John   237
Uslar Pietri, Arturo   237

Valenzuela, Luisa   238
Valera, Juan   238
Vallbona, Rima de   238
Valle-Inclán, Ramón del   239
Vega, Ana Lydia   239
Vercors   240
Vernon, Lawrence   240
Verreault, Sabine   240
Villiers de L'Ise-Adam, Count   240
Viramontes, Helena Maria   241

Wackenroder, Wilhelm Heinrich   241
Walker, Alice   241
Walser, Martin   241
Walser, Robert   242
Walsh, Rodolfo   242
Walter, John   242
Warren, Robert Penn   242
Watson, Sheila   242
Waugh, Evelyn   242
Weatherhill, W. D.   243
Weidman, Jerome   243
Weil, Sylvie   243

Weinzweig, Helen   243
Weldon, Fay   243
Wells, H. G.   243
Welty, Eudora   245
Wendt, Albert   247
Wescott, Glenway   247
West, Nathanael   248
West, Paul   248
West, Rebecca   248
Wharton, Edith   248
Wiebe, Rudy   252
Wiechert, Ernst   252
Wilde, Oscar   252
Wilding, Michael   252
Williams, Charles   253
Williams, Joy   253
Williams, William Carlos   253
Wilner, Herbert   253
Wolcott, Richard   254
Wolf, Christa   254
Wolfe, Thomas   255
Wolff, Tobias   255
Woolf, Virginia   255

Wright, Richard   256
Wright, William   256
Wurlitzer, Rudolph   256

Xianyong, Bai   256

Yamamoto, Hisaye   257
Yamauchi, Wakako   257
Yeats, Jack B.   257
Yehoshua, Abraham B.   257
Yourcenar, Marguerite   257
Yushkevich, Semën   258
Yuson, Alfred A.   258

Zepeda, Eraclio   258
Zhang Jie   259
Zhang Kangkang   259
Ziethe, Wilhelm   259
Zola, Émile Édourard Charles
   Antoine   259
Zong, Pu   259
Zúñiga, Juan Eduardo   259
Zürn, Unica   260